CH0092266A

OXFORD STUDIES IN ANCIENT PHILOSOPHY

OXFORD STUDIES IN ANCIENT PHILOSOPHY

EDITOR: DAVID SEDLEY

VOLUME XXX

SUMMER 2006

OXFORD
UNIVERSITY PRESS

OXFORD
UNIVERSITY PRESS

Great Clarendon Street, Oxford OX2 6DP

Oxford University Press is a department of the University of Oxford.
It furthers the University's objective of excellence in research, scholarship,
and education by publishing worldwide in

Oxford New York

Auckland Cape Town Dar es Salaam Hong Kong Karachi
Kuala Lumpur Madrid Melbourne Mexico City Nairobi
New Delhi Shanghai Taipei Toronto

With offices in

Argentina Austria Brazil Chile Czech Republic France Greece
Guatemala Hungary Italy Japan Poland Portugal Singapore
South Korea Switzerland Thailand Turkey Ukraine Vietnam

Oxford is a registered trade mark of Oxford University Press
in the UK and in certain other countries

Published in the United States
by Oxford University Press Inc., New York

British Library Cataloguing in Publication Data
Data available

Library of Congress Cataloging in Publication Data

Oxford studies in ancient philosophy.—
Vol. xxx (2006).—Oxford: Clarendon Press;
New York: Oxford University Press, 1983–
v.; 22 cm. Annual.
1. Philosophy, Ancient—Periodicals.
B1.O9   180.'5—dc.19   84–645022
AACR 2   MARC-S

Typeset by John Waś, Oxford
Printed in Great Britain
on acid-free paper by
Biddles Ltd, King's Lynn, Norfolk

ISBN 978–0–19–928746–8
ISBN 978–0–19–928747–5 (Pbk.)

ADVISORY BOARD

Contributions and books for review should be sent to the Editor, Professor D. N. Sedley, Christ's College, Cambridge, CB2 3BU, UK. He can be contacted by e-mail on dns1@cam.ac.uk.

Contributors are asked to observe the 'Notes for Contributors to Oxford Studies in Ancient Philosophy', printed at the end of this volume.

Up-to-date contact details, the latest version of Notes to Contributors, and publication schedules can be checked on the *Oxford Studies in Ancient Philosophy* website:

www.oup.co.uk/philosophy/series/osap

CONTENTS

Contents

AMBIGUITY AND TRANSPORT: REFLECTIONS ON THE PROEM TO PARMENIDES' POEM

MITCHELL MILLER

LET me begin by distinguishing an ultimate and a proximate task for these reflections. The ultimate task, a perennial one for students of Greek philosophy, is to understand just what Parmenides lays open for thinking and speaking when, in the so-called Truth-section of his poem, fragments 2 through 8. 49, he isolates the 'is' (ἔστι) that is 'the steadfast heart of . . . truth' (1. 29). The proximate task is to explore the context Parmenides gives us for this ultimate task, the proem's account of the transformative journey to and through 'the gates of the paths of Night and Day' that brings the traveller into the presence of the truth-speaking goddess. We modern-day philosophers have generally been reluctant to pursue this exploration too closely, not only because we are accustomed to draw a sharp distinction between poetry and philosophy, a distinction that, arguably, did not take hold in the Greek world until Aristotle, but also, more to the point at present, because Parmenides' proem seems riddled with ambiguity. This is not wrong; indeed, as I shall try to show, its ambiguity is both more extensive and more central than has been recognized heretofore. But I shall also try to show that it is a resource, not a liability; by the close of these reflections I hope to have made compelling that and why bringing the ambiguity of the proem into good focus is key to a well-oriented turn to our ultimate task, understanding the 'is'.

For helpful responses to earlier versions of this essay, I owe thanks to colleagues and students at an APA Eastern Division meeting, an October meeting of the Society for Ancient Greek Philosophy, St Francis College, Southwestern University, Colby College, and Vassar College, and especially to James Barrett, Jill Gordon, Ed Halper, Phil Hopkins, Alexander Mourelatos, Alan Udoff, and the Editor of *OSAP*. Above all, I owe thanks to Rachel Kitzinger, whose ear for poetry and mastery of the sense and sound of Greek have helped me find my bearings at many points.

We shall proceed in three broad stages. I shall begin with a series of orienting observations on fragments 2 and 6, as well as a provisional indication of the historical-philosophical background that the proem recalls; our purpose will be to acquire questions and resources. In Section 2 we shall turn to the proem; I shall first draw on parallels with fragments 8. 50–61 and 9 in the Doxa section to give a general characterization of the significance of the image of arriving at the gateway, then lay out three fundamental ambiguities that must complicate, to say the least, any effort to understand the significance of the proem's image of passing through the gateway to the goddess. What first appears as a set of obstacles will, however, when considered more closely, reveal itself as a well-integrated means of passage; embracing these ambiguities, I shall try to show, lets us recognize Parmenides' manifold response to his two major philosophical predecessors, Hesiod and Anaximander, and gives us two distinct but complementary courses of thought (marked in fragment 6) for experiencing the 'truth' of the 'is'. In Section 3 we shall attempt to travel each of these courses, then reflect on the implications of their difference and their fit for the significance of the 'is'.

1. Preparatory questions and observations

(a) *A first reading of fragment 2; basic questions*

Parmenides first articulates the 'is' in fragment 2:

> εἰ δ' ἄγ' ἐγὼν ἐρέω, κόμισαι δὲ σὺ μῦθον ἀκούσας,
> αἵπερ ὁδοὶ μοῦναι διζήσιός εἰσι νοῆσαι·
> ἡ μὲν ὅπως ἔστιν τε καὶ ὡς οὐκ ἔστι μὴ εἶναι,
> Πειθοῦς ἐστι κέλευθος (ἀληθείῃ γὰρ ὀπηδεῖ),
> ἡ δ' ὡς οὐκ ἔστιν τε καὶ ὡς χρεών ἐστι μὴ εἶναι,   5
> τὴν δή τοι φράζω παναπευθέα ἔμμεν ἀταρπόν·
> οὔτε γὰρ ἂν γνοίης τό γε μὴ ἐόν (οὐ γὰρ ἀνυστόν)
> οὔτε φράσαις.[1]

Come, I shall tell you, and you, having heard, preserve the account,
These are the only routes of enquiry there are for thinking:
The one—that . . . *is* and that it is not possible [for] . . . *not to be*—

---

[1] For Parmenides' Greek, here and below, I borrow, with a few differences noted, from A. P. D. Mourelatos, *The Route of Parmenides* [*Route*] (New Haven, 1970), appendix IV, pp. 279–84.

Is the path of persuasion, for it attends upon truth;
The other—that . . . *is not* and that it is right [for] . . . *not to be*— 5
This unturning route, I point out to you, is one from which
    no learning ever comes,
For you could not know *what-is-not*, as such, for it cannot be
    brought about,
Nor could you point it out.

There are a number of observations to make here. First, the goddess picks out or highlights the 'is' by pointedly suppressing its subject (and, possibly, predicate). The effect is to reverse the usual order of the conspicuous and the inconspicuous: by eliding the normally conspicuous subject (and, possibly, predicate), the goddess brings the normally inconspicuous 'is' to the front and centre and challenges us to reflect upon it. Second, she sets the 'is' into an adversative contrast with its negation, 'is not' (2. 5). If on 'the one [route of enquiry]' one thinks 'that' (or 'how') its elided subject 'is', on 'the other [route]' one thinks 'that' (or 'how') its elided subject 'is not'. But, third, this contrastive pairing of the two routes belies a deeper, asymmetrical connection between them: the first route is essentially constituted as a response to the impossibility of the second. The goddess marks out the first route by closely conjoining[2] her articulation of the 'is' with the declaration that its negation, 'not to be' (μὴ εἶναι), 'is not possible'. Thus, the first route bears an internal relation to the second: its thinking 'that' or 'how . . . is' arises, if not out of, then in close connection with the attempt to think the negation of the 'is'—that is, to think 'that' or 'how . . . is not'—and the recognition of its impossibility. The goddess provides the insight at the core of this recognition in her critique of the second route in the closing lines of fragment 2. 'No learning ever comes' from the second route, she tells the traveller, because the enquiry that proceeds upon it tries to take up what, because it 'cannot be brought about' (οὐ γὰρ ἀνυστόν, 2. 7)[3]—that is, because it cannot be constituted as an object or determinate content, much less, then, as an object for thought—cannot be 'know[n]' or 'point[ed] out' (2. 7-8). This imponderable is τό γε μὴ ἐόν, 'what-

---

[2] Note τε καί, the tightest possible pairing expression, in 2. 3 and 2. 5.

[3] ἀνυστόν, 'to be accomplished; practicable' (LSJ), derives from ἀνύειν 'to effect, accomplish'. LSJ also lists three narrower senses of great interest for understanding Parmenides: 'to make . . . to be . . .', 'to make [an image]', and 'to finish [a journey]' (LSJ s.v. 3, 4, and 5, respectively).

is-not, as such' (2. 7), a 'what' (τό . . .) whose 'is' (or 'being', . . . ἐόν)
is subjected to negation ('not', . . . μή . . .) and which thinking seeks
to take up precisely and exclusively as it suffers this negation; the
goddess indicates this restrictive focus by the particle γε, the force
of which I have tried to convey with 'as such'. Asserting not only
'that . . . is not' but, as the basis for this, that 'it is right [for] . . . not
to be' (2. 5), the thinking that proceeds on the second route gives
itself—or, more precisely, tries and fails to give itself—such a pure
'what-is-not' as its object. By contrast, the thinking that proceeds
on the first route, recognizing that the very formation of such a
(non-)object 'is not possible' (2. 3), turns away from it and affirms,
instead, 'that' or 'how . . . is'.

The vagueness of these formulations is deliberate; their chief
value is to let some of the sets of questions emerge that are important
for interpreting Parmenides' '. . . is'. I would single out, to begin
with, these five: (i) Does the 'is' have an implied subject? About
what—if, indeed, about anything specific at all—does the thinking
that proceeds on the first route say 'is'?[4] And if there is an implied
subject of some sort, why does Parmenides elide it? (ii) In what
sense or senses should we hear the 'is'? What, if anything, does
this 'is' signify?[5] (iii) What, if anything specific, does Parmenides
intend to call to mind when he has the goddess speak of 'what-is-
not, as such'? How do the possible specifications of the '. . . is' that
are invited by questions (i)–(ii) bear on any possible specification
of 'what-is-not, as such', and vice versa? (iv) Through the voice of
the goddess, Parmenides lays claim to the discovery of the route

[4] To put this in familiar grammatical terms, does the '. . . is' imply a specific
subject, of which it is asserted? Does Parmenides intend a subject for 'is' but elide
it in order to turn our focus to the normally inconspicuous 'is'? The analogous
questions could be asked, note, with regard to the possibility of an implied predicate.

[5] To put this question in terms of familiar scholarship, does the 'is' signify existence, identity, or truth, or is it better understood syntactically, as an 'is' of predication, or, again, does it cross the line between significance and function in the
way that, especially, 'speculative predication', as proposed by Mourelatos, *Route*,
ch. 2, and rearticulated by P. Curd, *The Legacy of Parmenides* [*Legacy*] (Princeton,
1998), does? (See n. 63 below.) Does it involve not just one but rather some interplay of these senses and functions, as Charles Kahn ('Parmenides and Plato', in V.
Caston and D. Graham (eds.), *Presocratic Philosophy: Essays in Honor of Alexander
Mourelatos* (Aldershot, 2002), 81–93) has recently reiterated? Or, perhaps, are these
very distinctions questionably or poorly attuned to ancient Greek, as Lesley Brown
('The Verb 'to Be' in Ancient Philosophy: Some Remarks' ['Verb'], in S. Everson
(ed.), *Language* (Companions to Ancient Thought, 3; Cambridge, 1994), 212–36)
has argued, implying choices that the Greek ear would not have heard, at least as
we do?

on which one thinks 'that', or enquires 'how', '. . . is'. But he has the goddess disclaim the second route. Whom does she target in identifying the second route? Who, if anyone, takes it as 'right [for] . . . not to be'? (v) Finally, Parmenides' elision of the subject (and, perhaps, the predicate) of the '. . . is' is part of a larger act of elision. In bringing the '. . . is' front and centre, he lets fall from view the context within which the '. . . is' emerges. This *may* signal the indifference of the '. . . is' to its context—but it may also, instead, signal the first stage in the transformation of this context; that is, it may mark a departure from the context that will put thought in position to return to it with new understanding of its meaning and significance. Without begging this question, we can hope that identifying the context would help give us our bearings in trying to respond to questions (i)–(iv). Accordingly, we need to ask: does Parmenides indicate the context within which the two routes emerge, even as he prepares to elide it in fragment 2?

(b) Fragment 6; two encounters with the negation of being?

Before proceeding, we should pause to recognize a complication. In fragment 6 the goddess once again distinguishes two 'routes'. Are these in some way redescriptions of the two routes of fragment 2, or—an alternative view held by many—is the second route in fragment 6 a third route overall, set apart from the two routes in fragment 2? Fortunately, we do not yet need to venture too deeply into the difficult syntax of the opening clause of 6. 1 (the proem will help us with this later), nor do we need to address the question of the lacuna in the text at 6. 3.[6] At this point we need only to observe

---

[6] The main verb is missing in the oldest manuscripts. My supplement, ἄρξω, is suggested by A. Nehamas, 'On Parmenides' Three Ways of Inquiry', *Deucalion*, 33/4 (1981), 97–111. This runs parallel with the earlier suggestion of ἄρξει, 'you shall begin', by N.-L. Cordero, 'Les deux chemins de Parménide dans les fragments 6 et 7', *Phronesis*, 24 (1979), 1–32. (Both have repeated their proposals, first arrived at independently, in more recent work—Nehamas in his 'Parmenidean Being/Heraclitean Fire' ['Fire'], in V. Caston and D. Graham (eds.), *Presocratic Philosophy: Essays in Honor of Alexander Mourelatos* (Aldershot, 2002), 45–64, and Cordero in *By Being, It Is* [*By Being*] (Las Vegas, 2004).) The traditional and more widely accepted reading, going back to a Renaissance edition in 1526 and adopted by Diels, is εἴργω, 'I restrain' or 'hold [you] back'. If we adopt the traditional reading, we must take the goddess to intend to 'hold' the traveller 'back' only from the thinking of the negation of being, whether in the sense of the 'nothing' (μηδέν) of 6. 2 or in the sense of the thought of 'not to be' (οὐκ εἶναι) of 6. 8, and not from the affirmation of being that goes along with each of these. I adopt the Cordero–Nehamas alternative because it avoids the need for this special pleading.

the difference between the two characterizations of the encounter with the negation of 'being' in 6. 2 and 6. 8–9. Here is fragment 6, with the key phrases underlined:

χρὴ τὸ λέγειν τε νοεῖν τ' ἐὸν ἔμμεναι· <u>ἔστι γὰρ εἶναι,</u>
<u>μηδὲν δ' οὐκ ἔστιν·</u> τά σ' ἐγὼ φράζεσθαι ἄνωγα.
πρώτης γὰρ σ' ἀφ' ὁδοῦ ταύτης διζήσιος ⟨ἄρξω⟩,
αὐτὰρ ἔπειτ' ἀπὸ τῆς, ἣν δὴ βροτοὶ εἰδότες οὐδέν
πλάττονται, δίκρανοι· ἀμηχανίη γὰρ ἐν αὐτῶν   5
στήθεσιν ἰθύνει πλακτὸν νόον· οἱ δὲ φοροῦνται
κωφοὶ ὁμῶς τυφλοί τε, τεθηπότες, ἄκριτα φῦλα,
<u>οἷς τὸ πέλειν τε καὶ οὐκ εἶναι ταὐτὸν νενόμισται</u>
<u>κοὐ ταὐτόν,</u> πάντων δὲ παλίντροπός ἐστι κέλευθος.

It is right for what is there for discourse and understanding[7] to be;
    <u>for it is there[8] to be,</u>
<u>Whereas nothing cannot [be]</u>; that is what I bid you consider.
For [I shall begin for] you from this first route of enquiry,
And then next from the [route] on which mortals knowing nothing
Wander, two-headed; for helplessness in their   5
Breasts guides their wandering mind; and they are borne along
Both deaf and blind, dazed, tribes without discernment,
<u>By whom to be and not to be have come to be taken as the same</u>
<u>Yet not the same</u>; and the path of all is backward-turning.

Taken by itself, the route marked in 6. 1–3 seems to fit well with the first route the goddess describes in 2. 3: in the compound clause that ends 6. 1 and begins 6. 2, it is the impossibility that 'nothing' '[be]' that secures the 'right'-ness or propriety of saying 'to be' (ἔμμεναι) of 'what is there for discourse and understanding' (6. 1), and this correlates with the way that, in fragment 2, it is the impossibility

---

[7] Thus λέγειν τε νοεῖν τ'. Mourelatos has argued persuasively, I think, that ' "thinking" (νοεῖν) functions in Parmenides not as a psychological but as an epistemic term, that it expresses the incisive and sure apprehension of what-is, or truth . . . Parallel comments apply to "speaking". It is clear that Parmenides treats, on the one hand, νοεῖν and, on the other, λέγειν, or φάναι, or ὀνομάζειν as cognate processes' (*Route*, 164). Accordingly, following his suggestions (ibid.), I shall translate νοεῖν as 'understanding' and λέγειν, when paired with νοεῖν, as 'discourse'.

[8] This clause could also be translated 'for it can be', in which case we would have the same use of ἔστι signifying possibility that, on my reading, we have in 6. 2. This, however, would fail to convey the way in which ἔστι in 6. 1, heard existentially, resonates with the idea of presence for . . . that is expressed by the preceding ἐόν and with the idea of existence that is expressed by the preceding ἔμμεναι. By the same token, the οὐκ ἔστιν of 6. 2 could be translated 'is not', but this would lose the intensification of the denial of existence that is expressed by the denial of possibility and that is so appropriate to μηδέν. (I owe thanks to Rachel Kitzinger for discussion of this variety and interplay of uses.)

of 'what-is-not, as such'—'for it cannot be brought about' (2. 7)—
that moves thought to turn back to affirm 'that' or 'how . . . is'
(2. 3). In 6. 4–9, however, the goddess brings us to consider the
negation of 'being' under what appears to be a different aspect:
here, in the view of 'two-headed mortals', 'to be and not to be'
(τὸ πέλειν τε καὶ οὐκ εἶναι) are 'the same and yet not the same'; it
is not the isolated 'what-is-not, as such' but rather the apparently
contradictory linking of 'not to be' with 'to be' that is problematic.
So we must add the following to the questions we gave ourselves
at the end of the previous subsection: (vi) What is the 'backward-
turning path of all' that the goddess refers to at 6. 9, and how does
it link 'to be' and 'not to be'? (vii) How does this second 'route', in
6. 4–9, relate to the 'route' in 6. 1–3? Do they, each encountering
the negation of 'being' in its own way, lead to different destinations,
or do they somehow converge? And, (viii), how do these 'routes'
relate to the 'routes' in fragment 2? How should we understand the
relation between Parmenides' distinct pairings in 2 and 6?

(c) Background: notes on Hesiod and Anaximander

My project in this essay is, of course, an affirmative response to (v).
I want to try to show that Parmenides gives us in the proem the
context for the discovery of the '. . . is'. First, however, we need to
provide ourselves with some key historical background. The central
image in the proem is the gateway 'of the paths of Night and Day'
(1. 11 ff.), presided over by 'much-punishing Justice' (1. 14). In
its details this image resonates with Hesiod and Anaximander, and
our ability to appreciate its significance for the discovery of the
'. . . is' will depend on our ability to recognize and, what is more,
let our imagination be guided by these allusions.[9] Hence this set of
preliminary notes.

(i) *Hesiod's recognition of the play of opposites.* Parmenides' reference to the 'House of Night' at 1. 9 and his forceful opening locative
adverb 'There' (ἔνθα) in 1. 11 recall Hesiod's description of the underworld in the *Theogony*,[10] and Parmenides' image of the gateway

---

[9] On Parmenides' rightful presumption of this ability in his hearers, see K. Robb,
Literacy and Paideia in Ancient Greece (Oxford, 1994), esp. p. 5.

[10] Hesiod structures the description, 720–819, as a series of pointings, each begun
with an opening ἔνθα. See 729, 734, 736, 758, 767, 775, 807 (=736), 811. This is an
ingenious way to proceed, for it allows him to keep a certain order in his discourse

will remind his Greek hearer of Hesiod's vivid portrayal of the interplay of the personified Night and Day at 748–55. By referring
to a 'great threshold of bronze' (μέγαν οὐδὸν χάλκεον, 749–50) and a
'door' (cf. θύραζε, 750), Hesiod conjures up a gateway on the border
of the underworld.[11] On the far side and underneath, containing
the House of Night, lies Tartarus, a 'great chasm' (*Theogony* 740).
Night and Day, Hesiod sings,

                                              draw near to each other
and speak a word of greeting as they exchange places [ἀμειβόμεναι]
        over the great threshold
of bronze; when the one is about to go down, the other comes
out the door, and the house never holds them both within at once
but always, when one of them is outside the house, faring over the earth,
the other stays inside, waiting for its due time for travel to arrive;
the one brings to those on the earth far-flashing light,
while the other holds Sleep, brother to Death, in her arms,
[and she is] destructive Night, veiled in dark clouds.

That this is mythopoeic depiction makes all the more remarkable
the keen sense for the logic of opposites that it expresses. Night and
Day are mutually exclusive, strict alternatives each to the other;
in having them 'speak a word of greeting' as they pass each other
over the threshold, however, Hesiod makes poignant the way in
which their alternation is a form of sharing and collaboration. Each
requires the other in order, through their very contrast, to be itself,
and so they share a home and yield, each to the other, an equal share
of the diurnal period to 'fare over the earth'. By their interplay they
express just the knowledge that Hesiod makes it his mission to
teach, 'how much greater is the half than the whole' (*Works and
Days* 40).

Hesiod expresses this keen sense for the play of opposites in
two further ways as well, and since both are at work in the allu-
sive content of Parmenides' proem, we need to note them here.
First, Hesiod recognizes the way in which the specifically temporal alternation of night and day fits together with the specifically
spatial distribution to opposed loci of their spatial analogues. At
Theogony 123–5 he pairs Erebus, the darkness of the underworld,

without thereby attributing any subordinative or even interrelating structure, hence
any intrinsic integration, to Tartarus itself.

[11] M. L. West (ed.), *Hesiod:* Theogony (Oxford, 1966), ad loc.

with Night, and he makes them the parents of their correlative opposites, Aither, the sheer radiance of the upper sky, and Day. Thus
the principles of light and dark fit together in different ways—ways,
indeed, that themselves in their own difference also fit together—to
structure both the time and the space of the world. Second, and still
more remarkably, Hesiod appears to recognize the way in which the
very lack of differentiation stands over against differentiated totality, and so stands with it to constitute a still higher totality. In his
cosmogony he builds up an image of the whole of the world as a set
of nested pairings of the internally differentiated with the absence
of differentiation. To trace this from micro- to macro-structure:
within the earth, the fertile hills and forests stand over against
the barren sea (129–32); within our over-world, in turn, the thus
differentiated whole of the earth stands over against the open sky
(126, 133); and finally, within the cosmos as a whole, the thus differentiated over-world stands over against 'dark and murky' (729),
storm-filled (742–3) Tartarus, a 'great chasm' (740) precisely in
that, far beneath the very 'roots of earth and sea' (727–8), it lacks
any such internal differentiation and structure within itself.[12]

(ii) *Anaximandran justice and the Apeiron*. Whereas the figure
of the gateway of the paths of Night and Day resonates with Hesiod, the figure of 'much-punishing Justice [who] holds the keys
of interchange' (1. 14) resonates with Anaximander. I have translated Parmenides' word ἀμοιβούς as 'interchange' in order to preserve its echo of Hesiod's ἀμειβόμεναι, 'as they exchange places',
at *Theogony* 749 (quoted above). But Parmenides' word also carries the ethico-legal significance of retribution or requital and fits
together with 'much-punishing' to recall Anaximander's recognition of the 'moral necessity' (τὸ χρεών)[13] that governs the cosmos.
Anaximandran justice is in play in two ways in Parmenides' image.
Most obviously, the regular alternation of Night and Day conforms
to the cyclical pattern in which opposites, each one 'perishing into'
and, conversely, 'coming to be out of' the other,

---

[12] For sustained exegesis, see M. Miller, '"First of all": On the Semantics and
Ethics of Hesiod's Cosmogony' ['First'], *Ancient Philosophy*, 21 (2001), 251–76; also
'La logique implicite dans la cosmogonie d'Hésiode', *Revue de métaphysique et de
morale*, 82 (1977), 433–56.

[13] This and the fragment quoted below are reported by Simplicius, *In Phys.*
24. 18–21 Diels (=DK 12 B 1+A 9), cited in G. S. Kirk, J. E. Raven, and M.
Schofield, *The Presocratic Philosophers*, 2nd edn. [*Presocratics*] (Cambridge, 1983),
§101a, p. 107.

διδόναι γὰρ αὐτὰ δίκην καὶ τίσιν ἀλλήλοις τῆς ἀδικίας
κατὰ τὴν τοῦ χρόνου τάξιν.

pay penalty and retribution to each other for their injustice
according to the assessment of time.

Anaximander, it is usually thought, has in mind the hot and the
cold, very possibly in combination with the dry and the wet, and
refers especially to the rhythm of the seasons.[14] For either of a pair
of opposites to exist for a time is for it to suppress the other, and that
is an injustice; hence it must 'pay' the proportionate 'penalty' of
'perishing' so as to let that other 'come to be' and exist for an equal
time. But this second existence, even while a just compensation for
having suffered the earlier crime of suppression, is also in its own
right a new crime of suppression, and so requires a new 'penalty';
hence the second opposite must also 'perish' in its turn so as to
let the first 'come to be' again. Thus, summer heat gives way to
winter cold, and winter cold again to summer heat, endlessly—
or, similarly, day gives way to night, and night to day, over and
over—all in accord with the requirements of justice. Though his
motif of crime and punishment represents the harshness of justice
in contrast with Hesiod's motifs of a 'greeting' and the sharing of
time and a home, still, Anaximander's 'moral necessity' fits well
with Hesiod's image of day and night 'exchanging places' on the
'threshold'. Hence Parmenides' integration of the two in his figure
of the gateway 'of the paths of Night and Day' ruled by 'much-
punishing Justice'.

We shall come to the second, less obvious presence of Anaximandran justice later, when our discussion of the proem invites it.
To be ready for that moment, however, we need to pause here to
note the connection of justice with his conception of the *archē*, the

[14] He also seems, like Hesiod, to have recognized a spatial analogue to the temporal
interplay of opposites. His obscure account of the sun, moon, and stars as apertures
in great rotating tyre-like wheels made of a solid, bark-like night on the outside
and filled inside with fire gives equal place to night and fire. As Charles Kahn
has argued very persuasively in *Anaximander and the Origins of Greek Cosmology*
[*Anaximander*] (New York, 1960), 159–63, the qualitative associability of the pairs
hot and cold, dry and wet, and (mediated, I suggest, by fire and night) bright and
dark invites us to recognize as a distinctively 'Milesian view' the recognition of a
'pattern of elemental dualism' (162). Kahn takes as evidence of this Parmenides'
own designation, in the Doxa section of the poem, of Fire or Light and Night as the
two forms privileged by 'mortals'. For discussion suggesting how rare and dense
should also be included in this nexus, see the remarks on fragment 4 in sect. 3(*b*),
esp. n. 55 below.

'source' of the cosmos itself, as 'unlimited' or 'boundless' or 'indeterminate'.[15] To compress a momentous and complex insight to its
core: Thales had made the revolutionary claim that the 'source' of
all things is water, but Anaximander, on the strength, arguably, of
his recognition of the justice that regulates opposites, saw that this
could not be. For water, or the wet, to be the source for all else would
imply the permanent suppression of the dry, a crime that 'moral
necessity' could not—and in observable fact, does not—permit.
Anaximander saw the positive implication of this impossibility in
its full generality. Since to grant the status of *archē*, 'source', to
any power that has an opposite—that is, to any qualitatively determinate power—would be to endorse this injustice, the *archē* must
be something qualitatively indeterminate. Accordingly, he distinguished from the opposites a qualitatively indeterminate stuff that
somehow gives rise to them,[16] and so to the world structured by
their interplay. This world, moreover, he was the first to conceive
as spherical in shape, with the column drum-shaped earth at its
centre and the great wheels of night-sheathed fire that are the stars,
the moon, and the sun lying concentrically and at the angle of the
ecliptic around it. Outside this world-sphere, 'surrounding' it entirely and 'embracing' it (περιέχον),[17] he held, lies the Apeiron, the
indeterminate and boundless stuff that is, somehow, its 'source'.

[15] Anaximander's word, ἄπειρον, is remarkable not only for what it means but also
for the transparency with which it bears this web of meanings; it is tempting to
think that we can witness in Anaximander's choice of it his very thought process
as he objects to Thales and reconceives the source and shape of the world-whole
accordingly. ἄπειρον is constructed out of an alpha-privative, meaning 'un-', and
either πεῖραρ (or πεῖρας), meaning 'end, limit, boundary', or the root of the adverb
πέρα, meaning 'beyond, further, beyond measure'. It invites us to think of something
'boundless' in the distinct but complementary senses of something that, since it is
neither limited by any bordering other nor set into contrast with any qualitatively
specific other, is both unchecked in its outward reach and without any internal
qualitative determinateness. And, indeed, the reports of Anaximander's teaching
suggest that he did have both these senses in mind.

[16] On this obscure process see Kirk, Raven, and Schofield, *Presocratics*, §121 and
commentary.

[17] This key word and idea is reported by Aristotle at *Phys.* 3. 4, 203^{b}7–8. On the
spherical shape of the world, 'surrounded' by the ἄπειρον stuff, see Kahn, *Anaximander*, esp. 76–81, 233–9. For a fascinating dissent, see Dirk Couprie, 'The Visualization of Anaximander's Astronomy', *Apeiron*, 28 (1995), 159–81, and Robert
Hahn, *Anaximander and the Architects* (Albany, 2001), 200–18; but I find no trace
of Couprie's cylindrical world-structure in Parmenides' allusions to Anaximander.

2. The proem: towards the gateway and the route(s)

We turn now to the proem. Here, for the sake of a common point of departure as we proceed, is the text and a provisional translation.

ἵπποι ταί με φέρουσιν, ὅσον τ᾽ ἐπὶ θυμὸς ἱκάνοι,
πέμπον, ἐπεί μ᾽ ἐς ὁδὸν βῆσαν πολύφημον ἄγουσαι
δαίμονος, ἣ κατὰ πάντ᾽ ἄ⟨ν⟩τη⟨ν⟩[18] φέρει εἰδότα φῶτα·
τῇ φερόμην· τῇ γάρ με πολύφραστοι φέρον ἵπποι
ἅρμα τιταίνουσαι, κοῦραι δ᾽ ὁδὸν ἡγεμόνευον.   5
ἄξων δ᾽ ἐν χνοίῃσιν ἵει σύριγγος ἀυτήν
αἰθόμενος (δοιοῖς γὰρ ἐπείγετο δινωτοῖσιν
κύκλοις ἀμφοτέρωθεν), ὅτε σπερχοίατο πέμπειν
Ἡλιάδες κοῦραι, προλιποῦσαι δώματα Νυκτός[19]
εἰς φάος, ὠσάμεναι κράτων ἄπο χερσὶ καλύπτρας.   10
ἔνθα πύλαι Νυκτός τε καὶ Ἤματός εἰσι κελεύθων,
καί σφας ὑπέρθυρον ἀμφὶς ἔχει καὶ λάινος οὐδός·
αὐταὶ δ᾽ αἰθέριαι πλῆνται μεγάλοισι θυρέτροις·
τῶν δὲ Δίκη πολύποινος ἔχει κληῖδας ἀμοιβούς·
τὴν δὴ παρφάμεναι κοῦραι μαλακοῖσι λόγοισιν   15
πεῖσαν ἐπιφραδέως, ὥς σφιν βαλανωτὸν ὀχῆα
ἀπτερέως ὤσειε πυλέων ἄπο· ταὶ δὲ θυρέτρων
χάσμ᾽ ἀχανὲς ποίησαν ἀναπτάμεναι πολυχάλκους
ἄξονας ἐν σύριγξιν ἀμοιβαδὸν εἰλίξασαι
γόμφοις καὶ περόνῃσιν ἀρηρότε· τῇ ῥα δι᾽ αὐτέων   20
ἰθὺς ἔχον κοῦραι κατ᾽ ἀμαξιτὸν ἅρμα καὶ ἵππους.
καί με θεὰ πρόφρων ὑπεδέξατο, χεῖρα δὲ χειρί
δεξιτερὴν ἕλεν, ὧδε δ᾽ ἔπος φάτο καί με προσηύδα·
ὦ κοῦρ᾽ ἀθανάτοισι συνάορος ἡνιόχοισιν,
ἵπποις ταί σε φέρουσιν ἱκάνων ἡμέτερον δῶ,   25
χαῖρ᾽, ἐπεὶ οὔτι σε μοῖρα κακὴ προὔπεμπε νέεσθαι
τήνδ᾽ ὁδόν (ἦ γὰρ ἀπ᾽ ἀνθρώπων ἐκτὸς πάτου ἐστίν),
ἀλλὰ Θέμις τε Δίκη τε. χρεὼ δέ σε πάντα πυθέσθαι
ἠμὲν ἀληθείης εὐκυκλέος[20] ἀτρεμὲς ἦτορ

---

[18] I follow A. H. Coxon, *The Fragments of Parmenides* [*Fragments*] (Assen, 1986), 158, in reading ἄντην in place of the universally disputed ἄτη.

[19] Punctuation was, of course, added only later, and editors disagree about whether to put a comma at the end of the line, thereby dividing προλιποῦσαι δώματα Νυκτός from εἰς φάος. Among those who do put a comma here are L. Tarán, *Parmenides* (Princeton, 1965), 7; Mourelatos, *Route*, 279; and Cordero, *By Being*, 185. Among those who do not are D. Gallop, *Parmenides of Elea* [*Elea*] (Toronto, 1984), 48; Kirk, Raven, and Schofield, *Presocratics*, 242; and Coxon, *Fragments*, 160. On the underlying issue see subsect. (*b*)(i) below.

[20] Without wanting to make much hang from this, I have a slight preference

ἠδὲ βροτῶν δόξας, ταῖς οὐκ ἔνι πίστις ἀληθής. 30
ἀλλ' ἔμπης καὶ ταῦτα μαθήσεαι, ὡς τὰ δοκοῦντα
χρῆν δοκίμως εἶναι, διὰ παντὸς πάντα περ ὄντα.[21]

The mares that bear me the lengths my spirit might reach
Were escorting me, when they took and set me on the storied route
Of the divinity who bears onwards throughout the man who knows;
On that route was I borne, for on it the much-discerning mares
    were bearing me,
Straining to pull the chariot, and maidens were leading the way. 5
And the axle in its sockets, ablaze, gave out the war-shriek of a pipe,
For it was being driven hard by the two whirling
Wheels at both ends, whenever the Daughters of the Sun hastened
To escort me, after passing from the House of Night[22]
Into the light, having lifted their veils from their heads. 10
There stand the gates of the paths of Night and Day,
And a lintel and threshold of stone hold them together;
And they themselves, ethereal, are filled with great doors,
Of which much-punishing Justice holds the keys of interchange.
Appeasing her with gentle words, the maidens, 15
Persuading, showed her why for them she should lift the bolted bar
Quickly from the gates; and these in their casing made
A yawning chasm as they were thrown back

for εὐκυκλέος here, following e.g. Tarán, *Parmenides*, 16–17, and Kirk, Raven, and Schofield, *Presocratics*, 242; others, including Mourelatos, *Route*, 154–5, and Coxon, *Fragments*, 168–9, argue well for εὐπειθέος. There is a semantic felicity in having the goddess describe the 'truth' as 'well-rounded' just before turning the traveller's attention back to the 'opinions of mortals', at 1. 30, and showing him the implications of the 'truth' for the best or strongest version of these, at 1. 31–2. We shall discuss this in sect. 4 below.

[21] There is wide, if not deep, support for the reading περῶντα (e.g. Tarán, *Parmenides*, 8–9, 214; Gallop, *Elea*, 21; Kirk, Raven, and Schofield, *Presocratics*, 242–3; Coxon, *Fragments*, 51, 170) over περ ὄντα in the final clause of 1. 32. But I have a slight preference for the reading περ ὄντα ('just being') as it is argued for by G. E. L. Owen in 'Eleatic Questions' ['Questions'], *Classical Quarterly*, NS 10 (1960), 84–102, repr. in R. E. Allen and D. Furley (eds.), *Studies in Presocratic Philosophy*, ii (Atlantic Highlands, NJ, 1975), 48–81, esp. 49–55, and by Mourelatos, *Route*, esp. 210–16. The unusual ὄντα, rather than ἐόντα, appears also at 8. 57. Both Owen and Mourelatos note that this text is better attested, and Mourelatos argues with persuasive precision that the primary sense of περῶντα would be 'piercing through', not 'pervading' (Tarán; Kirk, Raven, and Schofield) or 'permeating' (Gallop) or 'ranging through' (Coxon). Under those translations, it should be noted, περῶντα would fit very well with 9. 3 ('all is full of . . .') and would be very appealing. On the other hand, a chief virtue of περ ὄντα is that it exhibits a use of 'is' on which we should expect Parmenides, with his keen attention to the ontological commitments of cosmological dualism, to seize. See subsect. 4(*b*) below.

[22] Should there be a comma here? See n. 19 above.

And caused the bronze axle-posts to revolve interchangingly
    in their sockets,
Being attached with pegs and rivets. This way, then, straight
    through [the gates],   20
Did the maidens guide the horses and chariot along a broad way.
And the goddess received me kindly, and took my right hand
In hers and spoke to me, addressing me thus:
'Youth, companion to immortal charioteers
Who reaches our home with the mares who bear you,   25
Welcome! For no evil fate has sent you forth to travel
This route (for indeed it is beyond the beaten track of ordinary men),
But propriety and justice. And it is right that you should
    learn all things,
Both the steadfast heart of well-rounded truth
And the opinions of mortals, in which there is no true trust.   30
But nevertheless you shall learn these as well, how for what
    are deemed [to be]
It would have been right that they be eminently, just being all things
    in every way.²³

I shall begin with a general reflection on the significance of the
journey to the gateway; our primary resource for this will be the
goddess's ironically delivered statement of the 'opinions of mortals'
(1. 30), in the Doxa section (8. 50–fr. 19). Then we shall bring to
focus the three key ambiguities in the proem's description of the
journey to, and the passage through, the gateway. This, I hope, will
position us to experience the emergence of the '. . . is'.

(a) The general significance of the arrival at the gateway

Why, then, does the youth journey to the gateway? But this is poorly
phrased. Only in the very beginning of the proem is he travelling
'the lengths my spirit might reach' (1. 1). This self-directed travel
turns out to be but the first phase of a journey in which the powers
that 'bear' (1. 3, 1. 4) and 'guide' (1. 5) him—the 'much-discerning
mares' (1. 4) and Daughters of the Sun (1. 8)—and, indeed, the
course itself, the 'storied route of the divinity' (1. 3), are revealed
to be superhuman. Moreover, the lines just preceding his arrival at
the gateway seem to portray the journey itself as an experience of
ecstatic transport; the chariot reaches such an intensity of speed,
'its axle . . . driven [so] hard by the two whirling wheels' (1. 7–8),

---

²³ On the translation of lines 31–2, see n. 26 below.

that it catches fire and gives forth a fierce, uncanny screech, 'the war-shriek of a pipe' (1. 6). It is no wonder that in her greeting to the youth the goddess begins by reassuring him that 'no evil fate' (1. 26)—euphemistic for madness or death—has brought him to her.[24] All of this reshapes our question: what is the extraordinary achievement symbolized by the youth's arrival at 'the gates of the paths of Night and Day' (1. 11)?

Both the structure of the proem as a whole and the specific content of the goddess's formulations of the 'opinions of mortals' make the Doxa section our key place to begin in seeking an understanding of this. Structurally, the poem moves in a circle: the youth travels to the goddess in the proem, hence from the region of human understanding to that of the divine; in fragments 2–8. 49 the goddess teaches him 'the steadfast heart of well-rounded truth' (1. 29); then, at 8. 50 ff., she guides him back to the region of human understanding, presenting from that point on 'the opinions of mortals' (1. 30, cf. 8. 51). What she presents correlates closely—with but one major difference, which we shall discuss shortly—with what is expressed by the image of the arrival at the gateway in the proem. From the side of the Doxa section: by telling the traveller that she presents to him 'the opinions of mortals' so that 'no thought of mortals shall ever outstrip you' (8. 60), she grants these 'opinions' the status of the deepest possible human insight; that 'no thought *of mortals*' can 'outstrip' these 'opinions' implies that they can be surpassed only by going on to her own specifically divine wisdom. From the side of the proem, correlatively: the gateway is the last structure the youth sees before passing through it and into the presence of the goddess—hence it signifies what human understanding grasps at the limit of its reach, the last (or, as we shall see, nearly the last) insight we at-

---

[24] Peter Kingsley's two books on Parmenides, *In the Dark Places of Wisdom* [*Dark*] (Inverness, Calif., 1999) and *Reality* (Inverness, Calif., 2003), stand out from all other recent commentary for the utter—indeed, deeply passionate—seriousness with which they recognize in the proem an experience of spiritual transport. It is very difficult to assess as a truth claim Kingsley's fascinating identification of Parmenides as an Apollonian *iatromantis*, a 'healer-priest', who is reporting back to 'mortals' what he has learnt from an underworldly 'incubation' and meeting with Persephone. My own more philological approach leads me to agree, however, that the proem (and, hence, the poem as a whole) is inspired by and seeks to re-create some such initiatory and transformative experience; that Parmenides tries to evoke this experience in the proem implies that the depth of attunement to the order of the world that it enables is necessary if the hearer is to share in the goddess's insight.

tain from the human side of the boundary between human and
divine.

The content of the two passages informs and supports this correlation. Here, beginning in each case with the 'opinions of mortals'
and then turning to the proem, are the key substantive parallels:
(*a*) mortals 'have become accustomed in their thought to name two
forms' (8. 54); 'Night and Day' (1. 11) are a paradigm case of such
a pair. (*b*) These 'two forms' are Night (8. 59)—just as in the proem
(1. 11)—and 'fire of flame' (8. 56) or 'light' (9. 1), close kin both to
each other and to Day (1. 11), which bears the '*light*' of the *fiery* sun
to those dwelling on the earth (Hesiod, *Theogony* 755). (*c*) The two
forms are in themselves and in their powers 'opposites' (8. 55), as,
of course, are Night and Day. (*d*) And they are 'equals' (9. 4), as are
Night and Day. (*e*) The two forms, since the 'features' of 'all things'
are explained as the expressions or effects of their 'powers' (9. 1–
2),[25] are together the causes of 'all' (9. 3), analogously as Night and
Day provide the two basic contexts that at every moment condition
everything in the world. In all these ways, the goddess's formulation of the 'opinions of mortals' in effect spells out as doctrine
the symbolic content of the youth's arrival at the gateway. The vision of the gateway, 'filled with [the] great doors [of each path]'
(1. 13), represents the insight that there are two fundamental principles, opposite and equal to one another, that stand as the causes
of the 'features' (9. 2) of all else: 'all is full of light and obscure
night together' (9. 3). The thinking that achieves this insight, in
turn, has detached itself from the seemingly orderless multiplic-
ity and heterogeneity of the world as we ordinarily experience it
and reached the recognition of the underlying order that makes it
a whole ($\pi\hat{\alpha}\nu$, 9. 3) and gives the multiple and heterogeneous the
secondary status, relative to the two forms, of appearance. Thus
understood, the arrival at the gateway marks the achievement of
comprehensive insight into the fundamental powers and structure
of the world.

As for the one major difference that breaks the correlation of the
'opinions of mortals' and the gateway, the goddess signals this in
advance at 1. 31–2. After telling the youth that he must 'learn . . .

---

[25] The 'signs' (8. 55) of fire of flame are its 'bright[ness]', its 'gentle[ness]' (that
is, its rarity or dispersedness), and its 'light[ness]' (8. 56–7); those of Night are its
'dark[ness]', its 'dense[ness]', and its 'heav[iness]' (8. 59). Fire and Night have the
'powers' to produce these 'features' (9. 2) in things.

both the steadfast heart of well-rounded truth and the opinions of
mortals' (1. 29–30), she adds that he must also learn

ὡς τὰ δοκοῦντα
χρῆν δοκίμως εἶναι, διὰ παντὸς πάντα περ ὄντα.

> how for what are deemed [to be]
> It would have been right that they be eminently,[26] just being
> all things in every way.

Her pointed χρῆν ('it would have been right') indicates a past obligation that mortals have not met: to what they 'deem [to be]',
namely, the two forms, mortals ought to have granted the status
of δοκίμως εἶναι, 'be[ing] eminently' or 'with distinction', for these
forms 'just *are* all things in every way'[27]—that is, as we have heard
her explain from the point of view of mortals, they are the ultimate
principles whose 'powers' account for all the 'features' of everything else. At 9. 4 the goddess will fulfil this obligation and make
the necessary correction of the 'opinions of mortals': by her obscure final clause, 'to neither belongs any nothingness' (οὐδετέρῳ
μέτα μηδέν), she asserts that neither of the two forms suffers any
negation; that is, drawing on 1. 32 to put this positively, each 'is'
so 'eminently', 'with' such 'distinction', that it is not subject to
any lack or negation. The implication for our understanding of the
vision of the gateway is important: to recapture the way the figure
of the gateway expresses the best human insight *prior to* the correction the goddess warns us of at 1. 31–2, we must *not* make this

---

[26] I translate τὰ δοκοῦντα as 'what are deemed [to be]' in order to convey its focus
on the things that mortals in their δόξαι ('opinions') take as basic. The imperfect
χρῆν expresses a past (and still present) obligation that has gone unfulfilled (Smyth,
Greek Grammar [*Grammar*] (Cambridge, Mass., 1963), §1774). δόκιμος means 'esteemed' and 'excellent' (LSJ s.v. 1 and 2); nicely capturing its combination of subjective appraisal and objective worth, Owen comments that '[i]n Herodotus the sense
"renowned" becomes common, but never with the implication that the renown is
not wholly deserved' (*Questions*, 70 n. 13). It is in an effort to convey this double
sense of a thing's being held in high regard or granted distinction, on the one hand,
on account of its genuine stature, on the other, that I have translated the adverbial δοκίμως as 'eminently'. Owen's 'genuine', following its uses to mean 'really' or
'genuinely' in Aeschylus and Xenophon (*Questions*, 51, and LSJ s.v. 3), captures
only the objective aspect, but the punning resonance in δοκίμως of δοκοῦντα requires
that we try to convey the subjective aspect as well.

[27] It is important to underscore, however, that this last is the goddess's formulation
as she greets the traveller in fragment 1, not in the Doxa; in the Doxa she does *not*
say 'is' explicitly, for there, by the 'deceptive order of [her] words' (8. 52), she is
representing, as if in their own voice and language, the opinions of mortals, and
mortals have not discovered the '. . . is'.

correction; even at their best, then, mortals not yet instructed by the goddess—that is, Parmenides' predecessors—think that each of the two forms is somehow afflicted by 'nothingness'. This gives us an additional question: (ix) what is this 'nothingness', and in what way(s) are the two forms, as they are understood prior to the goddess's intervention and correction in the Doxa section, subject to it?

(b) *The three ambiguities*

In the preceding account of the figure of the gateway, I have deliberately held back from invoking the Hesiodic and Anaximandran resonances in it, and I have not tried to interpret either the location of the gateway or the actual passage through it. All of this we must now attempt. As we do, we shall find ourselves confronted with three fundamental ambiguities in Parmenides' language. One's first response will be, almost surely, to turn away from these as obstacles to understanding. (Indeed, no scholar I know of has acknowledged all three, much less accepted that which he has acknowledged as both deliberate and positive in its substantive implications; I too, until risking this essay, have shared in this aversion, fearing the chaos that opening up to the ambiguities might let loose.) But, remarkably, these ambiguities are, *even as obstacles*, also constitutive of the way to the experience of the emergence of the '. . . is'.

Let me take up each of the three—and, where the poem invites this, its historical resonance—in turn.

(i) *First ambiguity: descent to the underworld, ascent to the Apeiron.* The most extensive—and, though only in part, well known—of these ambiguities presents itself when we try to locate 'the gates of the paths of Night and Day'. If, on the one hand, Parmenides' early reference to the female divinity ('the divinity who bears me', 1. 3)[28] who bears on her 'storied route' 'the man who knows' moves us to think of Circe's guidance of Odysseus' descent into Hades (*Odyssey* 11), we shall be predisposed to envisage the proem's journey as a *katabasis*, a 'descent' into the underworld.[29] And we shall

---

[28] The Greek—δαίμονος, ἥ . . .—makes the divinity's gender explicit by making the relative pronoun, 'who', feminine.

[29] This view was first argued by J. S. Morrison, 'Parmenides and Er', *Journal of Hellenic Studies*, 75 (1955), 59–68; W. Burkert, 'Das Prooemium des Parmenides und die Katabasis des Pythagoras', *Phronesis*, 15 (1969), 1–30; and D. Furley, 'Notes

feel confirmed in this when we hear of the 'House of Night' (1. 9) and when, with his Hesiodic 'There . . .' (ἔνθα . . ., 1. 11), Parmenides situates the traveller before the gates; for these, as we have noted in recalling *Theogony* 748–55, are located at the very edge of the world, dividing it from Tartarus. Does Parmenides prepare us to meet the waiting goddess, a Demeter- or Persephone-like figure, in the 'great chasm' of Tartarus?

If, on the other hand, our imagination is caught by the image of the 'Daughters of the Sun' (1. 8), we shall be drawn instead to see their 'escort[ing] me . . . into the light' as an ascent.[30] And we shall feel confirmed in this by the characterization of the gates as 'ethereal' (1. 13)—for the Aither, as we noted in discussing Hesiod, is the radiance of the upper sky. Two further details in the passage also seem to support this interpretation. If we take the unveiling by the Daughters of the Sun (1. 10) to reflect their sense of having come home when they pass 'into the light' (1. 10),[31] then, since this is their last gesture before the chariot halts in front of the gateway, it will be natural to locate the gateway in the light. What is more, the phrase Parmenides uses to describe the chariot's course through the opened gates, 'this way, then, straight through them' (τῇ ῥα δι' αὐτέων, 1. 20), is an all but exact quotation[32] of the phrase Homer uses at *Iliad* 5. 752 to describe how Hera, seeking Zeus at the very peak of Olympus, steers her chariot up through the 'gates of sky' (πύλαι . . . οὐρανοῦ, 5. 749). Does Parmenides, then, prepare us to meet the waiting goddess, a Zeus-like figure, in the space above the world?

Remarkably, we seem to be in a stand-off. Should 'ethereal' over-rule the reference to the House of Night, or vice versa? Should 'this way, then, straight through them' overrule 'There . . .', or vice versa? Or, a third possibility, is it the very undecidability of the direction of the journey that Parmenides intends? This third alternative begins to acquire plausibility if we focus on the exquisite

on Parmenides', in E. N. Lee, A. P. D. Mourelatos, and R. Rorty (eds.), *Exegesis and Argument: Studies in Greek Philosophy Presented to Gregory Vlastos* (Assen, 1973), 1–15. It has been adopted by Gallop, *Elea*, 6–7, among others.

[30] This interpretation goes back at least as far as Sextus. It has been reaffirmed against Morrison's and Burkert's challenges (cited in n. 29) by Coxon, *Fragments*, 9–10, 14–15, 161–2, 170–1, and very recently by Kahn, 'Parmenides and Plato', 90–2, and Cordero, *By Being*, 27–30.   [31] Coxon, *Fragments*, 161.

[32] Parmenides writes τῇ ῥα δι' αὐτέων; Homer's τῇ ῥα δι' αὐτάων differs only in the use of alpha for epsilon in αὐτάων, and that is simply a matter of dialect.

indeterminateness of Parmenides' syntax in the key clause at 1. 8–10. At issue is how εἰς φάος ('Into the light'), the opening phrase of line 10, fits into the ὅτε ('whenever') clause in lines 8–10. When we hear it, do we link it with the subject and finite verb, σπερχοίατο πέμπειν | Ἡλιάδες κοῦραι ('the Daughters of the Sun hastened to escort me'), in lines 8–9, or do we link it with the intervening and immediately preceding participial phrase, προλιποῦσαι δώματα Νυκτός ('after passing from the House of Night'), that ends line 9? Parmenides' syntax, which I have preserved in my translation, allows one to construe the connections equally well either way. The two construals, however, invite and reflect opposite visualizations, with the journey going in opposite directions to opposite destinations. Thus, if one links εἰς φάος with σπερχοίατο πέμπειν | Ἡλιάδες κοῦραι, one will see the Daughters of the Sun, having just 'pass[ed] from the House of Night', now 'hasten[ing] to escort' the traveller 'into the light'; thus heard, the proem describes an ascent to the 'ethereal gates'. But if one links εἰς φάος with προλιποῦσαι δώματα Νυκτός, one takes 'the light' as the destination of the Daughters' initial passage 'from the House of Night', and one will see this passage, now completed ('after passing . . .'), as only the first leg of a longer journey in which, having initially come out of their home in the underworld and into the light of the over-world to pick up the traveller, they next 'hasten to escort' him to the gateway. And in so far as the gateway, as that 'of the paths of Night and Day', is on the border of the underworld, the Daughters will be escorting him back towards Tartarus.[33]

Note, moreover, how the detail of the Daughters' unveiling can be—and for one visualizing the passage this way, will be—easily assimilated to the construal of the journey as a descent. One who is caught up in this way of visualizing the journey will take the aorist participle ὠσάμεναι ('having lifted', 1. 10) to indicate a prior action, and so to imply that the Daughters 'lifted their veils from their heads' before they 'passed from the House of Night into the light'. And this timing, one will think (using the same argument we made earlier but now to the opposite conclusion!), aptly reflects

---

[33] To mark the obvious: neither punctuation, which is added only later, nor oral performance, which is, alas, irrecoverable, can be the basis for resolving the ambiguity. Scholarly consensus, moreover, is that since hexameter is a stichic metre with, therefore, the line as its determining unit, a pause at the end of each line would be normal; but in this case it would not indicate how Parmenides' syntax is to be construed. I owe thanks to Rachel Kitzinger for this observation.

the Daughters' feeling at home in that House, which, as powers associated with Day, they share with Night.[34]

But we have not yet reached the climax of this first ambiguity. This comes with the pivotal moment of the arrival at the gateway, the opening up of the 'yawning chasm' (1. 18). To put ourselves in position to appreciate what Parmenides offers us, we must first suspend this translation, which, as translations almost always do, selects some one possibility to the exclusion of others, and so conceals as well as reveals the sense(s) of its original. Parmenides' Greek is the stunning noun–adjective construction χάσμ' ἀχανές. It is built from χάσμα, 'chasm', and ἀχανές, which I have so far translated 'yawning'. Notice that both terms have the same stem, χα (*cha*), which bears the sense of 'opening' or (to invoke two English cognates) 'gap' or 'yaw'.[35] Hence the stem of the following adjective repeats the sound and sense of the stem of the initial noun. Thus, on one level they form a tightly integrated unity. But on another—if, indeed, it makes sense to speak of 'levels' at all in analysing such a play of meanings—the adjective opposes the noun.[36] The Hesiodic resonance of Parmenides' χάσμα, first of all, brings us to see the vast, dark abyss of the 'great chasm' of Tartarus[37] stretching *beneath* us. This is the culminating moment of the image of the journey as descent. The kinaesthetic grip of this sight makes it all the more striking that the following ἀχανές, even while echoing the sense of 'opening', effectively reverses the spatial orientation of our experience of the 'chasm'. Let me explain by providing some philological background. Parmenides' 1. 18 gives us the earliest surviving appearance of ἀχανές in Greek poetry. The next appearance is in a now lost play by Sophocles; it is preserved only in a later lexicon of Sophoclean vocabulary[38] in which we are told that it expresses

[34] What should not be lost sight of in this indeterminateness—whether one takes the unveiling as evidence that the Daughters are coming home to 'the light' or takes it as a sign of their feeling at home in the 'House of Night' or finds this undecidable—is the more fundamental and invariant value of the unveiling: it is a gestural announcement of the revelatory experience to come.

[35] Moreover, *cha* and 'gap' and 'yaw' all bear this sense with a certain onomatopoeia. Notice the comportment of the throat and mouth in uttering these sounds. This onomatopoeia is most completely accomplished by Greek χάσκειν ('to yawn'—which translation, of course, repeats just the same sound–sense performance as χάσκειν).

[36] There is, moreover, a third level to consider as well, which we shall turn to in subsect. (ii)[α] following.   [37] *Theogony* 740, as noted in subsect. 1(*c*)(i) above.

[38] Fragment 1030 Pearson (as reported in LSJ s.v. II.1) = *Tragicorum Graecorum Fragmenta*, iv. *Sophocles*, ed. S. Radt (Göttingen, 1977), 612.

the sense of open space spreading 'over the labyrinth on account of its not having a roof'. This meaning has a long life. LSJ also cites an instance of it from the second or third century CE in the phrase ἀχανὴς καὶ ἀνώροφος νεώς, 'an open and roofless temple'. In these uses ἀχανές signifies the openness overhead, above the upper reaches of the structures—in these examples the high walls of the labyrinth, the column tops and lintels of the temple—that define our local place below. If we let this spatial orientation reinforce Parmenides' 'ethereal' at 1. 13 and itself be further reinforced by his evocation of the Homeric 'gates of sky' at 1. 20, then ἀχανές opposes the sense of place and direction that the Hesiodic resonance of χάσμα so strongly invites: the chasm that 'yawns', yawns *overhead*, and we find ourselves gazing up, not down, through the open gateway and into the void above, not below, the world!

If we allow ourselves to feel and be guided by this oppositional force in ἀχανές, moreover, we also open ourselves to an otherwise unsuspected complexity in the historical resonance of Parmenides' imagery. In Hesiod there is no thought of anything above the upper limit—Aither and sky—of the world; to go beyond the world, one must descend into the 'chasm' of Tartarus. In Anaximander, by contrast, the world is a sphere with the earth at the centre; accordingly, there can be no thought of an underworld. Every path leads outward to the limit of sky. One can, however, at least in thought, go beyond the world by such ascending, for beyond the world-sphere, 'surrounding' and 'embracing' (περιέχον) it in every direction, is its ἀρχή ('source'), the ἄπειρον. This, then, is what would 'yawn' overhead, on the far side of the 'ethereal gates', for one transported there: the indeterminate, boundless, unlimited stuff that 'embraces' and is somehow the 'source' of the world.

Does the traveller, then, descend to the lower limit of the world to gaze down through the gateway into the dark 'chasm' of Tartarus, or does he ascend to the upper limit, the 'ethereal' height, of the world-sphere to gaze up into the limitless stretches of the Apeiron? It would be a mistake, I think, to choose: Parmenides interweaves pointed cues for each reading, and in χάσμ' ἀχανές he brings the two together into a balanced conjunction of opposites. Nor, further, should we settle for the negative, epistemologically weighted position that Parmenides intends nothing more than to reflect the confusion of 'two-headed' mortals (6. 5) who posit two forms, then 'wander' (6. 5) inconsistently between the privileging of the one and the privileging of the other. This possible reading has the virtue of acknowledging that the evidence points in both directions at once; but in so far as it treats the ambiguity as an expression of the confusion of mortals, it turns away before noticing a deeper, more positive philosophical content that Parmenides may be inviting us to recognize.[39]

What is this content? First, Parmenides appears to set before us an analogy of thought-form that unites the apparently opposite paths of his two great predecessors. In making it impossible—or, rather, possible only through a demonstrably arbitrary choice—to experience the journey as either a descent alone or an ascent alone, he compels us to feel the draw of both, and this puts us in position to discern, beyond their differences, the underlying structure that they share. Thus he points to the universal pattern that shapes our best human enquiry into the order of the world. Even while one proceeds imagistically, the other conceptually, and while their thinking moves in apparently opposite directions and to locatively and qualitatively contrasting ultimates, still, both Hesiod and Anaximander alike move from the heterogeneous plurality of the phenomenal world to the discernment of pairs of opposites that, in the interplay of mutual physical displacement and logical complementarity, account for the basic order, both spatial and temporal, of that heterogeneous plurality. This is the pattern of thinking to which, with the one major correction she introduces at 1. 31–2, the goddess gives her ironic blessing in the Doxa section of the poem.

Secondly—and here we begin to move into uniquely Parmenidean territory—Parmenides also marks and exposes as deceived the further move from the opposites to a prior 'one' that both Hesiod and Anaximander, in their different ways, attempt.[40] The 'great chasm' of Tartarus, we saw, is that region not subject to the to-

---

[39] Accordingly, I disagree with the surface, at least, of Mourelatos's view (reiterated by Curd, *Legacy*, 19, esp. n. 52, and A. Hermann, *To Think like God: Pythagoras and Parmenides* (Las Vegas, 2004), 176–78) that Parmenides deliberately leaves 'the topography of the journey . . . blurred beyond recognition' (*Route*, 15). This suggests that Parmenides seeks to prevent a clear sense of the direction and course of the journey from forming in the first place (see 41), whereas I am arguing that he elicits a clear, and clearly contradictory, double sense of this. But as I hope will be clear from my argument below, I very much agree with what I take to be the substance of Mourelatos's point: 'Parmenides uses old words, old motifs, and old images precisely in order to think new thoughts in and through them' (39).

[40] For Hesiod's own quite un-Parmenidean reservations about this priority, however, see Miller, 'First'.

pographical and elemental articulation that makes the over-world a differentiated whole. The Apeiron, in turn, is a boundless and qualitatively indeterminate stuff that both precedes and somehow sources, outside of itself, the qualitatively determinate opposites whose just interplay structures the world. Both, accordingly, must be located beyond the space of the differentiated and determinate, and in this analogous 'beyond' they are not opposites to the world but, rather, privations of the structure that constitutes it. But this is to say that each alike is arrived at not by the discovery of any intrinsic character but, rather, by removing the opposites. This is the significance of Parmenides' subtle but, in its critical bearing on both Hesiod and Anaximander, devastating account of the formation of the χάσμ' ἀχανές, the 'yawning chasm', of 1. 18. Even as he compounds Hesiod's underworldly 'chasm' with the Anaximandran Apeiron that 'yawns' above the world, he discloses the abyss itself *as a product of the opening of the gates*. It is '[the gates] in their casing' (ταὶ . . . θυρέτρων), 'as they were thrown back' (ἀναπτάμεναι), that 'made' (ποίησαν) the 'yawning chasm' (1. 17–18). With this touch Parmenides invites us to appreciate the full uncanniness of Tartarus and the Apeiron: each is an artefact and an expression of absolute negation, a pure absence of the opposites, and so in itself *nothing*. This Hesiod and Anaximander have missed, each mistaking sheer absence for a positive presence, the void that the removal of the opposites constitutes for an ultimate 'something'. In exposing this deception, Parmenides frees himself to encounter this nullity, the pure absence of the opposites, for what—to speak with unbridled paradox—'it' 'is', and so allows his thought to be borne by 'it' through the gateway.

(ii) *A second and a third ambiguity*. That Tartarus and the Apeiron are in each case only an absence or nothing is, I shall try to show in Section 3, the recognition that opens the way (sticking, for the moment, to Parmenides' figurative language) through the gateway to the goddess. But to prepare for this opening of the way, we need first to acknowledge two further ambiguities; like the first, these too will both complicate and orient our thinking as we seek the '. . . is'.

[α] *The '(un)yawning chasm'?* Parmenides' 'yawning chasm'— χάσμ' ἀχανές—has still one more strange gift to offer. We have noted its onomatopoeic echoing of the χα-; hence my English effort to repeat in the adjective 'yawning' the idea and the sound of the noun 'chasm'. At the very centre of the compound we hear the -a-, the first sound in the adjective ἀχανές and, at the same time, a trace of the elided final -α of χάσμ' that it displaces. Given the dominance of the sound and the idea of χα-, 'opening', it is natural to take that -a- as an alpha-intensive; in this function it heightens the idea of the stem to which it is prefixed. (Smyth gives as examples of the alpha-intensive ἀτενής 'stretched, strained', in which the initial ἀ- intensifies the sense of the stem of τείνω 'stretch', and ἄπεδος 'level', in which the ἀ- intensifies the sense of the stem of πέδον 'ground'.[41]) But, strikingly, the ἀ- may equally well be heard as an alpha-privative, which cancels or takes back the idea of the stem to which it is prefixed; indeed, this is the more frequent and familiar function of the prefixed ἀ- in Greek, well known to us in countless English cognates such as 'atheist' (cf. ἄθεος), 'anodyne' (cf. ἀνώδυνος), 'asymmetry' (cf. ἀσυμμετρία), 'apolitical' (cf. ἀπολιτικός), etc.[42] Hence, surprisingly, ἀχανές can mean not only 'wide-mouthed' (LSJ s.v. II) but also 'not opening the mouth' (LSJ s.v. I), not only 'yawning' (LSJ s.v. II) but also 'narrow' (LSJ s.v. I).

How should we respond to this ambiguity? Every translation I have seen fails to express it.[43] In so far as this reflects a preference for the alpha-intensive reading, it is understandable and right. To translate, as we noted earlier, requires making choices, and it would do an injustice to Parmenides' χάσμ' ἀχανές to choose 'un-yawning' over and to the exclusion of 'yawning'. The gates are, after all, 'thrown back' or 'open', ἀνα-πτάμεναι, and it is only by passing 'this way, then, straight through' the opening they make that the traveller reaches the goddess. At the same time, to fail to indicate the alpha-privative sense at all, hence to fail to indicate the ambiguity, is also to leave hidden a forewarning of the very mistake that reflection on the first ambiguity has exposed in Hesiod and Anaximander. Just in so far as the 'chasm' is not a separate *something* beyond the gates but rather the *nothing* that their 'being thrown back' 'makes', it is not in itself a positive object or determinate content for thought. In this sense, even as it seems to invite consciousness to take it up, we discover when we try to do so that there is nothing there—no

---

[41] Smyth, *Grammar*, §885.4.

[42] Smyth, *Grammar*, §885.1, gives the first two examples, LSJ the second two.

[43] This includes my own 'Parmenides and the Disclosure of Being', *Apeiron*, 13 (1979), 12–35. It was Rachel Kitzinger who first pressed me to account for my presumptive neglect of the alpha-privative sense.

'it' at all—for consciousness to take up in the first place. As the privation or absence of the opposites, 'it' resists being constituted as 'an' 'it', as in itself a separate intentional object. Parmenides, as we have already noted, will have the goddess explain this in 2. 7–8: 'what is not, as such'—that is, taken by itself—'cannot be brought about', and so cannot be 'known' or 'pointed out'.

But, of course, it is within the context of the act of trying to point 'it' out that the goddess declares this very act impossible. In terms of the imagery of the proem, it is as a 'chasm', as an 'opening' that 'yawns' before the traveller, that the 'chasm' is also 'un-opening', 'un-yawning'. So we need to hear both the alpha-intensive and the alpha-privative senses of ἀχανές together.

[β] *The way(s) the gates open.* If the 'chasm' is 'un-yawning' as well as 'yawning', how is it possible for the traveller to pass 'this way, then, straight through' it? Part of the force of the contradiction is to turn us away from a literal understanding of its significance. We need to understand the meaning of the image of the χάσμ' ἀχανές in a way that makes its ambiguity appropriate. Just what is this strange nullity that both invites and resists thought and that, in this very resistance, is somehow none the less transitional to the thought of the '. . . is'? But here we need to step back, for such a direct and single-minded focus both forgets and falls prey to the very difficulty that the χάσμ' ἀχανές poses: the thought that it resists is the thought that tries to take it up by itself, 'as such' (γε, 2. 7). We should therefore pursue it instead in the larger context of relations in which it first seems to present itself. How is it, then, that the gates first 'make' the 'chasm'?

Here we encounter the third ambiguity: Parmenides gives us two essentially different descriptions of how the gates swing open. These descriptions come only a line apart, and they are conveyed by two participles, ἀναπτάμεναι (1. 18) and εἰλίξασαι (1. 19), that modify the same noun ('these [gates]', ταὶ [πύλαι], 1. 17), are in the same tense (the aorist), and are not linked by any third term that might subordinate one to the other. Parmenides once again invites us to confront and interpret a contradiction. To explicate by translating: in the first description, at 1. 18, it is by 'being thrown back' (ἀναπτάμεναι) that the gates 'make' the 'chasm'. The Greek term signifies a flinging (-πτάμεναι) open or back (ἀνα-), with the strong presumption that the two gates are pushed back together and in the same direction. In this case, the 'chasm' will be constituted by *the absence of both gates together*. In the second description, at 1. 19–20, the gates are said to open in such a way that they 'caused the bronze axle-posts to revolve (εἰλίξασαι) interchangingly in their sockets, being attached with pegs and rivets'. The adverb 'interchangingly', ἀμοιβαδόν, refers us back to Justice's 'keys of interchange', κληῖδας ἀμοιβούς, 1. 14—and so, also, both to Hesiod's image of the 'exchang[e] of places' (cf. ἀμειβόμεναι, *Theogony* 749) by Night and Day as they enter and depart their shared home and to Anaximander's account of the 'moral necessity' that requires the regular alternation of the opposites. Here the doors are depicted as swinging in opposite directions, the one swinging back while the other swings forward. In this second depiction, the 'chasm' will be 'made' by the absence *now of one* of the gates (which swings back while the other swings forward), *now of the other* (which now swings back while the first swings forward), *alternately*.

Here as before, it is at first tempting to look for a way to defuse the contradiction—or, indeed, simply to ignore it. The latter has been the universal practice of previous commentators, so far as I know.[44] If we look away, however, we risk missing what may be a first indication in the text of how to understand the initially puzzling distinction between the two routes in fragment 6. (Recall Section 1(*b*) above.) If we key from the first description of the gates' opening, the 'chasm'—that is, the absence they 'make' by 'being thrown back' together—will be the absence of them both at once. If, on the other hand, we key from the second description, the 'chasm' will be first the absence of one of the gates as it swings back, even as the other, swinging forward, becomes present, and then the absence of this other as *it* swings back while the first gate swings forward and becomes present. Is there not a prima facie correlation of these two images with the two characterizations of the routes in fragment 6? Is Parmenides anticipating with these contradictory depictions the two different ways of encountering the negation of being that he distinguishes in fragment 6? The absence of both gates at once appears to fit with the unqualified 'nothing' (μηδέν) in

---

[44] I have not attempted a complete canvassing, but I find no acknowledgement of this ambiguity in Tarán, *Parmenides*; Kirk, Raven, and Schofield, *Presocratics*; Mourelatos, *Route*; J. Barnes, *The Presocratic Philosophers*, 2 vols. (London, 1979); Gallop, *Elea*; Coxon, *Fragments*; R. McKirahan, *Philosophy before Socrates* (Indianapolis, 1994); Kingsley, *Dark* and *Reality*; Curd, *Legacy*; Kahn, 'Parmenides and Plato'; or Cordero, *By Being*.

6. 2, while the alternation of the absence of one (together with the presence of the other) and the absence of that other (together with the presence of the one) fits well with the 'path' of 6. 8–9 that, as the cycling between the 'being' (τὸ πέλειν, 6. 8) of one of the opposites at the expense of the 'non-being' ([τὸ] οὐκ εἶναι, 6. 9) of the other and the 'being' of that other at the expense of the 'non-being' of the first, is 'backward-turning' (παλίντροπος).

3. Passing through the gates—the emergence of '. . . is' for 'understanding'

Our guiding thought in this essay is that Parmenides gives us in the proem the context within which the '. . . is' first emerges from inconspicuousness to become a referent for philosophical insight. This insight is the achievement of the 'discourse and understanding' (λέγειν τε νοεῖν τ', 6. 1) of the goddess in the Truth section (fragments 2–8. 49) of the poem. My heuristic hope has been that by letting ourselves be informed and oriented by the parallels between the proem and the Doxa and by the proem's historical resonance, we shall find ourselves in position to experience the emergence of the '. . . is', and so to rise to the level of the goddess's 'discourse and understanding'. This, if we can accomplish it, will be our own enactment of the traveller's passing through the gateway.

Our recognition of the third ambiguity has given us two distinct courses of thought to pursue. We shall attempt to think through each in turn.

(a) 'The gates . . . thrown back'—being guided by 'nothing'

Let us begin by putting ourselves in the position of the traveller and reconstructing the situation of enquiry one more time. To arrive at 'the gates of the paths of Night and Day' (1. 11) is to reach the 'naming' of 'two forms' (8. 53, 9. 1) that, by their 'powers', account for the 'features' of 'all things' in the world (9. 1–3); presided over by Justice (1. 14), they are 'opposites' in every way (8. 53) and 'equals' in their exercise of causal power (9. 4). And to be poised there, our inspiring guides asking for passage through the gateway, is to be asking—but now of the two forms themselves—the questions that first led us beyond the heterogeneous plurality of things. What, in

turn, might lie beyond the two forms? What, just as they are basic
to 'all things', might be basic to them? Persuaded of the 'propriety
and justice' (1. 28) of our enquiry,[45] Justice unbars the gates, and
'these in their casing made | A yawning chasm as they were thrown
back . . .' (1. 18). In its resonance, this 'yawning chasm', χάσμ'
ἀχανές, summons to mind both the 'great chasm' of Tartarus, the
abyss of the underworld, in Hesiod and the Apeiron, 'yawning'
above, beyond the boundary of the world-sphere, in Anaximander.
But even as he elicits these associations, Parmenides also undercuts
them: the 'chasm' is 'in the casing' of the gateway, and it is 'made';
it is not, then, a region or a stuff beyond the gateway but rather
the very lack of the gates, 'thrown back', within it. What appears
as beyond and independent to one gazing into the open gateway is
just that—an appearance from the human side—and, indeed, less
than that: as the emptiness 'in the casing' that is 'made' by the gates
being 'thrown back', it is *nothing*, a pure absence or privation.

Here, finally, is the moment of passage:

> This way, then, straight through [the gateway],
> Did the maidens guide the horses and chariot along a broad way.
> And the goddess received me kindly, . . .
>
> (1. 20–2)

The way we understand the traveller's passing into and through the
gateway, I would argue, makes all the difference for our appreciation
of the goddess's disclosure of the '. . . is'.

If, on the one hand, we neglect the manifold ambiguity of the
text, letting its difficulties disappear in favour of the formation of a
consistent image, we gain a clear and straightforward symbolization
of the traveller's surpassing the dualism of mortals and attaining
the higher standpoint of the welcoming goddess. This clarity and
straightforwardness come at great cost, however: Parmenides' challenge to the presumption of there being *something* beyond the two

---

[45] 'Propriety and justice' are the goddess's words, in effect thematizing the significance of Justice's decision to grant the traveller passage through the gateway. This
gives us yet another web of questions: (ix) in what sense of justice is it just for one
who has attained the 'naming' of 'two forms', the limit of the reach of the 'opinions
of mortals', to pass beyond this to the 'discourse and understanding' of '. . . is'? In
what way is Justice's character as 'much-punishing', that is, as requiring alternation
and balance, relevant and in play here? And in so far as in some way it is in play, is
there a reciprocal or complementary 'propriety and justice' to the mirroring return
from the discourse and understanding of '. . . is' to the two forms, as Parmenides
has the goddess execute this at 8. 50 ff.?

forms goes forgotten; that the 'chasm' is, as ἀχανές, 'un-yawning' as well as 'yawning', hence a closure as well as a site of passage, is ignored; and in our ongoing picturing of the journey, our own mode of thinking remains undisturbed and, so, untransformed. We have an unproblematic picture of the transport from human to divine consciousness and, on that account, have ourselves undergone no such transport at all.

If, on the other hand, we keep the first and second ambiguities firmly in mind, we seem to face an insuperable obstacle. To pass through the gateway is—to bring into focus the philosophical depth of the symbol—somehow to take up the *nothing*, the pure absence or privation of the opposites, in thought. But the second ambiguity has brought home the difficulty of this: if the 'chasm' is, as 'yawning', apparently an opening or site of passage, it is also, as 'un-yawning', not an opening but a closure. Thus, thought appears to be blocked. The 'chasm', a *nothing* or absence or privation, is precisely not something that we can think into. It cannot be constituted as an object and remain itself; it cannot be taken up in thought by itself, 'as such' (γε, 2. 7); and these very utterances of mine, precisely by their failure to express their point without at the same time performatively contradicting it, show why: each starts from the presumption of an 'it', and this is just what, as *nothing* or absence, it is not. 'What-is-not, as such, . . . cannot be brought about' (2. 7).

And yet 'this way, . . . straight through [the gateway]', the traveller does pass. Does the insuperable resistance, then, that the *nothing* offers itself provide the decisive occasion for the transformation of consciousness and the transition to the goddess's insight? To see how this might be so, we need to work patiently, step by step, through a series of distinct recognitions that, in the experience of the thinking they trace, belong to one manifold intuition. Consider: (*a*) as the gates are 'thrown back', their withdrawal constitutes the 'chasm', the emptiness 'in the casing'. That is, as we turn in thought away from the opposites, seeking what other than them may be still more fundamental than and basic to them, what begins to present itself to mind—since, after all, the opposites themselves account for 'all things'—is nothing further, no third thing, but just their absence. (*b*) An emptiness first presents itself as an altering of context: the gates fly backward, and the casing empties out. But at the end of this event, the emptiness is invisible, vanished, so to speak, in the presence of what lies within or beyond it. Analogously, the *nothing* or absence of the opposites, even as it begins to present itself, fails to complete itself, fails to constitute itself as an object or determinate content that can be taken up in thought. (For, to step again into inescapable paradox, this is its very nature, namely, not to be an 'it' with a nature, a specific character, in the first place.) (*c*) But this failure, even as it leaves us without an object, is not fruitless; for in the very experience of it, we learn not to picture but rather, as the attitude that underlies and turns this surrender into receptivity, to open up to the lack of an object as the condition for something altogether different in kind. And this frees us to experience—bear with me here! I am straining for helpful language—the functioning of referral. For the *nothing* or absence, even while it fails to take a form that thought could 'know' in the sense of 'pointing it out' (2. 7–8) as one content among others, is none the less the absence or the privation *of* . . ., and the thinking that is capable of not trying to take 'it' up 'by itself' thereby opens itself up to the dynamic of this '*of* . . .'. (*d*) If we were less patient than Parmenides, we might now jump to the assumption that the 'chasm', 'un-yawning', refers us back to the opposites; for it was as the opening left by the gates, that is, as the absence *of* the opposites, that it first 'yawned'—began to present itself—before us. But this would be too quick, for it would cost us the crucial insight that, for Parmenides, is the attainment of the company of the goddess. The *nothing* or absence of the opposites is indeed the negation of them—but not of them as, when in enquiring into the basis of the heterogeneous plurality of the world, we first brought them to view. Then it was their reciprocal difference that, making for their complementarity, let us pair them together in mind. Parmenides evoked this beautifully by his image of the essentially bipartite gateway, in which the opposed courses of Night and Day are placed side by side, 'held together' from without by the lintel and threshold (1. 12). But the *nothing* or absence of the opposites is the negation not specifically of Day (that negation is the work of Night) or specifically of Night (that negation is the work of Day), nor is it merely the conjunction of these negations; accordingly, it refers us not to the one and then the other, nor even to the conjunction of the two in their complementarity. Rather, it is the negation of *the very being* or *presence* that, as it is made subject to negation, they share. It is this that *nothing* threatens, this that their absence is the absence *of*. To try to think this counterfactually: if the negation of them could 'be brought about'—that is, if it could

'be made to be' or 'finished' (ἀνυστόν, 2. 7)[46]—then they would be
denied their very being. But it cannot 'be brought about' (not if
it is *nothing*), and so their very being cannot be denied. What the
negation does do, however, even as it fails to take form as an object
for mind, is refer to that of which it is the negation, *the being, as
such*, of the two, and so, in calling this out of inconspicuousness,
provide the occasion for νοεῖν (2. 2, 6. 1), that is, for thought to
'understand' it. (*e*) Finally, however, this 'as such' is dangerous.
'Being' too, in a way that makes it oddly akin to its very absence, is
not a separate object. As the being *of the two forms*, it too has the
character for mind of a functioning referral. To focus our attention
on it is, accordingly, to be referred to what it is the being *of*, that is,
to the two forms—now, however, under the newly disclosed aspect
of their very being. Thus we are led to bring them to mind in their
fundamental unity or affinity in kind *as beings*.

   This experience of the passage through the gateway gives us
the basis, I think, for an understanding of the obscure 6. 1–2.[47]
Why, we want to ask the goddess, does she declare that 'it is right
for what is there for discourse and understanding to be' (χρὴ τὸ
λέγειν τε νοεῖν τ᾽ ἐὸν ἔμμεναι, 6. 1)? Here I take as the subject of
the 'to be' (ἔμμεναι) the substantive 'what is there' (in Greek the
substantivized participle τὸ . . . ἐόν); the closely conjoined infinitives
'for discourse and understanding' (λέγειν τε νοεῖν τ᾽) function to
limit the meaning of the participle,[48] restricting and specifying the
context in which 'what is there' (τὸ . . . ἐόν) presents itself. And I
take it that Parmenides' reference to 'discourse and understanding'
(λέγειν τε νοεῖν τ᾽) is pointed: he refers to the modes of consciousness
that we achieve only in so far as we detach from the need for image-
bound consciousness, namely, the seeing and hearing (cf. 6. 7: 'deaf
and blind') and the thinking that is still dependent for its content on
things as they are given to seeing and hearing (cf. 6. 6: 'wandering
mind', and 6. 7: 'without discernment'), that grips even Hesiod
and Anaximander. Accordingly, we are asking the goddess why it
is 'right' for the *being* that is taken up by the 'understanding' that

---

[46] Recall n. 3 above.
[47] For a sample of the different construals of 6. 1–2, see Gallop, *Elea*, 30–1 nn. 15
and 16, and his apparatus on p. 61. Mourelatos, *Route*, p. xv, declares that 'undeniable
syntactic ambiguity . . . make[s] gratuitous any attempt to obtain from these lines
positive information regarding Parmenides' philosophical doctrine'.
[48] Smyth, *Grammar*, §2006. I owe thanks to Rachel Kitzinger for illuminating
discussion of this syntax with me.

we have just traced to have its status *as being* in the first place. Her
explanation (cf. 'for', γάρ, 6. 1),

ἔστι γὰρ εἶναι,

μηδὲν δ' οὐκ ἔστιν,

(6. 1–2)

for it is there to be,
Whereas nothing cannot [be],

refers us to the two fundamental moments in that complex 'understanding'. She sets her declaration of the manifestness or presence
of being—namely, 'it *is there* to be'—into the context of the thought
of the impossibility of 'nothing'. That is, she gives us, as if to be
considered, the *nothing*, only then, in a beautifully dexterous con-
signing of it to its own impetus, to declare that it 'cannot [be]'. Had
we not thought into the passage through the gateway, we might be
puzzled over the connection of these two thoughts, 'it is there to be'
and 'nothing cannot [be]'. But our reconstructive reflections have
shown us the fit that the goddess now invokes: it is precisely by its
referring, even as it itself fails to be constituted as an object, to the
very being that it negates that it lets this being emerge and become
manifest to mind.

(b) 'The gates' . . . 'revolving interchangingly'

Let us now attempt to pass through the gateway by the second
course. In 1. 19, recall, Parmenides says that the gates, unbarred
by Justice, swung open in such a way that they 'caused the bronze
axle-posts to revolve interchangingly in their sockets' (1. 19). In
this second image the 'chasm' is 'made' by the gates swinging in
opposite directions: while the one swings forward, the other swings
backward, then vice versa. Since this is how the gates must open at
dawn and at dusk to let Night and Day pass side by side, the one
coming forth to 'fare over the earth' while the other 'goes down' into
Tartarus, the image recalls their 'exchange of places' in Hesiod.[49]
But it also fits the analogue of this exchange in Anaximander, the
'backward-turning path of all'[50] (6. 9) that is manifest, for instance,
as the cyclical interchange of summer heat and winter cold. Each

---

[49] *Theogony* 749, 750, 752, slightly modified, all cited within the longer quote in
subsect. 1(c)(i) above.

[50] Some argue that 'all' refers not to all things but to all men. See e.g. Mourelatos,
Route, 77 n. 7. But though all live under its sway, only a few, the most eminent

opposite, by its own time of existence having denied such time to the other, must then 'pay penalty and retribution' to that other by 'perishing into' it, and so allowing the other to have its time of existence. Thus the 'chasm' that the gates 'make' by swinging open 'interchangingly' signifies (in Hesiodic terms) the 'going down' into the underworld or (in Anaximandran terms) the 'perishing into' its opposite or (now in Parmenidean terms) the reduction to a *'what-is-not'* (τό γε μὴ ἐόν) or *'nothing'* (μηδέν) that each opposite must suffer as both the consequence of and the precondition for the presencing or coming to be of the other.

As before, the key to passing through the gateway will turn out to be attending to the second ambiguity, the way in which the 'chasm', even as it 'yawns' before us, is also 'un-yawning'. But the different way in which the 'chasm' is 'made' points to the different context in which the *nothing* here begins to present itself: the manifold connections of being and not-being in the 'backward-turning path'. At 6. 8–9 the goddess points to this manifold when she says that 'mortals' have come to take[51] 'to be and not to be as the same | Yet not the same'. In the interplay of the opposites in Hesiod and Anaximander, we can identify a double knot of sameness and difference. Take Anaximander's pair of hot and cold as a paradigm. In any definite time and place, the hot's coming to be is absolutely dependent upon the cold's ceasing to be, and vice versa. For each of the opposites in the cycle, the 'being' of the one, here and now, cannot be separated from the reduction of the other to 'not being', hence to the status of a 'what-is-not' (2. 7). And conversely, the reduction of one to the status of a 'what-is-not' cannot be separated

thinkers, have discovered and articulated the structure of the cycle of opposites. So I find it more plausible to take 'all' to refer to all things as, in accord with the fundamental insight of these few, these things are governed by this cycle. One of those few was Heraclitus, and some, most recently Daniel Graham ('Heraclitus and Parmenides', in V. Caston and D. Graham (eds.), *Presocratic Philosophy: Essays in Honor of Alexander Mourelatos* (Aldershot, 2002), 27–44), have found in Parmenides' word παλίντροπος ('backward-turning') an allusion to Heraclitus 22 B 51 DK. This is possible but, I think, unlikely. On the side of its possibility, Graham identifies other wordplays in Parmenides that remind one of Heraclitus. None of these, however, seems pointed in its critical thrust. This includes even Parmenides' use of παλίντροπος here in fragment 6; whereas Parmenides seems to refer to a cycle over time, Heraclitus in fragment 51 seems to refer to the simultaneous and reciprocal production of one opposite by another. On the question of the relation between Heraclitus and Parmenides, see Nehamas, 'Fire'.

[51] Parmenides puts this in the passive voice: 'to be and not to be have come to be taken [νενόμισται] to be the same and not the same'.

from the 'being' of the other. Accordingly, 'to be' and 'not to be', in so far as they are inseparable, may 'be taken' to be 'the same'—'and yet', in so far as their subjects differ, they may also 'be taken' to be 'not the same'.

Or so, prior to Parmenides' closer reflection on the 'chasm', it seemed. As with the first course of thought, so here, we can best recover Parmenides' insight if we distinguish and work through, step by step, a series of recognitions that are really integral moments in one manifold intuition. (*a*) Each opposite, presenting itself initially as a qualitatively determinate sensible presence, precludes the appearance of the other; for instance, when and where the hot prevails, the cold cannot be. (*b*) But if, with Parmenides, we pause to consider this 'chasm' of the cold, we discover that it is, rather, this very not-being of the cold that cannot be. With a qualification we shall come to, this is once again the recognition of 2. 7–8: 'what-is-not, as such, . . . cannot be brought about', hence cannot be 'known' or 'pointed out'. That is, to fall again into illuminatingly self-undermining language, it cannot be constituted as an object or determinate content for thought, for it is its very nature to be, 'by itself' (γε, 2. 7), precisely the negation or lack of any such nature and determinateness.[52] (*c*) This is the moment of apparent impasse. The 'chasm' is 'un-yawning', no passageway after all—unless, as before, we learn the lesson its very closure has to teach us: if we accept, in the failure of 'what-is-not' to constitute itself as an object or content for thought, that we cannot take it up 'by itself', we free ourselves to experience the force of its referral beyond itself. (*d*) Here we encounter the difference from the first course that requires the qualification I just anticipated. As before, the not-being *of* . . ., even as it itself fails to stand alone for thought, refers us on beyond itself to what it is the *not* or negation *of*. And analogously as before, this referent is the opposite not in its immediate qualitative presence but rather in its very being—for it is this, as we saw, that the negation, i.e. the reduction to not-being, threatens, and so lets

[52] This, note, is why any account of the world that invokes it as if it were an intelligible content for thought—as does Anaximander's account of the cycle of opposites—is deceived, and it is in order to avoid this deception that the goddess makes the reform of the 'opinions of mortals' in fragment 9 that she first warned the traveller of at 1. 31–2. 'To neither [of the two forms]', she declares at 9. 4, 'belongs any nothingness'. Thus—but only when she comes to present the 'opinions of mortals' at 8. 50 ff. and in fragments 9–19—she arranges that what we mortals 'deem [to be]' we deem 'to be eminently', purging from our best mortal account any reduction of what-is to the status of what-is-not.

emerge for νοεῖν, 'understanding'. But in addition, the negation of the very being of the opposite refers us as well to the very being *of the opposite's other*; that is, it refers us to the conjunction of the being of the one with the being of the other. For in the relation of opposites, the one cannot be what it is unless its other, both providing and receiving the contrast in the context of which each has its proper specificity, also is what it is. And this means that when negation threatens the being of the one, it necessarily threatens the being of the other as well. (*e*) Thus—now to bring (*c*) and (*d*) together—we are guided, even as the absence that guides us absents itself, so to speak, from thought, to the 'understanding' (νοεῖν) of the way *the very being of* each requires *the very being of* the other, and so to the reciprocal necessity by which, as *being* to *being*, each is conjoined with the other.

This movement and insight, I think, are the crux of fragment 4:[53]

λεῦσσε δ' ὅμως ἀπεόντα νόῳ παρεόντα βεβαίως·
οὐ γὰρ ἀποτμήξει τὸ ἐὸν τοῦ ἐόντος ἔχεσθαι
οὔτε σκιδνάμενον πάντῃ πάντως κατὰ κόσμον
οὔτε συνιστάμενον.

Consider what are absent, and see how they are, nevertheless, steadily present to mind;
For [mind] will not cut off what-is from holding fast to what-is—
[For what-is] neither scatters in every direction everywhere in order
Nor solidifies.

Let me prepare the way for a reading of this with several orienting observations. Parmenides' beautiful—and, alas, only awkwardly translatable—opening imperative, λεῦσσε, urges a meditative attentiveness. It is cognate with λευκός 'light, bright, clear',[54] and means 'look upon . . ., gaze at . . .', with the connotation of letting an otherwise hidden intelligibility 'dawn' on one or 'come to light'. To convey both these aspects, process and goal, I have written two verbs in place of Parmenides' one: 'Consider . . ., and see how . . .'. Second, the effect of his paratactic play with ἀπεόντα and παρεόντα in

---

[53] It is a virtue of this second course of thought that it provides a rich context for interpreting this otherwise enigmatic sentence, 'the most disputed of all [the] "fragments"' (Cordero, *By Being*, 16). Mourelatos, *Route*, p. xv, chooses not to 'attempt . . . an interpretation' of fragment 4 on account of its 'syntactic . . . ambiguities coupled with loss of context . . .'.

[54] And with Latin *lux* (LSJ s.v.).

4. 1, 'what are absent' and '[what are] present', respectively, and of
his substantive reference to 'dispersal' and 'solidification' in 4. 3–4
is to turn our thought to Anaximander's conception of opposites.
The polarity of dispersal and solidification (or, more familiarly,
of rarefaction and condensation) constitutes a fundamental axis of
possibility for the states of bodies; Anaximander's prime successor
Anaximenes picked these out as the basic opposites underlying all
other physical conditions in the world, and in this he is probably
reinterpreting Anaximander's fundamental pair, the hot and the
cold; certainly dispersal (as in thawing, melting, and evaporating)
and solidification (as in condensation and freezing) are conspicuous effects of the powers of the hot and the cold, respectively. The
goddess seems to allude to this when, articulating the opinions of
mortals in 8. 55–9, she declares 'gentle' (in the sense, presumably,
of 'yielding')[55] and 'dense' as 'signs' of the two forms, 'fire of flame'
and 'night', respectively. The key point is this: as 'opposites' (8. 55),
they are exhaustive alternatives; a body must be in the state of, or
be undergoing the process of, either 'dispersal' or 'solidification'.
This gives us the point of departure, I suggest, for understanding
the sense of the goddess's term 'what are absent' (ἀπεόντα) in 4. 1.
She asks us to contemplate qualitative states that, in the perceptible
presence of their opposites, are 'absent'. That is, she asks us—to
put this in the terms she used in characterizing the Anaximandran
'backward-turning path' in fragment 6—to consider states that, in
the 'being' (cf. 'to be', 6. 8) of their opposites, are 'taken' to suffer
'not being' (cf. 'not to be', 6. 8). To repeat our examples: when and
where it is night, it is not day; when and where the cold prevails, the
hot must be absent; if a stuff grows compact, solidifying, it cannot be
dispersing. And yet, the goddess now urges us to 'see', this alternation of perceptible states is itself opposed by their 'steady presence
to mind' or 'thought'. 'What are absent' are 'nevertheless'—that is,

---

[55] Taking ἤπιον (8. 57) in this very material sense—namely, of a body's offering no
resistance to whatever enters the space it occupies—makes intelligible Parmenides'
otherwise puzzling assignment of it to 'fire of flame' (8. 56); in no other sense is
fire 'gentle', and in this sense it is paradigmatically so. Further, what is 'yielding' in
this sense is opposed to the resistant character of whatever is πυκινόν, 8. 59, 'dense,
close-packed'; and since the resistant character of what is πυκινόν is based on its
density, we may take the yielding character of what is ἤπιον to be based on its being
maximally loose-packed or internally dispersed, the paradigm for which is, again,
'fire of flame'. Thus, by the opposition of ἤπιον and πυκινόν in 4. 3–4 Parmenides
integrates the rare and the dense into the goddess's reconstruction of the 'opinions
of mortals'.

even in their absence—also unfalteringly 'present'. How so? In 4. 2 the goddess indicates what we must come to understand. When she says that 'mind' (or 'thought') 'will not cut off what-is from holding fast to what-is', she implies that the senses, by contrast, do 'cut off' 'what-is' from 'what-is', and we have seen that this is so: in their sensible presence, qualitative opposites are mutually exclusive; when and where either one of them is, the other cannot be. If, however, we step back to contemplate this 'cannot be', this denial of being, already we are turning from the sensible absence of the qualitatively determinate to the intelligible presence of its being, and since, in the relation of opposites, neither one can be what it is unless its other also is what *it* is, we find ourselves turned, now in 'thought', to the 'holding-fast', the requirement, by *the being of* each opposite to *the being of* the other. Thus our initial 'consideration' of 'what are absent' is transformed into the recognition of the necessary conjunction of 'what-is' with 'what-is'.

(c) The fit of the two courses

We are now in position to reply to the questions we raised earlier under (vii) and (viii).[56] To begin with, the two courses we have just traced do, it appears, correspond to the two 'routes' distinguished in fragment 6,[57] and these, in turn, are complementary versions of the first 'route' distinguished in fragment 2, the 'route of enquiry' on which one 'thinks' 'that (or how) . . . is and that it is not possible [for] . . . not to be' (2. 3). Both turn on the discovery of this impossibility; in each, it is the resistance to thought posed by 'what-is-not, as such', that provides the occasion for the discovery of the thought of being. But 'what-is-not' arises for consideration, so to speak, at different points in the two courses of reflection, with the consequence that being emerges at different points as well. In the first course, the *nothing* that is the absence or negation of the two forms at once, even as it fails, taken by itself (γε, 2. 7), to be thinkable, none the less refers thought on to the being, as such, of the two forms together; in the second course, the *nothing* that is the absence

---

[56] To recall these from sect. 1(*b*): (vii) How does this second 'route', in 6. 4–9, relate to the 'route' in 6. 1–3? Do they, each encountering the negation of 'being' in its own way, lead to different destinations, or do they somehow converge? And, (viii), how do these 'routes' relate to the 'routes' in fragment 2? How should we understand the relation between Parmenides' distinct pairings in 2 and 6?

[57] Recall 6. 3 and 6. 4, as discussed in sect. 1(*b*) above.

or negation of each of the two in turn, as this absence is implied by the sensible presence of the other, refers thought on to the very being of each of the two in its requirement of—and its being required by—the very being of the other. Though the two vistas that these referrals open up for thought are distinct, they dovetail, fitting together as complementary aspects of the same order. In the first, the being, as such, of the two forms refers thought on to these as beings, bringing them to mind as 'of a single kind' (μουνογενές, 8. 4);[58] in the second, the 'holding-fast' (4. 2, cf. 8. 25) of the being of each to the being of the other reveals the two as integral, each to the other, in the being that, brought together to constitute a 'whole' (οὖλον, 8. 4), they thereby share. Hence, whereas in the first vista the being as such of the two discloses them in their affinity as beings, in the second the fit or coherence of being with being (or, to say the same, of what-is with what-is) implies the transcending of their distinctness by what presents itself, accordingly, as their being, as such.

4. Postscripts

These remarks are offered as provisional. At the very outset of this essay I distinguished the 'proximate task' of studying the proem from the 'ultimate task' for which, I hope, this study might provide us with good orientation, the task, namely, of interpreting the 'is' as Parmenides lays it before us in the Truth section of the poem. All that we have said so far must be put to the service of that interpretative task—and, too, be put to the test by it. This next phase of the project must be deferred to the future. In anticipation, however, let me mark the distance we have come by bringing into focus the provisional light the proem casts on the first two sets of questions we posed regarding fragment 2.[59]

---

[58] I follow Mourelatos, *Route*, 95 n. 3, as well as Kahn, *Anaximander*, 157 n. 1, Tarán, *Parmenides*, 88–93, and Owen, 'Questions', 101–2, in favouring this reading over μουνομελές, 'single-limbed', which is preferred by Gallop (*Elea*, 64–5) among others, and οὐλομελές, 'whole-of-limb', which is favoured by Diels–Kranz. This reading allows the larger conjunction at 8. 4, οὖλον μουνογενές τε, 'whole and of a single kind', and this pair answers beautifully, as I try to explain in the next few sentences, to the different accents of the thought of *being* provided by the two courses we have traced, with the first course revealing the two forms as, *qua beings* (ἐόντα), 'of a single kind' and the second course revealing them, in the requirement of the *being of* each by the *being of* the other, as integral to each other, and so constituting a 'whole'. [59] See subsect. 1(*a*) above.

(a) The subject(s) of the '. . . is'

Question (i) asked: does the 'is' have an implied subject? If our understanding of the significance of the image of the gateway presided over by 'much-punishing Justice' is well taken, then our answer will be a qualified yes. The proem situates the discovery of the thought of the 'is' at several key moments of enquiry into the basic principles responsible for the heterogeneous plurality of the world. It is when, after identifying the 'two forms' (8. 53) whose 'powers' account for the 'features' of 'all things' (9. 1–2), we then go on to seek what may lie beyond them that, in the experience of the χάσμ' ἀχανές, we have occasion to discover their being, as such. Or, to turn to the second course, it is when, having recognized that the sense-perceptual presence of each of the 'two forms' requires the sense-perceptual absence of the other, we then contemplate (λεῦσσε, 4. 1) this absence that we have occasion for the 'understanding', beyond sense, of how the very being of each 'holds fast' to the very being of the other. In both of these moments of breakthrough, then, it is the 'two forms' that are the subject of—and, indeed, are subject to a transformation of the way they are disclosed to mind by the emergence of—the '. . . is'.

But there are two important qualifications to add. First, the generality of my reference to 'the two forms' is deliberate. As we have noted, by interweaving allusions to Hesiod and to Anaximander in the proem's account of the journey to the goddess, Parmenides makes it problematic for us to privilege any one particular pair of opposites; while the gateway is 'of the paths of Night and Day', the Anaximandran Justice that presides over it regulates the hot and the cold in the changing of the seasons. If (as, surely, Parmenides' intended Greek hearers would have done) we hear both the Hesiodic and the Anaximandran resonances together, we shall be led to recognize them as analogues, and so as examples of a more universal pattern of thought. It is, then, any discernment of a fundamental two that Parmenides both acknowledges by his compound figure of Justice and the gateway and then claims to surpass by having the traveller pass through the gates to the goddess.[60]

---

[60] This point is reinforced, I think, by the way Parmenides has the goddess formulate the 'opinions of mortals' in the Doxa section. Though the goddess does pick 'fire of flame' (or Light) and Night over, for instance, the hot and the cold and the rare and the dense, etc., she also stresses that 'there is no true trust' in 'the opinions of mortals' (1. 30, cf. 8. 50–1); thus she leaves this question open. What

Nor, indeed, is it even certain that these fundamental principles need be two rather than some other number. Here the proem gives us a question to pursue when, in taking up the 'ultimate task', we turn to fragment 8:[61] if some larger number of forms were to have the same integrality, each to each of the others, that the balanced enclosure of the gateway and the precise alternation of the swinging of the gates suggest the 'two forms' must have, would Parmenides regard the set of these as an equally valid possible subject of the '. . . is'?[62]

However this may turn out, the key help the proem gives us is this: it is not the heterogeneous many given in sense experience that are the subjects of the '. . . is' but, rather, the several 'forms' that mortals identify as their basic causes. It is these that, if we can learn from the occasion for insight provided by the χάσμ' ἀχανές, will emerge for thought in the radically new light of their being.

is more, when Parmenides shifts from 'Day' in the proem to 'fire of flame' in 8. 56 and then to 'Light' in 9. 1, she indirectly acknowledges the instability—or, to put a more positive face on it, the openness to reconsideration and redefinition—of 'the opinions of mortals'. Parmenides' primary concern is with the metaphysical status of any such causes, not their particular identity.

[61] And, I would add, the so-called 'Cornford fragment': 'Such, changeless, is that for which as a whole the name is "*to be*"'. See Gallop, *Elea*, 90–1.

[62] With her insightful opening reflection on the implications of the fact that Parmenides' successors gave no arguments in defence of their positing more than one fundamental principle, Curd (*Legacy*, 1–2) throws open the door—initially left ajar by Mourelatos, *Route*, 132–3—to the possibility of reading him as open to pluralism. (Consider, for example, Empedocles' four elements or Anaxagoras' infinite number of qualitatively different 'seeds'.) On the same grounds I would add the distinct but analogous point (which, however, Mourelatos and Curd reject) that since his successors also felt no need to give special arguments in defence of making their fundamental principles complementary opposites, that is, 'enantiomorphic' pairs (Curd, *Legacy*, 107–8), the door should also be open to reading Parmenides as a dualist. (Consider, for example, Empedocles' pairing of 'love' and 'strife', or the atomists' pairing of 'full' and 'void'.) Indeed, if we are to take our bearings from Parmenides' successors' responses to him, it was not the number of principles but, rather, their integrality—paradigmatically but not exclusively achievable by complementary opposites, the being of each of which requires the being of the other—that Parmenides stressed. (Consider in this light how even the unrestrainedly pluralistic Anaxagoras claims such integrality both in the beginning—'all things were together' (fragment 4)—and once and for all—'in everything there is a portion of everything' (fragments 11 and 12). These fragments appear in Kirk, Raven, and Schofield, *Presocratics*, as §468 and §§476, 481, respectively.)

(b) The significance(s) of the 'is'

Question (ii) asked: in what sense or senses should we hear the 'is'?
What, if anything, does this 'is' signify? As interpretative work on
the Greek verb 'to be', much of it concerned directly with Parmenides' 'is', has developed in the past half-century, both the array
of distinctions to be drawn and the array of connections problema-
tizing them have multiplied. This has occasioned pointed and illuminating second thoughts about the aptness to Greek, and to philosophical Greek in particular, of some of the ways of categorizing
senses and syntactical patterns that have become staples of modern
logic and philosophy of language.[63] Working through all this in a
systematic way would be much too large a project to undertake
here. None the less, we can draw pointedly from the resources of
this discussion—and, equally important, mark its limits—in making explicit what we have seen the proem to imply regarding the
sense(s) of the '. . . is'.

The first of the two courses through the gateway has brought
us to the thought of the being, as such, of the two forms together;
the relevant sense appears to be existential. The second course has

---

[63] To acknowledge much too briefly several of the major contributors: at the
forefront of the work throughout this recent period is Charles Kahn ('The Greek
Verb "to Be" and the Concept of Being', *Foundations of Language*, 2 (1966), 245–65;
'The Thesis of Parmenides', *Review of Metaphysics*, 22 (1969), 700–24; *The Verb
'Be' in Ancient Greek* (Dordrecht, 1973); and 'Parmenides and Plato'), who long
ago called attention to the locative cast ('is *there*') of the existential sense of Greek
ἔστι ('there is'), to the irreducibility of the veridical sense ('is true, truly so, is the
case') to either the existential or the predicative senses (or, turning this round a
bit, the existential implications but formally predicative structure of the veridical),
and—recently joining Lesley Brown, 'Verb'—to the disanalogy of the distinction of
the 'complete' ('*x* is') and 'incomplete' ('*x* is *y*') uses with our familiar distinction
of existential ('*x* exists') and predicative ('*x* is *y*') uses. (The expression '*x* is', by
analogy with 'John teaches', admits of expansion by '. . . *y*', or, say, '. . . Greek', as in
'*x* is *y*', 'John teaches Greek', and just as 'John teaches' may be derived from 'John
teaches Greek', so may '*x* is' be derived from '*x* is *y*'; neither of these conditions
is true of '*x* exists' in relation to '*x* is *y*'.) Further, Alexander Mourelatos, *Route*,
ch. 2, in a brilliant recognition, qualified in 'Determinacy and Indeterminacy, Being
and Non-Being in the Fragments of Parmenides' (*Canadian Journal of Philosophy*
(1976), suppl. vol. ii. 45–60), and very recently renewed and rearticulated by Patricia
Curd (*Legacy*, 39–40), long ago introduced the notion of 'speculative predication'
to single out predications in which the predicate lays bare the very nature of the
subject, what it 'really' or 'truly is', rather than just an attribute of it. (Consider, for
example, 'all things are matter and energy', or, to cite Mourelatos's own citation of
Xenophanes fr. 29, 'The things which come to be and grow are all of them earth
and water' (*Route*, 60).) He noted how, in '*x* is really *y*' or '*x* is truly *y*', the 'is' has
existential and veridical force; '*x* is really, or is truly, *y*' suggests that '*y* exists' and/or
'is true, or truly is the case'.

brought us to the thought of the very being of each of the two forms, as this being stands in a relation of mutual requirement with the being of the other. Here the sense of being is twofold. Were, for example, Light to be reduced to nothing, there would also *be* no Night; that is, Night would not exist. But we can also accentuate this differently and say, there would be no *Night*; that is, without Light, Night could not *be Night*, could not *be what it is*. Travelling on the second course, then, we hear both the 'is' of existence and the 'is' of identity.

But this, already complex, is only the beginning of the reflection the proem prepares us to pursue. These emergences of being, recall, occur at crucial moments of the larger enquiry in which, seeking the 'forms' fundamental to all else, mortals arrive at the gateway—that is, come to understand and to say,

πᾶν πλέον ἐστὶν ὁμοῦ φάεος καὶ νυκτὸς ἀφάντου . . .
All is full of Light and obscure Night together . . .
(9. 3)

Notice how, in 'order[ing]' '[her] words' 'deceptive[ly]' (8. 52) so as to give voice to the perspective of mortals, the goddess elides the 'is'—that is, the expression of the being, as such—of the two forms. Her 'is', ἐστίν, copulative with 'all' and 'full', serves to direct attention away from itself and to the two forms in their eminence as the principles basic to 'all things'. This is good mimetic irony, for the 'is' she elides is exactly what, since mortals have not paused to experience the imponderability of 'what-is-not, as such', they have not yet found occasion to discover. None the less, this 'is' is implicit and there 'for discourse and understanding' (6. 1)—as, we can now see in retrospect, her reversal of this elision in the elision of 2. 3 serves to bring out. What is the sense of this implicit 'is'? We might bring out the point of 9. 3 by restating it as

all things are really (or truly) Light and Night.

This gives us a speculative predicative 'is' with strongly veridical force. Interestingly, if we try to express this same insight but with a reversal of subject and predicate, to wit,

Light and Night just are all things,

we recover the goddess's own language in the opening of the Truth section when she describes the ultimate principles that mortals posit—that is, the 'two forms'—as

> . . . just being [περ ὄντα] all things in every way.
>
> (1. 32)

And if we now expand this quotation to include all of 1. 31–2, we can hear the goddess herself highlight the implications of existence and of identity that this (inverted) speculative predication bears within it:

> But nevertheless you shall learn these as well, how for what
>   are deemed [to be]
> It would have been right that they be eminently, just being all things
>   in every way.

This 'be[ing] eminently' implies the being, as such (that is, the existence) of the two forms together and, as well, the being-what-it-is (that is, the being in the sense of identity) of each form by virtue of the other's also being-what-*it*-is, that we have discovered by travelling the two courses through the gateway. With her adverb 'eminently'[64] the goddess indicates the transcending of any negation that we have witnessed for ourselves in imaginatively reconstructing each of the two experiences of the χάσμ' ἀχανές and that she declares at 9. 4 with her enigmatic '. . . to neither belongs any nothingness'. In the context of the question of the sense(s) of the '. . . is', then, the proem prepares us to see that it is meant in a host of intelligibly interrelated senses. The search for the basic principles of the cosmos invokes a speculative-predicative 'is' with strong veridical force, and the thinking that enters into the experience of the impossibility of thinking 'what-is-not, as such' brings to the fore the senses of existence and identity that are implicit in that speculative-predicative/veridical 'is'. Rather than choose between these various senses, we need to acknowledge and mark their interplay.[65]

In doing so, however, we need to be both circumspect and bold. Circumspection is required if we are to preserve our historical sense, our appreciation for the strangeness of the past: even while we let

---

[64] Here Owen's translation of δοκίμως as 'genuinely' or 'really' ('Questions', 51) makes my point more clearly than my 'eminently'. But as indicated in n. 26, 'eminently', taken with 'be', is intended to include this meaning.

[65] Kahn, 'Parmenides and Plato', stresses such interplay.

these distinctions of senses help us secure an analytical clarity in hearing the 'is', we must resist the anachronism of letting ourselves assume that we are recovering the terms of Parmenides' own self-understanding. Boldness is required, in turn, if, our energies quickened by this appreciation of strangeness, we are to risk opening up to the provocative vitality of Parmenides' language; that is, to say this in a way that articulates in one sentence our project and its most important finding: we need to let the poetry of the proem lead us into the experience of the epiphanous power of the 'is'. By 'poetry' I do not mean to speak of the peculiar beauty or grace of Parmenides' verse (I must leave that to others better qualified than I);[66] rather, I mean to remind us one last time of the surprisingly Heraclitean power of the ambiguity of his imagery. By generating contradictions, he provides occasions for intellectual transport, and in doing this, he gives us access to the power that, if we give ourselves to these occasions, his core referents, *'what-is-not, as such'* and *(the)* *'being'* *(of . . .)*, show themselves to have, the power to detach us from, then turn us back to, the ultimate principles of the world, disclosing them in a hitherto unsuspected light in the process. The study of these principles as, in this light, they 'are there for discourse and understanding' (6. 1)—the study of them, accordingly, in their status *as beings*—is the 'ultimate task' for which the proem prepares us.

Vassar College, New York

BIBLIOGRAPHY

Barnes, J., *The Presocratic Philosophers*, 2 vols. (London, 1979).

Barrett, J., 'Struggling with Parmenides' (unpublished paper presented at the Ancient Philosophy Society meetings, 2003).

Boehme, R., *Die Verkannte Muse: Dichtersprache und die geistige Tradition des Parmenides* (Berne, 1986).

Brown, L., 'The Verb "to Be" in Ancient Philosophy: Some Remarks'

---

[66] See R. Boehme, *Die Verkannte Muse: Dichtersprache und die Geistige Tradition des Parmenides* (Berne, 1986); R. Cherubin, 'Parmenides' Poetic Frame', *International Studies in Philosophy*, forthcoming; E. D. Floyd, 'Why Parmenides Wrote in Verse', *Ancient Philosophy*, 12 (1992), 251–65; Mourelatos, *Route*, 34–5; and T. Popa, 'The Reception of Parmenides' Poetry in Antiquity', *Studii clasice*, 34–6 (1998–2000), 5–27. I have also benefited from James Barrett's 'Struggling with Parmenides', a paper presented at the Ancient Philosophy Society meetings, 2003.

['Verb'], in S. Everson (ed.), *Language* (Companions to Ancient Thought, 3; Cambridge, 1994), 212–36.

Burkert, W., 'Das Prooemium des Parmenides und die Katabasis des Pythagoras', *Phronesis*, 15 (1969), 1–30.

Cherubin, R., 'Parmenides' Poetic Frame', *International Studies in Philosophy*, forthcoming.

Cordero, N.-L., 'Les deux chemins de Parménide dans les fragments 6 et 7', *Phronesis*, 24 (1979), 1–32.

—— *By Being, It Is* [*By Being*] (Las Vegas, 2004).

Couprie, D., 'The Visualization of Anaximander's Astronomy', *Apeiron*, 28 (1995), 159–81.

Coxon. A. H., *The Fragments of Parmenides* [*Fragments*] (Assen, 1986).

Curd, P., *The Legacy of Parmenides* [*Legacy*] (Princeton, 1998; reissued in 2004 by Parmenides Publishing Co.).

Floyd, E. D., 'Why Parmenides Wrote in Verse', *Ancient Philosophy*, 12 (1992), 251–65.

Furley, D., 'Notes on Parmenides', in E. N. Lee, A. P. D. Mourelatos, and R. Rorty (eds.), *Exegesis and Argument: Studies in Greek Philosophy Presented to Gregory Vlastos* (Assen, 1973), 1–15.

Gallop, D., *Parmenides of Elea* [*Elea*] (Toronto, 1984).

Graham, D., 'Heraclitus and Parmenides', in V. Caston and D. Graham (eds.), *Presocratic Philosophy: Essays in Honor of Alexander Mourelatos* (Aldershot, 2002), 27–44.

Hahn, R., *Anaximander and the Architects* (Albany, 2001).

Hermann, A., *To Think like God: Pythagoras and Parmenides* (Las Vegas, 2004).

Kahn, C., *Anaximander and the Origins of Greek Cosmology* [*Anaximander*] (New York, 1960).

—— 'The Greek Verb "to Be" and the Concept of Being', *Foundations of Language*, 2 (1966), 245–65.

—— 'The Thesis of Parmenides', *Review of Metaphysics*, 22 (1969), 700–24.

—— *The Verb 'Be' in Ancient Greek* (Dordrecht, 1973).

—— 'Parmenides and Plato', in V. Caston and D. Graham (eds.), *Presocratic Philosophy: Essays in Honor of Alexander Mourelatos* (Aldershot, 2002), 81–93.

Kingsley, P., *In the Dark Places of Wisdom* [*Dark*] (Inverness, Calif., 1999)

—— *Reality* (Inverness, Calif., 2003)

Kirk, G. S., Raven, J. E., and Schofield, M., *The Presocratic Philosophers*, 2nd edn. [*Presocratics*] (Cambridge, 1983).

McKirahan, R., *Philosophy before Socrates* (Indianapolis, 1994).

Miller, M., 'La logique implicite dans la cosmogonie d'Hésiode', *Revue de métaphysique et de morale*, 82 (1977), 433–56, trans. Louis Pamplume.

(The English original appeared in *Independent Journal of Philosophy*, 4 (1983), 131–42.)
—— 'Parmenides and the Disclosure of Being', *Apeiron*, 13 (1979), 12–35.
—— ' "First of all": On the Semantics and Ethics of Hesiod's Cosmogony' ['First'], *Ancient Philosophy*, 21 (2001), 251–76.
Morrison, J. S., 'Parmenides and Er', *Journal of Hellenic Studies*, 75 (1955), 59–68.
Mourelatos, A. P. D., *The Route of Parmenides* [*Route*] (New Haven, 1970).
—— 'Determinacy and Indeterminacy, Being and Non-Being in the Fragments of Parmenides', *Canadian Journal of Philosophy* (1976), suppl. vol. ii. 45–60.
Nehamas, A., 'On Parmenides' Three Ways of Inquiry', *Deucalion*, 33/4 (1981), 97–111.
—— 'Parmenidean Being/Heraclitean Fire' ['Fire'], in V. Caston and D. Graham (eds.), *Presocratic Philosophy: Essays in Honor of Alexander Mourelatos* (Aldershot, 2002), 45–64.
Owen, G. E. L., 'Eleatic Questions' ['Questions'], *Classical Quarterly*, NS 10 (1960), 84–102; repr. in R. E. Allen and D. Furley (eds.), *Studies in Presocratic Philosophy*, ii (Atlantic Highlands, NJ, 1975), 48–81.
Popa, T., 'The Reception of Parmenides' Poetry in Antiquity', *Studii clasice*, 34–6 (1998–2000), 5–27.
Radt, S. (ed.), *Tragicorum Graecorum Fragmenta*, iv. *Sophocles* (Göttingen, 1977).
Robb, K., *Literacy and Paideia in Ancient Greece* (Oxford, 1994).
Smyth, H., *Greek Grammar* [*Grammar*] (Cambridge, Mass., 1963).
Tarán, L., *Parmenides* (Princeton, 1965).
West, M. L. (ed.), *Hesiod:* Theogony (Oxford, 1966).

ZENO UNLIMITED

PIETER SJOERD HASPER

1. Introduction

WHEN it comes to Zeno's paradoxes, it is difficult to distinguish interpretation from attempts at solving them. How to make sense of arguments which are deliberately paradoxical and thus challenge the basics of common sense, without finding out what is wrong with them? This interplay between historical interpretation and philosophical analysis is often fruitful enough, sharpening our view of what is going on in the arguments under consideration. However, the balance of power in the interplay is easily disturbed, as the perceived clarity of philosophical analysis may come to guide our interpretative efforts at the expense of our sensitivity to the details of the historical evidence.

The philosophical framework in which Zeno's paradoxes are studied today is dominated by concepts and arguments derived from mathematics. It is a common theme in much of the present-day literature, both historical and systematic, dealing with Zeno's paradoxes that they can be solved or at least made to disappear by the application of modern mathematical concepts.[1] The nicest example in this respect is provided by two of Zeno's paradoxes in which the summation of an infinite series of regularly decreasing terms and the set-theoretical representation of such a series seem

[1] The most influential work, both systematically and historically, is by Adolf Grünbaum, in *Modern Science and Zeno's Paradoxes* (Middletown, Conn., 1967) and the relevant sections of *Philosophical Problems of Space and Time*, 2nd edn. (Dordrecht and Boston, 1973). It was primarily the influence of Gregory Vlastos, in articles to be quoted below, that definitely turned the mathematical approach into the cornerstone of the historical interpretation of Zeno. Other authors, such as Michael White in a work with the significant title *The Continuous and the Discrete: Ancient Physical Theories from a Contemporary Perspective* (Oxford, 1992), extended this approach to the interpretation of other ancient philosophers on matters of continuity and infinite divisibility.

to play a crucial part. The most familiar of these is the so-called
Runner Paradox, also known as the Dichotomy or the Stadium.
Zeno argues there that a Runner who wants to get from A to ω will
first have to reach a point B, halfway on the road to ω; to get from
B to ω he will again have to reach a point halfway, and so on; therefore he will never reach ω. Perhaps somewhat less familiar is one
half of Zeno's Second Paradox of Plurality, where he argues that an
entity divided in the same way as in the Runner Paradox is actually infinitely large. If we may believe the mathematically inspired
interpretation and solution, these two arguments fail to provide a
real paradox—Zeno was just mistaken, perhaps excusably so, but
still mistaken. In the case of the Second Paradox of Plurality, how
could the whole divided into the infinite series of parts with lengths
$\frac{1}{2}$, $\frac{1}{4}$, $\frac{1}{8}$, and so on ever be infinitely large? From the definition of the
sum of an infinite series as the limit, if there be one, of the infinite
series of partial sums, it is absolutely clear that the sum of this particular series is just 1—the length of the original whole. In the case
of the Runner Paradox, one may adopt the same solution, if one
thinks that the crux of Zeno's argument is that the infinite series
of periods of time needed to traverse the infinite series of lengths
is supposed to be infinite in length. Matters are only slightly more
complicated if one takes the point of the Runner Paradox to be that
it is impossible to reach the end-point of the journey for lack of
a final step. For then one may argue that in order to traverse the
whole distance it is enough to traverse all the 'halves' and to reach
all the infinitely many points at this side of the end-point, because,
as modern mathematics tells us, an interval on the reals excluding
that one limit does not differ in terms of measurement from the
union of that same interval and the singleton containing that one
limit; in the end one will have traversed the same distance.

In this article I want to argue that the mathematical approach to
these two Zenonian paradoxes is completely off the mark and thus
has steered their interpretation in the wrong direction. I shall be
mainly concerned with arguing that it is off the mark from a historical perspective, and maintain that the reason why Zeno, when he
devised these arguments in the fifth century BC, thought that the
Runner would never arrive at ω and the infinitely divided entity
would be infinitely large has nothing to do with faulty arithmetic or
other more intricate mathematical considerations. Rather, his paradoxical conclusions derive from a conceptual problem, a problem

which still does not seem to be immediately solvable. The main
idea driving these two paradoxes, I shall explain, is that a whole
of parts is nothing more than these parts together. Moreover, this
idea will be seen to be at work in many of Zeno's other arguments.[2]
As a by-product of this historical analysis, however, it will appear
that the modern mathematical solution is also off the mark from a
philosophical perspective, as the analysis shows that what is needed
is not a mathematical solution, but a conceptual cure limiting our
tendency to apply this whole–part principle.

2. 'So large as to be unlimited'

According to Simplicius' report, Zeno argued in his Second Paradox of Plurality that 'if there are many things, . . . they are . . . large,
so large as to be unlimited'. As far as we know, Zeno's reasoning
consists of two parts. First he states in a kind of preamble that what
is without size does not exist. Then he uses this statement to reach
his paradoxical conclusion. Simplicius tells the story twice:

[Z]eno [says] these things [i.e. that whatever has no magnitude or mass or
any bulk cannot be] [in order to prove] that magnitude is possessed by each
of the many things—unlimited things, because there is always something
in front of what is being taken, because of the division *ad infinitum* [ὅτι
μέγεθος ἔχει ἕκαστον τῶν πολλῶν καὶ ἀπείρων τῷ πρὸ τοῦ λαμβανομένου ἀεί τι
εἶναι διὰ τὴν ἐπ᾽ ἄπειρον τομήν]. (*In Phys.* 139. 16–18 Diels)[3]

And:

[The infinity] in magnitude [he proved] . . . [by means of the dichotomy].
For after he has proved that 'if what is has no magnitude, it cannot be',
he continues: 'But if it is, each must have some magnitude and bulk and
the one part of it must be apart from the other [ἀπέχειν αὐτοῦ τὸ ἕτερον ἀπὸ
τοῦ ἑτέρου]. And of the part which juts out [περὶ τοῦ προύχοντος] there is
the same account, for this as well will have magnitude and some part of it
will jut out [προέξει αὐτοῦ τι]. Now it is the same to say this once and to

---

[2] So often, indeed, that we may safely assume that it held sway over Zeno's own
thinking and was much more than an idea he encountered in the arguments of his
opponents and used dialectically against them. Consequently I shall treat this idea
thus, indulging even in presenting Zeno as rejecting because of it certain conceptual
possibilities which he may not have dreamt of.

[3] In this article I supply phrases and words which are necessary to make the
translation comprehensible, but do not change the sense; these are indicated by
square brackets. Real additions, on the other hand, stand between angle brackets.

be saying this always, for no such part of it will be the last nor will a part not be related to another [οὔτε ἕτερον πρὸς ἕτερον οὐκ ἔσται]. Thus if there are many things, it is necessary that they are small and large, small so as to have no magnitude, large so as to be unlimited [μεγάλα δὲ ὥστε ἄπειρα εἶναι].' (*In Phys.* 140. 34–141. 8 Diels)

As appears from the final lines of Simplicius' report, the paradox we are concerned with here is part of a larger whole, the second half of which consists of the thesis that if there are many things, each of these things is unlimitedly small. This thesis is probably based on the consideration that only sizeless things are indivisible and thus the only things out of which, as ultimate units, the whole of reality consists if there are many things. This other half we shall briefly consider later on.

The preamble of the paradox, the argument for the thesis that what does not have size does not exist, we shall discuss in what follows. The first aim is to find out exactly how the argument goes in the second part.

In the second, more elaborate, summary of the second part Zeno seems to describe a procedure of division which generates a series of parts without a final one, as every 'front part' taken is recursively divided into two:

In this diagram part Bω is the part jutting out of the whole Aω, or, as Simplicius phrases it in the first summary, the part 'in front of'[4]

---

[4] A more suitable translation of πρό here would be 'in the front of'. That this is a possible translation appears from the use of πρό by Plato, *Parm.* 165 A–B 3: πρό τε τῆς ἀρχῆς ἄλλη ἀεὶ φαίνεται ἀρχή . . . ἔν τε τῷ μέσῳ ἄλλα μεσαίτερα τοῦ μέσου. The two clauses are clearly meant to be completely parallel. As the things in the middle can only be more central than the previously taken middle if they are parts of that previously taken middle, the parallel shows that the beginning πρὸ τῆς ἀρχῆς is a part of the previously taken beginning. Thus it is the beginning in the front of the beginning.

This construal of πρό absolves Simplicius from an accusation of misunderstanding levelled against him by G. Vlastos, 'Fränkel's *Wege und Formen frühgriechischen Denkens*', in his *Studies in Greek Philosophy*, i. *The Presocratics* [*Studies*] (Princeton, 1993), 164–79 at 171 [originally in *Gnomon*, 31 (1959), 193–204 at 196], and H. Fränkel, 'Zeno of Elea's Attacks on Plurality' ['Attacks'], in R. E. Allen and D. J. Furley (eds.), *Studies in Presocratic Philosophy*, ii. *The Eleatics and Pluralists* (London, 1975), 102–42 [originally in *American Journal of Philology*, 63 (1942),

Aω; part Bω is then 'apart from' the other part of the whole Aω, that is, apart from AB.[5] It appears that Zeno thinks that the existence of such an unlimited series of parts constitutes sufficient reason to conclude that the many things 'are so large as to be unlimited'. What line of thought could have brought Zeno from the one to the other?

2.1. *Fallacy or failing interpretation?*

The most influential account of Zeno's reasoning in this paradox is provided by Gregory Vlastos.[6] He reconstructs the argument as follows:

(1) There is a series of parts without a final part—cf. the diagram.
(2) Therefore there is an infinite number of parts.
(3) Each of these parts has some size—cf. the statement in the preamble.
(4) Therefore the whole of these parts has an infinite size.

According to Vlastos's interpretation, Zeno must have made an arithmetical mistake. Somehow he thought that the sum of such a series would exceed any limit. This would, however, be surprising, for not only would we then have to assume that Zeno failed to do some simple arithmetic (it would have escaped his notice that summing a series consisting, for example, of the terms $\frac{1}{2}$, $\frac{1}{4}$, $\frac{1}{8}$, $\frac{1}{16}$, and so forth, would never get one beyond 1), but also that he did not understand his division procedure by way of a diagram as drawn above.[7] In an attempt to find a mitigating explanation, Vlastos claims that history tells us that knowing that the partial sums of such a series never exceed a certain limit—stated for the first time explicitly by Aristotle (*Phys.* 3. 6, 206^{b}3–11)—is compatible with

---

1–25, 193–206], at 118 and n. 70. According to them, Simplicius misunderstood the phrase προέξει αὐτοῦ τι as: 'some [part] will be more in front than it', as would appear from the fact that he thought that Zeno argued that there would always be something 'in front of what is being taken' (πρὸ τοῦ λαμβανομένου). Their accusation falls flat on the translation proposed here.

[5] G. Vlastos, 'A Zenonian Argument against Plurality' ['Zenonian Argument'], in *Studies*, 219–40 at 225–6 [originally in J. P. Anton and G. L. Kustas (eds.), *Essays in Ancient Greek Philosophy* (New York, 1971), 119–44 at 122–3] has convincingly shown that we should not interpret ἀπέχειν ('being apart from') in such a way that it implies a separation by a gap, but only in terms of having distinguishable parts.

[6] See his 'Zenonian Argument', 233–7 [129–32].

[7] Cf. Vlastos, 'Zenonian Argument', 234 [130].

committing the same fallacy as Zeno's. Vlastos points to Epicurus and Simplicius.[8] Just as they could not have been so stupid as to forget this, but must have made a more subtle error, it is possible that Zeno fell into the same hidden trap rather than committing a blunder. That subtle error, Vlastos proposes, is the assumption that there is a smallest term to the series.[9]

Against this interpretation I have two objections. A first small point is that none of the passages from Epicurus or Simplicius employs this particular division procedure yielding an infinite series of unlimitedly decreasing terms. Everywhere one encounters the reasoning that if there is an infinite number of parts, all of them having size, they will together form a whole of infinite size.[10] And generally that is true—it may only be false if for every size the number of parts larger than or equal to that size is finite, only the number of parts smaller than that being infinite.[11] Thus Zeno would really stand alone in having committed this fallacy.

More important, however, is the second objection. How could Zeno ever have thought that there is a smallest part without there being a final term to the series of ever-decreasing terms? I take that to be just as impossible as the idea that Zeno did not understand what his division procedure as represented in the diagram amounted to.[12]

Dissatisfied with an interpretation imputing such a fallacy to Zeno, a number of scholars have tried to ascribe a better argument to him. From Vlastos's reconstruction they retain (2)–(4), but they deny that Zeno based (2) on (1). Instead he would adopt a division procedure yielding an infinite number of *equal* parts. For if all parts have size, as is indeed claimed in (3), then the size of the whole will

[8] Epicurus, *Ep. Hdt.* (ap. D.L. 10) 56–7; Simpl. *In Phys.* 142. 14, 168. 34–169. 1, 459. 23–4, 460. 23–4, 462. 3–5 Diels and *In De caelo* 608. 16 Heiberg; cf. Eudemus ap. Simpl. *In Phys.* 459. 25–6 Diels.

[9] Vlastos, 'Zenonian Argument', 234–5 [130–1]; cf. D. J. Furley, *Two Studies in the Greek Atomists* [*Two Studies*] (Princeton, 1967), 69.

[10] This is incontestable as far as the passages from Simplicius are concerned, but with regard to Epicurus it may be controversial. However, I have not been able to find any literature on the issue and it would take us too far to discuss the matter here.

[11] A possible reason against such a presupposition is that it would be rather coincidental: if one has an infinite variety in size, why then are the different sizes not distributed equally?

[12] Despite the attempts by Vlastos, 'Zenonian Argument', 235 [131], to convince us that it is quite possible to make such a mistake.

be infinite.[13] The only method to ensure such an infinity is by way of a division through and through: that is, a division according to which *both* parts produced by a division are divided recursively. It should be such a division that Zeno had in mind.

The problem with this interpretation, however, is that it is difficult to square with the evidence. Perhaps that is why scholars often simply shift the discussion to an argument which has been ascribed to Zeno, and which does contain a division through and through:

[S]ince it is everywhere alike, if divisibility belongs to it, it will be divisible everywhere alike, and not divisible here, but not there. Let it then be divided everywhere. It is then clear that again there will remain nothing and it will have vanished, and if it is to be composed, again it will be composed out of nothing. For if something will remain, it will not turn out to be divided everywhere. Hence it is also clear from these points that what is will be indivisible, partless, and one. (*In Phys.* 140. 1–6 Diels)

Simplicius quotes these lines from Porphyry, who ascribes them to Parmenides. Simplicius himself, however, and before him Alexander of Aphrodisias, think that they are from Zeno. Not so long ago Stephen Makin argued very convincingly that Zeno is indeed the author.[14] That does not imply, however, that it is the same reasoning as the one we are discussing.[15] The only one to have argued the case for argumentative identity between the fragment taken from Porphyry and our paradox is Abraham. He makes two points: first that one should not interpret the use of τὸ προῦχον ('the thing jutting out') in such a way that it implies a kind of ordering of parts, but rather that it signifies a symmetrical relation between parts, just as is the case with ἀπέχειν ('being apart from'); and secondly, that τὸ προῦχον does not refer to one specific part, but has a generalizing

[13] G. E. L. Owen, 'Zeno and the Mathematicians', in his *Logic, Science and Dialectic: Collected Papers in Greek Philosophy* [*LSD*] (London, 1986), 45–61 at 48, esp. n. 10 [originally in *Proceedings of the Aristotelian Society*, 58 (1957–8), 199–222 at 146], also seems to interpret Zeno along these lines.

[14] 'Zeno on Plurality', *Phronesis*, 27 (1982), 223–38 at 227–9.

[15] W. J. Prior, 'Zeno's First Argument concerning Plurality', *Archiv für Geschichte der Philosophie*, 60 (1978), 247–56 at 254–5, seems to presuppose the identity of the two arguments. S. Makin, 'Zeno of Elea' ['Zeno'], in E. Craig (ed.), *The Routledge Encyclopedia of Philosophy*, vol. ix (London, 1998), 843–53 at 847, claims that 'it is easy enough to reformulate' our paradox in such a way that it becomes identical to the argument in the Porphyry fragment. Only J. Barnes, *The Presocratic Philosophers*, 2nd. edn. (London, 1982), 246, mentions in passing the possibility of a difference between the two arguments.

meaning: 'every part jutting out'.[16] Interpreted thus, Zeno would have argued that each of the two parts in a whole which are apart from each other has itself two parts which are apart from each other, and so forth. The number of parts then turns out to be infinite and the size of the parts will always be the same.[17]

Against this interpretation I also have two objections. First, it gives the impression of being very contrived. Why would Zeno then not have written 'And of *both these parts* there is the same account', instead of the rather clumsy sentence as it stands? Moreover, even if one were to accept Abraham's account of προὔχειν, πρό in πρὸ τοῦ λαμβανομένου ('in front of what is taken') remains very awkward if it does not imply an asymmetrical relation. Second, Abraham, as well as the other scholars who claim that Zeno's reasoning here is the same as in the Porphyry fragment, must assume that Zeno first allowed a division through and through to be completed, and then ascribed size to the *ultimate* parts resulting from such a division. I cannot see how this fits with Zeno's contention that 'no such part of it will be the last'. How can ultimate parts—and only they can be infinite in number, if they are to be equal in size—fail to be final parts? Moreover, the phrase 'nor will a part not be related to another' must refer to a relation between a part of stage n of the division procedure and a part of stage $n+1$.[18] To ultimate parts this does not apply.

2.2. *No arithmetical argument*

If we may believe the existing literature, then, we have two options: either we impute to Zeno a blatant fallacy or we accuse him of being imprecise in his choice of words. In itself that is already a rather unsatisfactory situation. One further reason to be dissatisfied with this rather limited choice is that both interpretations are built on a point which cannot be traced back to the sources. The point is this: while disagreeing on the justification for (2), they both think that Zeno's reasoning ran along steps (2)–(4), by way of an arithmetical argument. One may question this point, however, for if we read the

---

[16] W. E. Abraham, 'The Nature of Zeno's Argument against Plurality in DK 29 B 1' ['Nature'], *Phronesis*, 17 (1972), 40–52 at 42–3.

[17] At least the parts do not constitute an infinite series of regularly decreasing size in such a way that the partial sums never exceed a certain limit. For the sake of convenience I assume that in this division through and through each part taken is divided exactly in the middle.   [18] *Contra* Abraham, 'Nature', 43.

text carefully, we do not find anything corresponding to (3). We find only the statement from the preamble, that what does not have size does not exist, but this statement is not used to ascribe size to all the parts.[19] Instead, Zeno invokes this statement for each part in front taken separately, in order to argue that each part in front still has size, and therefore still has a part jutting out. So this statement is used to justify the infinite divisibility of magnitudes, since no division can yield a part without size and thus without any further part. (Zeno here relies on the premiss that everything which has size has parts.)

It could be objected, though, that if we do not find (3) in Zeno's actual words, we do find it in Simplicius' summary preceding them. For does his statement that Zeno meant to prove 'that magnitude is possessed by each of the many things—unlimited things, because there is always something in front of what is being taken, because of the division *ad infinitum*' not suggest that there are unlimitedly many things (cf. (2)) each of which has size (cf. (3))? Now this objection is based on the commonly assumed interpretation that the phrase μέγεθος ἔχει ἕκαστον τῶν πολλῶν καὶ ἀπείρων means that the many are unlimited in a numerical sense,[20] so that the reasoning (2)–(4) becomes the only viable reading of the summary. That interpretation fails, however, for thus the number of the many, first given as just 'many', would subsequently be specified as 'unlimited', leaving the many only to be the parts generated by the division procedure described in Zeno's actual words. However, that fails to fit those words at two places. First, Zeno starts with: 'If it is, *each* must have some magnitude . . .', that is, each of the many, and in this place certainly not each of the (infinitely many) parts generated in the division procedure. And second, in the conclusion it is stated that the many things are large so as to be unlimited. But that is a conclusion Zeno is not entitled to if his many things are the parts generated in the division procedure, for it is the wholes of those parts, not the parts themselves, which allegedly are so large as to be unlimited.

This problematic interpretation can be avoided, however, once we become aware that we are not obliged to read ἀπείρων as referring to the infinite number of the many. For it can simply be taken as short for Zeno's actual conclusion that the many things are *so large*

---

[19] As Vlastos, 'Zenonian Argument', 224–5 and 236 [122 and 131], acknowledges.
[20] e.g. Makin, 'Zeno', 847.

as to be unlimited (μεγάλα . . . ὥστε ἄπειρα), with the italicized words
left out.[21] If we read Simplicius' summary in this way, there is no
temptation whatsoever to adopt the reading that according to him
Zeno argued from (2) and (3) together to (4).

Taking stock of the interpretative situation, then, we may conclude that there is not much we can say about Zeno's reasoning
with the support of or even in harmony with either Simplicius' testimony or Zeno's own statement. Any interpretation which ascribes
to Zeno some kind of arithmetical argument, by multiplying something an unlimited number of times, is inconsistent with his actual
words. Moreover, the basis of such a multiplication, that the term to
be multiplied is of some magnitude so as to be available for multiplication, cannot be found in the available evidence. Not everything
is uncertain, as we do know for sure that the construction Zeno had
in mind is the one considered first, according to which there is an
unlimited series of ever-decreasing parts. However, it appears that
this is Zeno's sole ground for the conclusion that each of the many
is so large as to be unlimited. How are we to make sense of that?

3. Zeno's version of the Runner Paradox

The question how to make sense of Zeno's step from the existence
of an unlimited series of ever-decreasing parts to the unlimited size
of the whole is all the more urgent, since, as I shall argue in the
present section, Zeno must have made exactly the same step in his
Runner Paradox. Only now Zeno does not apply this argument to
a distance, but to the time needed to traverse a track divided in that
Zenonian way: that time will be unlimited and therefore there will
be no motion along that track.

3.1. *Doing away with Aristotle's testimony?*

There is much that is disputed about Zeno's version of the Runner Paradox. It starts with the construction: did Zeno envisage a
division procedure exactly the same as in the Paradox of Plurality
discussed above (the so-called 'progressive' version), or did he have

---

[21] It is with this interpretation in mind that one might be tempted to adopt the
emendation of ἀπείρων into ἄπειρον, so that it says something about μέγεθος: 'each of
the many things has size, namely an unlimited [size].' This emendation is proposed
by Fränkel, 'Attacks', 111 and 134 n. 45; I do not think it is necessary.

a runner in mind who could not reach any halfway point, because he had to reach the one before first (the 'regressive' version)? The ancient tradition prefers the latter version,[22] and it lingered on for a long time.[23] I shall take it, however, as having been established that Zeno had the progressive version in mind:

<pre>
A   B   C   D   E F ω

|_____|_____|_____|___|__|_|
</pre>

(with the runner starting at A).[24]

A construction, however, is not enough—we need an argument for Zeno to derive his paradoxical conclusion, and that is where opinions really differ. One opinion in the debate, or so it is treated, despite being our primary source for this paradox, is Aristotle's.

---

[22] See Simpl. *In Phys.* 1013. 7–10 Diels and Philop. *In Phys.* 81. 8–12 Vitelli; cf. S.E. *PH* 3. 76 and *M.* 10. 139–41.

[23] For example, W. K. C. Guthrie, *A History of Greek Philosophy*, ii. *The Presocratic Tradition from Parmenides to Democritus* (Cambridge, 1965), 92, could still give the regressive version as Zeno's without any comment; cf. W. D. Ross, *Aristotle's* Physics: *A Revised Text with Introduction and Commentary* [*Physics*] (Oxford, 1936), 658–9, and Owen, 'Zeno and the Mathematicians', 51 [149]. Some later authors, such as R. D. McKirahan, Jr., 'Zeno', in A. A. Long (ed.), *The Cambridge Companion to Early Greek Philosophy* (Cambridge, 1999), 134–58 at 143, and Barnes, *Presocratic Philosophers*, 262, still suggest that it does not really matter which version we adopt.

[24] Even if we assume that the two main passages in Aristotle, *Phys.* 6. 9, 239^{b}9–14, and 6. 2, 233^{a}21–31 (both 29 A 25 DK), are neutral on the construction (though see n. 32), we may conclude, from Aristotle's exposition of the Achilles as well as from the existence of a modified, counting version of the paradox, that Zeno had the progressive version in mind. For Aristotle says about the Achilles:

[The Achilles is the argument] that the slowest one will never be caught up with while running by the fastest. For the pursuer has first to go whence the pursued one started, so that the slower one must always be somewhat ahead. This is the same argument as the one by dichotomy [i.e. the Runner], though it differs in that the magnitude taken in addition is not cut into two. (*Phys.* 6. 9, 239^{b}14–20 = 29 A 26 DK)

Despite what Ross, *Physics*, 659, says, the last line would be quite misleading if there were no 'magnitude taken in addition' in the case of the Runner too. That the counting version is a mere modification of the Runner appears from Arist. *Phys.* 8. 8, 263^{a}7–11 (cf. *De lineis insecabilibus* 968^{b}1–2):

[S]ome present the same argument [i.e. the Runner] by way of different questions, assuming that together with the moving one should count first the half-motion, with each half coming up, so that with having traversed the whole motion it follows that one has counted an infinite number.

This would be inconsistent with the regressive version of the Runner.

According to him, Zeno made the incorrect assumption that it is not possible to make a run divided in this way in a limited time:

> That is why Zeno's argument [i.e. the Runner] makes the false assumption that it is not possible to traverse unlimited things or to touch unlimited things singly over a limited time. For both length and time, and in general everything continuous, are called 'unlimited' in two ways: either according to division or by their extremities. The things then which are unlimited according to quantity it is not possible to touch over a limited time, but the things which are so according to division it is possible to touch in that way, for the time too is itself unlimited in this way. Hence traversing what is unlimited occurs over an unlimited and not over a limited time, and the touching of unlimited things [occurs] with unlimited, not with limited, things. (*Phys.* 6. 2, 233ᵃ21–31 = 29 A 25 DK)

And referring back to this passage, Aristotle proclaims later:

> In the first discussion about motion we tried to solve [the Runner Paradox] on the basis of the point that the time has unlimited things in itself. For it is not absurd at all if over an unlimited time someone traverses unlimited things: and the unlimited is similarly present in both length and time. . . . [T]his solution is sufficient with regard to the questioner (for it was asked whether it is possible to traverse or to count unlimited things over a limited time) . . . (*Phys.* 8. 8, 263ᵃ11–17)

As the questioner may be identified with someone posing the Runner Paradox in the same way as Zeno did, Aristotle once again clearly states his conviction that Zeno's argument as presented by himself turns on the impossibility of traversing an unlimited number of stretches within a limited amount of time.[25]

There are few scholars, however, who accept Aristotle's testimony;[26] most prefer a Zeno who says that it is impossible to complete an unlimited series of runs without qualification.[27] As may be judged from the abundant explicit as well as implicit references in the literature to the philosophical discussions about Zenonian problems starting at the beginning of the twentieth century and

---

[25] Cf. already Ross, *Physics*, 73–4.

[26] Among them are Ross, *Physics*, 73–4, and, tentatively, R. Sorabji, *Time, Creation and the Continuum: Theories in Antiquity and the Early Middle Ages* (London, 1983), 324.

[27] G. Vlastos, 'Zeno's Race Course. With an Appendix on the Achilles' ['Race Course'], in *Studies*, 189–204 at 192–3 [originally in *Journal of the History of Philosophy*, 4 (1966), 95–108 at 96–7]; McKirahan, 'Zeno', 145; Barnes, *Presocratic Philosophers*, 266; cf. the ease with which Makin, 'Zeno', 848, goes over to this version of the argument.

really taking off in the 1950s,[28] their preference seems mainly motivated by philosophical interest, even though they can also call upon Aristotle, this time by invoking the continuation of the previously quoted passage:

> However, though this [earlier] solution is sufficient with regard to the questioner (for it was asked whether it is possible to traverse or to count unlimited things over a limited time), with regard to the matter and the truth it is not sufficient. For if someone leaves the length aside and refrains from asking whether it is possible to traverse unlimited things in a limited time, but makes these enquiries in the case of the time itself (for the time has unlimited divisions), that solution will not be sufficient any more. (*Phys.* 8. 8, 263ª15–22)

Still, as even here Aristotle distinguishes so sharply between the two versions, the onus is on those who wish to reject Aristotle's testimony; putative philosophical interest should not tip the scales against solid authority. However, this preference for what is believed to be a philosophically more interesting Zeno may be backed up by an argument in the form of a *reductio*. Suppose Aristotle were right and Zeno did indeed argue that traversing an unlimited number of stretches would take an unlimited amount of time. Why should he think so? The only answer available, it seems, is that Zeno assumed that the time of traversal is not infinitely divisible, but has smallest parts, so that the unlimited number of stretches, by each taking at least a minimal period of time to traverse, together will take an unlimited time. Moreover, this seems also to be the point Aristotle makes against Zeno in the first of the quoted passages.[29] As Vlastos pointed out, however, it would be surprising if Zeno had made such an assumption. For in the Achilles the same series of stretches is generated by way of an immediate pairing of each stretch with a member of a similar unlimited series of ever-decreasing subperiods of time (though a different pairing for each of the two movers: see n. 24 for Aristotle's testimony).[30] Therefore, we had better not believe Aristotle.

[28] For references, see the works of Grünbaum mentioned in n. 1, which contain extensive discussions of attempts to construe arguments showing that it is impossible to complete an infinite number of tasks, without further qualification.

[29] Vlastos, 'Race Course', 191 [95–96]; Ross, *Physics*, 73; McKirahan, 'Zeno', 145; cf. Barnes, *Presocratic Philosophers*, 265.

[30] Vlastos, 'Race Course', 192 [96]. This is the third of three reasons given by Vlastos to doubt Aristotle's testimony, the other two being that Aristotle nowhere even implies that Zeno actually said that it is impossible to traverse the stretches in

3.2. Taking Aristotle's testimony seriously

This is the only real argument on offer against Aristotle's account of Zeno's version of the Runner Paradox. I think it is unconvincing, for two reasons. Firstly, there are other indications that Aristotle's account does derive from Zeno's original version. Secondly, the argument itself fails on two points: there are more, and more important, lessons to be drawn from the Achilles than the one above, lessons which point in another direction; and Aristotle does not fault Zeno for thinking that time consists of indivisibles with size.

3.2.1. *Remarkable vocabulary*   To start with the first reason, if we go through Aristotle's analysis of the Runner Paradox in *Physics* 6. 2 as quoted above, we encounter two uses of vocabulary which may strike one as a little awkward. The first concerns the verb 'touching' (ἅπτεσθαι), which is used as a kind of synonym for 'traversing' (διιέναι). Now the whole of Aristotle's discussion of which this analysis of Zeno's argument is a part centres around the conception of moving over a distance x in a time T and the concomitant proportionality between x and T for each moving object; Aristotle argues on the basis of this proportionality from the divisibility of the one medium of motion to the divisibility of the other ($232^b20–233^a17$) as well as from the unlimitedness of the one to the unlimitedness of the other ($233^a31–^b15$). Moreover, Aristotle's distinction between two kinds of *unlimited* is drawn within the context of this 'continuous' conception, as one might call it: the entity which may be unlimited according to division, because it can be divided to infinity, or unlimited by extremities, because it may be infinite in extension, is a continuous entity, like a length or a period of time,[31]

a limited time, and that given his solution, Aristotle has an interest in representing Zeno thus. Aristotle's statement at *Phys.* 8. 8, $263^a16–17$, however, that 'it was asked whether it is possible to traverse or count unlimited things in a limited time' provides sufficient evidence to discard the first reason. The second reason looks suspect anyway, but appears even weaker if one takes the order of presentation in *Physics* 6. 2 into account: Aristotle first makes his point about there being two ways of being unlimited, in the context of a larger discussion about correspondences between magnitude and time ($233^a13–21$, continued at 233^a31), and then applies this point to Zeno's Runner Paradox—an application that, strictly speaking, he could have done without in the context. This does not leave him much interest in misrepresenting Zeno.

[31] See esp. *Phys.* 6. 2, $233^a24–6$, quoted above, but also $233^a17–21$: 'And if either of them, no matter which [ὁποτερονοῦν] [referring to "time" and "magnitude" in $^a16–17$], is unlimited, the other is also, and in the way the one is, the other also: for

not a discrete series, as the distinction would then not make sense. While the verb 'traversing', used here with an object referring to an unlimited discrete series, lends itself very easily to reframing into the continuous mode, that does not apply to the notion of 'touching', with its strong emphasis on the discrete structure of the run. The tension between these two modes becomes most clear in the sentence in which Aristotle makes his crucial point: 'The things then which are unlimited according to quantity [τῶν μὲν . . . κατὰ τὸ ποσὸν ἀπείρων] it is not possible to touch over a limited time, but the things which are so according to division [τῶν δὲ κατὰ διαίρεσιν] it is possible to touch in that way, for the time too is itself unlimited in this way [οὕτως ἄπειρος].' Though grammatically Aristotle uses the plural form in the first part of the sentence, it is obvious that the two occurrences of 'things which are unlimited' cannot be interpreted in the discrete mode, since the distinction, as pointed out above, does not then make sense. Therefore the plural here is a generalizing plural, referring to a plurality of things each of which is unlimited. Thus these things are continuous entities like lengths and periods of time—to which the verb 'touching', in fact demanding a discrete series as its grammatical object, is then applied. The vocabulary of 'touching' seems therefore not to fit very well with Aristotle's discussion.[32]

A second remarkable element in Aristotle's analysis concerns the phrase 'with unlimited, not with limited, things' in the last sentence (233ᵃ28–31). As also appears from the clearly intended parallel between the first and second half of that sentence, it must refer to the series of periods of time together making up the whole period needed for the whole run.[33] In itself there is something clumsy and,

example, if the time is unlimited by extremities, [so] also is the length by extremities, while if by division, [so] also is the length by division, and if by both, [so] also is the magnitude by both.'

[32] It is also the verb 'touching', in combination with 'singly' (καθ᾽ ἕκαστον), which suggests the progressive version of the construction. It should also be noted that in *De lineis insecabilibus* 968ᵇ2–3 the identity of 'touching singly' and 'counting' is invoked as a rather unproblematic premiss in a counting version of the Runner Paradox, a version which is inconsistent with the regressive version of the construction.

[33] Though in itself it could also refer to the series of acts by which the series of stretches is touched; in that case the first half of the sentence would testify to Aristotle's temporal interpretation of the phrase. A temporal interpretation seems more likely because in the Achilles Zeno does work with an unlimited series of periods of time. On the other hand, it may be easy enough—even for Zeno himself—to slip from the one interpretation to the other.

I would say, un-Aristotelian about the construction of *touching a
series of stretches* <u>*with*</u> or <u>*by way of*</u> (bare dative) *a series of periods
of time*; there is certainly no parallel in the *corpus Aristotelicum*.
Moreover, it emphasizes the discreteness of the temporal aspect of
the run, rather than the extensional, continuous aspect, as if it is
only the unlimited number of periods that is bothersome.

It was, of course, to be expected that there would be a tension
between a continuous and a discrete aspect, for without the former
there would be no room for Aristotle's solution, while without
the latter there would be no Runner Paradox. However, the verb
'touching', together with a discrete notion of 'unlimited things',
with regard to the distance covered and especially the time needed,
makes the tension between Aristotle's solution and Zeno's paradox
all the more palpable, in a way that could have been avoided by
Aristotle, if he had so wished, without any damage to his own
argument. The best explanation for their presence, it seems to me,
is that these elements go back to Zeno himself.[34]

3.2.2. *Defending and clarifying Aristotle's testimony*   These considerations already go some way towards establishing that Zeno
did indeed argue that since the run can be divided in the familiar
Zenonian way, the time needed for the run, to touch all these parts,
consists of an unlimited series of periods, and that that is problematic because a run taking an unlimited series of periods of time takes
an unlimited time, the only way to complete a run being to take a
limited time and therefore a limited series of periods. However, the
argument given above, as most clearly articulated by Vlastos, might
still deter one from accepting this version as Zeno's. To remove any
remaining doubts, we therefore need to deal with that argument.

The first point I want to make is that the fact that the construction
of the Achilles depends on the infinite divisibility of time cannot be
used, as Vlastos does, to establish that Aristotle wrongly criticized
Zeno for denying the ever-divisibility of time. The problem with
such a use is that it gives Aristotle an inconsistent position, for
Aristotle states explicitly that in his eyes the solution of the Achilles

---

[34] In *De lineis insecabilibus* too, a tract transmitted in the *corpus Aristotelicum* and,
to say the least, very closely associated with Aristotle, the verb 'touching' is used
when and only when the Runner Paradox is discussed (968^a18-^b4 and 969^a26-34).
Moreover, in the counting version of the Runner given in *De lineis* 968^a23-^b4, the
notion of counting is identified with that of touching singly, as if the touching version
is some kind of original to which other versions must be linked.

must be the same as that of the Runner (*Phys.* 6. 9, 239ᵇ25–6). But Aristotle cannot sensibly maintain against the Achilles that Zeno falsely assumes that time consists of smallest parts. Given that Zeno must hold that time is infinitely divisible if he is to have an argument in the Achilles,[35] the only conclusion we should draw from the above is that Aristotle cannot have accused Zeno of time-atomism.

There is yet more to be learnt from Aristotle's discussion of the Achilles. In his presentation of it (see n. 24), he states its conclusion as:

(c) The slower will never be caught up with while running by the faster,

which he represents as deriving from

(p) The slower must always be somewhat ahead (ἀεί τι προέχειν).

The mistake in the argument he identifies in the following way:

Assuming that what is ahead [τὸ προέχον] is not caught up with is false. For as long as [ὅτε] it is ahead, it is not caught up with. However, it is caught up with all the same [ὅμως], if, that is, one will grant that it traverses a limited [distance]. (239ᵇ26–9)

Assuming (c) to be unambiguous and paradoxical, we see that Aristotle objects to the step from (p) to (c), and in particular to the interpretation of 'always' which would justify this step. As has already been explained by others,[36] Zeno's argument seems to depend on the ambiguity of this term and thus on the ambiguity between:

(p1) During every period of the endless series of periods of the race the slower must be somewhat ahead,

and:

(p2) During the whole (period) of time the slower must be somewhat ahead.

Aristotle's objection is most easily interpreted as drawing precisely this distinction, for he is willing to admit that 'as long as [the

---

[35] If Zeno surreptitiously adopted a kind of time-atomism in the Achilles, the speed of both contestants must have decreased in such a way that they would not be able to reach the end anyway—but there would be nothing paradoxical about that.
[36] e.g. McKirahan, 'Zeno', 150; cf. Barnes, *Presocratic Philosophers*, 275, though Barnes gives a very curious reconstruction of the argument.

slower] is ahead, it is not caught up with', which is related to (p1), but refuses to subscribe to the unqualified principle that 'what is ahead is not caught up with', which is related to (p2), a refusal he justifies by referring to the possibility of traversing (any) finite distance.

As pointed out above, according to Aristotle this solution is the same as the one provided against the Runner Paradox. Now as a matter of fact, it is very easy to find an ambiguity at the heart of Aristotle's analysis of the Runner: '[B]oth length and time, and in general everything continuous, are called "unlimited" in two ways: either according to division or by their extremities.'[37] Two sentences later, the emphasis is again on the need to disambiguate: '[F]or the time [of the run] too is itself unlimited in this way [i.e. according to division]', i.e. not by extremities. So taken at face value, Aristotle does not criticize Zeno for assuming that time is not infinitely divisible, but rather for failing to distinguish between two meanings of the term 'unlimited'.

Staying very close to the terminology and phrases from Aristotle's discussion, we may thus reconstruct part of the argument in the version targeted by Aristotle as follows:

(1) Touching unlimited things singly requires unlimited things to touch with.[38]
(2) Therefore touching unlimited things singly requires an unlimited time.
(3) Therefore it is not possible to touch unlimited things singly in a limited time.[39]

According to Aristotle, the step from (1) to (2) is acceptable only if the time is unlimited in the sense of unlimited according to division, while the correctness of the step from (2) to (3) depends on the time being unlimited in the sense of unlimited by extremities (of course, given that in (3) the time is limited in the extensional sense, but that is clearly the sense needed). Against the step from (2) to (3) Aristotle insists, at 233ᵃ27–8, that the possibility of touching unlimited things singly in a limited time—the negation of (3)—is compatible with the time being unlimited according to division, and, at 233ᵃ28–31,

---

[37] Cf. also Aristotle's statement that 'in the way the one is [unlimited], the other is also' at 233ᵃ18.

[38] Cf. 233ᵃ30–1.

[39] The incorrect proposition, as Aristotle states at 233ᵃ21–3.

that there is thus nothing problematic[40] about touching unlimited things with unlimited things, i.e. in a time unlimited according to division.[41]

This distinction between two senses of 'unlimited' is basically the same as that between the two senses of 'always' in the Achilles, for 'in a time unlimited according to division' is in the context equivalent to 'during every period of the endless series of periods of the run', while 'in a time unlimited by extremities' is equivalent to 'during the whole of time'. Thus, to make the point once again, if Aristotle had meant to accuse Zeno of assuming time to consist of minimal parts, he surely did not express himself very clearly.[42] We therefore had better take Aristotle at his word and interpret him as faulting Zeno for jumping from one sense of 'unlimited', namely 'unlimited according to division', to the other sense, 'unlimited by extremities'.

All this is enough to dismantle the argument against believing Aristotle's testimony about the Runner Paradox. For with the argument (1)–(3) suggested by Aristotle's diagnosis, we have an alternative to the quasi-arithmetical derivation of the infinity of the time needed to make the whole run, which forms the core of that argument. According to Aristotle, Zeno took the existence of an unlimited number of periods of time, one for each stretch of the Zenonian run, as sufficient reason for the infinity of the time needed to make the whole run. And why should we distrust the authority of Aristotle?

---

[40] Cf. *Phys.* 8. 8, 263ᵃ13–14: 'There is *nothing absurd* if someone traverses unlimited things in an unlimited period of time.'

[41] The solution of the Runner Paradox offered in *De lineis insecabilibus* is exactly the same:

> Zeno's argument does not establish that something in locomotion touches in a limited time unlimited things *in just that same way* [ὡδὶ τὸν αὐτὸν τρόπον] [sc. of being (un)limited]. For the time as well as the length are called unlimited as well as limited, and have the same divisions. (969ᵃ26–31)

Though this passage too has always been interpreted as objecting against Zeno that he assumes time to consist of indivisibles (see e.g. M. Timpanaro Cardini (ed., trans., and comm.), *Pseudo-Aristotele:* De lineis insecabilibus (Milan, 1970), 55 and 84), the emphasis on the ambiguity hidden in Zeno's argument is clear enough.

[42] The fact that the author of *De lineis insecabilibus*, who follows Aristotle so closely in dealing with this paradox, presents an argument *deriving* an atomistic conclusion from Zeno's paradox (968ᵃ18–23 and ᵃ23–ᵇ5), while he does not indicate in any way that there might be an atomistic premiss involved, makes it all the more unlikely that Aristotle had such an analysis in mind.

4. From 'unlimited series' to 'without limit' to 'unlimited'

Thus both in the Second Paradox of Plurality and in the Runner Paradox we see Zeno arguing immediately from the existence of an unlimited series of ever-decreasing parts to the unlimitedness of all these parts together, an inference which cannot be accounted for by ascribing some kind of arithmetical reasoning to Zeno. In this section I shall propose an argument which does fill the gap, an argument, moreover, for which relevant parallels from antiquity can be cited and whose underlying idea can be attributed to Zeno on the basis of solid evidence. I shall phrase this argument in terms of Zeno's argument that each of the many is so large as to be unlimited; in the next section I shall discuss its application to the Runner Paradox.

4.1. *No limit, no end*

The argument is very simple, consisting of one premiss and two steps. The premiss is that Zeno by his construction has shown that:

(1) Each of the many consists of an unlimited series of ever-decreasing parts, without a final part,

from which he may go on to:

(2) Therefore each of the many is so large as to be without limit.
(3) Therefore each of the many is so large as to be unlimited.

The idea behind this proposal is not new; more than half a century ago Fränkel already suggested interpreting 'unlimited' in terms of 'without limit'.[43] Fränkel does not mention it, but the same idea can already be found in Plato's *Parmenides*, where at 165 A 5–C 5 Parmenides concludes that something that, as he has just argued, does not have a limit or end (A 6–7: οὔτε πέρας . . . ἔχων) is unlimited or infinite (C 3: ἄπειρα); he does so even while explicitly contrasting 'having a limit' (C 4: πέρας ἔχοντα) and being unlimited or infinite. Moreover, the appropriateness of this idea in the present context is confirmed by the fact that the ground Parmenides gives for the

---

[43] Fränkel, 'Attacks' 119–20.

absence of a limit, being that there is no ultimate unit to be found, is closely related to Zeno's Second Paradox of Plurality (A 7–B 4).[44]

However, the way in which Fränkel subsequently reconstructs Zeno's reasoning from (1) to his conclusion does not seem correct. For Fränkel takes what one might call the constructivist approach: according to him, the point of Zeno's introduction of a division procedure yielding an infinite series of unlimitedly decreasing parts is that such a division cannot be completed, so that in fact the series as a whole will never be there, for lack of a last step to finish its construction.[45] The problem with this approach is again that it does not fit Zeno's actual words. For they suggest the following line of reasoning: each part has size, so that it *has* parts itself, of which the front part has size, so that it again *has* parts, and so forth; therefore there *is* no last part, but each part taken *has* a subpart; therefore the whole of all these parts is large so as to be unlimited. Moreover, as we shall see later on, given his own principles, Zeno could not have taken the constructivist approach anyway. Thus Zeno assumes he shows by argument that all the parts of the infinite series are actually there: although the construction used in the proof to describe the series is never completed, the series thus described is already there in reality.

By severing Fränkel's suggestion from his constructivist interpretation, and understanding it in the context of an interpretation according to which all parts of the infinite series do really exist, one may comprehend the first step of Zeno's argument, from (1) to (2), very easily. He takes an object, stipulates that it be divided in the familiar way, and concludes that the object does not have a final part. Therefore the object does not have a limit.

---

[44] As may also be judged from the use of πρό in exactly the sense required by Zeno's argument (see n. 4) and perhaps from the use of λαμβάνεσθαι as well.

[45] Fränkel, 'Attacks', 119–20, conceives of the argument in terms of 'measuring the thickness of an object', 'reaching the ultimate surface', and 'covering the whole distance'. He explicitly uses Aristotelian vocabulary when he says that the object constructed thus does not have 'an actual and existing plane surface', yet 'still has a potential limit for its extension'. Not only is this pretty vague, but it also seems inconsistent with Fränkel's interpretation of the conclusion, that the object is unlimited in the sense of not having a limit or end. Perhaps for this reason, McKirahan, 'Zeno', 139, does adopt the same constructivist approach, but not Fränkel's translation of the conclusion. Instead he reads it as saying that each of the many things is so large that it does not have a limited number of parts. 'So large that it has an unlimited number of parts' seems, however, a strange construction. Moreover, in this way the parallel with the conclusion of the other half of the paradox disappears, because there it is said that each of the many is so small as to have no magnitude at all.

Fränkel's constructivist interpretation may be part of the reason why his proposal has not been accepted by others. A more important factor, however, is probably that (2) does not appear to get Zeno very far. After all, there does not seem to be anything remarkable or paradoxical about the conclusion that an object may be divided in such a way that it does not have a final part. Only if the conclusion were that an object because of that becomes infinitely large, i.e. if (3) becomes true on the grounds of (2), has Zeno achieved something with which he can fight those who claim that there are many things. Moreover, in antiquity everyone, including our source Simplicius, understands Zeno as saying that each of the many things is infinitely large.[46] And even if Zeno were to have thought that something that has no limit in the sense of a final part is infinite in the sense of infinitely large, is he then not guilty of a rather simple equivocation very similar to the one Aristotle describes in the case of the Runner Paradox? For why should Zeno's opponent not simply accept the absence of a limit to each of the many things, without committing himself to the conclusion that each of the many things is infinitely large?[47]

However, I do not think that there is anything wrong with the step from (2) to (3), from *without limit* to *being unlimitedly large*. There is therefore no reason to deny Zeno that step, and thus to prevent him from drawing a conclusion which is problematic for his opponents. For how else could something be limited and finite, except by having a limit or end?

This view was also held in antiquity. We encounter the step already in Aristotle:

If the definition of *body* is *that which is bounded by a plane* [τὸ ἐπιπέδῳ ὡρισμένον], there cannot be an unlimited body [σῶμα ἄπειρον]. (*Phys.* 3. 5. 204ᵇ5–6)

Though strictly speaking the inference here is from the presence of a limit to the finitude of a body, we are allowed to draw the conclusion that everything which is infinite is so because it is not bounded by a plane, i.e. because of the lack of a limit. An even clearer parallel to Zeno's inference from *without limit* to *infinite* can be found in Plutarch, in his work *De communibus notitiis adversus*

⁴⁶ The most explicit passage in Simplicius is *In Phys.* 141. 15–16 Diels. For the objection, cf. Furley, *Two Studies*, 68.
⁴⁷ Cf. Furley, *Two Studies*, 68–9.

Stoicos, where he states the following objection against Stoic ideas about limits:

[I]t is against the common conception that there be no extremity in the nature of bodies, nor anything first or last at which the body terminates, but that the subject, by always making an appearance beyond what has been taken, be reduced to infinity and indefinitude [ἀεί τοῦ ληφθέντος ἐπέκεινα φαινόμενον εἰς ἄπειρον καὶ ἀόριστον ἐμβάλλειν τὸ ὑποκείμενον]. For it will not be possible to conceive of one magnitude being larger or smaller than another, if it belongs to both alike to proceed with their parts to infinity [εἰ τὸ προϊέναι τοῖς μέρεσιν ἐπ' ἄπειρον ἀμφοτέροις ὡσ⟨αύτως⟩ συμβέβηκεν]. (1078 E–F)[48]

However one interprets this not quite pellucid passage, it is clear that according to Plutarch the mere absence of a final part is sufficient for infinity of size.

Moreover, it was not only in antiquity that they held this view, for if one takes a look at the modern mathematical representation of lengths of objects, one can also draw the same conclusion. Whether one represents a length by an open interval (a, b) on the real number-line, without the boundary-points represented by a and b being part of the length, as a closed interval $[a,b]$, with the boundary-points included as parts, or as a half-open interval $(a,b]$ or $[a,b)$, there is no escape from the fact that the length has limits: in every possible representation the points corresponding to the real numbers a and b.

4.2. *Limits as separate parts*

Though it may be the case that even according to the modern mathematical representation it does not make any difference to the presence of a limit whether the length is represented by an open or closed interval, the same model does point to a distinction to be drawn. For there remains a difference between the two representations: in the representation by a closed interval the limit does indeed constitute an independent, in the sense of removable, part of the interval, while in the representation by an open interval the limit is not a part of it in this sense. We need to distinguish, then, between having a limit or end and having a limit or end as an independent part. Thus, in order to escape from Zeno's conclusion we

[48] I leave out ⟨τι⟩, which in several editions, among them the one by H. Cherniss (ed. and trans.), *Plutarch's* Moralia, vol. xiii (Cambridge, Mass., and London, 1976), 812, is inserted before τοῦ ληφθέντος.

may, on the basis of this distinction, object that while he may have shown that (1) each of the many consists of an unlimited series of ever-decreasing parts, without a(n independent) final part, still that is not enough to give him the conclusion that (2) each of the many is so large as to be without limit (without qualification).[49]

This accusation, however, is based on the idea that it is possible that a body has a limit or end without having it as an independent part of that body. It may seem that it is not so difficult to conceive of such a possibility. To give an example of one conception (i), if we put all the parts of the infinite Zenonian series next to each other, will we not always remain at one side of a certain line we could draw? Or, on an alternative conception (ii), if we remove the parts one by one in a Zenonian way from the original object, are we not working towards some boundary of the body, a boundary which may not be an independent and removable part, but which still in one way or another is a part of that body, in the sense that it is always connected with the body and moves with it?

4.2.1. No limits which are not parts   These two conceptions correspond to two ways of conceiving of a limit without turning it into an independent part. According to the first conception (i), a limit is that at which something happens—for example, where two objects touch each other, or where an object ends (in case the limit is between an object and absolute vacuum). Thus a limit turns out to be a plane which has one object at one side of it and another object at the other side. In itself, however, the limit is not part of either object and does not belong to it, but is completely independent. This independence also shows itself by the fact that one can conceive of a limit where nothing really happens, e.g. in the middle of a homogeneous object. Such a limit is therefore a geometrical rather than a physical entity in the sense that it belongs conceptually to the space in which objects exist rather than to the objects themselves.[50]

Even to us, however, this conception of a limit does not readily suggest itself. After all, what else but the surface which is its limiting boundary do we touch when we come into contact with a body?

[49] Or, alternatively, that he has shown that (2) each of the many is so large as to be without any (independent) limit, but that that is not enough to conclude that (3) each of the many is so large as to be unlimited. This way of making the point, however, seems somewhat contrived.

[50] For this conception of limits, see A. Stroll, *Surfaces* (Minneapolis, 1988), 40–6 and 47–50.

And does this surface not move with the body? One may wonder, therefore, whether Zeno would have thought of this conceptual possibility. This doubt will be reinforced by considerations to be advanced in the next subsection, for there we shall see that implicit in many of Zeno's arguments is a principle according to which a body should be able to take care of itself with respect to being limited and thus cannot leave it to a limit which is independent from it and does not constitute a part of it. What is more, in his paradox of place Zeno poses a problem for a similar entity:

'If place is something, in what will it be?' (Arist. *Phys.* 4. 3, 210^{b}22–3 = 29 A 24 DK)

[I]f [place] is one of the things which are, where will it be? For Zeno's puzzle requires some account. For if everything which is is in a place, it is clear that there will also be a place of place, and so on *ad infinitum.* (Arist. *Phys.* 4. 1, 209^{a}23–5 = 29 A 24 DK)

This problem exists only if one assumes that everything which there is is in a certain place. The idea behind this assumption seems to be that the being of material bodies, which involves occupying a place, serves as the standard for existence and being something. Obviously limits conceived of as places where something happens or may happen with objects cannot meet that standard.

4.2.2. *No limits as abstract parts*   As indicated above, the second conception (ii) of a limit without turning it into an independent part of an object seems more natural to us as well. We conceive of a limit in this sense by way of a kind of limiting procedure: the limit of a whole is grasped through an infinite series of nested, ever-decreasing parts of the whole—a procedure related to the division procedure Zeno employs in the present paradox.[51] However, in order to ensure that this limit thus grasped does not become an independent part of the whole, but rather an abstract entity which belongs inseverably to the whole and is dependent on it, the limit must be construed in terms of the whole converging series of nested parts; thus the limit is not an independently existing entity *found* at the end of the series.[52]

This conception of a limit is not acceptable to Zeno either. The

[51] See Stroll, *Surfaces*, 46–50.

[52] This conception of limits one encounters in the work of Whitehead. For an exposition of it, see D. W. Zimmerman, 'Could Extended Objects Be Made out of Simple Parts? An Argument for "Atomless Gunk"', *Philosophy and Phenomenologi-*

problem he has with it is that this method presupposes that with each step in the approximation procedure a new part is created rather than found.[53] That appears from two closely related ideas which often recur in Zeno's arguments. Firstly, he believes that a whole of parts is nothing more than the sum of the parts of which the whole consists; the parts have ontological priority and the whole exists merely by virtue of the parts. This idea alone would already be sufficient for a rejection of the proposed abstraction procedure, for with each step in the approximation procedure the part divided in that step stops existing independently, as it becomes a whole consisting of, and thus dependent on, the two parts into which it is divided. It is therefore impossible to define the limit in terms of a whole series, since all prior terms of that series do not really exist any more. Secondly, in a number of passages Zeno makes the further assumption that an entity which is divisible is in fact already divided. Then the abstraction procedure becomes completely vacuous.

The first idea can be recognized, for example, in the so-called Paradox of the Millet-Seed, in which Zeno concludes, on the basis of the premiss that a bushel of millet-seeds produces a(n audible) sound when falling, that one millet-seed, and even a minute part of one millet-seed, must produce a sound too.[54] This step is most easily explained by ascribing to Zeno the idea that the whole bushel produces sound *because* each of its parts separately produces sound. Another context in which we may discover this idea is in the other half of the Second Paradox of Plurality, where Zeno argues that 'each of the many things is so small as not to have any magnitude'. The only thing we know about this half is what Simplicius tells us:

[The other conclusion] he proves after showing that nothing has magnitude because each of the many is the same as itself and one. (*In Phys.* 139. 18–19 Diels)[55]

cal Research, 56 (1996), 1–29 at 17–19, and primarily his 'Indivisible Parts and Extended Objects: Some Philosophical Episodes from Topology's Prehistory', *Monist*, 79 (1996), 148–80 at 160–5.

  [53] It may thus be called 'constructivist'.
  [54] See Arist. *Phys.* 7. 5, 250ᵃ19–21, and Simpl. *In Phys.* 1108. 18–28 Diels.
  [55] οὐδὲν ἔχει μέγεθος ἐκ τοῦ ἕκαστον τῶν πολλῶν ἑαυτῷ ταὐτὸν εἶναι καὶ ἕν. I take οὐδέν to be the grammatical subject, for otherwise one would have to supply 'each of the many things' as subject, which seems a little awkward in the context. However, the sense is unaffected either way.

Vlastos provides the following plausible reconstruction:

(1) Each of the many is self-identical and one.
(2) Everything which is self-identical and one is partless.
(3) Everything which has size has parts.
(4) Therefore each of the many is sizeless.[56]

Accepting premiss (2) is equivalent to supposing that a whole of parts is not self-identical and one, but a mere sum of the parts, without any real self-identity and unity.[57]

The argument of the preamble to our paradox of division also seems to presuppose the ontological priority of the part over the whole. The argument goes as follows:

> In [this paradox of plurality] he proves that whatever has no magnitude or mass or any bulk cannot be. 'For if it were to be attached to something else that is,' he says, 'it would not make that any larger. For as it is no magnitude, it is, when attached, not capable of contributing anything to a magnitude. And in this way, then, that which is attached would be nothing. And if the other thing will not be in any way smaller with it being detached, nor again will increase with it being attached, it is clear that that which is attached was nothing, no more than that which is detached. (Simpl. *In Phys.* 139. 7–15 Diels)

Given the truth of the premiss that something sizeless cannot contribute to the size of that to which it is attached, the plausibility of this argument for what Aristotle calls 'Zeno's principle' (*Metaph.* B 4, 1001^{b}7–10), hangs completely on the truth of the premiss that what does not contribute to the size when it is attached, nor diminish the size when it is detached, is not.[58] However, why should we accept that premiss? If we look at Zeno's reasoning, the point to notice is that it is based on the notions of attachment and detachment. The concept thus introduced is that of *being a part*. Zeno

---

[56] Vlastos, 'Zenonian Argument', 220 [118–19], points to a parallel in Melissus, which we know from Simpl. *In Phys.* 87. 6–7 Diels: 'If it is, it must be one; but being one, it must be body. But if it were to have bulk, it would have parts, and not be one any more.'

[57] Compare also a remark in the pseudo-Aristotelian treatise *De Melisso Xenophane Gorgia*. In the context of an exposition of Xenophanes' one god, the author considers the case that Xenophanes would have claimed that his one god was 'the one': '[If that were the case] what [is it that] prevents the god from rotating, caused by the parts of the god moving to each other? For indeed he will not declare such a one to be many, as Zeno does' (*MXG* 4, 979^{a}3–5). The author assumes that Zeno would have withheld the predicate 'one' from things having parts.

[58] See Vlastos, 'Zenonian Argument', 223 [121].

seems to imagine a situation in which a point-like entity is attached
to or detached from an entity having size. The criterion of existence for a part which he apparently applies is that each part should
contribute to the size of the whole of which it is a part. This criterion can be analysed into two components. The first is that basic
entities have size, mass, and bulk. If that is not the case, there could
be entities having independent existence without having size, and
Zeno's whole argument falls through. At the same time this is a
plausible idea which could be contested only by philosophers like
Plato, who assume that there are abstract basic entities which do
not share in the three dimensions of space. The second component
is that a whole of parts is nothing more than the parts of which
it consists. Without this component the postulated basic entities
with size could have parts without size, e.g. properties such as
warmth, shape, as well as their limits—as someone like Aristotle
would claim. If, on the other hand, a part is ontologically prior to
the whole, those parts must be basic entities, and therefore have
size.[59]

The second idea which makes it impossible for Zeno to accept
limits as abstract, dependent parts is a modalized version of the
first idea. If a whole of parts is nothing more than a plurality of
parts, without its own unity, and exists in virtue of those parts, then
that in itself does not mean that a unity, something which thus has
no parts, could not be divis*ible*, but only that with the division that
unity goes out of existence, and two new unities come into being.
A modalized version of this principle, however, would rule out that
what is a unity could ever become a plurality (and vice versa). This
modal principle is ascribed to Zeno by Philoponus:

[S]uppose what is continuous to be one. Then since what is continuous is
ever divisible, it is always possible to divide what is divided into several
parts. If that, then, is the case, what is continuous is therefore many. Hence
what is continuous will not be one. (*In Phys.* 43. 1–3 Vitelli)

Though this passages strikes me as being a reconstruction rather
than a report, in itself Philoponus' ascription is correct. For example, premiss (3) in the argument for the infinite smallness of

[59] It should be pointed out that if we analyse the argument thus, we do not have
to accuse Zeno of arguing in a circle by presupposing that 'what is has magnitude',
as Arist. *Metaphys. B* 4, 1001^{b}10, and following him, Makin, 'Zeno', 846, do. On
the other hand, we do not have to assume either that he had taken over the crucial
premiss from his opponents, as Vlastos, 'Zenonian Argument', 222 [120], claims.

each of the many things, which says that everything with size has parts, entails, in combination with (2) the partlessness of what is one, that everything with parts is not one, but already many and divided. Conversely, in the context of the argument (3) does only not lead to Zeno's conclusion if having parts is understood in terms of being divisible but not yet divided. Therefore Zeno's use of (3) commits him to the idea that something divisible into parts is already divided into parts which are actually present and do not form a unity. Similarly, as we saw above, Zeno assumes in our paradox too that all the parts of the infinite series of parts already exist in full actuality before they are marked off or described through a division procedure.

Finally, in the so-called Porphyry fragment Zeno argues that an object cannot be divisible everywhere, because if it were divided everywhere, it would have been divided into sizeless entities, so that, absurdly, something with size would consist of sizeless entities. From this he infers that that object is not divisible everywhere (and even that it is nowhere divisible, because it is everywhere alike). As I have shown elsewhere,[60] this argument is valid only under the presupposition that something which is divisible is already divided. For showing that it is absurd that an object is divided everywhere is not enough to show that it cannot be divided everywhere, only that it cannot be divided everywhere at the same time. However, if we understand 'divisible everywhere' in terms of separation of already divided parts, the conclusion does follow, since something that is separable everywhere into already divided parts already consists of sizeless entities. So again we see that Zeno adheres to the idea that a whole of parts is already divided and is not a unity, but a plurality.

Because of these two principles it is impossible for Zeno to conceive of a limit as something that in an abstract and dependent way forms a part of a concrete object. Since he also rejects limits which are not a part of an object in any way, there is only one conception of limits left to him: limits as independent parts. The crux of his paradox of division, however, is that there is no such final part, so that the conclusion that the object is unlimited in size is inescapable.

What is more, even if there were such a limit to the unlimited series, whether as an independent part after the whole unlimited series of parts or, on the alternative conception (i) of a limit, as the place where the body ends, it would not make any difference. For

[60] In 'The Foundations of Presocratic Atomism', *OSAP* 17 (1999), 1–14 at 12.

if that final item is independent, so is the unlimited series without
that final item: it has to take care of itself, also with regard to having
a limit, on the same ground, that a whole of parts is nothing more
than these parts together, so that the whole has the properties it has
only because of the contributions of each of its parts separately. It
is clear that the unlimited series cannot take care of itself in this
respect, and thus cannot be stopped from going on and on.[61]

On his own principles, therefore, Zeno is justified in concluding
that each of the many things is so large as to be unlimited.

5. Parts of time

So Zeno's idea behind his Second Paradox of Plurality was, if I am
right, that because (i) a whole is made up of an unlimited series of
parts and (ii) nothing more, (iii) it does not have a final part or limit,
and therefore (iv) is unlimited in size. In principle this argument is
applicable in the case of the Runner Paradox as well, for there we
have (i) a period of time needed for the whole run which is made up
of an unlimited series of periods of time as parts, and Zeno clearly
presupposes that (ii) this series exhausts the whole period of time,
as there is little point in drawing a conclusion about the whole if the
series on which the conclusion is based does not exhaust the whole.
Moreover, we may assume that also in the case of time Zeno holds
on to his idea that any whole of parts is nothing more than those
parts together, so that any series of parts has to have a final part if it
is to be limited—a requirement the unlimited series of things with
which the stretches are touched obviously cannot meet.

However, it may be objected that it is merely an assumption
that Zeno applied his conception of parts and wholes invariably
to the domain of time as well as spatial magnitude. What is the
evidence for it? For if the assumption is dropped, it will not do
simply to repeat all the considerations given in the previous section
in order to justify (iii) and (iv) in the case of the Runner Paradox.
Moreover, one may then also question Zeno's assumption of (ii).
A kind of counter-example will make the point more perspicuous.

---

[61] This notion of an object having to take care of itself with respect to having a
limit also appears in the passage from Plato's *Parmenides* referred to at several points
above, when Parmenides states that because of its infinite divisibility an object 'itself
appears not to have a beginning or a limit or a middle *with regard to itself* [πρὸς αὑτόν]'
(165 A 6–7).

Suppose the Runner, whose running now is conceived of not in the Zenonian way, but in a way in accordance with our normal understanding, has completed the run in a finite time and we take the moment of completion as the present. Then we may divide the (finite) time needed to complete the run into two parts: the part which is now, namely the moment of completion, and the part before the present moment, i.e. the (relative) past (in so far as it is part of the time of the run, of course). The problem now is that it seems that with this present moment we have a part of the whole run whose presence undermines the argument (i)–(iv). For it may be objected that the unlimited series of periods of time whose existence Zeno has established does not exhaust the whole period of time, as there is still one part left; thus described, assumption (ii) would be discredited. Alternatively, it may be said that this present moment can be seen as a dependent part of the whole period of time, which period may thus be exhausted by the unlimited series in so far as it concerns separable parts, but would still be limited. Finally, if we reinterpret Zeno's phrase 'the unlimited things' with which the Runner touches the unlimited stretches in terms of the subruns as actions in time, rather than the mere temporal dimension of these actions, we may even argue that with the present moment we have an analogue to the line in space at which something happens to an object. Thus conceived, the present moment could function as an independent but abstract limit to the run, so that that would not be unlimited in time.

Moreover, in contrast to the case of the division paradox, where he could point out that something without size does not exist, Zeno cannot respond to all of this by denying that there is such a present moment. For in his Paradox of the Arrow he does accept the existence of the present moment, the now.

However, it is the same Paradox of the Arrow which provides the evidence that Zeno could not accept this counter-example and even that he applied his part–whole principle in the temporal realm. The first point I want to make is that the counter-example is inconsistent with the way Zeno thinks about the relation between the past and the present. He rather thinks of them as different, independent *stages* in time, even though in the Paradox of the Arrow he holds that the now is without duration and therefore without room for movement. Plato had already noticed this, as appears especially from the following passage from his *Parmenides*, where Parmenides remarks about the object of discussion, the one:

Does it not stop becoming older when it hits upon the now? It does not become, but is then already older, is it not? For if it were going on, it could never be caught by the now. *For a thing going on is in such a state that it touches both, the now and the later, letting go of the now and getting hold of the later, becoming between the two, the later and the now.* (152 B 6–C 7)[62]

One can recognize in this passage a concern with issues similar to those raised by Zeno in the Arrow and the Runner (no movement in the now, the relation between a process and its goal or limit): they are part of Plato's recasting of Zeno's arguments. Apparently Plato thinks that the conception of the now as an independent time between the past and the future was involved in those arguments.[63] Plato's analysis that a conception of past, present, and future as independent stages standing next to each other is involved in Zeno's paradoxes is confirmed if we look at Aristotle's testimony about the Paradox of the Arrow. For its basic premiss is that:

(n) The flying arrow is always in the now,

which means that the flying arrow is always in the present.[64] The idea behind this premiss is that it is in the now that everything happens and not in the past or the future. Now if the now were seen as something which merely provided a limit to the (relative) past and the (relative) future, as in the counter-example sketched above, it would be in some way a part of them, so that the claim that everything which happens, happens only in the now, and has, in so far as it happens, nothing to do with the past or the future,

[62] Trans. adapted from M. L. Gill and P. Ryan, *Plato:* Parmenides (Indianapolis, 1996).

[63] A similar conception seems to underlie two earlier passages, 151 E 6–152 A 2 and 152 B 3–6.

[64] Thus I subscribe to the interpretation of the Arrow as outlined by J. Lear, 'A Note on Zeno's Arrow', *Phronesis*, 26 (1981), 91–104. That this is the correct interpretation also appears from the fact that if we replace 'the now' in (n) with the more neutral 'instant', so that we get:

(n*) The flying arrow is always in an instant,

we have a premiss that is by no means as compelling as (n). Whereas it seems a matter of course that the arrow cannot be in the past or in the future, but 'always in the now', there is nothing questionable in the contrary of (n*), that is, in the arrow being over a period rather than in an instant, unless one surreptitiously derives (n*) from (n).

comes out false. For if the now is the limit to the past period, we somehow, in however weak a sense, conceive of this now as being in that period, and thus in the past period.

What is more, Zeno's argument in the Arrow can also be shown to rely in two related inferences on the idea that a whole of parts is nothing more than the parts together. The first inference is the argument which is needed to turn the now as used in (n) into a durationless instant (which it must be not only if it is to be used by Zeno as a time in which there is no room for motion, but also if it is going to serve as a limit, as in the counter-example sketched above). The only way to do so is by means of an unlimited division procedure at whose end it is found as a separate entity. The argument starts with the idea that there are three periods next to each other: the past, the present, and the future. Then one applies recursively the idea that part of the present is not really present: it is in the past or the future. For each stage of this thinning out of the now it remains true that there are three separate periods. Therefore there is, once one has finished this procedure, a durationless now which is still not part of either the past or the future; rather it is an independent entity standing between and next to the past and the future, as a quasi-period without duration.

The crucial step in this argument, which has become known as the argument for the retrenchability of the now,[65] is that it is impossible that one should consider a part of the present as a time which has been or is yet to come. Hidden behind this step is Zeno's part–whole principle. For only given this idea can we infer that if the present is a whole of parts, some of which are past or future, it is called present only because of the part which is *really* present. For without this idea there is no order of priority between a whole and its parts, and thus no notion of a *real* present; the one present time, e.g. the present month, may then without any problem contain a past and a future time, e.g. a past week and a future week.[66]

Because of this way of conceiving of the present moment, Zeno is also justified in the second inference in which we may recognize the idea that a whole of parts is nothing more than those parts together.

[65] See e.g. Owen, 'Aristotle on Time', *LSD* 295–314 [originally in P. Machamer and R. Turnbull (eds.), *Motion and Time, Space and Matter* (Columbia, Oh., 1976), 3–27] at 302–3 [11–12].

[66] Cf. J. Westphal, 'The Retrenchability of "the Present"', *Analysis*, 62 (2002), 4–10, who in fact gives the same diagnosis of the argument, saying that it commits the fallacy of composition.

In order to conclude that an arrow which does not move in the present does not move over the whole period of its flight either, he must assume that a period of time is just a collection of moments which are, have been, or will be present.[67] This conception of a period of time as a mere sum of present moments follows naturally from Zeno's way of thinking of the present as a dimensionless but independent stage of time.

So once again it is Zeno's view of the relation between parts and wholes, now applied to temporal entities, that blocks the attempt to find a way of escape from his paradoxical conclusions. For according to that view, the moment of completion of a motion is completely severed from the time of the motion itself as well as the other way round, so that in itself that time of motion, being divided into an unlimited series of periods, does not have a limit in any way. Therefore in the case of the Runner Paradox too Zeno is perfectly justified, given this view, to infer the unlimited size of the time needed for the motion from its consisting of an unlimited series of ever-decreasing parts.

6. Philosophical interest

While discussing Zeno's version of the Runner Paradox, I mentioned that philosophical interest seems to motivate the almost universal preference for a Zeno who argues that it is impossible to move because it is impossible to traverse an unlimited series of stretches, without further qualification. This preference would have been well founded if Zeno had indeed, as has always been supposed, derived the paradoxical conclusion that an unlimited series of ever-decreasing parts has an unlimited size by way of an arithmetical argument. As it is, however, there is no trace of an arithmetical argument to be found in the sources, either for Zeno's Second Paradox of Plurality or for his Runner Paradox. Instead we see an immediate transition from the unlimitedness of the series to the unlimitedness in size of the whole of the series.

This step is to be accounted for by ascribing to Zeno an implicit argument according to which the absence of a final part to the series of ever-decreasing parts is sufficient for the conclusion that

[67] Compare Aristotle's criticism of Zeno: '[He assumes] that the time is composed of nows' (*Phys.* 6. 9, 239^{b}31–2).

the whole of such a series is of unlimited size, for lack of a limit. The most important idea behind this inference is the notion, which we may call quasi-atomistic, that any whole of parts is a plurality without any real unity to it, a mere sum, which for its properties is completely dependent on those parts, each of which separately contributes something to that whole, while those parts, on the other hand, are completely independent from each other and thus also from the whole.[68] It is this idea which, on the one hand, rules out limits as dependent parts of a whole, while on the other hand it also severs the unlimited series of parts into which some whole is divided from any possible limit and demands that it be on its own, also with regard to having a limit.

Not only is this account of Zeno's inference more faithful to the direct evidence about Zeno himself and to the way his first interpreters responded to him, but it is also philosophically more interesting. Of course, the conclusion that objects and motions are infinite because they consist of an infinite series of parts is outrageous, but hardly more so than the conclusion that there is no motion because it is impossible to complete an unlimited series of runs. More importantly, however, this account also explains why the idea that it is impossible to complete an unlimited series of runs appeals to us. Somehow we naturally conceptualize a motion as something which has to stand on its own, also with regard to bringing the moving object to its final destination. But having divided a motion into an unlimited series of smaller motions and seeing that each of these motions brings the object closer to the finish, we wonder what motion makes the final contribution: we want a final step—which is not there.

The only way, therefore, to get rid of the conceptual problem posed by Zeno is to limit the domain of application of his part–whole principle. In the light of our almost natural inclination to apply this principle, however, it is not enough merely to deny or ignore the principle, and to declare, with the modern mathematical solution, that to traverse all the 'halves' and to reach all the infinitely many end-points of these 'halves' is sufficient for traversing the whole distance. According to mathematical theory, there may not be a difference in terms of measurement between an interval excluding

---

[68] Only the modalized version of this idea is really atomistic, as strictly speaking the idea as described does not rule out that what is a whole without parts at least could have been a whole with parts.

the end-point and one including it, but that amounts to nothing more than ignoring the underlying idea of Zeno's paradoxes and thus the demand for an independent limiting part. What is needed is an explanation of why and how we may conceptualize in such a way as to avoid applying Zeno's part–whole principle. It is only after giving the right diagnosis of Zeno's argument in the Second Paradox of Plurality and the Runner Paradox that we may start thinking about such a cure.[69]

University of Groningen

BIBLIOGRAPHY

Abraham, W. E., 'The Nature of Zeno's Argument against Plurality in DK 29 B 1' ['Nature'], *Phronesis*, 17 (1972), 40–52.

Barnes, J., *The Presocratic Philosophers*, 2nd edn. (London, 1982).

Cherniss, H. (ed. and trans.), *Plutarch's* Moralia, vol. xiii (Cambridge, Mass., and London, 1976).

Fränkel, H., 'Zeno of Elea's Attacks on Plurality' ['Attacks'], in R. E. Allen and D. J. Furley (eds.), *Studies in Presocratic Philosophy*, ii. *The Eleatics and Pluralists* (London, 1975), 102–42 [originally in *American Journal of Philology*, 63 (1942), 1–25, 193–206].

Furley, D. J., *Two Studies in the Greek Atomists* [*Two Studies*] (Princeton, 1967).

Gill, M. L., and Ryan, P., *Plato:* Parmenides (Indianapolis, 1996).

Grünbaum, A., *Modern Science and Zeno's Paradoxes* (Middletown, Conn., 1967).

—— *Philosophical Problems of Space and Time*, 2nd edn. (Dordrecht and Boston, 1973).

Guthrie, W. K. C., *A History of Greek Philosophy*, ii. *The Presocratic Tradition from Parmenides to Democritus* (Cambridge, 1965).

Hasper, P. S., 'The Foundations of Presocratic Atomism', *OSAP* 17 (1999), 1–14.

Lear, J., 'A Note on Zeno's Arrow', *Phronesis*, 26 (1981), 91–104.

McKirahan, R. D., Jr., 'Zeno', in A. A. Long (ed.), *The Cambridge Companion to Early Greek Philosophy* (Cambridge, 1999), 134–58.

Makin, S., 'Zeno on Plurality', *Phronesis*, 27 (1982), 223–38.

[69] On another occasion I hope to argue that we may perhaps cure ourselves from applying Zeno's part–whole principle in the realm of motion, but that we will not be able to do so in the case of tangible objects. Thus there would still not be an end to the havoc created by Zeno's argument.

—— 'Zeno of Elea' ['Zeno'], in E. Craig (ed.), *The Routledge Encyclopedia of Philosophy*, vol. ix (London, 1998), 843–53.

Owen, G. E. L., 'Zeno and the Mathematicians', in *LSD* 45–61 [originally in *Proceedings of the Aristotelian Society*, 58 (1957–8), 199–222].

—— 'Aristotle on Time', *LSD* 295–314 [originally in P. Machamer and R. Turnbull (eds.), *Motion and Time, Space and Matter* (Columbia, Oh., 1976) 3–27].

—— *Logic, Science and Dialectic: Collected Papers in Greek Philosophy* [*LSD*] (London, 1986).

Prior, W. J., 'Zeno's First Argument concerning Plurality', *Archiv für Geschichte der Philosophie*, 60 (1978), 247–56.

Ross, W. D., *Aristotle's Physics: A Revised Text with Introduction and Commentary* [*Physics*] (Oxford, 1936).

Sorabji, R., *Time, Creation and the Continuum: Theories in Antiquity and the Early Middle Ages* (London, 1983).

Stroll, A., *Surfaces* (Minneapolis, 1988).

Timpanaro Cardini, M. (ed., trans., and comm.), *Pseudo-Aristotele: De lineis insecabilibus* (Milan, 1970).

Vlastos, G., 'Fränkel's *Wege und Formen frühgriechischen Denkens*', in *Studies*, 164–79 [originally in *Gnomon*, 31 (1959), 193–204].

—— 'Zeno's Race Course. With an Appendix on the Achilles' ['Race Course'], in *Studies*, 189–204 [originally in *Journal of the History of Philosophy*, 4 (1966), 95–108].

—— 'A Zenonian Argument against Plurality' ['Zenonian Argument'], in *Studies*, 219–40 [originally in J. P. Anton and G. L. Kustas (eds.), *Essays in Ancient Greek Philosophy* (New York, 1971), 119–44].

—— *Studies in Greek Philosophy*, i. *The Presocratics* [*Studies*] (Princeton, 1993).

Westphal, J., 'The Retrenchability of "the Present"', *Analysis*, 62 (2002), 4–10.

White, M. J., *The Continuous and the Discrete: Ancient Physical Theories from a Contemporary Perspective* (Oxford, 1992).

Zimmerman, D. W., 'Could Extended Objects be Made out of Simple Parts? An Argument for "Atomless Gunk"', *Philosophy and Phenomenological Research*, 56 (1996), 1–29.

—— 'Indivisible Parts and Extended Objects: Some Philosophical Episodes from Topology's Prehistory', *Monist*, 79 (1996), 148–80.

THE FUNDAMENTAL CONFLICT
IN PLATO'S *GORGIAS*

JAMES DOYLE

T HE action of Plato's *Gorgias* is easily described. It is the late fifth century BC. Gorgias, the world-famous Sicilian orator, is visiting Athens. He has just finished giving a display of his rhetorical virtuosity before an audience. He is with two friends and admirers—Polus, a young and avid student of rhetoric, and Callicles, a man of burning political ambition—as Socrates and his friend Chaerephon come upon the scene. After a brief opening conversation, Socrates talks at some length with Gorgias, Polus, and Callicles in turn. These three conversations are of increasing length and intensity; the last of them takes up well over half the dialogue and includes some bitterly hostile exchanges. The dialogue begins with these words:

CALLICLES. This is how they say you're supposed to approach a war or a battle, Socrates.
SOCRATES. What's that? Are we late for a feast, as the saying goes?[1]
CAL. You certainly are, and a most elegant feast it was. Gorgias has just finished showing us all kinds of beautiful things.
SOC. But this is all Chaerephon's fault, Callicles: he made us linger in the market place. (447 A 1–8)

Greek word order is far more flexible than English, and Plato has chosen to make the first words of Callicles' admonition—the first words of the dialogue—πολέμου καὶ μάχης, which means 'war and battle'. As with several of his dialogues, Plato seems to have chosen

© James Doyle 2006

This paper is the text, lightly revised, of a talk given to the Department of Politics at the University of Virginia in April 2004. I would like to thank Colin Bird for the invitation, and the audience for comments.

[1] Presumably Callicles is invoking a proverb along the lines of 'first at a feast, last at a fight'. See Olympiodorus, *Commentary on Plato's* Gorgias, trans. R. Jackson, K. Lycos, and H. Tarrant (Leiden, 1998), 1. 3; also E. R. Dodds, *Plato's* Gorgias: *A Revised Text with Introduction and Commentary* [*Gorgias*] (Oxford, 1959), 188, and W. Hamilton, *Plato: Gorgias* (Harmondsworth, 1960), 19 n. 1.

the first words of the *Gorgias* as having a special significance in
relation to what follows.[2] The words 'war and battle' presage the
most contentious drama Plato ever wrote: Socrates' long conversation with—who else?—Callicles, which will not begin for another
thirty-four Stephanus pages. When Socrates threatens to bring his
conversation with Gorgias to a premature end, Callicles protests:
'I've been present at many discussions, but I don't know that I've
ever enjoyed one as much as this; I'd be happy for you to carry on
talking all day long!' (458 D 1–4) But once his own confrontation
with Socrates is under way, this tone of carefree badinage and warm
encouragement will deteriorate to the level of such exchanges as
the following:

CAL. This man won't stop talking rubbish. Aren't you ashamed at your
age, Socrates, to be setting verbal traps, and thinking it a godsend when
anyone makes a slip of the tongue? . . .
SOC. . . . My dear fellow, please adopt a gentler style of teaching—or I
may run away from your school!
CAL. You're being sarcastic, Socrates.
SOC. Not at all; I swear it by Zethus, whom you invoked just now in your
sarcasms at my expense.   (489 B 7–C 1, D 7–E 3)
CAL. I don't understand your subtleties, Socrates.
SOC. Oh yes you do, Callicles; you're just playing dumb. Take the argument
a little further.
CAL. What's the point of carrying on with this drivel?
SOC. So you may see what a wise teacher you are.   (497 A 6–B 1)

SOC. Discipline, then, is better for the soul than licence—contrary to what
you thought just now.
CAL. I don't know what you're talking about, Socrates. Ask someone else.
SOC. Here we have a man who can't bear being improved, by making
himself subject to what we're talking about: discipline.
CAL. I couldn't care less what you say. I was only answering you to oblige
Gorgias . . . What a bully you are, Socrates! If you take my advice, you'll
leave this subject alone, or discuss it with someone else.

(505 B 11–C 6, D 4–5)

Nowhere else in Plato does the reader get such a sense that the
gloves are off, and it is just this sense that gives the confrontation

---

[2] Scrutiny of Plato's first words begins with Proclus' commentary on the *Parmenides*. See M. F. Burnyeat, 'First Words: A Valedictory Lecture', *Proceedings of
the Cambridge Philological Society*, 43 (1997), 1–20 at 4–8; cf. P. Friedländer, *Plato*
(2 vols.; New York, 1964), ii. 245. See also my 'On the First Eight Lines of Plato's
Gorgias', *Classical Quarterly*, forthcoming (2006).

its uniquely urgent intensity. The opening exchange establishes a
light-hearted rapport between the *Gorgias*' main protagonists, but
forebodes in its very first words a subsequent degeneration into
naked hostility. This breakdown of the initially cordial relations
between Socrates and Callicles is one of the most dramatic and
alarming psychological reversals in all of Plato. I shall argue that
part of its meaning lies in a certain kind of opposition between
Socrates and Callicles. By this I do not mean the familiar fact that
Socrates and Callicles take opposed positions in their discussion
or that they descend into personal conflict; this is part of what
the whole reversal consists in, and so it is part of what has to be
explained. I mean that Socrates effectively represents himself and
Callicles as politically opposed archetypes: politically opposed to
such a degree that the entire terrain of political possibility is en-
compassed in the space between them. This is as yet, of course,
obscure and metaphorical; it will become clearer in the course of
the argument. Before we get to argument proper, we need to understand certain features of Socrates' conception of rhetoric, and how
that bears upon his understanding of the nature of philosophy and
politics.

With this in mind, let us return to the opening words, this time
considering the context in which they are spoken. Gorgias was the
most famous orator in the Greek world of his time. His embassy to
Athens in 427 BC caused a sensation and revolutionized the practice
of rhetoric.[3] Of the many Athenians who thought of themselves
as interested in intellectual culture, very few would have missed a
chance to attend a demonstration of Gorgias' rhetorical techniques.
Yet Socrates did not even show up! The opening exchange shows
more than it says: Callicles' mock-indignant words draw attention
to Socrates' late arrival, without registering its real significance:
Socrates thinks that rhetoric is a worthless, in fact a pernicious pursuit.
(His contempt for rhetoric, signalled by the dramatic construction
of the opening scene, is mirrored by Plato's own attitude, signalled
by his decision to have the *Gorgias* begin *after* the end of Gorgias'
rhetorical display—as if to intimate: 'What interest could such an
event hold for real philosophers who (as the subsequent dialogue
confirms) will naturally reject rhetoric for dialectic?') Socrates will
not make his disdain for rhetoric explicit until after Gorgias has
proven unable to produce a satisfactory definition of it, whereupon

---

[3] See D. Nails, *The People of Plato* (Indianapolis, 2002), 157.

Polus insists that Socrates give a definition of his own. He com-
plies reluctantly, because he is afraid that what he says may offend
Gorgias, and we can see why:

SOC. . . . The whole activity, of which what I call rhetoric is a branch, is
not admirable in the slightest.
GORGIAS. What activity, Socrates? Speak out, and don't spare my feelings.
SOC. All right, Gorgias: it doesn't strike me as having anything to do with
technai at all; rather, it's the sort of business that suits a shrewd and bold
spirit with a natural aptitude for dealing with men. I call the activity as
a whole *flattery*. It has many other branches, I believe, one of which is
cookery, which has the appearance of a *technē* but, as I understand it, is
not a *technē*, but a knack acquired through practice. What I call rhetoric
is another branch, along with cosmetics and sophistic: four branches,
each with its own activity.[4]   (463 A 2–B 6)

After the disclosure of Socrates' low opinion of rhetoric, much
of the dialogue can be understood in terms of Polus' and Callicles'
responses to it. Polus says that Socrates must nevertheless concede that those proficient in rhetoric have great power over others;
but Socrates, to Polus' mounting incredulity, denies precisely that.
His explanation of why they lack power requires him to expound
further theses which sound no less fantastic to Polus, such as that
happiness depends upon virtue, and that *it is better to suffer injustice than to inflict it*. Socrates' critique of rhetoric also provokes
Callicles to a sneering denunciation of philosophy: as in the opening exchange, he gives as good as he gets. Nothing else in Plato's
Socratic dialogues comes close to the finely wrought contempt for
Socratic philosophizing of Callicles' great speech, of which Dodds
wrote, with characteristic acumen, 'One is tempted to believe that
Callicles stands for something which Plato had it in him to become
(and would perhaps have become, but for Socrates)':[5]

I like philosophy in a young lad . . . but when I see an older man still
philosophizing and refusing to give it up, well, Socrates, in my view this
is a man who needs a good kicking. . . . He will never be a real man . . .
shunning the centre of the city and the market place where, as the poet

[4] I leave *technē* untranslated because all the going one-word translations ('art',
'craft', 'science', 'skill') are very misleading. Mathematics, astronomy, playing the
lyre, and making shoes are all examples of *technai*; the features of *technai* especially
relevant to this context are their having some measure of rational theoretical structure distinct from and governing their associated activities.
[5] Dodds, *Gorgias*, 14.

says, 'men win renown', he spends the rest of his life sunk in obscurity, whispering with three or four boys in a corner, and never coming out with anything grand or free-spirited or adequate to the occasion. (485 C 3–4, D 1–E 2)

The bulk of the long conversation with Callicles consists of Socrates' attempts to undermine the ideal of life—the pursuit of power and pleasure, uninhibited by respect for the 'conventional' virtues—which Callicles opposes to the Socratic pursuit of virtue through philosophy.

For all the distinctive intensity of the confrontation, it is still continuous with what went before it, at the level of the fundamental juxtaposition of ideas; in particular, with the opposition of rhetoric and philosophy, introduced in the dialogue's opening pages:

SOC. Now, are you willing to carry on with our conversation the same way as we did just now, Gorgias?—that is, asking and answering questions in turn, and postponing for another time the kind of long speeches Polus was trying to start in with.   (449 B 4–7)

It is a remarkable feature of the *Gorgias* that the contrast between speeches and interrogations is introduced so unobtrusively—as if it were a mere matter of formal convention, of no substantive import—only for it then gradually to assume a global ethical significance, as it becomes the defining opposition of the dialogue. At the same time, Socrates effects an association of rhetoric and philosophy each with their own constellations of ideas, which also stand opposed to each other. Rhetoric is characterized (i) as concerned only with persuading the audience, indifferent to the truth of the propositions of which they are persuaded (454 E, 459 A–C); (ii) as manipulating the appearance of good (centrally, pleasure) with no concern as to where the real good lies (464 B–465 D); and (iii) as having tyranny—the usurpation of political power—as its natural end (452 E). Socrates consistently depicts philosophy (or dialectic), on the other hand, as (i) ascribing to persuasion of the interlocutor a value strictly conditional upon the truth of the propositions he thereby comes to believe (495 A, 505 E–506 A, 471 E–472 C); (ii) concerned above all with the real good and indifferent to the apparent good (482 A, 494 E–495 A); and (iii) assigning no value to the accumulation of (so-called) political power for its own sake (468 C). As we shall see, Socrates does not associate the ideas within these two constellations merely analogically—he thought that there are important, necessary, inferential connections between, for example, (i) seeing extended speech-making as the paradigm intellectual activity and a corrupted ethical outlook that prizes the accumulation of brute power and denigrates the 'conventional' virtues, and between (ii) a commitment to philosophy, seeking the truth by brief question and answer, and the correct conception of how to live. This is not just because one is most likely to hit upon the correct way of life if one enquires into it philosophically: it is also a conceptual truth that the philosophical life consists partly, but essentially, of an enquiry into how best to live (cf. *Ap.* 38 a).

The very casualness with which this distinction, between speech-making and discussion, is introduced may lead us to suspect that it is too superficial, too much a matter of mere style of discourse, to bear the tremendous ethical and philosophical weight Socrates comes to place upon it. We may also object that it is in the end a distinction of degree rather than of kind: does an answer to a question posed in discussion not *become* a piece of speech-making once it exceeds a certain length, as in the *Symposium*? In a sense, these objections should be conceded. The distinction in question cannot literally be a matter of mere form. A 'discussion' with a sufficiently compliant or mesmerized interlocutor is surely not preferable, by any criteria that could interest Socrates, to a speech, as many passages in Plato's 'non-Socratic' dialogues illustrate all too well; the paradigmatic discussions recounted in the 'Socratic' dialogues, for their part, can easily be imagined read aloud by a single speaker, thereby becoming, technically, 'speeches'. As for the distinction being one of degree, Socrates himself concedes this in acknowledging that certain discussions make necessary long answers that amount to speeches (465 E 1–466 A 2). The distinction Socrates is really interested in is one that the distinction between speech-making and discussion characteristically stands for; and this is a distinction between the basic stances of orator and discussant as such: put briefly, the orator seeks to persuade, while the discussant seeks the truth.

Yet rhetoric in the *Gorgias* is opposed not only to philosophy or dialectic; it is also contrasted with another dominant theme: justice. In the hopelessly mismatched debate between Socrates and Polus, and in the long, climactic confrontation between Socrates and Callicles, Plato interweaves the dialogue's chief themes of rhetoric, justice, and well-being (*eudaimonia*). The juxtaposition of rhetoric and justice as defining themes of the *Gorgias* raises an important question for the twenty-first-century reader: what do these have to do with each other, that Plato thinks it a good idea to treat them together in the same dialogue? There is no prominent debate in the current journals of rhetoric or of political philosophy about important connections between these subjects, conceptual or otherwise. It is sometimes suggested that the yoking together of these themes strikes us as odd or dated because rhetoric played a far more important role in the ancient world, and especially in classical Athens. This may appear to be a reason for thinking that the *Gorgias'* relevance to our own urgent moral and political problems is limited by a dependence upon conceptions of politics and society that no longer apply. The important thing to understand about this way of thinking is that it gets everything completely the wrong way round. The *whole point* of Socrates' critique of rhetoric in his conversation with Polus is that it is simply a miscellany of tricks for getting people to think what you want them to think, and as such there is no unifying theory of it by reference to which it can be more profoundly understood: rhetoric is simply whatever mechanisms are used for the purpose of persuasion. Nothing in Socrates' arguments about rhetoric or its relation to justice turns on whether the mechanism in question consists of a man in a *himation* speaking to a crowd on a hill, words issuing from loudspeakers at Nuremberg, or images on a television or computer screen or on the cover of a magazine. The multiform proliferation in our own time of media of persuasion strongly confirms Socrates' view that rhetoric, in this broad sense, is not the kind of thing for which we should expect to be able to provide an underlying theory. It is not difficult to see important questions of justice about the use of all such means of persuasion, which have become immeasurably more powerful and intrusive in the last hundred years or so, and seem now to be entering upon a new period of positively pandemic expansion. The *Gorgias* may be unique among Plato's dialogues in being even more relevant to us than it was to his contemporaries.

Bearing in mind these observations about Socrates' conception of rhetoric and how that shapes his understanding of the nature of philosophy and politics, let us return to the confrontation with Callicles, and the dramatic reversal that represents. When an incredulous Callicles interrupts Socrates' conversation with Polus ('Tell me, Chaerephon: is Socrates being serious about this, or is

he joking?'), Socrates' response defers confrontation with a typically urbane appeal to what seems to be common ground:

My dear Callicles, if people didn't have certain feelings in common—some
sharing one feeling, some another—but some of us had unique feelings
unshared by the rest, it would not be easy to reveal one's experience to
one's neighbour. I say this because I've noticed that you and I actually find
ourselves in the same predicament. We are both lovers, and in each case
our love has two objects: mine is for Alcibiades the son of Cleinias and for
philosophy, while yours is for the people [δῆμος] of Athens and Demos the
son of Pyrilampes. Now, I observe that whenever your loves say anything
to you, for all your cleverness you find it impossible to contradict the
substance of what they say; instead you twist and turn this way and that.
If you say something in the assembly and the Athenian people disagree,
you change your story to what they want to hear; and you are the same
way with that handsome young man the son of Pyrilampes. In fact, you
are so far from being able to oppose your loves' wishes or words that, if
someone expressed surprise at the bizarre things they typically cause you
to say, you would probably tell them, if you were willing to tell the truth,
that unless someone stops your loves from speaking this way, you won't
stop saying these things either.
    So you should be ready to accept a similar answer from me, and not
be surprised at what I say, unless you can stop *my* love, philosophy, from
speaking this way. You see, my dear friend, she is always saying what you
are hearing from me right now, because she is far less capricious than *my*
other love. That son of Cleinias says something different every time he
opens his mouth; but philosophy always says the same thing: precisely
what amazed you just now, and you were there yourself when she said it.
(481 C 5–482 B 2)

Here we see some typically Socratic manœuvres: (1) the self-depre-
cating reference to his own libidinous nature and, more specifically, his mock obsession with Alcibiades (compare, of course, *Sym.*
215 A–219 D); (2) the disavowal of the *logos* in question as origi-
nating with himself; Socrates often tries to cast himself and his
interlocutor(s) alike in the role of co-operative followers of the *logos*; compare, for example, his quotation from Homer (*Il.* 10. 224)
in the *Protagoras*: 'when two men go looking together, one sees
before the other' (348 D 1), and, perhaps the most prominent and
curious case, the attribution of the *logoi* of the *Crito* to the 'laws
and the city of Athens' (50 A ff.), which seem to drown out Crito's
own *logoi* like the flutes of the Corybantes (54 D); (3) the yoking
together of the dynamics of *erōs* with the dynamics of philosophy

(cf. *Phaedo* 66 E 2, *Sym.* 210 A–212 B, *Phdr.* 244 A–257 B); and (4) the subtle disparagement of the interlocutor, although this is perhaps more typical of the *Gorgias* (and of the *Euthyphro*) than of Socratic procedure generally. Dodds writes of Socrates' reply that it is 'couched in playful terms which make the comparison inoffensive' (*Gorg.* 260) but I suspect he has missed a trick here. Socrates is using the same kind of rhetorical procedure as he did with Polus, exposing the commitments of the advocate of rhetoric as base and unworthy even on their own terms. He argued, in the face of Polus' exasperated incredulity, that since orators and tyrants do not attain their real good, even though that is what they (like everyone) really want, and power consists in doing what one really wants, orators and tyrants have no power. Some commentators have professed themselves unable to believe that this argument is intended seriously, on the ground that its conclusion cannot be seriously meant.[6] Yet there is reason to think of this as a saying we can intelligibly *hope* to be true. Polus and, especially, Callicles are obviously very much taken with the glamorous allure of political power. Callicles' position, as set out in his great speech, is a subtle and compelling one, brilliantly expressed. Unlike the modern 'moral sceptic', a merely notional figure, Callicles articulates a way of life that is not only a real option, but was to some extent a lived reality among many members of the political class to which he belonged, and had some of its roots in the heroic tradition with which all educated Greeks were imbued. There is nothing anomalous in his having inspired Nietzsche—not a superficial man—and there is nothing fantastic in Dodds's conjecture that he represents Plato's conception of what he might himself have become had he not quit politics.[7] Polus is in thrall to as much of Callicles' ideology as he understands, and for Socrates to tell Polus that tyrants actually have no power is to hit him where it hurts. If power is worth seeking, it makes perfect sense to hope that it is not, after all, what tyrants have found, so that

---

[6] See e.g. K. McTighe, 'Socrates on Desire for the Good and the Involuntariness of Wrongdoing: *Gorgias* 466 A–468 E', *Phronesis*, 29 (1984), 193–236, repr. in H. H. Benson (ed.), *Essays on the Philosophy of Socrates* (Oxford, 1992), 263–97; R. Weiss, 'Ignorance, Involuntariness and Innocence: A Reply to McTighe', *Phronesis*, 30 (1985), 314–22, and 'Killing, Confiscating and Banishing at *Gorgias* 466–468', *Ancient Philosophy*, 12 (1992), 299–315. My own view is that the genuineness of Socrates' conviction here is beyond doubt; see my 'Desire, Power and the Good in Plato's *Gorgias*' ['Desire'], in S. Tenenbaum (ed.), *New Directions in Philosophy: Moral Psychology* (Amsterdam: forthcoming [2006]).

[7] Dodds, *Gorgias*, 14, quoted above.

one can neutralize the attraction political power holds for people
like Polus by telling no more than the truth about tyrannical im-
potence.[8] This insight into the glamour of political power pervades
the *Gorgias*, and it shows that Plato, unusually among moralists, refuses to assimilate all vices to what is mean, conniving, and parasitic
in human beings. Nor is it easy to see how the *Gorgias'* conception
of moral danger can be made consistent with the assimilation of all
vice to ignorance, which Socrates seems to insist upon in many of
the shorter dialogues. Part of the 'latent content' of the argument
addressed to Polus is: 'You worship power, and desire to acquire
it more than anything else? Then forget about orators and tyrants,
because *they don't have any!*' In depicting Callicles as in thrall to
his 'two loves', the Athenian *dēmos* and Demos son of Pyrilampes, Socrates (anticipating the details of Callicles' position) may be
understood as saying: 'You think of your advocacy of rhetoric as of
a piece with a grand, forceful life, lived in accordance with "natural" rather than "conventional" justice, and in utter disregard of the
feeble subterfuges of the Lilliputian masses, by which they seek to
constrain strong and talented natures like your own. But here is the
reality of your life: you spend it in a mercenary sequence of changes
of opinion dictated by the necessity of keeping pace with the fickle
thinking of the *dēmos*—for all the world as if you were a desperate
lover seeking your beloved's approval. What's worse, it's distinctive of your very own view that the *dēmos* is to be despised—yet
here you are chasing after it and fawning upon it.' And it is hard to
avoid a further implication of the *dēmos*/Demos comparison: that
Callicles' ultimate purpose in flattering the *dēmos* is the same as
his purpose in flattering Demos: to ingratiate himself in order to
achieve physical gratification in a way that precludes respect for
either quarry—by screwing them, as one might say.

I want to suggest, then, that the force of the '*dēmos*/Demos' passage runs counter to its apparently mollifying content. Socrates
presents himself as pointing out something that he and Callicles
have in common, but his real purpose is to undermine the allure
of Callicles' conception of 'natural' justice, and thereby his conception of himself. But more than this: when understood in the
light of what comes later, this passage gives us a crucial clue as
to why Socrates and Callicles cannot in the end make dialectical contact: why, in other words, their views and personalities are

so fundamentally opposed that, unlike Socrates and Gorgias, or Socrates and Polus, they end up unable to take part in the same discussion.

This becomes clear, I suggest, if we look ahead to Socrates' argument at 509–12, that in a tyranny one must choose between doing and suffering injustice. He has claimed, in his conversations both with Polus and with Callicles, that it is worse to do injustice, although both are evils.

At 509 B–C Socrates responds at last to the charge that he should be ashamed at not being able to protect himself from injury or death (generally: from suffering injustice). It is interesting to compare the response here to the *actual* accusation, made with reference to Socrates' *hypothetical* trial and execution, with his response to the very same accusation made *hypothetically*, in the *Apology*, with reference to his *actual* trial and (impending) execution (28 B–30 B). There Socrates relied upon conventional notions of heroism and shame, comparing himself with Achilles, and insisting that there is nothing necessarily shameful about adhering to a course one knows will result in one's death. Here in the *Gorgias* he goes much deeper: the reason why there need be nothing shameful about it is that the most shameful and ridiculous condition is the failure to protect oneself against the worst of misfortunes or evils—and this is to *commit* injustice, not to suffer it.

Here he proposes that escaping the worse evil, doing injustice, requires only an effort of the will; but to avoid suffering injustice one must acquire 'some sort of power or skill': namely, either the power of tyranny itself, or the protection that comes with the tyrant's friendship. Clearly, in becoming a tyrant one is committed to doing injustice. But the same is true, Socrates argues, of becoming the tyrant's friend. For the tyrant fears and resents those who are better than himself, and has only contempt for those who are worse; so the person who desires his friendship must become *like him*—and it is impossible to imitate the tyrant without imitating his injustice:

SOC. So if a young man in a city like this were to ask himself: 'How can I get great power and ensure that no one can treat me unjustly?', the answer would seem to be this: by accustoming himself from an early age to liking and disliking the same things as his master, and by ensuring that he's as similar to him as possible. Isn't that right?
CAL. Yes.
SOC. Such a man will have achieved the goal of immunity from being

treated unjustly and of possession of great power in the city, according
to you and your friends.

CAL. Certainly.

SOC. But what about ensuring that he won't *commit* injustice? Not likely—
not if he's really going to resemble this ruler and wield great power
under him, since the ruler himself is unjust. No, I think that the man's
plan will be the exact opposite of this: to enable himself to commit with
impunity as much injustice as possible.   (510 D 4–E 8)

SOC. . . . If you suppose, Callicles, that anyone can furnish you with the
sort of know-how [*technē*] that will make you very powerful in this city,
without your thereby acquiring, for better or worse, the same nature as
its ruling class, then I'd say you're not thinking straight. It's not enough
to mimic these people: there must be a genuine natural likeness, if you're
going to make any real progress in the affections of the Athenian *dēmos*—
or of Pyrilampes' Demos either, for that matter. So whoever can make
you most like them is the man who will make you what you want to be:
a politician and an orator. Demos and the *dēmos* alike, you see, enjoy
hearing speeches made in accordance with their own nature, and hate
the reverse. Or perhaps you disagree, my dear fellow? Is there anything
to be said against this, Callicles?

CAL. What you say strikes me as impressive, Socrates, although I couldn't
say why. Then again, I'm in the same boat as a lot of the people you talk
to: I'm not entirely convinced.   (513 A 7–C 6)

The significance of this argument does not lie in its details, many
of which are questionable. Socrates seems to elevate sociological
rules of thumb to the status of exceptionless scientific laws; and
he treats only of the case where avoiding suffering injustice is
the very highest priority. Nevertheless, as Callicles himself (of all
people!) finds himself saying: 'What you say strikes me as impressive, Socrates, although I couldn't say why.' There is *something*
important in Socrates' argument, and perhaps it is this: *you must
take sides.* Unless you are literally a hermit, you cannot remain
above the fray: if you are not part of the solution, you are part of
the problem; if you are bent on avoiding suffering injustice, you
must ally yourself with evil. And surely there is truth in this.

Furthermore, this argument circles back to that elaborate simile
Socrates deployed at the start of his conversation with Callicles: the
comparison between his attitudes to Demos the son of Pyrilampes
and the Athenian *dēmos*. Callicles seeks above all to avoid being
the victim of (conventional) injustice: that is why he allies himself,
exactly in accordance with Socrates' argument, with the tyrant of

Athens: the people at large. And in slavishly imitating them, he cannot avoid committing injustice.

At 512 Socrates insists on a point familiar from the *Apology*: ensuring and preserving the quality of one's life must always take precedence over any attempt to prolong it. The attack on Callicles can thus be intensified: how do his acquisition of rhetorical skill, his pandering to the Athenian *dēmos*, his planned acquisition of political power, etc.—all of which are undertaken for the sake of physical security and gratification—improve the quality of his life (i.e. of his soul)? They do not: they only make it worse, because in imitating the *dēmos* he becomes enmired in injustice. Callicles himself is an object lesson in Socrates' thesis that the person who seeks to avoid suffering injustice will necessarily end up committing it.

The case of Socrates himself, of course, illustrates the other side of this thesis:

> So where power is in the hands of a brutal and uneducated despot, anyone in the city who's far superior to him will be very much feared by him, and he'll never be able to be on terms of genuine friendship with him. (510 B 7–C 1)

In the context of the argument, the consequences of failing to establish terms of genuine friendship with the 'brutal and uneducated despot' (a description that applies to the Athenian *dēmos*) include the liability to suffer injustice—up to, and including, death. And of course this is what befell Socrates: he refused to protect himself against the possibility of suffering injustice precisely because he knew that he could do so only by committing injustice (pandering to the *dēmos* and disobeying the god, which are fused in a single imagined case in the *Apology* (29 C–30 B), when Socrates envisages the *dēmos* allowing him to go free on condition that he give up philosophizing).

So in their respective courses of action, Callicles and Socrates serve as perfect exemplars of the two sides of Socrates' 'birds of a feather' argument. They have chosen opposite sides, and never the twain shall meet. This pessimism about the power of dialectic may seem to distinguish the *Gorgias* from the bland intellectualist optimism often taken to typify the Socratic dialogues. But then we remember Socrates' words to Crito:

> One should never do wrong in return, nor injure any man, whatever injury one has suffered at his hands. And Crito, see that you do not agree to this

contrary to your belief. For I know that only a few people hold this view or will hold it, and *there is no common ground between those who hold this view and those who do not, but they inevitably despise each other's views.* (49 C 8–D 4)

Plato saw that there was something attractive in Callicles' outlook, and it is exactly what attracted Nietzsche: the idea of a strong personality spurning the masses. Yet Socrates' conversation with Callicles shows that this is a mirage: the true entailment of Callicles' view is not the ability to rise above the masses, but the necessity of abasing oneself before them. The final irony is that it is Socrates, with his seeming allegiance to 'conventional' justice, who has the real opportunity of rising above the herd; and that is why they must kill him. Callicles has enslaved himself to Socrates' persecutors: no wonder, in the end, that they have nothing to say to each other.

University of Bristol

BIBLIOGRAPHY

Burnyeat, M. F., 'First Words: A Valedictory Lecture', *Proceedings of the Cambridge Philological Society*, 43 (1997), 1–20.

Dodds, E. R., *Plato's Gorgias: A Revised Text with Introduction and Commentary* [*Gorgias*] (Oxford, 1959).

Doyle, J., 'On the First Eight Lines of Plato's *Gorgias*', *Classical Quarterly*, forthcoming (2006).

—— 'Desire, Power and the Good in Plato's *Gorgias*' ['Desire'], in S. Tenenbaum (ed.), *New Directions in Philosophy: Moral Psychology* (Amsterdam, forthcoming [2006]).

Friedländer, P., *Plato* (2 vols.; New York, 1964).

Hamilton, W., *Plato: Gorgias* (Harmondsworth, 1960).

McTighe, K., 'Socrates on Desire for the Good and the Involuntariness of Wrongdoing: *Gorgias* 466 A–468 E', *Phronesis*, 29 (1984), 193–236; repr. in H. H. Benson (ed.), *Essays on the Philosophy of Socrates* (Oxford, 1992), 263–97.

Nails, D., *The People of Plato* (Indianapolis, 2002).

Olympiodorus, *Commentary on Plato's Gorgias*, trans. R. Jackson, K. Lycos, and H. Tarrant (Leiden, 1998).

Weiss, R., 'Ignorance, Involuntariness and Innocence: A Reply to McTighe', *Phronesis*, 30 (1985), 314–22.

—— 'Killing, Confiscating and Banishing at *Gorgias* 466–468', *Ancient Philosophy*, 12 (1992), 299–315.

PLATO AND ARISTOTLE ON THE UNHYPOTHETICAL

D. T. J. BAILEY

1. Introduction

IN the *Republic* Plato contrasts dialectic with mathematics on the grounds that the former but not the latter gives justifications of some kind for its hypotheses, pursuing this process until it reaches 'an unhypothetical principle'. But which principles are unhypothetical, and why, is rather dark. One reason for this is the scarcity of forms of that precious word, 'unhypothetical' (ἀνυπόθετος), used only twice by Plato (*Rep.* 510 B 7, 511 B 6) and just once by Aristotle (*Metaph.* 1005ᵇ14). But that very scarcity also suggests the intriguing possibility that Aristotle has Plato's text in mind when he uses the word, so we might expect to understand Plato better by grasping how Aristotle took him. That is a notoriously defeasible assumption since plenty of modern accounts of Plato want to save him from Aristotle's numerous critiques, and hence imply that the master of them that know frequently missed the point when it came to his own master. But surely we can be more confident that Aristotle will give us access to Plato when it appears not merely that he is dealing with the same topic, but using the same rare vocabulary to boot.

Hence the understandable temptation to turn to *Metaphysics Γ* for help in identifying Platonic unhypothetical principles. I shall argue that Aristotle is indeed thinking of Plato's text when he uses the word for 'unhypothetical', and further that what is explicitly an unhypothetical principle for Aristotle might well have been one

I am very grateful to seminar audiences in London, Oxford, and Atlanta, and in particular to those who read the piece and were kind enough to supply written comments, namely: Nicholas Denyer, Gail Fine, M. M. McCabe, David Sedley, and Christopher Shields. I regret that I have been unable to address all of their questions and concerns adequately.

for Plato too. But later I shall claim that their joint use of a much more common word in the same philosophical context is either coincidence or misunderstanding on Aristotle's part, for he must mean something different by it from what Plato means.

2. Plato and Aristotle share a similar conception of the unhypothetical

Let us begin with Aristotle's example of an unhypothetical principle. In chapter 3 of *Metaphysics* $\varGamma$ he is considering propositions that are true of all things whatsoever *qua* things-that-are: he refers to any such proposition at $1005^{b}14$ as unhypothetical. So the question is whether Aristotle is thinking of the same kind of principle as Plato at the end of *Republic* 6 and, by implication, *Phaedo* 101 E 1, where the hypothetical method is supposed to conclude in the discovery of 'something sufficient'. Initially, it seems that he is. For Aristotle tells us two things about these 'firmest principles of everything' that are surely true of the end-points of enquiry Plato has in mind:

(1) Unhypothetical principles are such that error about them is impossible [βεβαιοτάτη δ' ἀρχὴ πασῶν περὶ ἣν διαψευσθῆναι ἀδύνατον] ($1005^{b}11$–12). (I shall call this the incorrigibility condition.)

(2) Unhypothetical principles are necessarily the most intelligible principles [γνωριμωτάτην τε γὰρ ἀναγκαῖον εἶναι τὴν τοιαύτην] ($1005^{b}13$). (I shall call this the intelligibility condition.)

Now the incorrigibility condition is surely true of the end-points of Plato's hypothetical method too. That method proceeds roughly as follows (I am here drawing on both *Republic* 6 and the end of the *Phaedo*, necessarily compressing quite a bit). Make a safe hypothesis and then check to see whether its results cohere with one another (ἀλλήλοις συμφωνεῖ, *Phaedo* 101 D 5).[1] If they do not, the hypothesis is false and you had better start again. If they are coherent, put your original hypothesis among the set of results of another 'higher' proposition (presumably a more general one) and

[1] For an account of what this coherence consists in, see D. Bailey, 'Logic and Music in Plato's *Phaedo*', *Phronesis*, 50.2 (2005), 95–115.

see if it coheres in the right way with all of them, and so on. This is supposed to be a method we can continue so long as we might be wrong in supposing our current highest proposition true. Therefore the method comes to a stop only when we reach a proposition that we know we *cannot* be wrong in supposing true.[2] Only when we see that the highest proposition we have reached has this property will we know that there is no need to try justifying it further by putting it among the set of results for a still higher proposition. For we will realize that there is no such higher proposition, so no such further justification is possible.

From this we can tell that the intelligibility condition is true of Plato's unhypothetical first principle as well. For how is it that we will know when we have reached the highest proposition? What property will it have that allows us to recognize that there is no proposition still higher with which we can give a justification or explanation for it? Surely it will be the fact that it is utterly immediate to us. From our point of view nothing could explain it better than it explains itself. So there is neither need nor possibility of looking for an explanation for it. It is therefore as intelligible as any proposition can be.

But, Aristotle tells us, there is a third feature of (at least some) such principles, which is also characteristic of their unhypothetical nature:

(3) Unhypothetical principles are necessarily part of the equipment of anyone who grasps any of the things that are [ἦν γὰρ ἀναγκαῖον ἔχειν τὸν ὁτιοῦν ξυνιέντα τῶν ὄντων, τοῦτο οὐχ ὑπόθεσις] (1005^{b}15–16). (I shall call this the priority condition.[3])

Logically this condition seems different from the others. The incorrigibility and intelligibility conditions appeared to be both necessary and sufficient for being unhypothetical. But, for Aristotle at least, the wording of the priority condition makes out that satisfying it is *sufficient* for being unhypothetical without even carrying the implicature that such satisfaction is also *necessary* for being un-

---

[2] I grant that there might be other interpretations of what it is for a proposition to count as 'something sufficient'. But this seems to me to be the most plausible reading.

[3] For the purposes of this paper I am avoiding the difficult issue of whether the relevant concept of priority here is temporal or logical.

hypothetical.[4] Is there any interesting correspondence in the case of Platonic unhypothetical principles?

An answer to that question will turn on what kind of mental state Aristotle has in mind in his use of the verb for 'grasp'. Given the context, this state will obviously be some kind of knowing, but of a possibly non-luminous kind.[5] Take the example of Heraclitus. For Aristotle, Heraclitus will be someone who does indeed grasp some of the things that are, just by virtue of being rational (at least in some moods). In that case, he will know anything one needs to know of necessity in order to know anything at all. In that case, he will know, among other things, the Principle of Non-Contradiction (PNC).[6] But this knowledge will be non-luminous, at least for Heraclitus: for far from being in a position to know that he knows PNC, he mistakenly believes he has succeeded in denying it. So PNC is something Heraclitus knows without knowing that he does, or even (at least according to him) believing that he does.

Are there examples of such complicated mental attitudes towards the unhypothetical in Plato? Arguably there are, in the *Meno* at least. For one might take the result of the examination of the slave boy to be that, in some sense, he knew the theorem all along, by virtue of his soul's experiences in the discarnate state, but was not (at least at the start of the experiment) in a position to know that he knew it, or able to express this knowledge.[7] Now of course what the slave

---

[4] I am grateful to Terry Irwin for pointing this out to me.

[5] I owe this observation to Jimmy Doyle. Following Timothy Williamson, a mental condition C is (roughly) luminous if and only if whenever an individual is in C, that individual is in a position to know that C obtains. See T. Williamson, *Knowledge and its Limits* (Oxford, 2000), ch. 4.

[6] Given what I have said about the priority condition being merely sufficient for being unhypothetical, it is of course an assumption that PNC satisfies it. But given that PNC is not merely unhypothetical, but *paradigmatically* so, I think it is a plausible assumption to make.

[7] This interpretation requires a reading of the *Meno* different from that proposed by, among others, Gail Fine, in her 'Inquiry in the *Meno*', in G. Fine, *Plato on Knowledge and Forms* (Oxford, 2003), 44–65. According to her arguments, Socrates refutes his construal of Meno's Paradox of Enquiry by using the Theory of Recollection to show that one of its premisses—the claim that one cannot enquire into that which one does *not* know—is false. According to the interpretation sketched above, Socrates would be disarming the paradox by using the Theory of Recollection to show that a different premiss—the claim that one cannot enquire into what one *does* know—is false. The thought would be that, since the slave clearly can enquire into constructing a square double in area a given square, that must be because he already in some sense knows the answer: his immortal soul saw the truth in a discarnate state and, while the trauma of birth renders impossible his answering

boy knows latently but comes to think about actively by the end of the discussion is not itself something *unhypothetical*, for it is a truth derivable from prior propositions. So can we think of examples in Plato in which there is possibly non-luminous knowledge of *unhypothetical* principles, where it is *also* the case that being known in this way is sufficient but not necessary for being unhypothetical? I think we can, although I lack the space to defend the point in detail. Admittedly, the analogy of the Sun, used to illustrate the nature of the Form of the Good, rather suggests that when the Guardians come to know unhypothetical principles, their knowledge at least at that moment will be luminous. For surely one cannot look at so intensely illuminated an object as the Sun without being in a position to know that one is looking at the Sun. Even if not all perceptions are luminous, surely that one is, so it would seem that the knowledge this perception is used to illustrate should be luminous too. But equally surely, the Guardians will retain this knowledge even when they are no longer looking at the Sun or the real things it illuminates. They will continue to have this knowledge while descending back to the murky gloom of the Cave when their eyes become 'full of darkness' (*Rep.* 516 E 4–5). Arguably while in such a condition the Guardians, analogously to Meno's slave, will know what they learnt outside the Cave without being in a position to know that they know it (which might amount to their continuing to know the first principles of dialectic even when not doing dialectic, or attending to some object which cannot be treated dialectically, such as the sensible world). So arguably their knowledge of unhy-

---

Socrates correctly straight away, it does not follow that he is completely lacking in genuine knowledge about the theorem he eventually brings to mind. It might be thought that what Socrates says at 85 c 10–12 causes trouble for this interpretation, but in fact it does not. For of course, from the claim that *if* the slave is asked the same questions in many different ways, *then* he will end up knowing the answers as accurately as anyone, it just does not follow that he does not, at least in some sense, already know those answers. And Socrates' description of what the slave can accomplish if questioned further only a few lines later, at 85 D 4 ('recovering the knowledge from within him for himself'), surely suggests the interpretation on offer here. But it is not clear to me to what extent Fine and I are in disagreement. It strikes me as a perfectly reasonable interpretation of the Recollection Theory to suppose that Socrates is introducing the concept of forgotten knowledge in order to falsify, albeit in different ways, *both* premises that drive the Paradox of Enquiry, and not just the one Fine takes to be relevant. On the Fine line, forgotten knowledge is something you can enquire into that you *do not* know, just in so far as you have forgotten it. On my line, forgotten knowledge is something you can enquire into that you *do* know, just in so far as it is knowledge. And these two interpretations are quite compatible.

pothetical principles is possibly non-luminous. But can we find in Plato the further thought that the priority condition is (1) sufficient but (2) not necessary for being unhypothetical? Well (1) is easily accomplished. For if we suppose that one comes to know anything in the true sense only when it is recognized either as unhypothetical or as being dialectically inferable from something unhypothetical, then it will follow that anything you need to know in order to know anything will be unhypothetical. (2) is a little trickier to defend, but I think it can be done once we ask ourselves how many propositions are unhypothetical for Plato. It is not clear in the *Republic* (nor in related passages in the *Phaedo*) whether Plato wants to assert $(\forall x)$ $(\exists y)$ (If x is an enquiry, then y is its unhypothetical terminus) or $(\exists y)$ $(\forall x)$ (If x is an enquiry, then y is its unhypothetical terminus). If he means the latter, then very likely he will have a different conception of the unhypothetical from Aristotle. For if there is at least one unhypothetical principle at which all enquiries terminate, it will satisfy the priority condition: and if there is only one such principle, then satisfying the priority condition will be not only sufficient for being unhypothetical, but also necessary. But if he means the former, and there are a plurality of unhypothetical principles distributed over different subject matters, then it may be that, while of course knowledge of them will be necessary for knowledge of the subject matter in question, some need not be known by someone in order for him to know anything at all. For example, one needs to know unhypothetical truths of geometry in order to know geometric theorems properly, but that does not mean one must know unhypothetical truths of geometry in order to know *anything*. If there are a plurality of unhypothetical principles, satisfying the priority condition will be for Plato, as it is for Aristotle, sufficient but not necessary for being unhypothetical.

3. An example?

So there are compelling arguments for thinking that Plato and Aristotle share, at least roughly, the same conception of the unhypothetical. But it might be that these considerations can go only so far in allowing us to characterize Platonic unhypothetical principles along Aristotelian lines. For Plato is quite explicit that something like a principle Aristotle regards as paradigmatically unhypothetical is for him, at least in one context, *a hypothesis*. Aristotle's paradigmatically unhypothetical principle is this:

(A) (=PNC) For the same thing to hold good and not to hold good simultaneously of the same thing and in the same respect is impossible (given any further specifications that might be added against the dialectical difficulties) [τὸ γὰρ αὐτὸ ἅμα ὑπάρχειν τε καὶ μὴ ὑπάρχειν ἀδύνατον τῷ αὐτῷ καὶ κατὰ τὸ αὐτό· καὶ ὅσα ἄλλα προσδιορισαίμεθ᾽ ἄν, ἔστω προσδι-ωρισμένα πρὸς τὰς λογικὰς δυσχερείας]. (*Metaph.* 1005ᵇ19–22)

Which is surely, at least at first glance, similar to a principle Plato formulates in *Republic* 4:

(P) It is clear that the same thing will not do or suffer opposites in the same respect in relation to the same thing and at the same time [δῆλον ὅτι ταὐτὸν τἀναντία ποιεῖν ἢ πάσχειν κατὰ ταὐτόν γε καὶ πρὸς ταὐτὸν οὐκ ἐθελήσει ἅμα]. (*Rep.* 436 B 8–9)

I said just now that (A) is something like (P), but of course there are important differences. (A) uses negation to specify what it says is impossible—that something should hold and also *not* hold of something—while (P) speaks in terms of opposites. That is, the former supposes that contradictories cannot hold of the same thing while the latter supposes that contraries cannot. But even Aristotle is not embarrassed to express his principle in terms of contraries, as he does a few lines later at 1005ᵇ26–7. Meanwhile, the properties with which Plato's Socrates illustrates the consequences of his principle, rest and motion, are arguably themselves contradictories rather than mere contraries.[8]

Perhaps more importantly, (A) is modally stronger than (P). (A) says that such-and-such being the case is *impossible* (ἀδύνατον), while the strongest construal of (P) is that it says that such-and-such *will refuse to be the case* (οὐκ ἐθελήσει). This might make, in the end, a great deal of difference between the two philosophers, for Plato accepts that some things that never were, never are, and never will

---

[8] I owe this observation to Christopher Shields. Modern philosophers might feel uncomfortable with the thought that rest and motion are contradictories, for it seems there are plenty of things, abstract objects especially, which just are not the right kinds of thing to be at rest or in motion: for instance numbers or space–time points. But Plato certainly has no qualms about ascribing rest to his favourite abstract objects, the Forms.

be are nevertheless possible.[9] His language is scarcely stronger a few lines later at 436 E 8–437 A 2 when Socrates restates (P), saying that he *will not be disconcerted* by sophistic tricks on the matter or *persuaded any the more* that something might suffer or do opposites etc. But to say that there is nothing that could convince you that ¬*p* is significantly weaker than saying that ¬*p* is impossible. At any rate, the former is a statement about oneself, while the latter is a statement about the truth-conditions of *p*—namely that they must obtain no matter what.

These differences can be explained away partially by the difference in argumentative contexts. Given Aristotle's broad aim of determining the subject matter of metaphysics in Gamma, he will want the meatiest and strongest general principle he can formulate to be basic. Plato, by contrast, only wants something strong enough to deliver the conclusion that the soul has parts, a claim which may be independently plausible anyhow.[10] In his drive for generality, Aristotle will be interested in *any* properties that determine a complement class, not just properties with opposites, and he will want his principle to be as modally ambitious as possible. Meanwhile Plato will naturally speak of properties with opposites as things which *most obviously* cannot belong to the same thing in the same respect, and will be happy if that claim is just plausible enough for Socrates not to entertain any doubts about it.

But reference to the argumentative contexts is only a partial explanation, since it cannot account for the following difference. For Socrates, (P) is something to be *hypothesized*, as he says at 437 A 6–7: ὑποθέμενοι ὡς τούτου οὕτως ἔχοντος. Now Aristotle would say that since the incorrigibility, intelligibility, and priority conditions are true of (A) (and hence, let us suppose for the moment, also of (P)) then no one can *really* believe that either (A) or (P) is ever false. As he puts it at *Metaph.* 1005^{b}23–6, 'it is impossible for anyone to believe that the same thing is and is not, as some consider Heraclitus said—for it is not necessary that the things one says one should

---

[9] The *Timaeus* holds (41 A–B) that it is *possible* for the world to perish even though in fact it *never will* perish (a position with which Aristotle took umbrage in *De caelo* I. 11–12). For a discussion of the debate, see N. Denyer, 'Never Will and Cannot', *Proceedings of the Aristotelian Society*, suppl. 74 (2000), 163–78.

[10] And when he redeploys that fact in an argument in bk. 10, his language is as modally strong as Aristotle's. At 604 B 3–4 he asks whether 'when two opposite impulses occur in a man at the same time about the same thing, we say that *of necessity* there are two things in him'.

also believe'. But if one cannot really believe in a counter-example
to (A) or (P)—as Aristotle says Heraclitus cannot, despite what he
might say—then surely one cannot really believe that *there might
be* any counter-examples to those principles. In other words, one
cannot believe that either of them could have the provisional status
of *mere* hypotheses, propositions which might be false although we
treat them as true for the time being. So by the lights of *Metaphysics
Γ* 3, would Aristotle tell Socrates that he cannot really believe what
he says to Glaucon when he introduces (P) as a hypothesis?

I think not. We can see that Aristotle and Plato are actually
thinking in the same way once we consider the difference between
an unhypothetical truth and its formulation in a context. Socrates
says that he will treat (P) as a hypothesis so that he and his interlocutors are not compelled 'to prolong matters by going through
all such sophistries, confirming for ourselves that they are not true
[πάσας τὰς τοιαύτας ἀμφισβητήσεις ἐπεξιόντες καὶ βεβαιούμενοι ὡς οὐκ
ἀληθεῖς οὔσας μηκύνειν]' (437 A 4–6). (P) is treated as a hypothesis
not because it might turn out to be *false* later on, but rather because, *when formulated like that*, the principle invites a number of
questions and quibbles, mainly about what the precise respects are
in which nothing can be both *F* and the opposite of *F* (Aristotle recognized this too). And when an unhypothetical truth is formulated
as the sort of proposition that invites such questions and quibbles,
one is entitled to treat the formulation as a hypothesis.

For all that he does not say he will treat (A) as a hypothesis, there
is none the less the same acknowledgement that something is missing in his formulation from Aristotle. He specifies a few constraints
on the conditions of *F* holding and not holding of the same thing to
be impossible (that it be at the same time, and in the same respect),
but then leaves off from identifying other relevant considerations
in favour of a brief stage direction that such qualifications be taken
as read. While Socrates in effect says, 'we shall just suppose that
this principle is true and ignore the quibbles for the moment',[11]
Aristotle appears to be saying, 'we affirm a suitably qualified version of this principle, the details of whose qualification we shall not
bother to spell out at the moment'. So both philosophers state their

---

[11] *Soph.* 230 B is an indication that this is the right way of taking what Socrates
says in the *Republic*. For here we get a fuller statement, this time from the Eleatic
Stranger, of the kind of qualifications that need to be made in making clear and
explicit what the Principle of Non-Contradiction says is impossible.

principles with pretty much the same acknowledgement that the explicit formulation omits important points of detail. Thus while it initially seems an important difference that Socrates calls what he says a hypothesis while Aristotle calls his version unhypothetical, they are both aware of the fact that their actual formulations of the principle are sensitive to the context, and hence somehow inadequate. And in the case of Socrates, that his formulation is sufficiently opaque for him to treat what he says as a hypothesis is perfectly compatible with the fact that what it is a formulation *of* is unhypothetical.

This is as it should be. For surely we want to be able to begin investigations generally by saying 'Suppose *p*' for any value of *p* whatsoever, even 'Suppose that two twos make four' or 'Suppose that I am now inviting you to make a supposition'. If we could not formulate unhypothetical truths in a manner suitable for treatment as a hypothesis, then it would be impossible to carry out any kind of serious investigation into their nature, which is presumably one of the things that the completed science of dialectic will do. It will want, for instance, to know what is the hallmark of propositions that are known to be true once formulated in the right way, and in order to discover this it may be necessary to hypothesize the unhypothetical. To say that unhypothetical principles are immune from being hypothesized would be to misunderstand the force of the negative prefix in 'unhypothetical' for both Plato and Aristotle. In calling a principle unhypothetical, one is not going so far as to rule out the possibility of *expressing* the principle as a hypothesis. One merely says that such a principle, unlike others, can be formulated in a way that is sufficient for knowing it immediately once it is so formulated.

An illustration of the sort of thing I have in mind might help. Mathematicians usually treat basic arithmetical propositions as unhypothetical in the way Aristotle treats (A). But sometimes other mathematicians such as Frege treat the same propositions as hypothetical in so far as they suppose them to be true but try to formulate them more transparently. In doing this, they do not cast the kind of doubt on those principles that would mean they do not actually qualify as unhypothetical. Frege never doubted that $2 + 2 = 4$. But he thought, very reasonably, that you put the truth more transparently (if more technically) when you say that the set of all pairs, when related to itself by the addition relation, is identical to the set of all quartets. Or again, think of the Cartesian case in which one cannot be wrong in thinking that one exists whenever one is thinking. The formulation *cogito ergo sum*, for all its indubitability, is certainly the sort of thing for which one can demand some sort of explanation. For example, is it known to be true non-inferentially by some kind of immediate intuition? Or is it inferred via the major premiss 'All thinking things exist'? Such questions can still be raised about *that* famous formulation of the Cogito, even though what it expresses is arguably unhypothetical.

This much, then, by way of argument that Aristotle and Plato are speaking of the same thought in these two passages, and hence that PNC or something like it might well be unhypothetical for Plato too, even though Socrates explicitly hypothesizes his version of it. If they are more or less the same principle, and Aristotle describes his formulation of it with his master's word 'unhypothetical', I see no reason to resist the inference that Plato would have regarded the same principle as unhypothetical too.

4. Baltzly on the unhypothetical

Still, this is not much by way of illumination. We want other examples of Platonic unhypothetical principles before we will feel comfortable that we know what they are like. Fortunately at least one philosopher, Dirk Baltzly, has suggested an ingenious way of characterizing what might be meant by 'unhypothetical' *without* drawing directly on *Metaphysics Γ*, although a consideration of his arguments will ultimately lead us back there.[12] Instead he turns to the dialectic in the second half of the *Parmenides*, arguing that, for Plato, a proposition is unhypothetical if its contradictory could not even be formulated if its truth-conditions actually obtained.[13] So, according to the first deduction of the second part of the *Parmenides*, the proposition 'The One has some share of being' is unhypothetical (142 A ff.). Parmenides says, 'If something is not, could anything belong *to* this thing that is not, or be *of* it? Therefore no name belongs to it, nor is there an account or any knowledge or

---

[12] D. Baltzly, '"To an unhypothetical first principle" in Plato's *Republic*', *History of Philosophy Quarterly*, 13 (1996), 149–65, and 'Aristotle and Platonic Dialectic in Metaphysics Gamma 4', *Apeiron*, 32 (1999), 171–202.

[13] Baltzly, '"To an unhypothetical first principle" in Plato's *Republic*', 153.

perception or opinion of it.' If it really were true that the One has no being—that the One is not—then this could not be expressed in any form, for there would not be anything for an expression about the One to be about. Since this is so, the contradictory of the claim 'One does not have a share of being' is, Baltzly thinks, unhypothetical.

According to this interpretation Plato also holds that the claim that some of the kinds blend (*Soph.* 251 D 5 ff.) is unhypothetical, because if the truth-conditions of its contradictory arose and, among other things, Being were apart from everything (including itself), then one would not be able to say so, since that would involve predicating something (namely non-blending) of Being, which would involve saying that Being blends with something (namely non-blending). So if Being really were apart from everything, one could not truly express this[14] (I shall have more to say about the logic of this argument below).

I am not convinced by Baltzly's characterization, for a number of reasons. Firstly, it seems to me that the passages he speaks of have the style of *proofs*, and I hold that one of the reasons for calling the end-points of Plato's method 'unhypothetical' is that they are propositions which neither need nor admit of proof (even if, as I was just now arguing, we might be able to provide some lesser form of explanation for them by trying alternative formulations). As Aristotle argues when he comes to discuss PNC in *Metaphysics Γ*, it is impossible that *everything* should have a proof (ὅλως μὲν γὰρ ἀπάντων ἀδύνατον ἀπόδειξιν εἶναι, 1006ᵃ8), and in particular his favoured unhypothetical principle ought not to be susceptible to proof since it is an ultimate belief for anyone proving anything (διὸ πάντες οἱ ἀποδεικνύντες εἰς ταύτην ἀνάγουσιν ἐσχάτην δόξαν, 1005ᵇ32–3).

I think this must be so just as much for Plato too. For according to the end of *Republic* 6, an unhypothetical first principle[15] allows you to move step by step through every hypothesis used in reaching it, in a series of moves from which it is the completely adequate starting-point. But if it behaves like this, then even if it is not like

---

[14] And if Nicholas Denyer is right (as I think he must be) in thinking of expressions as themselves being kinds, one could not express anything at all, true or false. See N. Denyer, *Language, Thought and Falsehood in Ancient Greek Philosophy* (London, 1991), ch. 9.

[15] In speaking of '*an* unhypothetical principle' rather than '*the* unhypothetical first principle', I refer the reader back to the remarks in the main text of p. 106.

Aristotle's first principles in other respects, it ought not to be the kind of thing that can be proved—in which case it ought not to be the kind of truth entailed by the sophisticated arguments Baltzly discusses. For the principles he takes to be unhypothetical are entailed, on this story, by Plato's tacit premiss that whatever can be true can be said to be true when it is true. Hence any purported truth that would be falsified if it were expressed is in fact necessarily false, in which case the contradictories of such propositions are necessarily true. In other words we can prove the truth of Baltzly's principles to ourselves on the basis of the truth of another, metalinguistic, premiss.[16] But this ought not to be possible if they were really unhypothetical. For such principles, at least when properly formulated, are supposed to explain themselves better than anything *else* could. They let us know that they are true themselves, without relying on some further principle.

Baltzly has a ready reply to this objection. While one cannot give a *Posterior Analytics*-style proof of unhypothetical principles, Aristotle tells us at 1006ᵃ11–13 that one can at least give an *elenctic* proof of such principles (or at any rate, of his sample principle PNC), provided someone who denies it at least says something (ἔστι δ' ἀποδεῖξαι ἐλεγκτικῶς καὶ περὶ τούτου ὅτι ἀδύνατον, ἂν μόνον τι λέγῃ ὁ ἀμφισβητῶν). Baltzly could then defend his claim that the principles he finds in Plato are unhypothetical because they too are proved in a similar fashion. Those who posit the contradictory of his unhypothetical principles are refuted *out of their own mouths* just like Aristotle's opponent. If what they *said* were in fact true, then they would not have been able to say it. And, for both Plato and Aristotle, Baltzly holds, this is a kind of proof that what they say must be false, but *not* the kind of proof whose premisses would suggest that the proved theorem is too posterior to be unhypothetical.

Now exactly how Aristotle's elenctic proof is supposed to work is a matter of considerable debate, into which I do not intend to enter here. But it is significant, I think, to note a number of disanalogies between the elenctic proof and the ways in which Plato arrives at the propositions Baltzly thinks are unhypothetical, which tend to show that the latter would *not* be unhypothetical by Aristotle's lights, if

---

[16] Baltzly realizes this: see '"To an unhypothetical first principle" in Plato's *Republic*', 153. It is a merit of his account that he can explain why Plato might have held this metalinguistic premiss, given his view that 'philosophical conversation is an important pathway to truth . . . When the content of a claim is such that, were it true, it couldn't be expressed, this is ample reason to think that it must be false.'

there is supposed to be some non-accidental connection between being unhypothetical and being susceptible to *elenctic* proof, whatever that is precisely.

Firstly, Aristotle's elenctic proof seems to rely upon a kind of circularity (which, of course, Aristotle has freely admitted to at 1005^{b}32–3). *Any* possible proof of PNC will ultimately rely *in some sense* on the truth of that principle because *every* possible proof so relies on it. Now it might be that the reason Aristotle says that PNC admits of an *elenctic* proof rather than proof proper is that one can give a partial explanation of PNC with an argument whose premises must be in accordance with it. For why else say that you can prove PNC *in any way*, given that those who deny its truth (at least according to Aristotle)[17] are hardly going to be the sort of people who are impressed by proofs *of any kind*, if not by way of saying that such a proof will at least explain something about PNC?[18] One might argue that this fact makes any purported proof of PNC viciously circular. Alternatively one might defend Aristotle's proof as Michael Dummett defends a similar version, as being benignly rather than viciously circular, because PNC is not asserted in the proof, even if its truth is somehow relied upon.[19] But whichever of these opposing views is correct, there is no such circularity, benign or otherwise, to be found in Plato's arguments that the One has some share of being and that some of the kinds

[17] I pass over the fact that Aristotle seems to have held that no one actually *does* deny PNC—that is, no one actually *believes* PNC false, even though there may be some who *say* it is false: 'for it is not necessary that the things one says one should also believe' (*Metaph.* 1005^{b}23–4). It may well be that the elenctic proof establishes that no one really disbelieves PNC, whatever they may say to the contrary: but this is a consequence of the proof rather than a precondition for it. It is not enough, in advance of the proof, to assert that such people cannot *really* believe what they say: for certainly they will reply that they do believe what they say, and will be unimpressed by any gainsaying on Aristotle's part. For even if he is right, and they do not really believe what they say, if PNC is in fact false, as they *think* they suppose, then they will have no reason to suppose they are in the wrong about what they think they believe.

[18] A similar argument might be put against those who hold that Protagoras is meant to refute himself in *Theaet.* 177 C–179 B. According to this argument, that ought not to be what Plato is aiming at, for if refuting yourself is a bad thing because it involves you in saying something necessarily false, why should such a charge bother anyone who has denied the possibility of falsehood in the first place? See S. Waterlow, 'Protagoras and Inconsistency', *Archiv für Geschichte der Philosophie*, 59 (1977), 19–36.

[19] For an argument along these lines establishing the ultimacy of PNC, see M. Wedin, 'Some Logical Problems in *Metaphysics* Gamma', *OSAP* 19 (2000), 113–62 at 115–19.

blend. Parmenides' argument does not depend in any sense on the thought that the One has some share of being. It depends instead on the quite different and completely independent thought that *what is being meaningfully talked about must be there to be talked about.* Again, the argument in the *Sophist* that some of the kinds blend does not depend in any way on the truth of that thought, but on the principle that *what makes predications true (or even possible) is some kind of blending.* Doubtless these claims are supposed to provide explanations of why the principles are true. But such explanations are very different from the (benignly or viciously) circular kind of which Aristotle's elenctic proof is an example. Rather, they seem to be the sort of helpful explanations—prior premises, if you like— that you get from ordinary, *Posterior Analytics*-style proofs.

Secondly, and more importantly, there seems to be a difference in logical status between the contradictory of Aristotle's unhypothetical principle PNC and the contradictories of what Baltzly thinks are Plato's. The point is best introduced by considering an example from the great medieval logician John Buridan, who wonders whether the proposition 'No proposition is negative' is self-refuting or not.[20] It looks on the face of it as if it is. For if its truth-conditions arose, it could not be stated. But, Buridan goes on to argue, even though 'No proposition is negative' is not possibly *true*, it is at any rate *possible*. Provided we construe propositions as tokens of some sort—that is, as obviously contingent beings—it could well be that what the proposition *says* to be the case obtains, that in fact no propositions *are* negative, even though the proposition saying just that obviously would not exist, and hence would not be true, in such circumstances. This consideration seems to me to open up another distinction between PNC and Baltzly's principles. For one could argue that the contradictories of the latter, but not the contradictory of the former, express possibilities without being possibly true. After all, is there anything impossible about the One having no share of being—that is, is there not the possibility of the non-existence of the One, even if its actuality would render impossible any thought or expression about it? Or again, what is wrong with supposing that there might have been nothing at all, which would surely be the result if none of the kinds blended, even though one could not, of course, say or think that there was nothing at all in

[20] See G. Hughes (ed.), *John Buridan on Self-Reference: Chapter Eight of Buridan's* Sophismata (Cambridge, 1982), 37–9.

such circumstances, since there would not be anything to say or think it with?

Now it might be that the answer is 'No' in both cases, and that the contradictories of Plato's principles are supposed to be *neither* possibly true *nor* possible, that the One *must* have a share of being, and that at least some of the kinds *must* blend.[21] But if that is so, such metaphysical commitments are going to require rich arguments with pretty substantial further premisses. And this is not the case, at least for Aristotle, when we come to say that the contradictory of PNC is neither possibly true nor possible. Not only would it be impossible to express the contradictory of PNC if it were true (for any purported formulation under such circumstances would, according to Aristotle, no more express a denial of PNC than an affirmation of it, since everything would be indeterminate). But also what such a formulation would try but fail to express is not even a possibility. Even of a world without any propositions to be thought, written, or said (in so far as Aristotle could entertain such a possibility) he would surely maintain that it is still *never* the case that contradictory properties belong to the same thing at the same time in the same respect etc. The denial of PNC is neither possibly true nor possible. But Aristotle will regard this as a brute fact about the world, admitting of no very deep explanation. If you want an explanation of how or why a property had by a certain thing at a certain time in a certain respect excludes the privation of that property at that time in that respect, then tough luck. That is just the way things are at the most fundamental level, and explanations come to an end. By contrast for Plato, if there is not merely a connection, but a necessary one, between the One and its being, or the kinds and their blending, that looks without further ado like the sort of thing that might admit of explanation. I can only guess at such explanations, as follows, but at least they spring to mind without too much sweat. The One just is, necessarily, because it is a Form, and that is the way Forms have their being (by contrast with sensible things). And at least some of the kinds blend because some are by themselves incomplete, as are some of their linguistic correlates, verbs (ῥήματα). I am not at all trying to say that these are the *right* explanations for Baltzly's principles, only that they and their ilk are available. And the important point

---

[21] The former at least seems likely if the One of the deductions in the second part of the *Parmenides* is a Form.

is that they are *generalizing* explanations. They explain a particular fact (the One's having being necessarily; at least some of the kinds blending) by a more general one (Forms have certain properties, including being, necessarily; and some kinds, whether they blend or not, are somehow incomplete). I can think of no such generalizing explanation for PNC, not even the claim that some things must be determinate. For just as many things as are determinate abide by PNC. That things be determinate, and that they abide by PNC, are for Aristotle two ways of expressing exactly the same condition.[22]

This difference in susceptibility to explanation indicates, to me at any rate, that PNC and the principles Baltzly finds in Plato are rather different kinds of claim, admitting of rather different kinds of proof. From the above facts together with the previous suggestion that PNC may well be unhypothetical for Plato, we ought to infer either that those principles are *not* unhypothetical, or that unhypothetical principles can be a pretty heterogeneous bunch.

As things stand at the moment, the former conclusion is preferable. For suppose I am right in arguing that 'The One has no share of being' and 'None of the kinds blend' *might* be propositions which express possibilities without being possibly true. If *all* that is wrong with those propositions (and hence unhypothetical about their contradictories) is that they could not be expressed if they were true, then what is there to stop Plato admitting denials of genuine possibilities as unhypothetical? What is there to stop the apparently contingent claim 'Some proposition is negative' from being unhypothetical?

It is for this reason, I suppose, that Baltzly's second paper on this subject[23] turns to another Platonic passage, *Theaet.* 181 c–183 c 5, arguing that the contradictory of Heraclitus' claim 'All things change in every way' is unhypothetical on the grounds that if the Heraclitean claim were true then neither it *nor anything else* could be thought, written, or said.[24] This case, I think, shows up the

---

[22] For a helpful discussion of this thought, see V. Politis, *Aristotle and the* Metaphysics (London, 2004), ch. 5.

[23] 'Aristotle and Platonic Dialectic in Metaphysics Gamma 4'.

[24] These sorts of conditions also interest Baltzly in his first paper on the subject: 'Plato is interested in philosophical views which are such that if the conditions which would make them true obtained, those same conditions would make it the case that neither they, *nor anything else*, could *ever* be expressed in any way' ('"To an unhypothetical first principle" in Plato's *Republic*', 153, emphasis

heterogeneity of the principles Baltzly discussed in his first paper. For if the truth-conditions of 'The One has no share of being' arose, then while you could not express that proposition, since there would be no such thing to say anything about, you could none the less talk, and maybe even talk truly, about plenty of other things besides the One. (Similarly: if the truth-conditions for 'No proposition is negative' arose, then, while that proposition itself could not be expressed, plenty of others still could be, including the logically equivalent, and true under the circumstances, 'Every proposition is positive'). But it seems that the contradictory of 'All things change in every way' has a better claim to be unhypothetical, since if the truth-conditions of Heraclitus' claim arose, then, supposedly, *no propositions whatsoever*, true or false, could be thought, spoken, or written. The same is true of the principle from the *Sophist*, albeit for a rather different reason. If none of the kinds blended (and in particular nothing blended with being, including itself),[25] then one could not express that fact or any other—but not this time because the world would be too dizzyingly fluxy for one to think, write, or speak, but because there would be literally *nothing at all*. Heraclitus' problem is that he describes a possible world one could not talk or think about were it actual: an intolerably unstable and incoherent world, but a possible world none the less, in fact one in which one might get to grips with things semantically in the minimalist way in which poor Cratylus is said to have ended up, i.e. by pointing. Indeed, *some* think that there is a good sense in which Heraclitus' world is actual, for it is nothing other than the sensible world as characterized in Plato's middle dialogues. By contrast, the late-learners' problem is that they imagine a world that would in fact be non-existent, or empty. These are clearly two very different ways of *logoi* failing to have any applications. So it ought to be the case that the corresponding principles derived from consideration

---

added). But if only those conditions determine unhypothetical principles, the claim that the One has a share of being will not be unhypothetical, as I argue in the main text.

[25] The late-learners do not recognize blending; and yet they permit themselves identity statements. So arguably the fact of Being's being the same as itself does not involve any kind of blending. But, equally arguably, Being would be the same as itself even if it had no being (for arguments in this style see C. McGinn, *Logical Properties* (Oxford, 2000), ch. 2). Moreover, the wording of the non-blending hypothesis is as strong as my reading tries to express: it is the set-up in which *nothing* has the power to associate with *anything*, not merely anything *else*.

of such situations are rather different. But this might count against treating them *both* as unhypothetical.

5. Destroying hypotheses?

Let us leave these objections for the moment: for it is not my task, at least in this paper, to say what other principles are unhypothetical for Plato, but to cast doubt on the thought that these ones are. But there is one final piece of evidence that the principles Baltzly finds in the dialogues are unhypothetical, a clue which takes us back to *Metaphysics Γ*. Supposedly, what they all have in common is that their contradictories are, arguably, self-refutingly false. Plato thereby establishes their putatively unhypothetical truth by *destroying* their contradictories (or, better, showing how their contradictories destroy themselves). But there is some important connection for both Plato and Aristotle between unhypothetical principles and one of the Greek words for destroying, ἀναιρεῖν. Towards the end of *Republic* 7 Plato tells us that the mathematicians are only dreaming of being, on account of their not explaining their hypotheses, while the superior method of dialectic does something or other to hypotheses (to be discussed below) in order to secure them (τὰς ὑποθέσεις ἀναιροῦσα, ἐπ᾽ αὐτὴν τὴν ἀρχήν, ἵνα βεβαιώσηται, 533 c 8–9 in the text of J. Burnet, 533 c 9–D 1 in that of S. Slings (the punctuation here is that of Slings)). Meanwhile, in *Metaphysics Γ* Aristotle tells us that the person responsible for the force of the elenctic proof of PNC is not its proponent but its opponent, some character like Heraclitus: and the reason for this is that such a person submits to argument in the act of destroying it (ἀναιρῶν γὰρ λόγον ὑπομένει λόγον, 1006ᵃ26).

Initially we might expect these two forms of ἀναιρεῖν to mean the same, given the identical philosophical contexts—the nature of unhypothetical principles—and the proximity of the magic word for 'unhypothetical', ἀνυπόθετον. These conditions suggest that Aristotle and Plato must have been thinking along such similar lines that uses of forms of the same verb in different senses for each author would seem to be either surprising coincidence or error on the part of the later author. However, I am going to argue that we ought to take it as coincidence or error.

Firstly, let us run through the one argument of which I am aware for saying that the expressions mean the same. It is quite clear that in Aristotle's text, ἀναιρεῖν must mean 'destroying' or 'eliminating'.[26] The point is that the opponent who objects to PNC refutes himself, by 'abiding by speech' (i.e. speaking at all) in the act of trying to destroy it by asserting the contrary of its intelligibility, PNC. The sense of ἀναιρεῖν as 'to take up' is not available here. For even if we could get any sense out of such a translation, it would not convey the important point that it is the objector to PNC himself, rather than his opponent Aristotle, who is poignantly responsible for his own refutation, by virtue of making use of what he tries to destroy in the act of trying to destroy it. This is how Sextus Empiricus, for example, used exactly the same word to point out that his argument in favour of global scepticism about non-relative matters of fact destroys itself, much as a fire consumes itself once it has consumed everything else available (*M*. 8. 480–1). So anyone wanting to argue that Aristotle is following Plato in his use of this word ought to impute the same sense to Plato's use of ἀναιρεῖν in the passage from the *Republic*. In other words, they have to tell us what it means for a dialectician *to destroy hypotheses*. According to Baltzly, dialectic 'destroys hypotheses' by operating on contradictory hypotheses, one of which is self-refuting, the other of which is unhypothetical. Dialectic destroys the former by exposing its self-refuting nature, and destroys the latter by eradicating its hypothetical character.[27]

My disagreement with this is as follows. I find it hard to accept that, in *Republic* 7, ἀναιρεῖν is not a univocal verb, an expression for one and the same dialectical process, which on Baltzly's story it is not. There is the destruction of showing that a proposition is self-refutingly false, and the destruction of showing that a proposition is secure well beyond the provisional status it was taken to have at the start of an enquiry. These are *very* different kinds of destruction indeed, so much so that it seems too perverse to have the same name for them. But anyhow, even if ἀναιρεῖν need not be univocal, it just is not the case that the contradictories *of the mathematicians' hypotheses* are *ever* in consideration, either in the *Republic* or anywhere else in Plato. And it is on the topic of the mathematicians' hypotheses in *Republic* 7 that dialectic emerges as the more esteemed science. It is

---

[26] The latter is favoured by C. Kirwan (trans.), *Aristotle's* Metaphysics Books *Γ, Δ, E* (Oxford, 1971), 9.

[27] Baltzly, '"To an unhypothetical first principle" in Plato's *Republic*', 153; 'Aristotle and Platonic Dialectic in *Metaphysics* Gamma 4', 195.

what the mathematicians say for the sake of reaching their conclusions that is the object of the participle ἀναιροῦσα. But there is no call for such propositions as 'There are no such things as triangles' or 'There are no odd or even numbers' (or even 'A straight line is not a line which lies evenly with the points on itself')²⁸ to be destroyed by being exposed as self-refuting (even if such an unlikely thing could be done). For unlike the theses of Heraclitus, Parmenides, and the late-learners, no one (so far as I know) even professes to entertain such odd claims. Dialectic does not secure the propositions that are merely hypothetical in the mathematicians' mouths by treating their contradictories as hypotheses and then destroying them. Such a game would hardly be worth the candle, because their contradictories are at best based on misunderstandings, at worst *plainly* false (and not e.g. false because of some metalinguistic claim that what can be true can be stated when it is true). If we think of characters who did actually contradict some of what the mathematicians said (although we hear nothing of them in the dialogues)—I am thinking here of the Protagoras of *Metaph.* 998ᵃ37–9, who 'refutes' the geometers by saying that the circle touches a ruler not at a point²⁹— then the right tactic for making mathematics secure is surely not to argue that such people *have refuted themselves*, trying to say something that could not in fact be said if it were true, but only that they have misunderstood the mathematicians (which is something both Plato and Aristotle would say of Protagoras: the former, that he does not realize that the mathematicians hypothesize for the sake of the super-sensible world, the latter, that he is ignorant of the *qua*-operator).³⁰

Instead, I take it that when Plato speaks of the superiority of dialectic to mathematics, he has the same sort of problem with the

²⁸ This would be the contradictory of Euclid's fourth definition, 'A straight line is a line which lies evenly with the points on itself'.
²⁹ I avoid the question of whether or not the claim that the line touches a circle at a point would count as a hypothesis for Plato's mathematicians, or as a consequence of prior hypotheses.
³⁰ In Baltzly's defence, one might argue that Parmenides' claim that there is just *one* thing is inconsistent with the mathematicians' hypothesis that there are numbers i.e. *pluralities* of units; and further that one might destroy Parmenides' monist hypothesis by showing it to be self-refuting by e.g. arguing that if his hypothesis were true, then (*a*) it would have to exist in order to *be* true and (*b*) what it speaks of, the One, would have to exist to *make* it true, in which case (*c*) there are at least two things. But such a route would take us far from the texts and require deeply prejudicial interpretations both of Parmenides and of Plato's understanding of him.

mathematicians' starting-points as Frege had with the definitions
of later mathematicians. In the introduction to the *Grundlagen*, we
read the following complaint, in which one might get the sense
of Plato's problem if one understood 'hypothesis' for 'definition'
throughout:

> Most mathematicians rest content, in enquiries of this kind [sc. enquiries
> into the definitions of mathematical concepts], when they have satisfied
> their immediate needs. If a definition shows itself tractable when used in
> proofs, if no contradictions are anywhere encountered, and if connexions
> are revealed between matters apparently remote from one another, this
> leading to an advance in order and regularity, it is usual to regard the
> definition as sufficiently established, and few questions are asked as to its
> logical justification. This procedure has at least the advantage that it makes
> it difficult to miss the mark altogether. Even I agree that definitions must
> show their worth by their fruitfulness: it must be possible to use them
> for constructing proofs. Yet it must still be borne in mind that the rigour
> of the proof remains an illusion, even though no link be missing in the
> chain of our deductions, so long as the definitions are justified only as an
> afterthought, by our failing to come across any contradiction. By these
> methods we shall, at bottom, never have achieved more than an empirical
> certainty, and we must really face the possibility that we may still in the end
> encounter a contradiction which brings the whole edifice down in ruins.[31]

Barring only the talk of 'an empirical certainty', Frege's complaint
here seems to me to be very Platonic. For in so far as Plato's mathematicians have not justified their hypotheses and thereby do not
know them, to that extent their conclusions might, albeit contrary
to all expectation, turn out to be mistaken. Moreover, Frege seems
to hold that the best that can be expected of proofs conducted from
unexamined principles is that 'no link be missing in the chain of
deductions', which would correspond well with one way of taking
Rep. 510 D 2, where the mathematicians are described as proceeding to a conclusion coherently (διεξιόντες τελευτῶσιν ὁμολογουμένως).
The last word here can be taken as meaning that the mathematicians pursue their conclusion by means of coherent inferences, and
that this much alone can be said in their favour.[32] But as we know
from a famous passage in the *Cratylus* (436 B 12–C 7), where the illustration is a mathematical one, this is no guarantee that any such

[31] Gottlob Frege, *Die Grundlagen der Arithmetik*, trans. J. L. Austin (Oxford,
1950), p. ix.

[32] This line appears to be taken by, among others, M. M. McCabe, *Plato's Individuals* (Princeton, 1994), 73.

inferences are *true*. Such a guarantee could come only from this together with *knowledge* of the starting-points, which is precisely what Plato's mathematicians do not bother to acquire. For Plato, it seems that mathematics as practised in his day *might* track the truth no less than dialectic, but its practitioners do not know this because they do not strive for the intelligibility characteristic of the better science. They do not know, nor seek to know, *why* what they think they know is true, if in the end it is.[33]

But—and here we return to what might be meant by 'destroying hypotheses'—anyone who makes such points as I hold Plato and Frege both make on this score is concerned to bolster the starting-points of mathematics in some way other than by arguing that their contradictories are false, or even necessarily false. For Plato, no less than for Frege, the contradictories of mathematical starting-points just are not germane to the discussion at all. And any operation performed on those starting-points so as to remedy a deficiency in our understanding of them will only very queerly be said to involve some sort of 'destruction'. Consider a similar case. If you produce a valid argument by which you can infer *q* from *p*, then there is a sense in which you have destroyed *q*'s inconsequentiality with respect to *p*. Well, you can *talk* like that if you like; and it might even be that if you were prone to Plato's mystical moods in such intellectually refined contexts, you *would* actually want to talk like that. But if you cared for being understood as readily as possible, it is an oddly indirect and perverse way to put things. And for all his appealing mysticism we should not attribute such perversity to Plato unless we can help it.

Fortunately, Plato's texts generally carry some weight against translating ἀναιροῦσα as 'destroying' anyhow. For while Aristotle usually uses ἀναιροῦσα in its 'destructive' sense, which was certainly the dominant usage in his day, Plato hardly ever does, if at all. Forms of the verb occur most frequently in the *Laws*, active ones at 642 E 1, 870 D 3, and 914 A 3, middle ones at 914 B 6, 921 A 8,

---

[33] Hence Plato's repeated talk of the connection between mathematics and dreaming. At *Rep.* 533 B 9–C 1 the mathematicians dream of that which is (τὸ ὄν). The slave boy in the *Meno* has acquired beliefs about the geometrical theorem Socrates demonstrates 'as if in a dream' (*Meno* 85 C 9–10). I understand the haziness of their dreaming to indicate a lack of understanding rather than certainty. When the slave is advised, at 98 A, to tie down his beliefs with the αἰτίας λογισμῷ, the analogy with securing the statues of Daedalus (presumably by attaching them to something heavier than themselves) suggests the epistemological securing involved in relating beliefs to other more certain beliefs, which begets *understanding* of those posterior beliefs.

and 921 B 3. None of these forms, with a trivial exception I shall come to later, can mean 'destroy'. The active forms (at least the first and third) have the same sense as the occurrence at *Ap.* 21 A 6, referring to a god's action in ordaining or pronouncing on some matter (ἀνεῖλεν, 'replied', is the verb predicated of the Pythia when she tells Chaerephon that no one is wiser than Socrates). Of the middle forms, the first straightforwardly means 'take up for oneself' (the passage is discussing what to do with the man who holds to the principle that finders are keepers), while the other two again mean 'take up', referring to a contractor who has taken up a piece of work and charges a fee for it. Likewise, the occurrences of the verb in the *Phaedrus* at 233 C 2–3 and 243 C 5, both in the middle, have nothing to do with destruction but again connote a kind of taking up. Here it is the taking up of violent hostility (ἔχθρα)—English has the clichéd expression 'to take up the cudgels'—which the non-lover will not be brought to by teething-troubles in relationships according to the first passage, and which the second passage says is typical of the behaviour of lovers, at least according to the sort of speeches Socrates deplores in the recantation of his first speech. Obviously the point is not that such lovers *destroy* enmity. Rather, they take it up for themselves in their aggrieved passion. Furthermore, the uses of the verb in later sections of the *Republic* both involve taking up: the passive form at 614 B 4–5 refers to the taking up of dead bodies after a battle (cf. *Menex.* 243 C 6), and the middle form at 617 E 7 means 'take up for oneself' as at *Laws* 914 B 6. In fact, the only place I have been able to find in Plato where one might plausibly translate a form of ἀναιρεῖν as 'to destroy', besides our disputed *Republic* passage, is at *Laws* 870 D 3, where we are told that fears bred of cowardice and iniquity can bring men to murder: for instance, when such men ἀναιροῦσι θανάτοις those who might divulge their secrets. Here you could translate ἀναιροῦσι as 'they destroy' if you like. For such men, in removing their potential betrayers 'with death', obviously destroy them. But the presence of θανάτοις allows you even here to avoid that option and translate the whole expression as 'they take them away [i.e. despatch them] with death'.

Now even though Plato does not seem to use an available sense of a word in any other context, he might still be using it with that sense in our *Republic* 7 passage. But the plurality of kinds of 'taking up' that the verb means in active, middle, and passive forms—from the taking up of the wallet on the wayside, and the taking up of the cudgels in a lovers' tiff, to the taking up of an odd job for money—all this suggests that if we can tell any story at all about how dialectic might 'take up' hypotheses for its own ends, then we will be justified in translating ἀναιροῦσα as I am urging. Fortunately there is such a story. The idea would be that, just as you would take an object into direct sunlight if you wanted to have the best possible look at it, so likewise dialectic takes up and presents the mathematicians' hypotheses to the unhypothetical principle (ἐπ᾽ αὐτὴν τὴν ἀρχήν) with a view to explaining them in the light of that principle. This kind of 'taking up' will presumably involve arguing that any such hypothesis will bear the συμφωνεῖν relation from the *Phaedo* to the principle (which amounts to giving a justification or explanation for the hypothesis), so once it has been taken up into the hands of dialectic it lacks the unexplained, provisional status it had in the mathematicians' mouths. This is what it means to ἀναιρεῖν hypotheses, and it is surprising no one has suggested it before, especially given the claim in 533 D 2 (D 2–3 in the new OCT) that dialectic *draws upwards* (ἀνάγει ἄνω) the eye of the soul.[34] Nothing destructive is going on, and rightly so—dialectic is a method of reinforcing the starting-points of mathematics with a deeper understanding of them, rather than trying to expose the shaky foundations of the essential element in the Guardians' education. Such reinforcement involves grasping hypotheses and appropriately connecting them with the unhypothetical.[35] So it seems as if it is either from coincidence or misunderstanding that Aristotle should use the same word with a quite different sense when speaking about the same topic.[36]

I have argued that both philosophers share the same conception of the unhypothetical; that what is avowedly unhypothetical

[34] I am grateful to Bob Sharples for drawing my attention to this.

[35] My interpretation requires a repunctuation of the text, deleting the comma after ἀναιροῦσα, which is present in both editions of the OCT. (Slings's addition of a comma after ἀρχήν is quite compatible with my reading.)

[36] This disjunction is not meant to be exhaustive. There is at least one other possibility, suggested to me by Verity Harte, which I lack the imagination and space to discuss in any detail. It could be that Aristotle knew perfectly well what Plato was trying to say using ἀναιροῦσα in this context, but is for some reason twitting him by using the same word in a different sense. In that case the intertextual relation would not be one of coincidence or misunderstanding, but one of polemic. It might be relevant to this interpretation that Aristotle here uses the verb ὑπομένειν for a logical or dialectical relation, which Plato only ever does once, at *H. Ma.* 298 D 4 (and even that is debatable).

for Aristotle might also have been so for Plato; and that the intertextual relations on this topic are strong enough to cast doubt on some shrewd attempts to identify unhypothetical principles in Plato. But when it comes to the verb ἀναιρεῖν, I think those relations are constituted by either accident or mistake.

Corpus Christi College, Oxford

BIBLIOGRAPHY

Bailey, D., 'Logic and Music in Plato's *Phaedo*', *Phronesis*, 50.2 (2005), 95–115.

Baltzly, D., ' "To an unhypothetical first principle" in Plato's *Republic*', *History of Philosophy Quarterly*, 13 (1996), 149–65.

—— 'Aristotle and Platonic Dialectic in Metaphysics Gamma 4', *Apeiron*, 32 (1999), 171–202.

Denyer, N., 'Never Will and Cannot', *Proceedings of the Aristotelian Society*, suppl. 74 (2000), 163–78.

—— *Language, Thought and Falsehood in Ancient Greek Philosophy* (London, 1991).

Fine, G., 'Inquiry in the *Meno*', in G. Fine, *Plato on Knowledge and Forms* (Oxford, 2003), 44–65.

Frege, Gottlob, *Die Grundlagen der Arithmetik*, trans. J. L. Austin (Oxford, 1950).

Hughes, G. (ed.), *John Buridan on Self-Reference: Chapter Eight of Buridan's* Sophismata (Cambridge, 1982).

Kirwan, C. (trans.), *Aristotle's* Metaphysics Books Γ, Δ, E (Oxford, 1971).

McCabe, M. M., *Plato's Individuals* (Princeton, 1994).

McGinn, C., *Logical Properties* (Oxford, 2000).

Politis, V., *Aristotle and the* Metaphysics (London, 2004).

Waterlow, S., 'Protagoras and Inconsistency', *Archiv für Geschichte der Philosophie*, 59 (1977), 19–36.

Wedin, M., 'Some Logical Problems in *Metaphysics* Gamma', *OSAP* 19 (2000), 113–62.

Williamson, T., *Knowledge and its Limits* (Oxford, 2000).

Zeyl, D. (trans.), *Plato's* Timaeus (Indianapolis, 2000).

ARISTOTLE ON *EUDAIMONIA* IN *NICOMACHEAN ETHICS* 1

GEERT VAN CLEEMPUT

I n Aristotelian scholarship there is the vexed question of what *eudaimonia*, happiness or human flourishing, means for Aristotle. In the intellectualist interpretation of *eudaimonia* contemplation plays a dominant role, whereas 'inclusivism' is attractive to its adherents because it seems to offer an alternative to the allegedly unpalatable consequences of the intellectualist interpretation. This paper presents a close reading of the relevant texts on happiness in *NE* 1. The inclusivist interpretation of those texts is found to be unpersuasive. In *NE* 1 Aristotle sets the stage for the identification of contemplation as happiness. I offer a new reading of the *ergon* argument in support of an intellectualist position.[1]

1. The hierarchy of ends

There are many human activities, Aristotle begins, and all are undertaken for the sake of their ends. There are two kinds of activities,

© Geert Van Cleemput 2006

I wish to thank Professor Sedley for his many useful critical remarks.

[1] As a means of reconciling these interpretations I propose a 'communal' or 'political' interpretation of contemplation as happiness, for which I cannot argue here. Aristotle is concerned not merely with the *eudaimonia* of the individual, but also with the *eudaimonia* of the polis. The highest *eudaimonia* of the polis is the maximization of the highest good of the polis. Since contemplation turns out to be the highest good, perfect happiness of the polis consists of contemplation by those members of the polis who are capable of it: its citizens. This interpretation takes seriously Aristotle's statements in both the *Nicomachean Ethics* and the *Politics* that man is a being that belongs to the polis and that contemplation is perfect happiness. It also takes seriously the statement in the *Nicomachean Ethics* that the good of the polis is more divine than the good of the individual. Writers on Aristotelian *eudaimonia* have usually ignored the *Politics*. That is unfortunate because both the *Nicomachean Ethics* and the *Politics* deal with *politikē*. In both the topic of *politikē* is the highest human good. They should therefore be read and interpreted together.

those that are undertaken for the sake of an end which is produced beyond the activity itself, and those that are for their own sake, i.e. for the sake of the activity itself, irrespective of what may be produced beyond the activity itself. Some of these latter activities are more important than others; they have more value. Indeed, a certain activity may be undertaken for the sake of another activity or other activities. And this activity may be undertaken for yet another activity. So, bridle-making is for the sake of horsemanship and horsemanship for the sake of generalship. The activity at the end or top of the chain is more choiceworthy than the activities below. And the ends of the activities which are located higher in the hierarchy are more choiceworthy than the ends of the lower activities, since the lower ends are also for the sake of the higher ends (1. 1, 1094ᵃ1–16).

Aristotle continues:

And it makes no difference whether the activities themselves are the ends of the actions or something else beyond these, as in the case of the above-mentioned sciences.² (1. 1, 1094ᵃ16–18)

Aristotle says that the ends of architectonic pursuits are more choiceworthy than the ends of the pursuits under the architectonic pursuit. It does not matter if the ends of the pursuits are the pursuits themselves or something else (a product) beyond the pursuit. I understand the for-the-sake-of relation that is at work here and, indeed, in the rest of this work to be causal-normative, to use R. Kraut's phrase.³ The art of strategy is for the sake of victory: strategy causes the occurrence of victory. In addition, victory is the norm that regulates strategy. It is this kind of for-the-sake-of relation that operates between behaviour in accordance with the character excellences and contemplation. Aristotle is convinced that the character excellences are for the sake of contemplation.⁴

Character-excellent activities, for Aristotle, are not only for the sake of something else, but also for their own sake. The *energeiai* or *praxeis*, which are their own ends (1094ᵃ16–17), are character-excellent activities. This passage then says that, whether a pursuit

---

² *Epistēmē* does not have its technical meaning of demonstrative science here. It refers, more broadly, to any intellectual pursuit.

³ *Aristotle on the Human Good* (Princeton, 1989), 200–1.

⁴ I cannot argue for this here. See Kraut, *Aristotle on the Human Good*, and G. R. Lear, *Happy Lives and the Highest Good: An Essay on Aristotle's* Nicomachean Ethics (Princeton, 2004).

is a *praxis*, which is for its own sake (in addition to being for the sake of something else), or a *poiēsis*, which is only for the sake of the product it yields, the architectonic pursuit is always more choiceworthy than the pursuits below it. This passage is then very much compatible with the notion that contemplation is the final good and that character-excellent behaviour is for the sake of contemplation.

J. L. Ackrill disagrees. He complains that 'commentators have not been sufficiently puzzled as to what Aristotle has in mind'.[5] He thinks that it is not at all clear 'what is meant by saying that an action or activity is for the sake of another, in cases where the first does not terminate in a product or outcome which the second can then use or exploit'. He takes the distinction to which the above passage refers to be between (*a*) activities that have a product which the superior activity uses and (*b*) activities that have no products apart from themselves and are their own ends.

On Ackrill's reading character-excellent activities belong to category (*b*). Aristotle says that the activities of both (*a*) and (*b*) are for the sake of a higher good, *eudaimonia*. But how can this be for the activities under (*b*)? If they have no product beyond themselves, how can they be described as for the sake of another good? Ackrill says that only a part–whole concept of 'for-the-sake-of' can solve this puzzle. This concept implies that activities that are for the sake of *eudaimonia* are such in the way constituents of a whole are for the sake of that whole.

The problem with Ackrill's interpretation is that it requires that Aristotle introduce a new notion of 'for-the-sake-of' without his clearly saying that he is doing so. I believe there is no need to introduce a new notion, since the notion of 'for-the-sake-of' that Aristotle is using throughout does not need to cause the puzzlement that Ackrill experienced. The part–whole finality does not need to be introduced to solve the problems of unity of the *Nicomachean Ethics* that Ackrill believes are there. Ackrill unduly restricts the kinds of ends in the passage quoted above. He understands the category of ends (which are for the sake of) themselves to comprise only the activities that have no product or outcome which a second activity may then use, but are strictly and only for their own sake. This would exclude activities in accordance with the character ex-

---

[5] 'Aristotle on *Eudaimonia*', in A. O. Rorty (ed.), *Essays on Aristotle's Ethics* (Berkeley, 1980), 15–33 at 18.

cellences. These activities are for their own sake but also for the sake of something else. I cannot argue here that they are for the sake of contemplation.

Ackrill's rejection of this relationship forces him to read Aristotle's text in such a way that denies this connection. R.-A. Gauthier and J.-Y. Jolif do not deny the causal-normative reading that I defend, but claim that Aristotle is mistaken in offering it.[6] Moral actions, according to Gauthier and Jolif, belong to the category of actions that are undertaken for their own sake. How can it be, then, that they are part of a hierarchical series in which they are not at the top?

2. The final end

We have seen that Aristotle asserts that there are many kinds of ends. There is a hierarchy of ends, whereby the end for the sake of which something else is done is ranked higher. But what is now the most final end? Aristotle presents the following argument (1. 1, 1094^a18–22):

(T1) If there is some end of the things done which we want for itself,
(T2) and if we want the other (things) for it,
(T3) and if we do not choose all things for something else (for it will then go on *ad infinitum*, so that our desire will be empty and idle),
(T4) then it is clear that this end would be the good and the best.

Ackrill finds a fallacy in this argument: it is like saying that if everybody has a father, then one person is the father of everybody.[7] He formalizes the argument in the following way: $T1$ & $T2 = p$; $T3 = \neg q$, with q being 'the only alternative to p', which I take to mean that, for Ackrill, q is the negation of p;[8] and $T4 = r$. Ackrill renders the structure of the argument as follows: 'If p and not q, then r'.[9]

I think, however, that Ackrill has not formalized the argument

---

[6] R.-A. Gauthier and J.-Y. Jolif, *L'Éthique à Nicomaque: introduction, traduction et commentaire*, 2nd edn. (2 vols. in 4; Leuven and Paris, 1970), ii/1. 6–7, ad loc.

[7] Ackrill follows G. E. M. Anscombe in this. See W. F. R. Hardie. *Aristotle's Ethical Theory*, 2nd edn. (Oxford, 1980), 17.

[8] Since Ackrill further comments: 'in that case a proof of not-q would be a proof of p'.

[9] Since I take it that, for Ackrill, q amounts to being the negation of p—he indeed says that not-q is not an additional condition, which I contest in the main text—his reading may be formalized as 'if p and p, then r'.

correctly. It should be transcribed thus: $T_1 = p$; $T_2 = q$; $T_3 = r$; $T_4 = s$. The structure looks more like this: If $p \& q \& r$, then s. Ackrill sees T_1 and T_2 as constituting one premiss, with T_3 being the negation of the combination of T_1 and T_2. He says 'Nobody will suggest that not-q is here a condition additional to p.'[10] Well, that is exactly what I am suggesting. T_3 is a necessary premiss to be added to premisses T_1 and T_2 to reach the conclusion (T_4). In addition, a premiss, or two premisses, are presupposed, viz. that an end is a good and that the most final end is the best. These premisses, of course, are discussed in the opening paragraph of the *Nicomachean Ethics*.

The argument, therefore, is not fallacious. Ackrill dismisses Hardie's comment that this is a hypothetical argument.[11] But Hardie is right. Formally, the argument is hypothetical. The premisses T_1 and T_2 are not asserted as true. So, strictly speaking Aristotle has not established the truth of his conclusion. He only draws a hypothetical conclusion from hypothetical premisses and does so validly.

One may, of course, have doubts about the correctness of the premisses. Premiss T_2 in particular is crucial. Are the other things done for the sake of one final good? Ackrill certainly thinks this is not the case: humans have more than one goal. People have complex personalities and desires; they want to develop many aspects of their personality. One could reply, however, that it cannot be excluded, at least theoretically, that there are people who have one major goal in life which supersedes other subgoals which they may have. For example, one could be devoted totally to the imitation of Jesus Christ. It would be a difficult thing to realize, but it is not impossible to have such a goal and to be coherent in having such a good.

Aristotle presents the argument conditionally, but it is true that he more or less proceeds with the understanding that the conclusion describes a state of affairs, albeit a state that does not occur in all humans. Aristotle is himself probably fully aware of the fact that the behaviour of all people does not provide empirical evidence for his conclusion.

To conclude the discussion of this argument, we can say that it is not fallacious and that there is therefore no need to add an extra premiss, as Ackrill does,[12] to the effect that 'where there are two

---

[10] 'Aristotle on *Eudaimonia*', 25.   [11] *Aristotle's Ethical Theory*, 17.
[12] 'Aristotle on *Eudaimonia*', 26.

or more separate ends each desired for itself we can say that there is just one (composite) end such that each of those separate ends is desired not only for itself but also for *it'*. This added premiss serves only to prop up an inclusive view of the final good. The desired existence of an inclusive final good is merely read into this passage; it is not actually extracted from what the passage purports to argue for. If Aristotle were arguing that there is a composite end at the end of the chain, that would certainly be against the thrust of the language he actually uses: there is *one* thing at the end of the chain of desire. A composite of goods would really mean that there would be more than one good at the end of the chain.[13]

3. The three lives

In 1. 4 Aristotle agrees with most Greeks that *eudaimonia* is the highest practical good. To be happy is to live well and to do well.[14] In 1. 5 Aristotle begins to fill in what he means by *eudaimonia*. Different groups of people have different opinions on their preferred candidate. Aristotle has three candidates. The many, i.e. the most vulgar, think it is (physical) pleasure (1095^b14–22). Needless to say, Aristotle is not very taken by their choice.

But perhaps the second candidate, political life, can elicit more sympathy from him? People who lead this kind of life often call honour (τιμή) the goal of this life, but it is better, says Aristotle, to call *aretē*, excellence, its goal. Honour is too dependent on the opinion of others. If something is the final good, it should not be at the mercy of others. It ought to be completely up to us to achieve it. Excellence is up to us. But excellence is not flawless either. One could sleep one's whole life when in possession of excellence. This could scarcely be called a happy life. This criticism of *aretē*, of course, does not mean it plays no role in *eudaimonia*. In 1. 7 Aristotle will call excellent *activity*, as opposed to the mere (passive) possession of excellence, a state, the final good. The objection that *aretē* is a state as the goal of political life is obviously not sufficient to disqualify the political life from constituting the final good of man.

---

[13] See also Kraut, *Aristotle on the Human Good*, 219.

[14] τὸ δ' εὖ ζῆν καὶ τὸ εὖ πράττειν ταὐτὸν ὑπολαμβάνουσι τῷ εὐδαιμονεῖν (1095^a19–20). εὖ πράττειν may be taken in both its transitive (doing good things) and intransitive (flourishing) senses.

The third candidate is the life devoted to *theōria*, philosophical contemplation, the *bios theōrētikos*. Here Aristotle says only that he will investigate this kind of life in what follows. This seems to suggest already the importance of the theoretical life.

4. The formal criteria of *eudaimonia* (1): finality

After criticizing Plato's Idea of the Good in 1. 6, Aristotle sets out his own views in more detail in 1. 7. The most important argument for establishing his own candidate is the so-called *ergon* argument. Ackrill reads this argument as supporting a composite final good. Before we get there, my task is to offer a rebuttal of Ackrill's reading of the passages leading up to the *ergon* argument in which he claims to find further support for his reading. In these passages Aristotle, following Plato's lead at *Phileb.* 20 C–22 C, establishes some formal criteria for *eudaimonia*. He argues that *eudaimonia* is the most final end, and the most self-sufficient and most choiceworthy good.

To recognize the most final end, Aristotle divides ends into three categories:

Since the ends appear to be many and since we choose some of them for the sake of something else, like wealth, flutes, and, in general, instruments, it is clear that not all things are final [*or*: have the characteristic of an end]. The best thing appears to be something final. Therefore, if only one thing is final, that will be the thing sought [i.e. the final end], if there are more final things, the most final of them will be the thing sought. We call the thing which is pursued for its own sake more final than the thing pursued for the sake of something else, and the thing that is chosen never for the sake of something else more final than the things which are chosen both for their own sake and for the sake of something else. We call the thing that is always chosen for its own sake and never for the sake of something else absolutely final. (1097^{a}25–34)

With D. Keyt we may call the first category subservient ends.[15] They are not really ends, but, as Aristotle himself says, instruments toward ends. They occupy the bottom third of the hierarchy of ends. Keyt calls the second group subordinate ends. They are the ends that are chosen for their own sake but also for the sake of something else. Finally, at the top of the hierarchy is the final end, which is

---

[15] 'Intellectualism in Aristotle', in J. P. Anton and A. Preus (eds.), *Essays in Ancient Greek Philosophy*, vol. ii (Albany, NY, 1983), 364–87 at 365.

never chosen for the sake of something else, but always for its own sake. It is this end that Aristotle is targeting. This end, the most final end, is *eudaimonia* for Aristotle.

Aristotle continues the passage quoted above in the following way:

> *Eudaimonia* seems to be such *par excellence*, for we choose it always for its own sake and never for the sake of something else. Honour, on the other hand, pleasure, and reason and every excellence we choose both for their own sake (for we would choose each of these even if nothing would result) and also for the sake of *eudaimonia*, because we suppose that through them we shall be happy. Again, nobody chooses *eudaimonia* for the sake of the above ends or for the sake of anything else at all. (1097^b1–6)

Ackrill finds the degrees of finality to be indicative of an inclusive reading of *eudaimonia*. In his very short discussion of this passage he states that Aristotle is 'making a clear conceptual point, not a rash and probably false empirical claim'[16] when he says that, in addition to valuing pleasure and virtue themselves, we value them for the sake of *eudaimonia*. Since Ackrill does not accept that, for Aristotle, one particular good, such as contemplation, can constitute *eudaimonia*, it can only make sense to him that Aristotle makes a definitional point here. I accept that Aristotle is making a point about empirical facts. True, it is not the case that all people will say that they seek pleasure or excellence for the sake of happiness, but those who accept that *eudaimonia* consists in contemplation will confirm that to them pleasure and excellence, in addition to being pursued for their own sake, are valuable for the sake of contemplation. There is therefore no reason to import a part–whole relationship into the for-the-sake-of relationship in this passage.[17]

Keyt finds the thrust of the passage quoted to be 'that theoretical activity, the activity of *nous*, is a subordinate end that is included as one component among others of the ultimate end, happiness'.[18] At first sight, Keyt seems to have a point. *Nous*, reason, the faculty of the soul that will be identified in book 10 as the faculty whose

[16] 'Aristotle on *Eudaimonia*', 21.

[17] See also Kraut, *Aristotle on the Human Good*, 230–7, where he gives a more extensive explanation of why pleasure and excellence can be seen as for the sake of contemplation.

[18] 'Intellectualism in Aristotle', 366. A. Kenny, 'Aristotle on Happiness', in J. Barnes *et al.* (eds.), *Articles on Aristotle*, ii. *Ethics and Politics* (London, 1977), (London, 1977), 25–32 at 31, is also puzzled by this passage, but does not attempt to solve the problem.

activity is *theōria*,[19] finds itself here at the same, subordinate level as honour, pleasure, and every *aretē*, which we choose both for themselves and for the sake of *eudaimonia*.

I think there are three ways in which we can challenge Keyt's interpretation. First, a few pages earlier Aristotle dismissed *aretē* from being a candidate because it is not an activity. He makes much of the distinction between *aretē* and activity according to *aretē*. Similarly, we may suppose that he distinguishes between the faculty, *nous*, and its activity, *theōria*.[20] As just mentioned, he makes the actual distinction in book 10. We should therefore assume that Aristotle in the present passage does not go against his considered opinion about this distinction. If this is so, Keyt is not justified in construing from this passage an argument in favour of *theōria* being one component of a composite final good, since *theōria* is not even discussed here.

Second, *nous* is used in many ways in Aristotle. It certainly refers to the faculty of theoretical reason, as we have just seen. But it also seems to enter the realm of practical reason, notably in book 6.[21] Since Aristotle has not introduced his terminology for the different parts of reason, we should perhaps refrain from seeing any technical meaning of *nous* here. It may very well mean 'reason' in general. If this were the case, it would be premature to derive any substantial information on the content of the final good from these lines. We can therefore not use this passage to support the view that contemplation is a component of a composite final good.

Finally, a third objection denies that this passage represents Aristotle's own views. This objection, by P. Stemmer,[22] has Aristotle list the views on *eudaimonia* by proponents of the lives canvassed in 1. 5, i.e. the lives of pleasure, honour,[23] excellence,[24] and the mind. Since Aristotle does not give his own thoughts here, he is not favouring the doctrine of plural intrinsic goods. This eliminates a passage to which the inclusivists had looked to support their thesis. According to Stemmer, this passage states that the proponents

---

[19] e.g. at 10. 7, 1177ᵃ13–17.   [20] Kraut suggested this to me.
[21] 6. 11, 1143ᵃ35–6; 1143ᵇ2–3. J. A. Stewart, *Notes on the* Nicomachean Ethics *of Aristotle* (2 vols.; Oxford, 1892), i. 93, takes it to refer to practical reason.
[22] 'Aristoteles' Glücksbegriff in der *Nikomachischen Ethik*: Eine Interpretation von *E.N.* I, 7. 1097b2–5', *Phronesis*, 37 (1992), 85–110.
[23] Stemmer, ibid. 95–6, argues that Aristotle never considered honour an intrinsic good.
[24] Ibid. 98. The lives of honour and excellence refer to the political life.

of the above lives favour the view that only one good, i.e. pleasure, honour, excellence, or contemplation respectively, constitutes *eudaimonia* for them.[25] They do not, according to this objection, choose the good (that they happen to favour) for its own sake in addition to its being for the sake of *another* good,[26] *eudaimonia*. They choose their favourite good, such as honour or excellence, in so far as they identify their *eudaimonia* with it. Aristotle's own choice will be *nous*, one of the goods mentioned.[27]

5. The formal criteria of *eudaimonia* (2): self-sufficiency

In addition to being the most final good, *eudaimonia* has to be *autarkēs*, self-sufficient. Again, Aristotle follows Plato's lead in the *Philebus*. Self-sufficiency is a fundamental idea in Greek popular ethics, starting with the leadership by the Homeric *agathos* of his *oikos*. Both Plato and Aristotle reinterpret this basic idea in their moral philosophies:[28]

It seems that the same thing [i.e. that we choose other things for the sake of *eudaimonia*] results from (the argument of) self-sufficiency, for the final good seems to be self-sufficient. We are speaking about the self-sufficient not just for the individual who lives a solitary life, but also about the self-sufficient for the parents, children, wife, and in general the friends and fellow citizens, since man is by nature a being that lives in a community. But we should impose a limit, for if we extend self-sufficiency to include ancestors and descendants and friends of friends, it would progress *ad infinitum*. But we have to look at this again. (1097[b]6–14)

---

[25] Stemmer, 99.   [26] Ibid. 97.

[27] Stemmer, ibid. 93–4, also criticizes Kraut for using this passage to establish that other excellences in addition to contemplation are intrinsic goods for Aristotle. It is certainly true that honor is not an intrinsic good for Aristotle, nor is pleasure without some elaboration. This supports Stemmer's reading of this passage, but there may be a problem. While it is true that 1097[b]2–5 allows this interpretation, the next line, 'Nobody chooses *eudaimonia* for the sake of them or for the sake of any other thing at all' (1097[b]5–6), which Stemmer does not discuss, may cast some doubt. If it is the case that the proponents of these respective goods choose them because they, respectively, are *eudaimonia* for them, why phrase the sentence of 1097[b]5–6 in a way that separates those goods from their being *eudaimonia* for their respective proponents? But perhaps the term *eudaimonia* is a merely formal term in this sentence and Aristotle wants to stress the fact that, whatever its content for different people, it is the final good for all of them.

[28] See A. W. H. Adkins, *Merit and Responsibility: A Study in Greek Values* (Oxford, 1960), 241 n. 13, 348, 354 nn. 21 and 24; id., '"Friendship" and "Self-Sufficiency" in Homer and Aristotle', *Classical Quarterly*, NS 13 (1963), 30–45 at 44–5.

Aristotle is not concerned merely with the self-sufficiency of the individual *qua* individual, but also with his self-sufficiency consistent with being a member of a family and a polis, and with the self-sufficiency of the people around that individual. The individual's interests are necessarily intertwined with the interests of the community to which he belongs naturally.[29]

But what is self-sufficiency for Aristotle? He continues with some important lines:

We hold that the self-sufficient is that which taken alone makes life choiceworthy and lacking in nothing; we think that *eudaimonia* is such. Moreover we think that it is the most choiceworthy of all things, it not being counted with (the other goods). If it is/were counted, (we think that) it is clear that it is/would be more choiceworthy with the addition of the smallest of goods, for the (good) added would create an excess of goods. Of goods more is always more choiceworthy. *Eudaimonia*, then, appears to be something final and self-sufficient, since it is the end of things that are done. (1097[b]14–21)[30]

This passage has been debated since ancient times.[31] In recent times four different interpretations of it have been given. The key phrase is συναριθμουμένην δέ, which can be read as an indicative or as a counterfactual. Either grammatical interpretation has been offered to support an inclusive or an intellectualist interpretation. Ackrill[32] and others read συναριθμουμένην as a counterfactual. The second sentence of the above passage is then a *reductio* to prove that Aristotle presents inclusiveness as a characteristic of *eudaimonia*. Ackrill reads: *eudaimonia* is the most choiceworthy of all goods, since it is not counted among other goods, because it includes all of them. If *eudaimonia* were simply one among many other goods, it would be improved upon by adding whatever other good, even the smallest

---

[29] For an interesting view on how *eudaimonia* is not merely self-sufficient for the individual, but has implications for others, see Lear, *Happy Lives and the Highest Good*, 62–3, 196–207.

[30] τὸ δ' αὔταρκες τίθεμεν ὃ μονούμενον αἱρετὸν ποιεῖ τὸν βίον καὶ μηδενὸς ἐνδεά· τοιοῦτον δὲ τὴν εὐδαιμονίαν οἰόμεθα εἶναι· ἔτι δὲ πάντων αἱρετωτάτην μὴ συναριθμουμένην—συναριθμουμένην δὲ δῆλον ὡς αἱρετωτέραν μετὰ τοῦ ἐλαχίστου τῶν ἀγαθῶν· ὑπεροχὴ γὰρ ἀγαθῶν γίνεται τὸ προστιθέμενον, ἀγαθῶν δὲ τὸ μεῖζον αἱρετώτερον ἀεί. τέλειον δή τι φαίνεται καὶ αὔταρκες ἡ εὐδαιμονία, τῶν πρακτῶν οὖσα τέλος.

[31] The Greek commentators already disagreed on whether to read it in an intellectualist (Aspasius) or inclusive (Alexander) manner. J. Léonard, *Le Bonheur chez Aristote* (Brussels, 1948), 188–94, gives a brief overview of their interpretations. Léonard supports the contemplative reading.

[32] 'Aristotle on *Eudaimonia*', 21.

good. This newly acquired sum of *eudaimonia* plus this other good would be more choiceworthy than the original *eudaimonia*. Now this cannot be the case because we have seen that *eudaimonia* is most choiceworthy and it only is desired for its own sake and not for the sake of anything else.[33] This new sum would be less choiceworthy than it plus some other small good that may be added. We would then continue *ad infinitum*.

Standing on its own, this passage can bear Ackrill's interpretation. However, in the light of how I have interpreted the preceding chapters, there is no need to interpret it in the way Ackrill proposes. If we substitute contemplation for *eudaimonia* in the above passage, it becomes: contemplation is the most choiceworthy of all (goods), since it is not counted with other goods. If it were counted with other goods, it is clear that contemplation plus the smallest of goods would be more choiceworthy than contemplation alone. This, of course, Aristotle will reject. In book 10 he explicitly puts contemplation at the pinnacle of goods. It turns out that it is the only thing for the sake of which other goods, e.g. activity according to the character excellences, are pursued, which itself is not pursued for the sake of something else. Aristotle denies, then, that contemplation is pursued for the sake of contemplation plus some other good. It is this denial that is compatible with the present passage. In book 10, moreover, Aristotle will explicitly call contemplation the most self-sufficient good of all (10. 7, 1177ᵃ27–ᵇ1).

Perhaps additional support against the inclusivist reading may be adduced from the term μονούμενον at 1097ᵇ14. The self-sufficient is that which when *taken alone* makes life choiceworthy and in need of nothing. It would be a little odd to use this phrase if the self-sufficient turns out to be a collection of many goods or activities. How can you take this collection of goods *alone*? The self-sufficient as a single good would fit more elegantly with this expression.

Anthony Kenny—this is a third reading of this passage—agrees that the present passage supports the reading of contemplation as *eudaimonia*.[34] But he denies that συναριθμουμένην δέ is a counter-

---

[33] Indeed, it *alone* is desired both for its own sake and not for the sake of something else.

[34] *Aristotle on the Perfect Life* (Oxford, 1992), 24–6. See also his 'Aristotle on Happiness', 31; *The Aristotelian Ethics: A Study of the Relationship between the Eudemian and Nicomachean Ethics of Aristotle* (Oxford, 1978), 204–5; and 'The Nicomachean Conception of Happiness', in H. Blumenthal and H. Robinson (eds.), *Aristotle and the Later Tradition* (*OSAP* suppl.; 1991), 67–80. Kenny claims that his

factual clause. Instead he reads it as an indicative conditional: 'We think (happiness) most choice-worthy of all things, without being counted along with other things—but if it so counted[35] clearly made more choice-worthy by the addition of even the least of goods.'[36] Reading the passage in this way, Kenny finds it to mean that 'happiness is that activity, or good, which, if considered in itself and not conjoined with any other activity or good, is the most choice-worthy of all'.[37] In other words, for Kenny, Aristotle finds contemplation to be most choiceworthy because, taken by itself without the addition of any other good, contemplation is the most choiceworthy activity. Kenny accepts that contemplation, taken together with any other good, however small this good may be, is more choiceworthy than contemplation alone.

Lear presents a version of this indicative reading. She accepts that, for Aristotle, *eudaimonia* can be counted together with other things, but that its choiceworthiness does not depend on its being number one in a ranking, but on its being the most final end. As a final end it cannot be improved upon, but as a member of a rank it can be improved upon, e.g. by adding external goods to it.[38]

The grammar of the sentence certainly allows an indicative reading. Indeed, such a reading is the first one suggested by the grammar. But the indicative reading does not necessarily mean that Aristotle accepts that the conditional is true. The indicative merely means that, if the protasis is true, the apodosis is also true. The speaker, however, does not take a stance on the truth-value of the protasis. He merely makes a logical connection between the subordinate and main clauses.[39] Aristotle, therefore, on the indicative

interpretation is a traditional one. J. M. Cooper, in his review of Kenny's *Aristotelian Ethics*, in *Nous*, 15 (1981), 381–92 at 384, identifies this tradition as Christian, motivated by the desire to ensure that *eudaimonia* does not threaten the position of God as absolutely the best thing. S. R. L. Clark, *Aristotle's Man: Speculations upon Aristotelian Anthropology* (Oxford, 1975), 153–5, and R. Heinaman, '*Eudaimonia* and Self-Sufficiency in the *Nicomachean Ethics*', *Phronesis*, 33 (1988), 31–53, support an indicative reading of the passage and the intellectualist interpretation that Kenny extracts from this reading.

[35] i.e. along with something else, whatever that might be.
[36] *Aristotle on the Perfect Life*, 24.   [37] Ibid.
[38] *Happy Lives and the Highest Good*, 65–8.
[39] See H. W. Smyth, *Greek Grammar*, rev. G. M. Messing (Cambridge, Mass., 1956), §2298; W. W. Goodwin, *Syntax of the Moods and Tenses of the Greek Verb* (London, 1889), §402; R. Kühner and B. Gerth, *Ausführliche Grammatik der griechischen Sprache*, 2 vols. (Hanover, 1904), ii, §571.I and §573. That συναριθμουμένην

reading, does not accept the truth of the protasis. If he did, that would go against his doctrine of *eudaimonia*. If *eudaimonia* is that for the sake of which we do everything else, then we cannot say that *eudaimonia* plus an additional good is better than *eudaimonia* alone. *Eudaimonia* is such that it cannot be improved upon. It is clear that nothing can be the final good if it is made better by the addition of another intrinsic good. If contemplation turns out to be *eudaimonia*,[40] then, for Aristotle, contemplation plus another good is not more choiceworthy than contemplation alone. It is therefore better to adopt the counterfactual reading.

Since I am arguing that already in *NE* 1 Aristotle is presenting a view that is compatible with contemplation being *eudaimonia*, let us see if we can substitute contemplation for *eudaimonia* in the sentence we have been discussing, so that, at least, this passage does not offer ammunition against the intellectualist reading. For Aristotle, it makes no sense to speak of adding another good or, at least, good activity to contemplation, given what he understands the term 'contemplation' to mean. Any good activity is, in addition to its possibly being for its own sake, also for the sake of the highest good activity, contemplation. Whereas it may be possible to speak of adding a small good, such as having ice cream at certain moments, e.g. when one is relaxing from contemplating, to the good of *eudaimonia*, for Aristotle it makes no sense to add these two 'goods' to each other to achieve a sum of goods that is better and more choiceworthy than *eudaimonia* alone. The sense of 'good' when this term refers to having ice cream in the above circumstances and the sense of 'good' when it refers to *eudaimonia* are different. The goodness of *eudaimonia* implies that it is never pursued for the sake of anything else and indeed that other goods are pursued for the sake of it. The goodness of having ice cream has no such claims. Whereas it may be pursued for its own sake, i.e. for the sake of just having ice cream in a spare moment, it is always also for the sake of something else, e.g. in order to relax. This relaxation may,

δέ is a participle with a conditional meaning may be deduced from the preceding μὴ συναριθμουμένην, since μή is the negation of a participle with a conditional sense, οὐ being the negation of the other possible senses of the participle in the adverbial clause, e.g. causal, temporal, etc. (Goodwin, §832). Lear is therefore wrong in suggesting that μὴ συναριθμουμένην can have a causal meaning (*Happy Lives and the Highest Good*, 64).

[40] I agree with Kenny that this will be the case. But we are not yet in a position to argue for it, only that the μονούμενον passage allows for this reading.

in its turn, be pursued for the sake of its being able to help one concentrate better in order to contemplate. It is in this sense that Aristotle would say that it is impossible to add any other good to the good of *eudaimonia*.

S. White—and this is the fourth reading of the passage—accepts the indicative reading in the sense that Aristotle accepts the truth of the conditional, but denies, against Kenny, that it entails that happiness is a single good.[41] Aristotelian *eudaimonia* is a composite good for White. It is not a composite of all (possible) goods, as Ackrill wants it,[42] but of certain kinds of goods, the virtues. Composites of the virtues in different proportions satisfy the criterion of self-sufficiency. Aristotelian self-sufficiency is the absence of need. Rather than excluding the possibility of counting *eudaimonia* together with other goods, the present passage states that 'further goods *can* be added to [*eudaimonia*] and it *can* be made better. But to use this procedure to construct the best good possible, and to look for something so good that nothing ever *could* be added to it, would be to mistake the kind of self-sufficiency possessed by happiness.'[43]

White adduces a text from the *Rhetoric*:

It is necessary that the more goods are a greater good than the one or the fewer, when the one or the fewer are counted together.[44] (1. 7, 1363^{b}18–20)

This principle says that the sum of goods A, B, and C is better than the sum of goods A and B, and than goods A and B taken singly. It does not distinguish between the different kinds of goods. White uses this silence to plug *eudaimonia* into the list of goods to which the principle applies. His conception of Aristotle's *eudaimonia* as a composite of some goods allows him to do that. I am arguing that we are not allowed to put *eudaimonia* on the list of goods to which

[41] 'Is Aristotelian Happiness a Good Life or the Best Life?', *OSAP* 8 (1990), 97–137 at 119–20. White, 120 n. 23, is probably wrong in denying the possibility that the text can have a counterfactual meaning, although I agree that from a purely grammatical viewpoint the indicative reading would be the normal way of reading the text. White supports his version of the inclusive reading, against the 'comprehensive' reading of Ackrill, by appealing to the *Magna moralia* (127–36). He himself (127) admits that this work is probably not by Aristotle. We should therefore be cautious in using that text to support any reading.

[42] Kenny, *Aristotle on the Perfect Life*, 27–8, calls White's view on *eudaimonia* inclusive and Ackrill's view comprehensive.

[43] 'Is Aristotelian Happiness a Good Life or the Best Life?', 120.

[44] Keyt, 'Intellectualism in Aristotle', 365–6, cites this text and the *Topics* text which I discuss in the next paragraph in support of his inclusive interpretation.

the 'more-is-better' principle applies, precisely because *eudaimonia* is a different kind of good. *Eudaimonia*, be it excellent activity of the rational soul or contemplation, cannot be improved upon by adding just any good.[45]

Some confirmation of this can be found in the *Topics*, a text also quoted by White:

Further, the greater number of goods ⟨is more choiceworthy⟩ than the smaller number, either absolutely or when the one number is included in the other, the smaller number in the greater number. There is an objection if one thing is choiceworthy for the sake of another, for the two things are not more choiceworthy than the one thing, e.g. becoming healthy and health compared to health, since we choose to become healthy for the sake of health. (3. 2, 117ª16–21)

It is the objection in the second part that I am especially interested in. The 'more-is-better' principle receives an important challenge. The sum of becoming healthy and health, two goods, is not better than one component of this so-called aggregate. Becoming healthy is a means towards achieving the good of health. The sum of a means and its goal is not better than the goal alone, because the good of an end is not of such a nature that it can be added to the good of a means which is for the sake of it (i.e. the end).[46]

White agrees with the 'orthodox' interpretation when it appeals to this passage to disallow double counting a means towards happiness since it is already presupposed by happiness. The addition of such a means would not amount to making happiness more choiceworthy. White's point is that happiness can still be improved upon by adding *other* goods not presupposed by happiness. White says that 'Happiness . . . is not so good that it cannot be made better, but it is so good that it is always chosen for itself, with or without any other goods.'[47]

I argue that *eudaimonia* is *sui generis* in such a way that it cannot be counted together with other goods or that it cannot be improved upon in any way. In Aristotle's hierarchical world-view it makes no sense to speak of *eudaimonia* plus wealth as being better than *eudaimonia*. Wealth receives its goodness for a contemplator merely from its being a means toward setting up a situation in which contemplation can flourish. Wealth is good only in so far as it is used

[45] See also Kraut, *Aristotle on the Human Good*, 286–7.
[46] See also ibid. 283–6.
[47] 'Is Aristotelian Happiness a Good Life or the Best Life?', 123.

to promote excellent activity. Wealth cannot be counted separately from *eudaimonia* and added to it so as to create a 'better' composite. This does not mean that wealth is an actual part of *eudaimonia*. Rather, it is merely an essential condition for there to be *eudaimonia*. This can easily be confused with its being a part of *eudaimonia*. It is this confusion over the role of necessary conditions that is at the root of the inclusivist interpretation.

   To conclude: we have seen that there are four possible interpretations of the cited passage. The participle συναριθμουμένην δέ can be read as an indicative, which some take to support a non-inclusive view, whereas others find support for an inclusive reading in it. The participle can also be read counterfactually (admittedly a reading which grammatically is less obvious than the indicative reading), which again has been taken to support both an inclusive and a non-inclusive reading. I have taken the latter view. Aristotle's explicit description of contemplation as most self-sufficient in book 10 will make this view the most defensible. It is obvious that the passage discussed here cannot offer support for any reading in a decisive fashion, but we shall be able to identify more passages in book 1 which together make it highly likely that already in book 1 Aristotle had contemplation in mind as *eudaimonia*. One such passage is the so-called '*ergon* argument', which comes immediately after the συναριθμουμένην passage.

6. The *ergon* argument

In the famous *ergon* argument of 1. 7, or more correctly, in an addition to the argument proper, I find important support for an intellectualist reading. The *ergon* argument is part of an ongoing argument about *eudaimonia* and should be read in conjunction with the two preceding arguments for finality and self-sufficiency. I believe that this strengthens the case for a non-inclusive reading significantly.

   After presenting the formal characteristics of *eudaimonia*, which we discussed in the previous sections, Aristotle proceeds to say 'more clearly' what *eudaimonia* is. Perhaps the *ergon*[48] of man can

---

[48] *Ergon* is usually translated as 'function', a technical term. A. W. H. Adkins, 'The Connection between Aristotle's *Ethics* and *Politics*', *Political Theory*, 12 (1984), 29–49 (repr. in D. Keyt and F. D. Miller, Jr. (eds.), *A Companion to Aristotle's*

shed some light on the issue. The argument goes as follows (1. 7, 1097ᵇ25–1098ᵃ18):

(T1)   For just as the good and the 'well' for the flautist and the sculptor and for every craftsman, and, in general, for whatever has an *ergon* and a *praxis*, seems to lie in the *ergon*, this seems to be also the case for a human being, since/if indeed he has an *ergon*.[49]

(T2)   Do, then, the carpenter and the shoemaker have their *erga* and *praxeis*, while a human being has none and is, by nature, without *ergon*? Or just as there seems to be an *ergon* for an eye, a hand, a foot, and, in general, for each of the parts [of the body], could one posit also an *ergon* for a human being besides all those *erga*?

(T3)   What, then, could this be? Living apparently is common to plants, but we are looking for that which is characteristic. We should, therefore, exclude the life of nutrition and growth. Next would be the perceptive life, but it too is common to the horse, the ox, and every animal.[50]

(T4)   There remains, then, some sort of life of action of the [part] that has reason. Now this part has a part that obeys reason and another that has [reason properly] and is thinking.

(T5)   Moreover, since life is spoken of in two ways, we must posit the life as activity [as opposed to capacity], since this life seems to be called such more properly.[51]

(T6)   If, then, the *ergon* of man is an activity of the soul in accordance with reason or not without reason—

(T7)   and if we say that the *ergon* of a generic so-and-so and a good generic so-and-so, e.g. of a lyre-player and a good lyre-player, is the same and that this simply is so in all cases, when the eminence

Politics (Oxford, 1991), 75–93), makes a case for a non-technical translation such as 'task', 'work', or 'job'. He argues (44/90) that the nature of *ergon* 'is derived not from metaphysical biology but from Greek political practice from Homer onwards'. *Ergon*, related to the English 'work', in Greek mostly has the connotation of activity. It refers either to activity itself or to the result of an activity, a product. See *EE* 1219ᵃ13–17 and LSJ s.vv. πρᾶξις and ποίησις.

[49]   It is here that many moderns rebel, e.g. Hardie, *Aristotle's Ethical Theory*, 23. A knife is supposed to cut, an eye is supposed to see, but can we say that man *qua* man is supposed to do anything? Very much so, says Aristotle, and in the *ergon* argument he presents the foundation of his views.

[50]   He draws on his teaching on the levels of the human soul in *De anima* 2. 4. Against Léonard, *Le Bonheur chez Aristote*, 28–38, Gauthier and Jolif, *L'Éthique à Nicomaque*, ii. 56, argue that Aristotle here denies his teaching in *De anima*, since there he does not reduce the task of man to the task of his rational part.

[51]   Aristotle's metaphysical concepts of actuality and potentiality play an important role in his ethics; thus, for example, the distinction *hexis/energeia*. *Eudaimonia* is not merely excellence but excellent *activity*. Remember that *ergon* usually has the connotation of activity in Greek. See n. 48 above.

expressing excellence is added to the *ergon*, the *ergon* of the lyre-player being to play the lyre and the *ergon* of the good lyre-player to play well—

(T8) if this is the case—we take the *ergon* of man to be some kind of life and take this life to be activity and *praxeis* of the soul implying reason and we take the *ergon* of a good man to be his doing these things well and finely and each *ergon* is accomplished well according to its proper excellence—if this then is the case,

(T9) then the human good turns out to be activity of the soul in accordance with excellence,

(T10) and, if there are several excellences, in accordance with the best and most final one.[52]

At issue is how we should interpret what is usually taken to be the conclusion of the *ergon* argument, T10. What is this best and most final activity? Ackrill and the inclusivists translate τελειοτάτην as 'the most complete' and identify this activity as the composite of activities in accordance with all the virtues.[53] Ackrill rejects the idea that this conclusion refers to *theōria* as the most perfect virtue. He finds that 'there is absolutely nothing in what precedes that would justify any such restriction. Aristotle has clearly stated that the principle of the *ergon* argument is that one must ask what powers and activities are peculiar to and distinctive of man'.[54] *Theōria*, says Ackrill, does not qualify, because man shares it with Aristotle's god. 'In fact, practical reason . . . is really more' distinctive of man. This last remark certainly has prima facie plausibility.

Against Ackrill, I argue that the *ergon* argument is an argument, or, at least, part of an argument, for the identification of *theōria* with *eudaimonia* or that, at least, the stage is set for the identification of *theōria* with *eudaimonia*. Ackrill's criticism that the εἰ δὲ πλείους clause (T10) does not follow from the premises of the *ergon* argument is correct. However, it ignores the background against which Aristotle places the argument: the finality argument which precedes the *ergon* argument directly. In other words, the *ergon* argument should not be read independently from this background. It is a step in an ongoing argument about *eudaimonia*.

The *ergon* argument has been the subject of many controversies. It has been criticized for trying to do too much and for accom-

---

[52] T9: τὸ ἀνθρώπινον ἀγαθὸν ψυχῆς ἐνέργεια γίνεται κατ᾽ ἀρετήν, T10: εἰ δὲ πλείους αἱ ἀρεταί, κατὰ τὴν ἀρίστην καὶ τελειοτάτην.

[53] 'Aristotle on *Eudaimonia*', 27.   [54] Ibid.

plishing too little.[55] Let us then go back to the text to see what it does accomplish. At 1097ᵇ23–4 Aristotle wants to say more clearly (ἐναργέστερον) what *eudaimonia* is. 'More clearly' implies that he takes himself to have already said some significant things about it. What he will be saying now has to be read together with what he has said before about *eudaimonia*: *eudaimonia* is the most final good and it is self-sufficient.

7. The Platonic conception of *ergon*

Aristotle's use of the concept of *ergon* here (T1 and T2) has been widely read as having been inspired by Plato's use of it in *Rep.* 1, 352 D–353 B. Plato, through the mouthpiece of Socrates, defines the *ergon* of a horse as 'that which one can do either only or best with it' (352 E 2–3).[56] Plato presents the horse as a tool of man and its *ergon* is to do what man makes it do. At 353 A 10–11 he defines the *ergon* thus: 'that which either it alone or better than the other things accomplishes is the *ergon* of each thing'.[57] Aristotle's examples are more 'natural': eye, foot, hand, in addition to different activities of a human being *qua* doing those activities, i.e. as sculptor, carpenter. If it is the case that the parts of man, such as the eyes, feet, and hands, have *erga*, and if it is the case that the sculptor and the carpenter have *erga*, then *a fortiori*, says Aristotle, man[58] himself must have an *ergon*. This move has been widely criticized. Why indeed would man have only one kind of activity which is specific to him? It seems perfectly possible that man has several kinds of activities which are typical of him: reading books, doing politics, helping his neighbours, going to war, eating, sending his children to school, etc. Aristotle would respond that he has already anticipated such objections in the previous section. *Eudaimonia* has the characteristic

---

[55] Adkins, 'The Connection between Aristotle's *Ethics* and *Politics*', 33/79, who argues correctly against translating Greek value terms simply with our value terms, finds that the conclusion of the *ergon* argument is a purely formal definition, which has no moral content and which Thrasymachus could accept cheerfully. J. M. Cooper, *Reason and the Human Good* (Cambridge, Mass., 1975), 146, considers it too abstract to be informative.

[56] ὃ ἂν ἢ μόνῳ ἐκείνῳ ποιῇ τις ἢ ἄριστα.

[57] τοῦτο ἑκάστου εἴη ἔργον ὃ ἂν ἢ μόνον τι ἢ κάλλιστα τῶν ἄλλων ἀπεργάζηται.

[58] I use 'man' here and hereafter, because Aristotle is talking about man and not about woman. Woman stands at a lower level than man, according to Aristotle, and can at best only approach man in the pursuit of *eudaimonia*.

of a final end. It is not done for the sake of something else. Every other end is done for the sake of it. Even if some of those other ends which are typical of man may be done for the sake of themselves, they will also be done for the sake of *eudaimonia*, at least.

What human activity will qualify as the *ergon* of man? Aristotle reaches back to his studies of the soul in *De anima* 2. 3–4. Man has several activities. They can be classified in a hierarchical scheme. The lowest level is the nutritive and growing life: the life of plants. Above this level, there is the level of perception, which distinguishes animals from plants. Aristotle dismisses these two levels of life on the basis that they are shared with plants and/or animals (T3). We are indeed looking for something that is characteristic (ἴδιον) of man.

There remains only one level of life, the practical life or activity of the part of the soul that has reason. Now it happens that the part that has reason is really subdivided into two parts. One part, in Aristotle's words, obeys reason and the other is said to have reason and to think. The distinction which Aristotle makes here is, of course, of fundamental importance for his moral theory. He will return to it in 1. 13 and 6. 1.[59] As mentioned above, the excellences of these parts will be the intellectual and character excellences respectively.

This passage seems to offer support to an inclusive reading, and the proponents of such a reading appeal to it.[60] After discarding the nutritive and the perceptive parts and their activities, Aristotle settles on the activity of the rational part of the soul as the *ergon* of man. Since the rational part of man consists of two parts, the respective activities of those two parts should count as the *ergon* or the *erga* of man. The part that has reason will itself prove to have two parts: the part that studies unchanging objects and the part that deals with changing objects. *Theōria* is the activity[61] of

---

[59] Notice that Aristotle here talks about the rational part of the soul which can be subdivided into a part that 'has reason and thinks' and another part that 'obeys reason'. The soul further consists of two non-rational parts, the nutritive and the perceptive. At 1. 13, 1103ᵃ2, Aristotle speaks of a part that has reason fully or in its proper sense (κυρίως) as opposed to two non-rational parts, one of which is responsive to reason, whereas the other is not. In 6. 1, 1139ᵃ5–8, he returns to the distinction he made in the *ergon* argument between the two rational parts. See also *Pol.* 7. 14, 1333ᵃ16–30.

[60] Ackrill, 'Aristotle on *Eudaimonia*', 27, and T. D. Roche, '*Ergon* and *Eudaimonia* in the *Nicomachean Ethics*, I: Reconsidering the Intellectualist Interpretation', *Journal of the History of Philosophy*, 26 (1988), 175–94 at 182.

[61] *Sophia* is the theoretical excellence.

the first rational part and *phronēsis* is the activity of the second. Activity in accordance with the character excellences is activity of the other rational part, the part that obeys reason. If this is the case, the thrust of the *ergon* argument is to include activity according to the character excellences[62] and *theōria* in *eudaimonia*.

The inclusivists have a point here. The life of character-excellent activity should be included in *eudaimonia*. An argument could even be made that *theōria* is an activity which is shared by god or the gods and, as such, does not seem to be very characteristic of man, since he is not the only one who does it. I shall respond to this in a moment. At that time we shall also see why the inclusivists' view, viz. that the point of the complete *ergon* argument[63] is to present an inclusive view of *eudaimonia*, is wrong.

Aristotle continues his argument with T5. The capacity to behave in a certain way is not enough. We have to do something in actuality to be called happy. *Eudaimonia* is an activity. The capacity to behave rationally is less properly called the practical life or the life of action than the actual rational activity. This seems pretty straightforward. Capacity for a certain activity is at a lower level than the activity itself. This is an example of Aristotle's hierarchical world-view, which suffuses his ethics. Another such example will figure importantly in T10.

If man's *ergon* is activity in accordance with reason or not without reason, then, Aristotle concludes, the human good, i.e. *eudaimonia*, turns out to be activity of the soul in accordance with excellence.[64] But then Aristotle adds T10. Ackrill translates: 'the good for man turns out to be the activity of the soul in accordance with virtue,

---

[62] The rather heavy phrase 'activity in accordance with the character excellences' is a more correct rendering of what modern commentators often refer to as 'morally virtuous activity'. 'Morally virtuous activity' in modern parlance refers to any activity that is (morally) commendable. For Aristotle, *theōria* is also morally commendable, but he wants to distinguish it from other morally commendable activities, i.e. those in accordance with the character virtues. Our terms 'moral' and 'ethical' have lost their original Latin and Greek senses of 'relating to character', which is strongly connected to 'habitual': that is, character is formed through habitual activities. The terms 'ethical' and 'moral' gradually received the sense of 'morally (in our sense) commendable'. For Aristotle, commendability was contained in the term *aretē*. The term *ēthikē* simply referred to what was related to character. Activity in accordance with the character excellences, to Aristotle, is always 'morally' (in our sense) commendable, but activity in accordance with the intellectual excellences will, all things being equal, be more commendable. I think these distinctions are not always kept in mind.   [63] Or, the *ergon* argument plus its rider.

[64] ψυχῆς ἐνέργεια κατ' ἀρετήν (T9).

and if there are more than one virtue, in accordance with the best and most complete'.[65] I shall argue in a moment that the activity referred to in T10 is *theōria*. Ackrill rejects the reading that T10 refers to *theōria* because, in his opinion, 'there is nothing in what precedes that would justify any such restriction'.[66] Ackrill reads T10 in a way that strengthens his own interpretation of *eudaimonia*: that is, if there is more than one excellence, then the combination of all of them constitutes *eudaimonia*.

Ackrill reads τελειοτάτην here in the same way as he has done in other passages leading up to the *ergon* argument (1097^{a}25–34). He translates τέλειος as 'complete' and τελειοτάτην as 'most complete', which he then glosses as 'most inclusive'. But τέλειος is best translated as 'having the characteristic of an end' or 'final'.[67] τελειοτάτην is then 'having most of all the characteristic of an end'.[68] Against Ackrill we can say with Kraut that 'There is no justification for taking the most perfect virtue to be a composite of all virtues, unless Aristotle has already introduced the idea of a composite good, and has treated degrees of perfection in terms of greater inclusiveness. And this he has not done.'[69]

If Aristotle is already thinking here of *theōria*, then 'perfect' is certainly a better rendering of the meaning that Aristotle intends. *Theōria* has all the characteristics that are required for an end to be the most final one. It is desirable for its own sake and it is not for the sake of anything else. In addition, other ends are for the sake of it.

Indeed, if Aristotle intended an inclusive reading, he probably would have said so in a more unambiguous way, such as 'if there are several excellences, then in accordance with *all* of them'.[70] More importantly, in 10. 6–8 Aristotle clearly identifies perfect *eudaimonia* with *theōria* and uses language that is very similar to 1. 7.[71]

Ackrill further objects to reading T10 as implying that *theōria* is *eudaimonia*, on the grounds that this would go against the spirit of

[65] 'Aristotle on *Eudaimonia*', 28.
[66] Ibid. He calls *sophia* the activity in question in accordance with the virtue *theōria*. I think *sophia* is the virtue or excellence and *theōria* the activity in accordance with the excellence called *sophia*. See also n. 60.
[67] Ackrill does agree with this translation, but explicates it as 'inclusive' ('Aristotle on *Eudaimonia*', 28).
[68] Cf. Cooper, *Reason and Human Good in Aristotle*, 100 n. 10.
[69] *Aristotle on the Human Good*, 242.   [70] See Kraut, ibid.
[71] For example, at 10. 7, 1177^{a}17–18, Aristotle says that he has already identified contemplation as *eudaimonia* in the preceding argument.

the *ergon* argument, which is intended to isolate something distinctive of man. For Ackrill, (narrow) practical reason, i.e. the activity of reason apart from theoretical reason, is really more distinctive of man than theoretical reason.[72] On the face of it, Ackrill seems to be right. God also shares in theoretical reason, but is not encumbered by the limitations of man, who needs his practical reason to steer himself through the demands made upon him by the non-rational parts of his being, which is possible only in a body, unlike god's being. But Aristotle does include 'the part that has reason properly and is thinking' (1. 7, 1098ª4–5) in the distinctive element of man, the activity of which will also be included in the characteristic activity of man. Despite his narrow reading of πρακτική, Ackrill does not exclude *theōria* from the composite of excellences to which he thinks τελειοτάτην refers.[73]

I think that J. A. Stewart is right to include theoretical activity in πρακτική here.[74] However, if that is the case, how can we make sense of 'characteristic' (ἴδιον)? Ackrill's objection that theoretical activity, which we accept as being part of πρακτική, is not characteristic of man, since he shares it with god, creeps up again. The thrust of the *ergon* argument was to isolate the characteristic activity of man. God contemplates also, so contemplation cannot be characteristic of man. Why does Aristotle exclude nourishment, growth, and perception on the basis that they are shared with other beings, plants and animals, and not contemplation?

Kraut proposes the following solution to this puzzle.[75] Aristotle is not looking for something peculiar to man which sets us apart from *all* beings, but only for something that sets us apart from the lower classes of beings, i.e. plants and animals. He finds no textual reason to support the reading that our *ergon* must be absolutely unique to us. Such a reading would clash with 10. 7–8, where the gods are upheld as models to be imitated. This would be incompatible with the requirement that our good must consist in something that no god can do. Kraut reasonably supposes that books 1 and 10 should

---

[72] 'Aristotle on *Eudaimonia*', 27. See also his *Aristotle the Philosopher* (Oxford, 1981), 139. Similarly, H. H. Joachim, *Aristotle: The Nicomachean Ethics* (Oxford, 1951), 50, and A. Kamp, *Die politische Philosophie des Aristoteles und ihre metaphysischen Grundlagen* (Freiburg and Munich, 1985), 78.

[73] Kraut notices this inconsistency (*Aristotle on the Human Good*, 314 n. 4).

[74] *Notes on the* Nicomachean Ethics, i. 99, where he refers to an important passage in the *Politics*, 7. 3, 1325ᵇ16–21. See Kraut, *Aristotle on the Human Good*, 313 n. 3.

[75] *Aristotle on the Human Good*, 316–17.

and can be unified in one interpretation. Kraut also effectively answers the objection by Bernard Williams and others that a great many other activities are peculiar to man, such as making fire. Peculiarity, of course, is only one of several *necessary* features of our ultimate end. If an activity is shared with animals and plants, that will exclude it, but that does not mean that everything peculiar to man will do as the human good. Peculiarity to man is not a *sufficient* feature of any candidate.

But there are some problems. Kraut argues that Aristotle accepts Plato's definition of *ergon* of a thing in *Rep.* 353 A[76] as 'that which [that thing] either alone or better than anything else can do'.[77] But human beings are obviously not the best at contemplation; god is. Kraut is well aware of this, but he argues that in the *ergon* argument the type about which Aristotle is talking includes both god and man. This broad interpretation of the type in question is controversial, as Kraut realizes.[78]

I propose a different reading of the *ergon* argument which salvages Kraut's reading of *theōria* as (perfect) *eudaimonia*. I read T9 as the conclusion of the *ergon* argument. In other words, I exclude the rider (T10) from the argument proper. This reading accepts that the point of the *ergon* argument is to identify an activity that is absolutely peculiar to man. In this reading, the πρακτική life, the life of *praxis*, is the characteristic (ἰδία) life of man. πρακτική covers both contemplation and activities in accordance with the character excellences.[79] The part of the soul that has *logos* consists of two other parts, the part that obeys reason and the part that has reason properly and is thinking (1. 7, 1098ª3–4). There can be little doubt

---

[76] See nn. 55 and 56 above.   [77] *Aristotle on the Human Good*, 319 n. 12.
[78] In an earlier contribution, 'The Peculiar Function of Human Beings', *Canadian Journal of Philosophy*, 9 (1979), 467–78, Kraut did not put man and god together in one type, but rather proposed the concept of relative peculiarity. In the *ergon* argument Aristotle is interested only in setting man apart from beings *inferior* to himself. In this way we can say that activity in accordance with reason is the *ergon* of man because he is the only being that is given to activity according to reason and certainly is better at it than the beings inferior to himself, if we allow that some animals seem to display characteristics which suggest that they are capable of something resembling rational activity. In the article Kraut rejects the view that Aristotle accepted the Platonic conception of *ergon* in the *ergon* argument. In *Aristotle on the Human Good*, 319 n. 12, he thinks it is necessary to accept both Plato's definition of *ergon* and Aristotle's claim that it is our function to contemplate. If one does not accept Plato's definition, he thinks that there is no movement in the *ergon* argument.
[79] See *Pol.* 7. 3. I cannot argue for this here.

that theoretical reason is or belongs to the part which has reason. As Kraut mentions, *NE* 1. 13 presupposes this distinction, which will lead to the distinction between the intellectual and so-called character excellences.

The conclusion of the *ergon* argument proper is that the activity of the soul in accordance with excellence is the human good. This activity is with or not without reason. Since reason consists of both theoretical and practical reason, its activity will consist of both theoretical and (narrowly) practical activity.[80] Now, according to this alternative reading, it can be said that the combination of these two kinds of rational activities is absolutely peculiar to man.[81] In this way both activities of reason qualify as *eudaimonia*. The combination of these two rational activities is not found in any other species. Neither plants nor animals nor gods have this combination.[82] The combination of these two rational activities is the *ergon* of man. This is the conclusion of the *ergon* argument.

Then Aristotle makes a further move. He has already argued that *eudaimonia* is the most final good. Rational activity can be divided into the activity that has reason itself and that which follows reason. The first activity may be further subdivided into *theōria* and

[80] This practical activity can be described from two points of view: from the point of view of *phronēsis*, which commands the part of the soul that obeys reason to perform a certain excellent activity, and from the point of view of the part that obeys reason as character-excellent activities.

[81] Ackrill, 'Aristotle on *Eudaimonia*', 27, also prefers this reading. If we read the *ergon* argument, without its rider, ignoring the context, which, as I have argued above, offers strong support for the intellectualist reading, then Ackrill's position is clearly defensible: if the combination of practical and theoretical activities is our *ergon*, then our human good must consist, according to the *ergon* argument, in the excellent execution of those activities: that is, the human good is then a composite of different kinds of excellent activities. But the *ergon* argument has a context and it is followed by the rider 'and if there are several excellences, in accordance with the best and most final one' (1098ᵃ17–18). As we have seen, Ackrill finds the identification of *eudaimonia* with *theōria* an 'ill-fitting and at first unintelligible intrusion of a view only to be explained and expounded much later' (28).

[82] K. V. Wilkes, 'The Good Man and the Good for Man in Aristotle's Ethics', *Mind*, 87 (1978), 553–71, repr. in A. O. Rorty (ed.), *Essays on Aristotle's Ethics* (Berkeley, 1980), 341–58 at 345, considers and dismisses the view that this combination of contemplation and practical reasoning qualifies as ἴδιον on the grounds that 'there seems no reason of principle why it should not be further extended so as to overlap with the capacities of animals at one end as it already does with those of gods at the other'. However, the capacities man shares with plants and animals are not rational, whereas the capacity it shares with the gods is rational. The principle of rationality blocks the inclusion of the lower activities among the peculiarly human activities for the purposes of the *ergon* argument.

phronēsis, as discussed in *NE* 6 and *Politics* 7. Of those rational activities *theōria* will turn out to be the only one that is not for the sake of something else in addition to being for its own sake. Other activities will be for the sake of contemplation. Aristotle does not yet argue for these qualities of *theōria* here. He will do so in *NE* 6 and 10.[83] The rider (T10) thus goes beyond the *ergon* argument by distinguishing degrees of finality.[84] *Eudaimonia* is the most final good of man. Rational activity in accordance with excellence can be subdivided into theoretical and practical activity. Of these two activities the former will turn out to be more final, to have the characteristic of an end more than the other activity does, since theoretical activity will be only for its own sake whereas practical activity will also be for the sake of theoretical activity in addition to being for its own sake. Read in this way, the *ergon* argument is an integral part of an ongoing argument in book 1. The finality argument and the *ergon* argument combine to set the stage to identify contemplation as the highest form of happiness. While it is true that Aristotle does not explicitly mention contemplation, it is clear that he has it very much in mind. Book 10 will then explicitly identify contemplation as the candidate that satisfies all the criteria introduced in book 1.

The *ergon* argument proper establishes that the human good consists in rational activity in accordance with excellence. Both theoretical and practical activities qualify; both constitute the human good. *NE* 10 will explicitly identify both activities as happiness; theoretical activity will be the highest form of happiness and (narrow) practical activity will be the secondary form of happiness. In the rider to the *ergon* argument Aristotle says that activity in accordance with the best and most final excellence is happiness. He does not explicitly identify this excellence. However, the indications that he is talking about contemplation are very strong. The rider is incomplete in that it calls activity in accordance with one

---

[83] Aristotle has already set the stage for such a possibility when he distinguished between three different kinds of activities based on their degree of finality. See 1. 7, 1097^{a}30–4.

[84] Cf. Heinaman, '*Eudaimonia* and Self-Sufficiency in the *Nicomachean Ethics*', 37, who argues that T9 answers the question 'What life counts as *eudaimonia*?', while T10 answers the question 'What is the highest kind of *eudaimonia*?' See also Kenny, *Aristotle on the Perfect Life*, 29. My reading is an effort to counter H. J. Curzer's remark that 'on the intellectualist interpretation' T10 'is just awkwardly tacked on to the *ergon* argument's conclusion' ('Criteria for Happiness in *Nicomachean Ethics* I 7 and X 6–8', *Classical Quarterly*, NS 40 (1990), 421–32 at 430).

excellence (the best and most final excellence) the human good (i.e. *eudaimonia*) *tout court*. Aristotle could have avoided misperceptions had he used the term *perfect* or *most final* happiness. He will do so in book 10.

8. The final chapters of *NE* 1

In Book 1 of the *Nicomachean Ethics* Aristotle seems to prepare the way to identify *eudaimonia* with contemplation. The thrust of *NE* 1 seems to be that *eudaimonia* is not a composite. After the *ergon* argument Aristotle makes a few more statements which confirm that he is thinking about one activity, the best activity, and not a composite of activities. At 1. 8, 1099ᵃ24–31, he says:

> Happiness then is the best, the finest, and the most pleasant . . . For all (three) features are found in the best activities. And we say that happiness is these activities, or one of them, i.e. the best one.[85]

Happiness, or as we may anticipate, the highest form of happiness, consists of one activity. Note that the uncertain formulation ταύτας δέ, ἢ μίαν τούτων seems to anticipate the distinction that Aristotle will make in book 10 between perfect and secondary *eudaimonia*.

In *NE* 1. 9 Aristotle calls happiness blessed and divine. This probably suggests that he is thinking here of contemplation, an activity he will describe as divine in *NE* 10:

> Even if [happiness] is not sent by god but accrues through excellence and some kind of learning, it appears to be one of the most divine things, for the prize and goal of excellence appears to be the best thing and something divine and blessed. (1. 10, 1099ᵇ15–18)

A strong indication that happiness is set apart from the character excellences and that the happy man is quite different from merely character-excellent man is offered at 1. 12, 1101ᵇ21–7:

> If praise is for such things [i.e. being just and brave], then it is clear that for the best things there is no praise, but something greater and better. For we call the gods blessed and happy and call the godliest of men blessed. Similarly in the case of goods. Nobody praises happiness like justice but we call it blessed as something more divine and better.

[85] Cf. D. Devereux, 'Aristotle on the Essence of Happiness', in D. O'Meara (ed.), *Studies in Aristotle* (Washington, 1981), 247–60 at 253.

The just man and the brave man are praised. The gods and the godliest of men are called happy and blessed. Clearly, what sets these two categories apart is the activity in which they engage. The just and brave engage in the character excellences of justice and bravery, the gods engage in their activity, i.e. contemplation. It is this activity that the godliest men share with the gods. They contemplate and are called blessed precisely because of this activity.[86]

A few lines later we read:

It seems that this is the case because happiness is a principle. For we do everything else for its sake. We take the principle and cause of the goods to be something honourable and divine. (1. 12, 1102ᵃ2–4)

Aristotle calls *eudaimonia* an ἀρχή, a principle, for we do everything else for its sake. This ἀρχή we call honourable and divine. This is another indication that Aristotle is probably thinking here of contemplation, the only human activity which he calls divine. A composite of activities would not be divine.

10. Conclusion

In this paper I have argued that in *NE* 1 Aristotle anticipates the identification of contemplation with *eudaimonia*. The explicit identification will come in book 10, where Aristotle identifies contemplation with *teleia eudaimonia*. The hierarchy of ends sets the stage for contemplation to take the top spot. The formal criteria for *eudaimonia*, finality and self-sufficiency, point to contemplation since these criteria apply best to contemplation, as Aristotle will indicate in book 10. The rider to the *ergon* argument proper points also to contemplation. Finally, several remarks after the *ergon* argument make it clear that, already in book 1, Aristotle is thinking of one activity, a divine activity, as (perfect) happiness. This activity must be contemplation. Given these strong indications, the inclusivist position, which identifies happiness as a composite of activities and which could be supported by some isolated passages, including the *ergon* argument without its rider, appears to be severely weakened.

The inclusivist reading does not distinguish clearly between hap-

---

[86] See also Gauthier and Jolif, *L'Éthique à Nicomaque*, ii/1. 87, ad 1101ᵇ24. Note that this implies that secondary *eudaimonia*, as described in *NE* 10, is not blessed, but merely praised.

piness, which is an activity, and the happy life. The happy life will
turn out to contain both perfect (contemplation) and secondary
happiness (character-excellent behaviour), as described in 10. 6–8.
Moreover, Aristotle will not only be interested in the *eudaimonia* of
the individual, but especially in the *eudaimonia* of the polis. Indeed,
it is not the case that Aristotle's eminent happy person, the philosopher, will let his neighbour perish in his burning house because he
himself is perfectly happy philosophizing.[87] This fascinating story
lies, however, outside the scope of the present paper.

Antwerp/Thessaloniki

BIBLIOGRAPHY

Ackrill, J. L., 'Aristotle on *Eudaimonia*', in A. O. Rorty (ed.), *Essays on Aristotle's Ethics* (Berkeley, 1980), 15–33.
—— *Aristotle the Philosopher* (Oxford, 1981).
Adkins, A. W. H., *Merit and Responsibility: A Study in Greek Values* (Oxford, 1960).
—— '"Friendship" and "Self-Sufficiency" in Homer and Aristotle', *Classical Quarterly*, NS 13 (1963), 30–45.
—— '*Theoria* versus *Praxis* in the *Nicomachean Ethics* and the *Republic*', *Classical Philology*, 73 (1978), 297–313.
—— 'The Connection between Aristotle's *Ethics* and *Politics*', *Political Theory*, 12 (1984), 29–49; repr. in D. Keyt and F. D. Miller, Jr. (eds.), *A Companion to Aristotle's* Politics (Oxford, 1991), 75–93.
Clark, S. R. L., *Aristotle's Man: Speculations upon Aristotelian Anthropology* (Oxford, 1975).
Cooper, J. M., *Reason and Human Good in Aristotle* (Cambridge, Mass., 1975).
—— review of A. Kenny, *The Aristotelian Ethics*, in *Nous*, 15 (1981), 381–92.
Curzer, H. J., 'Criteria for Happiness in *Nicomachean Ethics* I 7 and X 6–8', *Classical Quarterly*, NS 40 (1990), 421–32.
Devereux, D., 'Aristotle on the Essence of Happiness', in D. O'Meara (ed.), *Studies in Aristotle* (Washington, 1981), 247–60.
Gauthier, R.-A., and Jolif, J.-Y., *L'Éthique à Nicomaque: introduction, traduction et commentaire*, 2nd edn. (2 vols. in 4; Leuven and Paris, 1970).
Goodwin, W. W., *Syntax of the Moods and Tenses of the Greek Verb* (London, 1889).

[87] A. W. H. Adkins, '*Theoria* versus *Praxis* in the *Nicomachean Ethics* and the *Republic*', *Classical Philology*, 73 (1978), 297–313.

Hardie, W. F. R., *Aristotle's Ethical Theory*, 2nd edn. (Oxford, 1980).

Heinaman, R., 'Eudaimonia and Self-Sufficiency in the *Nicomachean Ethics*', *Phronesis*, 33 (1988), 31–53.

Joachim, H. H., *Aristotle:* The Nicomachean Ethics (Oxford, 1951).

Kamp, A., *Die politische Philosophie des Aristoteles und ihre metaphysischen Grundlagen: Wesenstheorie und Polisordnung* (Freiburg and Munich, 1985).

Kenny, A., 'Aristotle on Happiness', in J. Barnes *et al.* (eds.), *Articles on Aristotle*, ii. *Ethics and Politics* (London, 1977), 25–32.

—— *The Aristotelian Ethics: A Study of the Relationship between the* Eudemian *and* Nicomachean Ethics *of Aristotle* (Oxford, 1978).

—— 'The Nicomachean Conception of Happiness', in H. Blumenthal and H. Robinson (eds.), *Aristotle and the Later Tradition* (*OSAP* suppl.; 1991), 67–80.

—— *Aristotle on the Perfect Life* (Oxford, 1992).

Keyt, D., 'Intellectualism in Aristotle', in J. P. Anton and A. Preus (eds.), *Essays in Ancient Greek Philosophy*, vol. ii (Albany, NY, 1983), 364–87.

Kraut, R., 'The Peculiar Function of Human Beings', *Canadian Journal of Philosophy*, 9 (1979), 467–78.

—— *Aristotle on the Human Good* (Princeton, 1989).

Kühner, R., and Gerth, B., *Ausführliche Grammatik der griechischen Sprache*, 2 vols. (Hanover, 1904).

Lear, G. R., *Happy Lives and the Highest Good: An Essay on Aristotle's* Nicomachean Ethics (Princeton, 2004).

Léonard, J., *Le Bonheur chez Aristote* (Brussels, 1948).

Roche, T. D. 'Ergon and Eudaimonia in the *Nicomachean Ethics*, I: Reconsidering the Intellectualist Interpretation', *Journal of the History of Philosophy*, 26 (1988), 175–94.

Smyth, H. W., *Greek Grammar*, rev. G. M. Messing (Cambridge, Mass., 1956).

Stemmer, P., 'Aristoteles' Glücksbegriff in der *Nikomachischen Ethik*: Eine Interpretation von E.N. I, 7. 1097b2–5', *Phronesis*, 37 (1992), 85–110.

Stewart, J. A., *Notes on the* Nicomachean Ethics *of Aristotle* (2 vols.; Oxford, 1892).

White, S., 'Is Aristotelian Happiness a Good Life or the Best Life?', *OSAP* 8 (1990), 97–137.

Wilkes, K. V., 'The Good Man and the Good for Man in Aristotle's Ethics', *Mind*, 87 (1978), 553–71; repr. in A. O. Rorty (ed.), *Essays on Aristotle's Ethics* (Berkeley, 1980), 341–58.

DOING WITHOUT MORALITY: REFLECTIONS ON THE MEANING OF *DEIN* IN ARISTOTLE'S *NICOMACHEAN ETHICS*

RICHARD KRAUT

1. Anscombe on moral duty

BEFORE Aristotle turns, in *NE* 1. 6, to a discussion of the Platonic theory of the good, he prefaces his criticism with the admission that he undertakes this investigation with some reluctance, because those who introduced the forms are his friends. He then adds that none the less he must go forward, and offers this justification for attacking their theory:

It will presumably be thought better, indeed one's duty, to do away even with what is close to one's heart, in order to preserve the truth, especially when one is a philosopher. For one might love both, but it is nevertheless a sacred duty to prefer the truth to one's friends. (1096ᵃ14–17)

I quote the recent translation of Roger Crisp because I want to focus on its use of the word 'duty' to convey Aristotle's meaning. The Greek term that Crisp is translating, when he takes Aristotle to mean that it is 'one's duty . . . to preserve the truth', is a verb: *dein*.[1] That Greek word will be the central topic here. Crisp is not alone in conveying the meaning of *dein*, in this passage, by means of the word 'duty': that was also the way W. D. Ross rendered Aristotle's

I am grateful to Terry Irwin and to audiences in Santa Clara, São Paulo, and Cambridge (England) for their criticism of a much shorter reading version of this paper. My special thanks go to David Sedley for his many helpful suggestions, and his proposal that I reduce the size of the inordinately large draft from which I began.

[1] *Aristotle:* Nicomachean Ethics (Cambridge, 2000). Throughout this paper, I will for the most part use the infinitive form, *dein* (δεῖν), but will switch to the third-person singular *dei* (δεῖ) either when I quote a text that uses that form of the verb or when I write a mixed Greek–English sentence that has a singular subject.

Greek.² But other translators differ: Terence Irwin uses 'right', both here and throughout much of his translation, as his preferred equivalent for *dein*;³ whereas Christopher Rowe for the most part uses 'should', switching occasionally to 'required'.⁴ Well, which is it: does *dein* mean 'duty' or 'right' or 'should' or 'required'? Does it mean different things in different contexts? Does our choice of which word to use, as a translation of *dein*, have any importance for our understanding of Aristotle?

Anyone who asks such questions must be mindful of G. E. M. Anscombe's paper 'Modern Moral Philosophy', published almost a half century ago, in which she argued that we should abandon such terms as 'moral duty', 'moral obligation', and 'moral wrongness', and looked back to Aristotle's ethics as an exemplar of a practical philosophy that is completely free of such notions.⁵ Now, neither Ross nor Crisp uses 'moral duty' as a rendering of *dein*, and so it might be thought that there is no conflict between their translation and Anscombe's insistence that Aristotle lacks any notion of moral duty, moral rightness, and the like.

But why should we abide by Anscombe's strictures and avoid coming into conflict with her? Why not say, in fact, that in this very passage Aristotle is saying that we philosophers have a *moral* duty to preserve the truth?⁶ The term 'moral' is used so extensively, and

² First published in 1925 by Clarendon Press, as part of *The Works of Aristotle*, under the editorship of Sir David Ross. Ross's translation can now be found in *The Complete Works of Aristotle*, ed. J. Barnes, vol. ii (Princeton, 1984).

³ *Aristotle:* Nicomachean Ethics, 2nd edn. (Indianapolis, 1999). Irwin's glossary (under the heading 'right') says: 'in the right contexts [*dein*] may convey awareness of an unqualified duty' (346).

⁴ *Aristotle:* Nicomachean Ethics (Oxford, 2002).

⁵ G. E. M. Anscombe, 'Modern Moral Philosophy' ['Modern'], *Philosophy*, 33 (1958), 1–19, repr. in *The Collected Philosophical Papers of G. E. M. Anscombe* (3 vols.; Oxford, 1981), iii. 26–43, and in R. Crisp and M. Slote (eds.), *Virtue Ethics* (Oxford, 1997), 26–44 (citations refer to the 1997 reprint). Her claim about Aristotle is made on pp. 26–7: one must be 'very imperceptive' if one 'professes to be expounding Aristotle and talks in a modern fashion about "moral" such-and-such' (27). She then offers an explanation of why a notion that is present in so much modern moral philosophy is missing in Aristotle: he lacks a '*law* conception of ethics' (31, her emphasis), according to which divine law provides the grounding for truths about what we ought to do. See T. H. Irwin, 'Aquinas, Natural Law, and Aristotelian Eudaimonism', in R. Kraut (ed.), *The Blackwell Guide to Aristotle's* Nicomachean Ethics (Oxford, 2006), 323–41, for the thesis that Anscombe fails to distinguish the voluntarist and naturalist traditions in moral philosophy, and that this undermines both her understanding of moral oughtness and her failure to recognize its presence in Aristotle.

⁶ In the glossary to his translation, Crisp has this entry for *dei*: it is 'not purely

to serve so many different purposes, that it would be foolhardy to deny that Aristotle is endorsing a perspective that should, in *some* sense, be called moral. We contrast strategic thinking and moral reasoning; surely what we find in Aristotle's ethical works falls far more comfortably in the latter category than the former. Similarly, we contrast doing something for purely aesthetic reasons and acting for moral reasons; again, it seems reasonable to say of the character types whom Aristotle admires that they act at least partly for moral reasons, and not for purely aesthetic reasons. Consider what we are likely to mean when we say about one of our contemporaries that he acts for moral reasons. Those words imply that he gives consideration to the good of others, and does not treat them as a mere means to his own ends; that he has a sense of justice, which calls upon him to treat others as equals; that he is not a mere partisan of a political faction, but also pays attention to the good of the larger community; that he blames and praises others only when he takes them to be responsible for their actions; that he tries to avoid doing what he takes to be shameful and criticizes others when they act shamefully; that he considers his actions to be justified only if he recognizes that anyone else similarly situated would also have been justified in undertaking those same actions. Now, Aristotle's thinking exhibits all of these features. He can therefore be said to have put forward a practical philosophy that occupies a moral perspective. Accordingly, it seems that there should be no objection to our taking him to mean (in the above passage) that he has a *moral duty* to put truth above friendship—or, if we prefer one of the other translations proposed, it seems that there should be no objection to our taking him to mean that it is *morally* right to preserve the truth, or that he is *morally* required to do so, or that, *morally* speaking, he should.

Despite Anscombe's philosophical stature and the importance of her essay as a contribution to moral philosophy,[7] it has had remarkably little influence on the way in which scholars who write about ethics in the ancient world think about their subject. Many of them continue to describe Aristotle's ethics, and ancient ethics

moral, but it does cover many cases of what we would call moral duty' (*Aristotle: Nicomachean Ethics*, 205). So he has, it seems, at least half a heart to go against Anscombe.

[7] It appears in the anthology of Crisp and Slote, cited above in n. 5, precisely for this reason.

in general, in terms that she would condemn. Here, for example, is what Julia Annas says: 'all ancient theories understand a virtue to be, at least, a disposition to do the morally right thing'.[8] The very title of her book, *The Morality of Happiness*, shows that Anscombe has had no effect on her; in fact, Anscombe is never mentioned in her book, and is not listed in its bibliography. If we want to find someone sympathetic to the contrast Anscombe drew between ancient and modern ethics, we have to turn to Bernard Williams, who was no less hostile than she to any form of thinking that relies on notions of moral wrongness, moral blame, and the like. But we do not find in Williams an extensive discussion of the question whether the notion of morality is missing from Greek ethical writings. Like Anscombe, he just took it to be obvious that it is. What he did try to show is that they are better off without it.[9]

In this paper, I come to the defence of Anscombe's historical thesis. I believe that Aristotle does not work with moral categories— that is, with such notions as moral rightness, moral wrongness, moral duty, and the like. I do not credit her with being the first to notice a significant difference between the terms that play a central role in ancient ethical theory and those that became prominent in the modern period. A difference of this kind was also noticed by Henry Sidgwick in the opening pages of his *The Methods of Ethics*, and was then dubbed, by C. D. Broad, in his discussion of Sidgwick, as a contrast between deontological and teleological uses of the word 'ought'.[10] That terminology has now become a standard feature of moral philosophy, and is most often used as a way of framing the debate between utilitarianism (or its contemporary successor, consequentialism[11]) and Kantian approaches to morality. Sidgwick's view, when put in these terms, is that modern

---

[8] *The Morality of Happiness* (Oxford, 1993), 9.

[9] See *Ethics and the Limits of Philosophy* (Cambridge, Mass., 1985), ch. 10 (174–96); and *Shame and Necessity* (Berkeley, 1993), 5–8. For criticism of Williams's reading of Aristotle, see T. Irwin, 'Aristotle's Conception of Morality', in J. Cleary (ed.), *Proceedings of the Boston Area Colloquium in Ancient Philosophy*, 1 (Lanham, Md., 1986), 115–43. He is responding to Williams, 'Philosophy', in M. I. Finley (ed.), *The Legacy of Greece* (Oxford, 1981), 202–55.

[10] *Five Types of Ethical Theory* [*Types*] (London, 1930), 162: 'Some people judge that there are certain types of action which ought to be done (or avoided) in all or in certain types of situation, regardless of the goodness or badness of the probable consequences. This is what I call the "deontological" application of "ought".'

[11] Utilitarianism takes the good to be pleasure, and demands its maximization; consequentialism holds that the good, whatever it is, should be maximized.

ethical thought, as represented by what he called the 'Intuitional view', uses 'ought' deontologically, whereas ancient moral philosophy uses 'ought' teleologically.[12] These terms are not always used uniformly—for example, Rawls's definition of them[13] differs from Broad's—and it is open to question whether they are useful categories. But, as a rough indication of where I am heading, it could be said that I will be portraying Aristotle as someone who has a striking affinity to teleologists of the modern era.

In coming to the defence of Anscombe's historical thesis, I leave aside her radical philosophical thesis, which was more fully developed by Williams, that we would do well to jettison such notions as moral duty, moral wrongness, and moral obligation. My own view is that these philosophical issues are far more complex than either of them supposes. The question whether these are fruitful categories of thought is, in my opinion, far from having been settled. I suggest that Aristotle can play an extremely helpful role in sorting out this issue: once it is recognized that he does not use the moral framework that has become part of common sense, he provides us with a stellar example of what a system of practical thought can look like when it operates without notions of moral rightness, moral wrongness, and the like.

2. 'Right' and 'morally right'

Our discussion will require us to take care not only with one of the key words of Aristotle's vocabulary (*dein*), but also with some of our own normative terms: 'right', 'wrong', 'moral', 'ought', 'should', and 'must'. I begin with them, before turning to *dein* itself. Since Aristotle's adjective *orthos* (normally translated 'right') and its cognates will also play an important role in our discussion, I pay special attention to our word 'right' (which Irwin uses frequently as a way of rendering *dein*) and its opposite, 'wrong'.

To put my cards on the table: I believe that *dein* should be translated 'should' in all of the important passages in which it figures in Aristotle's ethics. It is best to avoid 'duty', 'right', and 'required' as

---

[12] *The Methods of Ethics*, 7th edn. (Chicago, 1962), 3.

[13] *A Theory of Justice*, rev. edn. (Cambridge, Mass., 1999), 21–2. (All future references to Rawls will be to this edition.) I return to this issue later (sect. 14, esp. n. 28).

translations of *dein* (though 'right' is an appropriate way of translating *orthos*). As translations of *dein*, 'must' and 'ought' are almost
as good as 'should'; but I shall not have a great deal to say about
them. The most important point, in what follows, is that 'should'
is superior to 'right', 'duty', and 'required'. Grasping this point
will go a long way (though certainly not all of the way) towards
vindicating Anscombe.[14]

I begin with 'right' and 'wrong'. If I am baking bread, and it
comes out of the oven burnt, then I probably did something wrong.
But no one is likely to accuse me of any wrongdoing. I made a
mistake, all right; but I did no wrong. What is going on here? The
recognition of multiple meanings allows us to sort things out.[15] In
one sense, we apply 'right' and 'wrong' whenever we are assessing
the correctness or incorrectness of an action in some dimension. Am
I on the right train? Is this sweater the right gift for the occasion?
Is what he said right? No one would think to supply the word
'morally' to these uses of 'right' and 'wrong'. The question is not
whether I am on a train that is morally right—whatever that would
mean. In looking for the right gift, I seek something that would
be suitable—not morally right. If what he said is true, then it was
right—that is, true, whether or not his saying it was morally right
or wrong.

But on other occasions, to speak of right and wrong is to speak of
what is morally right or morally wrong. For example, when Rawls
says, 'The two main concepts of ethics are those of the right and
the good; the concept of a morally worthy person is . . . derived
from them' (21), he is claiming that moral rightness is one of the
central concepts of ethics. A good cook must know about how to go
right and avoid going wrong in the preparation of food. But a good
person—that is, a person who is 'morally worthy', as Rawls puts
it—must know something about which actions are morally right
and which morally wrong. By making this distinction between two
different meanings of 'right' and 'wrong', we can maintain that
there is no contradiction in saying that when you burnt the bread

[14] Anscombe calls 'should', 'needs', 'ought', and 'must' 'indispensable', and protests against equating them with 'is obliged', 'is bound', or 'is required to' ('Modern',
30). It is no part of her thesis that Aristotle lacks anything corresponding to the first
group of terms.

[15] Instead of claiming that 'right' has different *senses*, we might hold that there
are different *kinds* of rightness. For our purposes, it is not important to determine
which is the better way to avoid contradictions.

you did something wrong, even though you did nothing that was wrong: in its second occurrence, but not its first, 'wrong' means 'morally wrong'. (In what follows, I shall sometimes speak in an abbreviated way of rightness and wrongness, meaning, more fully, moral rightness and wrongness. Context often indicates whether the 'right' and 'wrong' being talked about are of the moral sort, and it would be tedious always to have to say 'morally right' when it is obvious that this is the sort of rightness we have in mind.)

3. 'Should', 'ought', and 'must'

It is crucial to realize that the use to which we put 'should', in our normative thinking, differs in an important way from the use to which we put 'morally right' and 'morally wrong'. They play different roles in the inferences we make. To see this, consider the following sociological platitudes:

> Many people attach great weight to doing what is morally right and avoiding what is morally wrong. They think that rightness and wrongness should figure in our deliberations in a special way: there are few, if any, circumstances in which they allow other considerations, besides right and wrong, to be given greater weight in their practical thinking. They say: 'It would be *wrong*, and for that reason alone I *should* not do it.' Or: 'I *should* do it, if only because it is the *right* thing to do.'

Notice how 'should' and 'right' operate in these sentences. The rightness of an act is what is referred to in the premiss of their argument; by contrast, the sentence 'I should do it' does not state their argument in favour of doing it, but instead reports the conclusion at which they arrive, on the basis of the consideration that doing so would be right.

'Ought' and 'must' play the same role as 'should'. It is intelligible to ask: 'Doing X is right, but ought I to do X?' So too: 'Doing X is right, but must I do X?' These questions ask whether the rightness of X is a reason, or a strong enough reason, to support the conclusion that I ought to or must do X.

There are, of course, differences between 'should', 'ought', and 'must'. 'Ought', when used in non-moral contexts, sounds stiff. I would not say that you ought to put the bread in the oven at noon;

rather, I would say that you should. But 'ought' and 'should' are interchangeable and equally at home in moral contexts. We say both that the governor ought to resign and that he should resign; these statements are equivalent in meaning and force. I would not understand someone who said, 'Not only is it the case that he should resign; it is also the case that he ought to resign.'

But it hardly needs to be pointed out that 'must' is a term that is more emphatic than either 'ought' or 'should'. If you have a position of authority over me, and you tell me that I must X, then you are not merely advising me to X, as you might be when you tell me that I should X or ought to X; you are requiring me to X. But 'must' has greater strength than 'should' and 'ought' in other contexts as well. Suppose my favourite band is in town, and I ask you whether I should take the day off to see them. If you reply, 'You must', you are urging me to do so with greater force than would have been the case had you instead merely said, 'You should'. (And it would have been a bit odd for you to say: 'You ought to'.) Even so, if you say 'you should' with great force and enthusiasm, your gestures and tone of voice will give your reply a force equivalent to that of 'you must'.

4. 'Moral duty'

The distinction to which I have called attention between the roles played by 'should' and 'morally right' applies to 'moral duty' as well. The fact that one has a moral duty to X can be used to support the conclusion that one should X or ought to X or must X. That one has a moral duty to X is one kind of reason, differing in its nature and weight from other sorts of reasons for acting. So, if Aristotle has beliefs about what one should do (as he no doubt does), it does not follow that his thinking is guided by assumptions he makes about what one has a moral duty to do. His thinking is guided by such assumptions only if he has some grasp of the distinctive kind of reason that is provided by moral duties.

We can describe the duties of an office without meaning to provide the basis for arguing that the person who occupies that office should undertake those duties. One of the duties of a member of the secret police, laid out in its rulebook, might be to torture prisoners. The fact that this is his duty provides no basis for saying that he ought to torture others. But when we say that someone has a duty to X, meaning that it is a moral duty, then we will be taken to mean that there is a reason in favour of his doing X, namely the very fact that X is his moral duty.

If that is what is meant by 'moral duty', and if we decide to read Aristotle as a philosopher who is guided by beliefs about duties (as expressed by means of the word *dein*), then no doubt Aristotle has a conception of *moral* duties. For example, if we take him to mean that he has a duty to preserve the truth, even at the cost of friendship, then what he must mean is that he has a *moral* duty to preserve the truth. After all, he cannot be taken to mean that some social role he occupies—some appointment he has received or office he occupies—requires him to tell the truth. He is not invoking the rules of some institution when he tries to justify his decision to criticize his friends. And so, if his thought is that he has a duty to tell the truth, then his idea is that this is his *moral* duty. Accordingly, the translations of Ross and Crisp are best interpreted to mean: it is better, indeed one's moral duty, to preserve the truth, even at the cost of friendship.[16]

5. Anscombe revisited

Now that we have taken care to distinguish the different roles played by such terms as 'should', 'ought', and 'must', on the one hand, and 'morally right', 'moral duty', and 'morally required', on the other, we are in a better position to make a decision about how to translate *dein*, both in the opening lines of *NE* 1. 6, cited above, but also in the passages where it helps Aristotle express his doctrine that virtue lies in a mean (Sections 7 and 9 below). We are also in a better position to evaluate Anscombe's thesis that Aristotle does not have the concepts of moral rightness, moral duty, moral obligation, and the like.

Her claim, as I understand it, is that Aristotle does not recognize the existence of the special kind of reason for action that people in the modern era speak of when they say: 'you should do it because it is morally right'. Her thesis is not that Aristotle lacks a word that means 'should' or 'ought' or 'must'. The fact that the word

---

[16] Crisp is therefore right to say, in his glossary, that *dein* 'cover[s] many cases of what we would call moral duty'—if it is right to take Aristotle's thinking to be guided by a notion of duty. See n. 6 above.

dein plays an important role in his ethics does not undermine her thesis—provided that 'should', 'ought', or 'must' are the best ways to translate that word. Nor does the fact that Aristotle uses *orthos*, which is properly translated 'right', prove her mistaken. For her claim is that Aristotle does not pick out the special kind of rightness that we distinguish from other forms of correctness and call 'moral rightness'; he is therefore innocent of the idea that there is a special kind of rightness that provides a distinctive form of justification for actions. It is only the generic kind of rightness—the rightness, for example, of a road that will lead one to one's destination—that he recognizes. The specifically moral kind of rightness that he fails to recognize is the one that plays a leading role in non-consequentialist philosophies of the modern era, and receives great weight in the deliberations of those who strive to be 'morally worthy persons' (to use Rawls's words once again).[17]

6. *Dein* in *NE* 1. 6

Let us now return to the point in *NE* 1. 6 at which Aristotle prefaces his critique of the universal good with a remark about truth and

---

[17] It might be thought that even if I am correct in maintaining that Aristotle's use of *dein* does not convey the idea of moral duty or moral rightness, some other word he uses does convey some such idea. But what would that be? Perhaps some will think that his notion of justice is rather close to our concept of moral rightness. I consider that suggestion in sect. 13. Another possibility is that for Aristotle the category of *kalon* (often translated 'fine', 'noble', or 'beautiful') is rather like our category of moral rightness or duty. That proposal can be found in J. Owens, 'The *kalon* in the Aristotelian Ethics', in D. O'Meara (ed.), *Studies in Aristotle* (Washington, 1981), 261–78. See esp. p. 263: 'the notion of the *kalon* carries with it intrinsically the aspect and the force of obligation. . . . It presents itself as something that *ought* to be done. In fact, the Greek term *kalon* and the impersonal *dei* . . . are used interchangeably in the *Ethics*' (his emphasis). He then cites, in a footnote: 2. 3, 1104^{b}10–12; 3. 6, 1115^{a}12; 4. 1, 1120^{a}9–1121^{a}4. But when one looks at these passages, one sees only that Aristotle will often say of one and the same action: one should (*dei*) do it, it is fine (*kalon*); but that he says both does not show that these expressions mean the same. In any case, the idea that being *kalon* is rather close to being morally right or a moral duty is not one that I find plausible. At one point (*NE* 1. 8, 1099^{a}24–31) Aristotle insists that *eudaimonia* and the activities in which it consists should be considered not only the best things (ἄριστα), but also the most pleasant things (ἥδιστα), and the finest things (κάλλιστα). (The same thought is expressed in the opening passage of the *Eudemian Ethics*: 1. 1, 1214^{a}1–8.) Here (and, I think, in many other such passages), one would be at a loss to know what to make of the suggestion that the category of the *kalon* is rather close to that of moral duty or moral rightness. *Eudaimonia* is the most morally dutiful thing? the thing that is most morally right? See too n. 25 below.

friendship. Here again is Crisp's translation of the part of it that is crucial for our purposes (1096^a14–15):

It will presumably be thought better, indeed one's duty, to do away even with what is close to one's heart, in order to preserve the truth.

Ross, as I noted, also uses 'duty' to render *dein*, and Irwin uses 'right'. For all of the subtle differences among their translations (a matter I set aside), they have something important in common: it is natural to take those translations to mean that, according to Aristotle, there are two types of reason in favour of saving the truth, even when this destroys what is one's own. First, it is better for us to do so; second, we have a duty to do so (on the Ross–Crisp reading), or it is right that we do so (on Irwin's). After all, when we tell someone that he has a duty to X, or that doing X is only right, we are offering one kind of reason in favour of X. The Ross–Crisp and Irwin translations imply that Aristotle is doing that sort of thing when he tells his readers not only that it is better to save the truth, but that it is, in addition, a duty, or only right.

Now contrast Rowe's translation of the relevant portion of the text:

But it would seem perhaps better, even imperative, certainly when it is a matter of saving the truth, to destroy even what is one's own.

What is Aristotle adding to his thought when he uses *dein* here? It would make no sense to reply: without it he would have failed to give one of his reasons in favour of saving the truth, namely that it is imperative to do so. That answer would make no sense, because to say that X is imperative is, in effect, simply to say that one must do X. And to say that some action is imperative or that one must perform it is not to offer an argument, even a highly schematic one, in favour of X. When we are searching for reasons in favour of X, we cannot cite, as one of the considerations in its favour, its imperativity, its being something that one must do, its 'must-ness'. (Nor, for that matter, its 'should-ness', its being something that one should do.) When we deliberate about whether to do X, and arrive at the conviction that we must, the fact that we must is our conclusion, not a reason for that conclusion. So, if we accept Rowe's translation, then the most natural answer to the question 'What does Aristotle add to his thought when he uses *dein*?' is: emphasis. When someone tells you, 'It is better to X; indeed, you must!', the second statement does not present a new consideration in favour of X: rather, the speaker is urging you, once again, and with greater emphasis, to X.

There is yet another possibility—one that was suggested to me by David Sedley, and to which I am greatly attracted. The sentence with which *NE* 1. 6 opens, and which immediately precedes the one that we have been looking at, reads: 'It is perhaps better [βέλτιον] to examine the universal [good] and puzzle over how it is said, even though such an enquiry is hard going because it was friends who introduced the forms' (1096ᵃ11–13). It seems to have escaped the notice of recent translators into English (as it escaped mine, until Sedley proposed his reading to me) that the 'better' (βέλτιον) of this opening sentence can be construed in a way that connects it to the 'better' of the next sentence, the one that we have been puzzling over. That is, the passage may be read as follows:

> It is perhaps better [βέλτιον] to examine the universal [good] and puzzle over how it is said, even though such an enquiry is hard going because it was friends who introduced the forms. But perhaps it *is* better [sc. to examine the universal . . .], and one should, for the preservation of the truth, destroy even what is one's own.

The chapter, so read, begins with the thought that it is better to consider the universal good; then notes a drawback of such an enquiry; then perseveres, affirming once again (and emphatically) that it is better to conduct such an enquiry; and then states the general principle that justifies doing so: one should place truth even above friendship. So construed, there is no reason to suppose that *dein* is emphatic, going beyond the force of 'better'. It can easily be construed as the equivalent of the less emphatic modal term 'should'. And if we find, as we shall (Sections 7, 9–11), that *dein* quite frequently means 'should' in Aristotle's ethical works, then there is no reason to read more than that into it here.

But what is most important about Sedley's proposal, for current purposes, is that it provides yet another way of reading the opening lines of 1. 6 in a way that does not have Aristotle offering two different kinds of reasons in favour of persevering with his enquiry into the universal good of the Platonists—one having to do with its being better to do so, the other having to do with its being morally right or a moral duty. So construed, our current passage would offer no support for what Crisp ('it 'cover[s] many cases of what we would call moral duty') or Irwin ('in the right contexts [*dein*] may convey awareness of an unqualified duty') say about *dein*.[18]

If we take Aristotle to be saying that there are two kinds of reasons in favour of saving the truth, one of them having to do with what is better, and the other having to do with what our duty is, or what is right, then we would expect him to show an interest, elsewhere in the *Ethics*, in exploring or explaining these two different kinds of consideration: reasons, on the one hand, having to do with what is good, better, and best; and reasons, on the other hand, having to do with what our duty is, or the rightness and wrongness of actions. At any rate, even if he does not investigate this second kind of reason, we would expect to find a recurring pattern of statements in which he offers two different kinds of consideration for or against various practices: those having to do with good, better, and best; and those having to do with duty, right, and wrong.

But in fact we find no such thing. What we find, on the contrary, is a way of approaching practical reasoning that assumes that all practical questions presuppose, as a starting-point, an understanding of what is good, better, or best. There is no theory of moral duty or moral right and wrong in Aristotle—either an explicit or an implicit theory—because he lacks these categories.

7. A general theory of what one should do

We should remind ourselves of some obvious points about the way in which Aristotle thinks about practical thinking. All deliberation begins from the assumption that something is good, and the process of deliberation consists in seeking a way (the best way) in which we may act so as to realize that good (1. 7, 1097ª15–24; 3. 2, 1111ᵇ26–1112ª13). Deliberation is a process that takes place in every sphere of practical activity: sculptors, cooks, architects— anyone whose line of work involves non-routinized thinking (3. 3, 1112ª34–ᵇ11)—needs to deliberate, no less than those who meet in assemblies and courts in order to resolve questions of war, peace, and justice. Success in deliberation requires a proper grasp of the end around which it is organized: an understanding of health, in the sphere of medicine; of wealth, in the sphere of household management; of houses, in the sphere of architecture (1. 7, 1097ª15–24).

[18] See nn. 3 and 6 above.

One can make some cross-field generalizations about how to succeed as a deliberator, no matter what one's sphere of deliberation
is; but by themselves, these generalizations are nearly useless. One
can, for example, advise the doctor, the head of the household, and
the architect to choose what is intermediate and to avoid excess and
deficiency; but no one would be knowledgeable in these areas if
that were all he knew. Aristotle says in 6. 1 that, somehow or other,
the study of the human good that he is undertaking in the *Ethics*
must go beyond the statements about the mean that he offered in
his treatment of the virtues in books 2 through 5.

When Aristotle makes these remarks in 6. 1, he uses the word
dei:

Since we said earlier that one should [*dei*] choose the mean . . . (1138^b18)

. . . one should [*dei*] work or relax neither too much nor too little . . .
(1138^b28)

. . . one would know nothing more, for example about what sorts of things
should [*dei*] be applied to the body . . . (1138^b30)

No one uses 'right' or 'duty' to translate *dei* in this passage. (Irwin
uses 'must' for the first two occurrences, and 'to be applied' for
the third; Rowe first uses 'must' and then switches to 'should' for
the next two occurrences; Crisp uses 'should' throughout; Ross
uses 'ought', then 'must', and then 'to apply'.) It is easy to see why.
Aristotle is assuming that we think in terms of *dein* in every practical
sphere, and that if we speak at a high enough level of generalization,
we can make the same point about how to answer questions that
involve this term. Just as the doctor *dei* apply medicines to the body
no more and no less than will enable him to restore the health of
his patient, so the sculptor *dei* take away neither too much nor too
little of the block of marble with which he is working. Now, the
sculptor does not ask himself: 'what is my moral duty with regard
to the statue I am trying to make?' Nor does he ask: 'in making this
statue, how can I do what is morally right and avoid doing what is
morally wrong?' He asks: 'what *should* I do (or *must* I do), in order
to make the statue turn out well?'

When we are deliberating in assemblies and courts as citizens, or
when we are trying to decide what to do for our friends and family,
and we use the word *dein* in our reasoning, in an effort to reach
a conclusion about which action *dei* to undertake, we are asking
precisely the same sort of question that the craftsman or technical

expert asks. The word *dein* does not mean one thing when used by a doctor who deliberates and another when used by citizens who are debating matters of war and peace in the assembly. At any rate, Aristotle gives us no reason to suppose that he thinks that the word *dein* is used differently in these contexts. On the contrary, he is at pains to emphasize that despite the great variety of their deliberative projects, each with its distinctive goal, they all have the same structure, share a common vocabulary, and employ a common set of precepts. What *dein* means, in these different contexts, remains the same, just as the terms 'excessive', 'deficient', and 'intermediate' mean the same. So, since the question that must be faced by the sculptor who is trying to deliberate well is not 'what is morally right for me to do?' but rather 'what should I do, in order to achieve the goal of my craft?', the question faced by co-deliberators in the assembly and courtroom is the very same question: not 'what is morally right to do?' but rather, 'what should (or must) we do, in order to achieve the good of our city?' What changes, when we ask questions about justice, friendship, war, and peace, rather than about medicine, sculpture, or poetry, is not the way the word *dein* is used, but the target towards which we look, as we seek answers to questions framed in terms of *dein*. Each of these targets is something good, but when we deliberate about war and peace in the public sphere or about friends and family in the private sphere, our target is the *highest* good, not some goal subordinate to it. Accordingly, our way of translating *dein* into English, and our construal of what it means, should not vary. It cannot mean 'morally right' or 'what is morally right' in the assembly, and 'should' in the workshop.

For Aristotle, the question 'what should [*dei*] one do?' is too general to admit of an answer. It requires a reduction into smaller parts: all questions about what one should do are to be tackled by specifying the sphere in which they are being posed, and that reduction is accomplished by positing some good as the goal to be achieved in that sphere. Once one breaks up the question 'what should one do?' into parts, each part reduced to a more tractable question, one will notice a pattern that emerges: in each sphere organized by its own particular kind of good, one can say that one must hit upon the mean, and avoid excess and deficiency. Further progress in each sphere towards answering the question 'what should one do?' can be made only by achieving a detailed and systematic understanding of the goal around which that sphere is organized.

Just as Aristotle believes that questions about *dein* are best handled by making them specific to some particular goal, so too with questions that involve the term *orthos*, which is universally translated 'right' or 'correct'. We praise a decision, in any sphere of practical reasoning, by saying such things as: 'what he decided to do is what he should do' or, more simply, 'he decided rightly'. So Aristotle says: 'Decision is praised more by reference to its being for what it should [*dei*] be, or to its being correctly [*orthōs*, rightly] made, whereas judgement is praised by reference to how true it is' (*NE* 3. 2, 1112ª5–7).[19] In the sphere of medicine, one decides rightly when one chooses the amount that is intermediate between excess and defect. Similarly, 'virtue is concerned with emotions and actions, things in which excess and deficiency go astray [ἁμαρτάνεται], while what is intermediate is praised and gets it right [κατορθοῦται]' (2. 6, 1106ᵇ24–8; Rowe, modified). He immediately remarks that there are many ways of going astray, but only one of getting it right (κατορθοῦν, ᵇ28–31): that is why being virtuous, like being skilled in any area, is difficult and deserving of admiration and praise.

It should be emphasized that Aristotle never says or implies that there is a special kind of rightness that deliberators must learn about when they meet in the assembly and the courtroom; or that there is one kind of rightness in the political sphere, and a different kind in all other deliberative contexts. Just as *dein* and his terms for excess and deficiency are treated as though they operate in the same way in all of the many deliberative spheres, so too with such terms as *orthōs* ('rightly') and *katorthoun* ('getting it right'). Of course, it is far more important to get it right when we deliberate as citizens than it is to get it right when one is trying to decide how much time to allow the cake to stay in the oven. But we need not say that, according to Aristotle, the difference in the importance of these two

---

[19] This is Rowe's translation. The Greek can also be construed to mean: 'And rational choice is praised for its being of what is right rather than its being correct, while belief is praised for being true' (Crisp). But what sense can be made of that? What distinction could Aristotle be drawing between being right (*dein*) and being correct (*orthōs*)? Crisp's construal of the Greek follows Ross, who makes this attempt to interpret Aristotle's meaning: 'And choice is praised for being related to the right object rather than for being rightly related to it'. Those sound like two different things—but what does that difference amount to? Irwin proposes that four Greek words be dropped, and translates thus: 'Further decision is praised more for deciding on what is right, whereas belief is praised for believing rightly.'

spheres is to be explained in terms of the different kinds of rightness that are involved in each sphere. Political deliberation is far more important, he holds, because it aims at the highest human good, not because it is to be evaluated in terms of a kind of rightness that is peculiar to that sphere.

Aristotle says that spite, shamelessness, grudgingness, adultery, theft, and murder are base (2. 6, 1107^{a}8–13); it is not possible ever to go right (κατορθοῦν) about them; to feel these emotions or act in these ways is already to go astray (ἁμαρτάνειν) (^{a}15–17). But to say that to engage in theft (or commit a murder, or begrudge a neighbour) is to go astray is not yet to put such actions or emotions into a different category from what bakers do when they fail to make good bread, or what sculptors do when they create ugly statues: all of them go wrong, though each in his own way. What makes the adulterer's (or thief's or murderer's) failure to go aright special, and deserving of punishment and dishonour, is that his action pertains not to some minor or subordinate good, but interferes with the political community's efforts to foster the highest good of its members, by violating the laws designed to promote that good. Rightness and wrongness in every sphere of practical activity are explained in terms of success and failure to achieve (perhaps even to aim at) some good.

This aspect of Aristotle's ethics will invite the same sort of criticism that some philosophers, working in the tradition of Kant, make against utilitarianism and consequentialism. Their charge against Aristotle will be that he is working with too simple a conception of the way in which ethical deliberation is structured. For, according to their way of thinking, we must be guided not only by a proper understanding of what is good for this or that person or this or that group of people, but also by a proper understanding of what is morally right—and indeed, considerations that pertain to what is morally right should be given even greater weight than those that concern what is good. If, as we deliberate, we discover that one of the options under consideration would require us to do something that is morally wrong, then that should rule it out, even if it does more good than the other alternatives. Or, if the moral wrong we would do is minor, and we would do a great deal of good by means of this minor infraction, then perhaps we would be justified in proceeding. But in any case, according to this way of thinking, the fact that an act is morally wrong is a serious criticism of it, and it is only in the most unusual circumstances that we would be justified in undertaking it. Those who hold that practical thinking should be structured in this way—paying serious attention to questions of right and wrong, and not merely to questions about good and bad—will accuse Aristotle of offering his readers at most half a moral philosophy: he completely ignores one of the most important factors in practical reasoning, namely moral rightness.[20]

It will not be an effective reply to this critique that Aristotle possesses the concept of correctness, as is made clear by his frequent use of *orthos* and its cognates. For the charge against Aristotle is that he fails to be guided by the special kind of rightness that we call moral rightness. As we have seen, for Aristotle there is no single standard of correctness in action, but rather as many standards of correctness as there are kinds of good at which we aim: what is correct in politics, for example, is that which achieves the good at which politics aims, just as what is correct in medicine is that which achieves the good at which medicine aims. So conceived, correctness is not something that can serve as a substantive guide to deliberation; it is not a source of reasons that are capable of providing a counterweight to considerations of goodness. There is no correctness in medicine that stands apart from the goodness to which the doctor should look; rather, our only way of getting a grip on correctness in medicine is to look to the good that is specific to that field of expertise. So the charge that will be made against Aristotle, by critics of utilitarianism who work within a Kantian framework, is not simply that he lacks a word or phrase that is equivalent to the English words 'morally right'. Rather, it is that his whole way of approaching the subject of practical reasoning leaves no space for the thought that an act that accomplishes some good none the less should not be done because it would be wrong to do it.[21]

---

[20] An even more severe expression of disappointment with Aristotle's project can be found in H. A. Prichard, 'Does Moral Philosophy Rest on a Mistake?' (1912), in *Moral Writings* (Oxford, 2002), 7–20 at 17. Prichard thinks our ordinary consciousness that (for example) it is morally right to pay our debts and tell the truth need not be and cannot be philosophically defended, and that therefore all investigations about what is good are of no moral significance.

[21] That of course leaves plenty of room for noting similarities between Aristotle and Kant—for example, their recognition of our capacity to subject our desires to rational evaluation. That commonality is emphasized by C. Korsgaard in 'From Duty and for the Sake of the Noble: Kant and Aristotle on Morally Good Action',

8. An alternative reading: two targets for deliberation

Is the reading I have proposed the only one that is possible? Let us consider an alternative. Doing so will bring to the fore some of the assumptions I have been making, and (I hope) will add further support to my reading.

Aristotle's opening move in the *Nicomachean Ethics* is to call our attention to the great importance of goodness in our thinking: 'every craft, every enquiry, and similarly every action and decision seems to aim at some good' (1. 1, 1094ᵃ1–2). His thought continues: if so many things aim at good, we had better try to come to a better understanding of what relationship all of these different goods have to each other. Upon reflection, we realize that some are pursued for the sake of others. So we had better see whether there is something for the sake of which all of the others are sought. And we had better come to an understanding of what it is, for if we achieve that understanding, then, like archers, we will be better able to hit our target (1. 2, 1094ᵃ18–24).

But is good the *only* thing we had better understand, if we want to live our lives as they should be lived? Surely not: Aristotle eventually turns his enquiry to a broad array of items that need to be investigated—justice, courage, pleasure, friendship, and so on. Yet there is one term that he does not reflect upon, though he uses it frequently, and that is the term that we have been discussing: *dein*. And even though he does not isolate this term as one that calls for philosophical reflection, it might be said—by someone who opposes the interpretation I have been offering—that his way of using *dein* indicates that it makes room for a way of thinking about actions that is independent of their goodness, fineness, or pleasantness. His way of using *dein*, according to this interpretation, indicates that some actions have the property of being such that we must do them. They have a must-ness or ought-ness or rightness: an imperatival feature that is quite different from their goodness or fineness or pleasantness. Aristotle does not carry out an investigation of this imperatival feature of certain actions, but he indicates by the way he uses the word *dein* that it forms a second target at which our actions should aim. His *Ethics* is devoted to the exploration of only one

in S. Engstrom and J. Whiting (eds.), *Aristotle, Kant, and the Stoics* (Cambridge, 1996), 203–36, esp. 217.

of these targets—the good—but his language indicates that there is another factor in practical deliberation that is equal in importance to the good, even though it is not one that he seeks to understand. According to this way of reading Aristotle, we should think of the *Ethics* as a work whose incompleteness its author would acknowledge: it has omitted a systematic investigation of the imperatival character of actions, in order to focus exclusively on their goodness and badness.

What textual evidence can be offered in support of this reading? Recall Aristotle's statement, which we examined above (Section 6), about the importance of seeking the truth, even when this brings one into opposition to one's friends. One might reject both the translation of Rowe ('perhaps better, even imperative, to destroy') and the proposed construal of Sedley ('perhaps it *is* better [sc. to examine the universal . . .], and one should . . . destroy . . .'), and instead take Aristotle to be offering two independent considerations in favour of preserving the truth: it is better to do so, and it is right (or a duty) to do so. And one might then draw a general conclusion: Aristotle assumes that in order to deliberate properly, one must pay attention to two equally important factors: the question of what is good, better, and best; and the question of what is right or wrong.

But if that passage were offered as the only piece of evidence in favour of the two-target reading of the *Ethics*, it would carry little weight. What the interpretation under consideration needs, in order to become persuasive, is evidence that Aristotle frequently deploys *dein* to express a central thesis, and does so in a way that implies that there is a difference between the goodness of an action and its rightness (that is, its being such that one must do it, even apart from its goodness). And it may look as though we find *dein* used in this way when Aristotle formulates, as he does so many times, his notion that virtue aims at a mean and lies between extremes of excess and deficiency. Consider one example: the generous person, Aristotle says, will give 'for the sake of the fine (*kalon*) and rightly (*orthōs*)' (4. 1, 1120ª24–5). 'For he will give to those whom *dei* and as much [as *dei*] and when [*dei*], and in all of the other ways that accompany right (*orthos*) giving. . . . Someone who gives to those whom it is not the case that *dei*, or does so not for the sake of what is fine [*kalon*] but for some other reason, is not generous' (ª25–9).

This is just one of many passages in which Aristotle uses *dein*, *orthos*, and *kalon* in his discussion of the way in which a virtuous person will deliberate. Impressed with the frequency with which *dein* appears in these passages, Nicholas White comes to the conclusion that there are two independent considerations that Aristotle directs us to take into account when we deliberate. Some of these considerations White, borrowing from Sidgwick, calls 'attractive': under this heading he places whatever is good, or fine, or pleasant. But, White insists, Aristotle is also attentive to a very different sort of reason: these are 'imperatival' notions, such as what one must or ought (*dei*) to do, or what it is right (*orthos*) to do. As White says: 'the virtuous person . . . will think of his action in *both* imperative and *attractive* terms, and will not focus especially on either the one type or the other'.[22] Of course, it is as obvious to White as it is to anyone who reads Aristotle that his ethical theory investigates one of these topics and neglects the other: Aristotle takes it to be a task for ethical enquiry to adjudicate among competing conceptions of good, but he offers no *theory* about which things are imperative or wrong, and what it means for them to have these characteristics. None the less, White would insist, Aristotle's frequent use of *dein* in his discussion of the mean indicates that deliberation and the appraisal of character must take into account what one must do, and not merely what it is good to do. Aristotle's ethical theory, therefore, is incomplete, because it does not subject to philosophical scrutiny every concept that must be employed by the ethical agent as Aristotle depicts him.

I would like to suggest that this way of reading the *Ethics* cannot be sustained, because it conflicts with the most natural way of reading its opening line: 'every craft, every enquiry, and similarly every action and decision seems to aim at some good'. I take Aristotle to be implying that anything worthy of the attention of a practical philosophy reaches out in some way towards an object that is assumed to be good. *Everywhere* we look in our practical thinking, we find ourselves thinking in terms of goodness. That is why he casts his net so widely, listing four types of things that can be seen to be striving for something good. He should not be taken to mean that the examples he gives (craft, enquiry, action, decision) exhaust the practical sphere, and that good is an object of aspiration only in these four spheres. Rather, we should take him to be saying that we could list more features of human life than these, and if we did so, we would discover that they too are a reaching out towards some-

[22] *Individual and Conflict in Greek Ethics [Conflict]* (Oxford, 2002), 118.

thing taken to be good. (The opening line of the *Politics* adds one
more: every association is constituted for the sake of some good.)
Good, then, is chosen as an object of Aristotle's study not because
it is one important topic among others, but because it is unique: it is
the organizing feature of all of human life. The image Aristotle uses
in *NE* 1. 2, drawn from archery, reinforces the idea that good is not
just one important item to be investigated, but one that sits at the
centre of ethical enquiry. We should not forget what an archer does:
as he stretches his bow, he takes aim at one and only one target. So
too, we, in living our lives, have one highest aim, and we are more
likely to hit it if we have a better grasp of what it is. This rules out
the idea that when we deliberate we should think of ourselves as
faced with the task of simultaneously hitting two targets, one constituted by what is good to do, and the other constituted by what is
our duty or what is right or imperative to do.[23]

If further evidence for this interpretation is wanted, we need
only look at the way in which the *Ethics* ends: Aristotle does indeed
say that his project has not yet been completed, but his reason for
saying this, of course, lies in the need for a study of politics and
the way in which cities are best organized. He takes himself to have
settled, in outline form, all of the topics that his students need
to learn—except one, namely, how to put his reflections about the
virtues, friendship, and pleasure into practice (10. 9, 1179ᵃ33–ᵇ4).
He believes that his theory has survived all of the testing to which it
should be subjected (10. 8, 1179ᵃ16–22), and must now be brought
closer to the point at which it can be put into action. Nothing of
the sort would have been said had Aristotle believed that he has
examined only one of the two major targets at which deliberation
must aim.

The proper conclusion to draw, then, is that the reason why the
Ethics contains no examination of *dein* or *orthos* is that for Aristotle
these terms do not designate a single aspect of our lives or a single
feature of our actions. To understand what it is to get things right,

[23] A double-target interpretation similar to White's is proposed by S. Broadie:
she believes that in general the *summum bonum* sought by Greek philosophers is not
meant to provide a 'single . . . standard of rightness'; it allows them to say 'that a
lot of actions are to be done or refrained from simply because they conform or fail
to conform to some familiar principle such as that one has a duty to keep promises
or to show gratitude to benefactors' ('On the Idea of the *summum bonum*', in C. Gill
(ed.), *Virtue, Norms, and Objectivity* (Oxford, 2005), 41–58 at 46). On this reading,
Prichard, 'Does Moral Philosophy Rest on a Mistake?', failed to recognize a kinship
between his own way of thinking about rightness and Aristotle's.

one does not study the single property of rightness, for there is no such thing; what we find instead are a motley of practical spheres in which people with different fields of expertise aim at different types of goal. One studies, in other words, one or another of the various types of good, in order to enhance one's ability to go right in this or that field. Similarly, Aristotle does not make a separate study of *dein*, as he does of virtue, pleasure, and friendship, because no one aims at must-ness or ought-ness or should-ness. One selects some goal that one takes to be good (or one is drawn to it, without ever having decided to seek it), and one draws conclusions about what *dei* to do—about what one must or ought or should do—in the light of that goal and one's understanding of it. The philosophical agenda of those moral philosophers who work in an anti-utilitarian and Kantian framework is rather different. For them, no discussion of ethics can be complete if it omits a treatment of moral duty or moral rightness, because these terms designate a distinctive kind of reason that must be given considerable weight, perhaps even absolute weight, in our deliberations. For them, goodness is only one kind of reason for action, and perhaps not even the most important one; rightness is no less important. There is no such duality in Aristotle, for there is nothing in him corresponding to that modern conception of rightness.

9. *Dein* in the doctrine of the mean

As I noted earlier, Aristotle often uses *dein* when he spells out his idea that virtue aims at a mean and lies between extremes of excess and deficiency. The generous person, for example, will give 'to those whom *dei* and as much [as *dei*] and when [*dei*]' (4. 1, 1120ᵃ25). One might translate: 'to the right people, in the right amounts, at the right time' (thus Ross, Irwin, and Crisp). Or: 'He will give to the people one should, as much as one should, when one should' (thus Rowe). I admit that in the many passages of this sort, all of which use *dein*, it makes little or no difference whether one uses 'right', 'should', or 'ought' to translate Aristotle's *dein*.[24] (I defend this point shortly.) Even so, I believe that 'should' is the better choice, because a translation should not gratuitously use different English

[24] Nicholas White, by contrast, holds that 'right' is not as good a choice as 'ought' or 'must', because it has a weaker 'imperatival' force than they (*Conflict*, 113–14).

words to render the same Greek term. There are other passages that use *dein*, aside from those that announce and apply the doctrine of the mean, and in these passages 'should', 'ought', or 'must' are significantly better choices than 'right', because 'right' would be misleading. We have just examined one of them (our passage from 1. 6), and we shall soon look at several others. If 'should' is the best word for rendering *dein* in those passages, as I think it is, then that is a strong reason to stick with 'should' as our translation of *dein* in passages that express the doctrine of the mean.

It might be asked: 'how can "right" be a misleading translation in some passages, but not misleading in others?' The answer is that when an *action* is called right—when it is said that it is the right thing to do—that could easily be taken to mean that it is morally right, and that failing to do it would be morally wrong. That is the great danger of taking Aristotle to be saying, in defence of speaking the truth even at the cost of friendship, that it is not only the better thing to do, but also the right thing to do. That makes it sound as though he recognizes the rightness of an action as a reason in its favour; in fact, a reason that is of a different sort from, and independent of, the action's relationship to what is good for us. The situation is rather different when Aristotle is made to say (for example) that the generous person will give at the right time. For it is unlikely that anyone will take that statement to mean that the right time for giving is to be determined by asking when it is morally right to give, or that in order to decide when is the right time for giving one needs to consider not just what is good for those involved, but what is morally right as well. When someone tells you that you are not on the right train, you naturally take the wrongness of the train to be a matter of its not going to your destination, or of its being a later train than the one you intended to take. You do not imagine that the rightness of the train has anything to do with morality. Similarly, it is natural to assume that when Aristotle is made to say that the generous person gives at the right time, he means that he gives at those times when his help will actually do some good—namely, when there really is a need for his aid, and the person who is the recipient of generosity really will benefit from some assistance. So long as we take Aristotle to be saying that the goodness accomplished by generous action is what makes certain times the right times for giving, no harm is done by translating *dein* by means of 'right'. But, as I have said, there is no reason to use 'right' when it would be no less accurate to use 'should' instead; and there are passages in which 'should' is by far the best way to render *dein*.

Some people believe that certain types of action should be performed only at certain times of the day, or times of the year, not because otherwise they will fail to do some good, but because there are religious rules that govern the timing of those actions. There is, for example, a religious prohibition against eating certain kinds of food on holy days, because God demands such abstinence. Similarly, there is a religious prohibition against handling money, even to assist others, on such days. If Aristotle were a religious philosopher who advocated obedience to the rules of a divinity, then we might take him to mean, when he says that a generous person will give at the right times, that it is impious and therefore morally wrong to give aid on certain days, and that the generous person will observe these rules. But Aristotle is not that kind of religious philosopher.

In certain circles, it is said that people of a lower social status are not 'the right people', and a stigma might be attached to associating with or helping these outcasts. Now, Aristotle is sensitive to social distinctions between those who are refined or elite (χαρίεντες, γνώριμοι) and the masses, and so it might be suggested that when he says that the generous person gives to those whom *dei* (1120ª25), he should be taken to mean that he gives only to people of high status. In that case, Aristotle's thought would be: one must not give to people of a certain type, not because doing so will fail to be good for them, but simply because these are people to whom it is morally wrong to give.

That would be a far-fetched attempt to defend 'right' as a translation of *dein* when it occurs in expressions of the doctrine of the mean. Aristotle of course does believe that a generous person will not devote his life to helping those who are natural slaves, and will not spend all of his time assisting the poor. But that is because he thinks that there is only so much that can be done to help these people: slaves are helped mainly by having firm masters, and the poor are helped mainly by protecting them from excessively oligarchical political systems. He does not simply label certain sorts of people 'the wrong sort', and he does not conceive of the generous person as someone who puts people into this category simply on the basis of their social status. Rather, he has an elaborate theory about which people will benefit from efforts to aid them, and which people are in the best position to offer these benefits. His conception of which people should be helped derives from his theory of well-being. He does not look to something beyond that theory as a way of deciding questions about who should receive the attention of generous people.

I have said that, for the sake of consistency, 'should' is the best translation of *dein* when that word is used to express the doctrine of the mean. But there is another reason for favouring it. Recall Aristotle's statement that the generous person gives to those whom *dei* (1120^a25). Here we have a third-person singular verb, used impersonally. The closest syntactic approximation to this in English would of course be another third-person singular verb, used impersonally. And that is: 'one should'. To choose 'right' as a translation here is to move away from the structure of the Greek sentence, and to put in the place of that structure an adjectival construction: 'he will give to the right people' takes the place of 'he will give to the people one should'. Nothing is gained by such a substitution, and misunderstanding is risked, for Aristotle is not here making the narrow point that only 'the right sort' (the refined and elite: οἱ χαρίεντες, οἱ γνώριμοι) will receive the generous person's attention, but the more general point that he will give to no one to whom he should not give.

But why not use 'must' for *dei* at 1120^a25, rather than 'should'? In that case, Aristotle will be made to say that the generous person will give to those to whom he must give, and as much as he must give, and when he must give. The reason why we should not take him to be saying this is obvious: in effect, his claim would be that the generous person will give only when the reasons in favour of doing so are extremely strong—so strong that it becomes appropriate to say, not merely, 'you should give', but 'you *must* give'. And there is no reason to attribute that idea to Aristotle. For he says nothing to suggest that the generous person will insist that the reasons in favour of helping others must reach a very high threshold of strength before he will aid them. He describes the generous person as someone who gives with pleasure (1120^a28)—in fact, as someone who might sometimes err by going too far in the direction of giving (1120^b5). Surely it cannot be incorrect to say of Aristotle's generous person that he gives whenever he *should*—and perhaps, occasionally, even when he should not. That statement of course allows it to be the case that he also gives on those occasions when he must—when the considerations in favour of giving are so strong that the highly emphatic 'must' is appropriate. In fact, to say 'one must' entails that 'one should'; and so the cases in which the generous person must give are included among those in which he should give. But 'one should' does not entail 'one must': for it to be case that you should hear a band play, it need only be good *enough*; it is only when they are truly exceptional that you *must* go. And for similar reasons, it would be a mistake to take Aristotle to mean that the generous person will give precisely when he must. He gives more often than that.

That creates a presumption in favour of 'should' and against 'must' in other contexts as well. Since it is clear that *dein* is to be translated 'should' in many passages—all those in which it helps express the doctrine of the mean—then, for the sake of consistency, it is reasonable to use the same term in other passages as well, unless the context provides a convincing reason to suppose that Aristotle is saying something stronger than is conveyed by 'should'.

Were we to survey the whole Greek corpus, we would undoubtedly find passages in which the best translation of *dein* is 'must'. Mathematical passages provide one good source of examples: when a proof is offered for the conclusion that this square *dei* be twice the size of that, only 'must' will do as a translation, not 'should'. But I am not convinced that there are any places in Aristotle's *Ethics* in which 'must' is clearly to be chosen as a translation over 'should'.

10. What the *akolastos* believes

Aristotle says that the self-indulgent or intemperate person (the *akolastos*) has the following belief: *dein* always to pursue the present pleasure (7. 3, 1146^{b}22–3; see too 1151^{a}23, 1152^{a}6). Should we take the *akolastos* to believe that one always *should* pursue the present pleasure? (Thus Rowe; Ross and Crisp use 'ought'.) Or that it is *right* always to do so? (Thus Irwin.)

Before answering this question, let us ask an easier one: should we take the *akolastos* to believe that it is his *duty* to pursue the present pleasure? No one, to my knowledge, has proposed 'duty' as a translation of *dein* at 1146^{b}23. Why not? Because the appeal of pleasure to the *akolastos* is not mediated through some connection

it might have with duty. Rather, his experience of life leads him
to believe that pleasure is the greatest good, and that is why he
pursues it.

If this is correct, then we should realize that it is an application
of a more general feature of Aristotle's thinking: he does not characterize *anyone* as a person who lives in a certain way because he
thinks he has a duty to do so. As Aristotle sees things, someone
who makes health (for example) his highest aim does so because
he has become convinced, whether by his own experience of life
or by listening to others, that this is the chief good. He does not
first become attached to the general idea of doing his duty, whatever that may consist in, and then, at a later point, see a connection
between duty and health. Rather, he somehow becomes convinced
that health is a great good, and so he thinks he should pursue it;
duty does not enter the picture.

The same applies to those individuals whom Aristotle assumes
are well brought up. They enjoy doing fine things, and they are
ashamed at the thought of doing anything unjust, indecent, or
harmful to others. They think of the virtues of courage and generosity as good in themselves. And because these things are so
good, they think they should pursue them. Again, duty does not
enter the picture.

The English word 'duty' names one kind of reason for acting,
and so when we say of someone that he believes that he has a duty
to X, that implies that when he does X, he does so because he thinks
that by X-ing he will be doing his duty. But the Greek term *dein*
does not operate in this way: it does not name one kind of reason for
acting. So, when Aristotle says that the *akolastos* believes that *dei* to
pursue pleasure, he is not ascribing to the *akolastos* any belief about
why pleasure should be pursued. 'Duty' would be a poor choice for
dein here, because 'duty' is a reason-giving word, and *dein* is not.
That is why 'should' is the better choice.

These points about the difference between *dein* and duty apply
with equal force to the difference between *dein* and right. To say
that an act is (morally) right is to give one kind of reason in favour
of performing it, just as to say that an act is a duty is to give one
kind of reason in favour of performing it. So, if we take Aristotle
to be saying of the *akolastos* that he believes that it is right always
to pursue the present pleasure, then we commit him to the thesis
that the *akolastos* is the sort of person who first asks himself, 'what

is the morally right thing to do?', and then proceeds to live a life of pleasure because he takes it that there is a connection between the rightness of an act and its pleasure. But, as we have seen, that is not Aristotle's picture.

The most accurate way to convey what the *akolastos* believes is to say that he thinks that he *should* always be pursuing the pleasure at hand, and he supposes this because he takes pleasure to be the greatest good. The advantage of using 'should' here is that it avoids any suggestion that *dein* by itself conveys a reason, as such terms as 'right' and 'duty' do. To say that you should do something is not yet to say why you should do it. That is the way *dein* works. Unlike 'duty' and 'morally right', *dein* does not play a reason-giving role.

11. Good humour and defective humour

Once we become aware that what one should do and what is morally right do not coincide, because the former is a more inclusive category than the latter, it should become obvious that Aristotle's discussion of the virtues has to do with the broader category, not the narrower one. When he guides us in the assessment of character, the question to which he directs our attention is this: does this person act and feel in the way that he should? He does not, as a modern moral philosopher might, recognize a distinctive subspecies of this question: does this person typically do what is morally wrong, or morally right? His method of classifying defects of character pays attention to doing and feeling something more than one should, or less than one should. He does not have an additional classification scheme according to which some defects involve doing something that it is not right to do, or feeling something that it is not right to feel.

Consider, for example, Aristotle's discussion of the virtue that has to do with social amusements, laughter, games, and play (*NE* 4. 8). We are told immediately (1128ᵃ1) that there are sorts of things one should (*dei*) say, and a way in which one should say them (and similarly for what one should listen to). The rest of the chapter gives illustrations of some of the most common failings in this area. Some people, for example, are eager to raise a laugh on every possible occasion; they are vulgar buffoons who have no regard for what is appropriate, and are insensitive to the pain they cause others (^{a}4–7). Others, at the opposite extreme, say nothing funny, complain about those who do (^{a}7–9), and make no contribution to the sociability that we need in order to relax (1128^{b}1–4).

Is Aristotle saying of certain jokes: it is morally wrong not to laugh at them? Or that we have a duty to laugh at them? It should be apparent that were we to use these words to convey what he is saying, we would be misunderstanding one of the points he is trying to make. There are things that the stiff, boorish person should find amusing. There are innocent pleasures that he could experience, but he misses them; and he never gives others these sorts of pleasures. It would be heavy-handed to say: he has a duty to laugh more often than he does. It would also be heavy-handed to say: it is wrong for him not to laugh. Or: he should laugh at this joke, because it is right to do so. Or: it is imperative that he laugh at this joke. Or: he must laugh at this. Or: he ought to. Of people whose inadequate sense of humour prevents them from appreciating wit one can only say: they should be enjoying that story, because it is funny. 'Should' is the best word to use when we express this sort of criticism; and so it is the best equivalent for Aristotle's use of *dein* in this chapter.

At the opposite extreme is the person who is amused by and laughs at too much. Now, a modern moral philosopher, employing the categories of moral right and wrong, might say that there are some jokes that it is wrong to tell or to listen to, whether or not one finds them amusing (and that if one does find them amusing, one is exhibiting a moral defect). But it would be a mistake to think that the moral wrongness of the jokes someone repeatedly tells is the only possible ground for criticizing his sense of humour. A sense of humour can be defective in all sorts of ways, and only some of them would be counted as moral failings. One can criticize an adult, for example, for having a puerile sense of humour. Or one can criticize someone whose constant punning becomes tiresome, or whose elaborate joking takes up too much of one's time. There are people whose craving to raise a laugh makes them a nuisance. And some people simply are not funny, though they constantly try to be. But we would not criticize any of these types for violating a duty, or acting wrongly. It is only one type of humour—cruel humour—that is wrongful. Once again, it is the word 'should' that is the most useful tool for expressing criticism: some people pun more than they should, or they take up more of our time with their jokes than they should, or they find scatological humour funnier than they should.

All of these defects fit easily into the category that Aristotle carves out in 4. 8 when he discusses those who go to excess in matters that have to do with amusements, laughter, and play. The defects involving excess that he discusses are of several sorts: he points out that some humour causes pain (1128ª7), and the word he uses here (σκώπτειν) refers to the kind of humour that consists in personal attacks ('hoot', 'mock', 'jeer', 'scoff at' are the meanings given by LSJ s.v.). But it is not only humour that causes pain in this way that Aristotle criticizes. Anyone who is undiscriminating in the kind of amusement and humour he enjoys will fall into the category of the vulgar buffoon. Aristotle thinks that the forms of play in which one should engage are those that are characteristic of a free person (1128ª18) who has been educated (ª21) and is refined (ª31), and he believes that such a person will refrain from using or listening with enjoyment to vulgar language (αἰσχρολογία, ª23). If someone asks, 'which of these ways of going to excess does Aristotle take to be morally wrong?', we should reply: 'none of them'. There is no basis for taking him to be thinking in terms of moral rightness or wrongness in this chapter.

On what grounds, then, can Aristotle say that one sort of person gets less pleasure from amusement than he should, and another gets more than he should? What stands behind these criticisms? Aristotle does not answer that question in his discussion of the pleasures of amusement, but presumably that is because he is assuming that all such questions are to be answered by drawing on a proper understanding of the human good. The person who gets little or no pleasure from amusement goes astray in that he fails to do something and feel something that is good for him. He misses one of the good things that human life has to offer. At the other extreme, the person who is excessive in the pleasure he takes in games, humour, and amusement is exhibiting a symptom of his lack of education and refinement: having been brought up poorly, he takes too little pleasure in the part of life that is not a matter of play and amusement, and so he substitutes for them the pleasures of making fun of people and using vulgar language. Aristotle's complaint about vulgar language could not be that using such words is a violation of a moral duty; rather, it is that if this is the sort of thing one enjoys, then there are other and better pleasures that one will be unable to give others and receive from them.

12. The absence of moral rightness
in Aristotle's analysis of the virtues

The point I have been making about Aristotle's treatment of pleasant amusements in 4. 8 should be generalized and applied to his treatment of *all* of the virtues of the soul. Moral duty and moral wrongness do not enter his repertoire of ideas in *any* of those portraits of character defects and virtues. All of his efforts are devoted to locating traits within his threefold scheme of excess, intermediate, and deficiency. Nothing he says in these chapters can be construed as a distinction between faults that involve moral wrongdoing and faults that do not.

For example, a modern moral philosopher discussing anger might say that the expression of anger is morally wrong when it is directed at someone who is not at fault; whereas someone who feels less anger than would be justified is showing a defect of character, but is not exhibiting a moral defect, because there is no wrongdoing involved in feeling less anger than one should. But this is not a distinction Aristotle makes.

Similarly, a modern moral philosopher would say, in a discussion of physical pleasure: someone who gets no pleasure from eating is not doing anything wrong, but someone else who takes pleasure in eating forbidden food (his child's pet cat, for example) is. Or, in a discussion of generosity: if someone asks for and deserves your help, because of the aid he has given you in the past, then it would be wrong to offer him nothing or too little in return; by contrast, if someone volunteers to help the needy but fails to do them any good because he did not realize how much money would be required, he has done nothing that is morally wrong.

According to any modern moral philosophy shaped by the Kantian tradition, the failure of a normal adult to take moral rightness as a reason for action, or to understand what moral rightness requires of us in particular situations, is a character defect of major proportions. That is why it is so important, for philosophers who fall into this category, to distinguish those defects of character that involve a failure to appreciate the demands of rightness from other sorts of defect. For Aristotle, however, there is no such thing as the rightness that provides a reason for action. He does not think of rightness in this way. Everyone, he assumes, aims at going aright (*orthōs*)—that is, hitting the mark at which he is aiming, that mark being something he takes to be good. The mistakes people make when they lack the virtues of the soul are caused by their failure to recognize or fully understand that target. They do not have two tasks—to understand what is right and also what is good—but only one: to understand and achieve what is good for themselves and others.

13. Justice and the priority of the right

Another way to see the gulf between Aristotle and one of the major traditions of modern moral philosophy is to notice a difference between the ways in which Aristotle and Rawls think about justice. For Aristotle, justice is a *good*; by contrast, Rawls puts this virtue into the category of what is *right*. Rawls's way of classifying justice is crucial to his effort to develop a moral theory that is superior to utilitarianism. He holds that individuals must do nothing that violates a principle of rightness, no matter how much good would be accomplished by such a violation: the right always takes precedence over the good, in that it sets the inviolable boundaries within which we are permitted to pursue our ends (93–5). By classifying justice as something that is right, Rawls claims for it the same status in our reasoning as any other species of rightness. That is the point he makes on the opening page of *A Theory of Justice*: 'Each person possesses an inviolability founded on justice that even the welfare of society as a whole cannot override' (3). This does not commit Rawls to denying that justice might also be a good; he can say that if someone's plans take a certain shape, it might indeed be good for him to conform his actions to the principles of justice, and certainly in many cases it will be good for people to be treated justly by their political institutions. But justice is already assured a place in our lives by virtue of the fact that it is right; it does not need to be good as well in order to have a claim on us so powerful that it defeats all other considerations.

By contrast, as I have said, Aristotle thinks of every virtue, including justice, as something that is good; in fact, the virtues of the soul, such as justice, courage, practical wisdom, and theoretical wisdom, are greater than any other kind of good. Now, just as Rawls is not prevented from considering justice to be a good by the fact that it is right (for the two categories are not mutually exclusive), so too Aristotle is not prevented from taking justice to be right by the fact that he assumes it to be good. That invites the question: does Aristotle in fact take justice to be right as well as good?

My answer is: no, Aristotle does not take justice to be right. And the reason why he does not do so is that he does not recognize the existence of such a thing as rightness—that is, *moral* rightness. It is not as though he recognizes the existence of that category, and places certain things in it, but holds that justice does not belong there. Rather, the category of moral rightness is not part of the framework of his practical philosophy. Once we have formulated the distinction between rightness and goodness as Rawls does, it becomes clear that Aristotle works without the former category. Of course, he thinks that one should be just. But that is because justice is a great good, both for the just person and for the community of which he is a part. Nothing in his way of thinking motivates him to give some protection to the claim that justice makes on us by placing it into some category other than that of the good—a protection we could then fall back on for those situations in which justice is not good. He sees no need to look for a different kind of reason in favour of justice besides its goodness, for the fact that it is one of the greatest of goods by itself assures it a secure place in our practical thinking.[25]

By contrast, Rawls has a conception of goodness according to which a person's plans or desires, so long as they are not irrational, determine which things are good for him. That, according to Rawls, is too lax a standard to serve as the foundation of just institutions, and the failure to appreciate this, he thinks, is one of the fatal flaws of utilitarianism. The problem with utilitarianism, he thinks,

---

[25] At this point a critic of my interpretation could try to revive the idea, which I dismissed earlier (n. 17), that for Aristotle the fine (*kalon*) is a conceptual tool for providing just such protection: if an action is fine, it might be thought, then it need not be good, for its fineness is by itself a sufficient reason in its favour. A consideration of that idea would take us far afield, because I cannot more fully discuss Aristotle's conception of the *kalon* here. But I am very doubtful that Aristotle could recommend anything as *kalon* if it were not already something that is advantageous (*sumpheron*) for someone. I consider this issue more fully in '*Agathon* and *Sumpheron*: *Nicomachean Ethics* 1094a1–2' (unpublished).

lies not in what it takes goodness to be,[26] but in its reliance on goodness alone (that is, its maximization) as the basis for all moral relationships, including those established by just institutions. We need to improve upon utilitarianism by turning to the concept of the right, and recognizing the superiority of reasons based on rightness to those based on the good, should the two conflict (as they certainly will, on many occasions). If someone's plans and desires take a certain shape, then Rawls would admit that his doing a certain amount of injustice would be in his interest. No matter: that person's injustice is wrong, and our attachment to justice must be based on its rightness, not on its being part of one's good.

It would be a mistake to think that Rawls's conception of the relationship between goodness and rightness is idiosyncratic, or that it is merely a theory of an academic philosopher who makes no contact with ordinary ways of thinking. On the contrary, his distinction between rightness and goodness, and their relationship to each other, should be recognized as the philosophical elucidation of a point of view that has a deep hold on the common sense of our time and place. According to our common-sense conception of morality, there are some things that we are morally required to refrain from, however much they would be to our advantage, because it would be wrong to do them. They are morally out of bounds, impermissible, forbidden, wrong—even if doing them would help us advance our plans and fulfil our desires. What is good for us is a matter of achieving our aspirations, hopes, desires, and plans; what is right, or a matter of duty, or morally required, is what places restrictions on our pursuit of what is good as we conceive it. The utilitarian tradition proposes that we abandon this ordinary framework, and think instead of rightness as simply a matter of maximizing the good. Rawls's principle that rightness is prior to goodness is not only a theoretician's attempt to develop an alternative to utilitarianism, but also an expression of a distinction that has taken hold in the modern moral consciousness.

As I have emphasized, Aristotle does have some notion of rightness—though not of moral rightness. He would say that someone who acts justly is getting it right ($\kappa\alpha\tau o\rho\theta o\hat{\upsilon}\tau\alpha\iota$)—just as an architect who supervises the successful building of a temple is getting it right. This sort of rightness, as I have said, is the achievement of

---

[26] 'I suppose with utilitarianism that the good is defined as the satisfaction of rational desire' (*A Theory of Justice*, 27).

a good, not a consideration that can compete with and even trump considerations of goodness, as *moral* rightness can.

Nor is the idea that certain types of reason should always be given greater weight than others alien to Aristotle's way of thinking. He holds that no matter how many external resources one might acquire by acting unjustly, or in a way that fails to accord with a virtue of the soul, one must refrain from pursuing or accepting them. But his reason could not be that it would be morally wrong to do so; rather, it is that certain types of good, namely those among them that are virtues, are always better to have than any other types of good. The idea that justice should take priority over other sorts of consideration has been in circulation for a very long time; but the thought that there is something called 'moral duty' or 'moral rightness' that trumps goodness is more recent.

We can none the less recognize some ways in which justice and injustice, as Aristotle thinks of them, have some features in common with the properties of moral rightness and wrongness. We normally accuse someone of doing something that is morally wrong only when his action has an effect on others besides himself, and does something to them about which they would be entitled to complain. Rightness and wrongness are, in other words, inherently other-regarding. For example, most people would deny that failing to take good care of one's teeth is morally wrong, even if they agree that one should, for the sake of one's health and peace of mind, make regular visits to the dentist. Now, Aristotle makes a similar point about justice: he holds that when the term 'just' ($\delta \acute{\iota} \kappa \alpha \iota o s$) is used in its broad sense, it involves doing good to some other person (*NE* 5. 1, 1129^{b}25–1130^{a}13).

Furthermore, he holds that it is not merely one part of virtue, but virtue as a whole (5. 1, 1129^{b}26). It is not entirely clear what he means by this, but perhaps his point is that whenever one acts justly, in the broad sense, one is also, at the same time, exercising some other virtue as well; and when one acts unjustly, in the broad sense, one is also, at the same time, exercising some other defect of character besides one's injustice.[27] For example, when one reacts more angrily than one should, and strikes someone in a situation that calls for restraint and negotiation, one is exhibiting both a vice having to do with proper control over anger and also the vice of injustice, in the broad sense. Justice, so conceived, has a much

---

[27] See my *Aristotle: Political Philosophy* (Oxford, 2002), 118–25.

wider range of application than any of the other character virtues that Aristotle discusses. And in that respect too, it has something in common with our ordinary notion of moral wrongness. For the category of moral wrongness, as we normally think of it, covers an extremely wide-ranging species of acts, including not only injustice but several other kinds of ill treatment of others.

These similarities between our notion of moral wrongness and *adikia* ('injustice') could be taken as grounds for identifying the two notions, i.e. for taking Aristotle's conception of justice and in-justice in the broad sense to be a conception of moral rightness and wrongness. And in fact, 'wrongdoing' is one way in which *adikia* is sometimes translated. But our notion of wrongdoing is closely linked with, and can only be explained by, the distinction we make between going morally wrong and going wrong in other ways. Re-call the point made earlier, in Section 2: if I burn the bread I am baking, I have done something wrong—but not morally wrong. I am not called a wrongdoer, even though I did something wrong, because 'wrongdoer' is reserved for those who do moral wrong. So, our use of 'wrongdoing' and 'wrongdoer' relies on our having the term 'moral', which we use in order to make a distinction be-tween what is morally required and what is merely required by the rules of some institution, and between moral duties and the duties that define an institutional role. Aristotle makes neither of these distinctions. We should not attribute to him beliefs about moral wrongdoing, because there is no basis for using our word 'moral' to describe what he believes. Of course, he does have beliefs about going wrong, just as he has beliefs about going right: the baker who makes a mess of his product goes wrong (ἁμαρτάνει) because he fails to achieve the good at which he aims. But his error is not an injustice, and Aristotle would not accuse him of *adikia*. We would be justified in taking his unwillingness to call a bad baker *adikos* to be an acquittal of *moral* wrongdoing only if we found the word 'moral' to be generally useful as a tool for understanding some of the statements he makes.

14. Teleological and deontological theories

Rawls says:

The two main concepts of ethics are those of the right and the good; the concept of a morally worthy person is, I believe, derived from them. The

structure of an ethical theory is, then, largely determined by how it defines
and connects these two basic notions. Now it seems that the simplest
way of relating them is taken by teleological theories: the good is defined
independently from the right, and then the right is defined as that which
maximizes the good. (21–2)

Later he adds: 'deontological theories are defined as non-teleologi-
cal ones' (26).[28]

That the concept of moral rightness is one of the main concepts
of ethics is, I have been suggesting, a partisan thesis. It will be
endorsed by those who, like Rawls, hold that rightness is no less a
source of justification than goodness. And, for all that I have said,
Rawls may be correct in maintaining that we need the concept of
moral rightness as much as, or even more than, we need the concept
of goodness. But his statement implies that it is common ground
among all moral philosophers that these are the two main categories
with which moral philosophy must work—the only question being
how to connect them to each other.

If we are asked whether Aristotle is a teleologist or deontologist,
in *Rawls's* sense of these terms, the best response we can make is
to say that not every practical philosophy employs the concepts
by means of which he makes this distinction.[29] This objection to
his classificatory scheme is not that his term 'deontological' is defined negatively, and can therefore encompass theories that differ
markedly from each other, in spite of the fact that neither is a

[28] Note how different this is from Broad's use of these terms (*Types*: see n. 10
above). For him, a use of 'ought' is 'teleological' if it is based on the good or bad an act
does, and is otherwise 'deontological'. Maximization does not enter his discussion.

[29] It must be kept in mind, however, that these terms are used differently by
different authors. Here, for example, is W. D. Ross: 'Aristotle's ethics is definitely
teleological; morality for him consists in doing certain actions not because we see
them to be right in themselves but because we see them to be such as will bring us
nearer to the "good for man"' (*Aristotle: A Complete Exposition of his Works and
Thought* (Cleveland, 1959), 184). Ross evidently means by this that, according to
Aristotle, virtuous actions are a mere means to good, and do not constitute a good,
for he immediately adds that the teleological component of Aristotle's theory is
incompatible with the distinction he makes at *NE* 6. 5, 1140^{b}6–7, between action
(which is 'valuable in itself') and production. Note too that if 'teleological' is used
as Broad does (*Types*: see n. 10 above), rather than as Rawls does, then Aristotle
should be classified as a teleologist after all: what one ought to do is always to be
determined by asking what is good or bad about what one does. Aristotle, in other
words, does not use *dein* in the way that Broad labels 'deontological'. It is for that
reason that I claimed (sect. 1) that there is a striking affinity between Aristotle and
teleologists of the modern era.

teleological theory.[30] Rather, it is that not all important practical philosophies should be studied with a view to how they connect rightness and goodness, since some of them either have or need no conception of rightness. It is only one recent tradition of moral philosophy—the one that is inspired by Kant's writings—that is shaped by its conception of the relationship between these two concepts.[31]

15. Limits on doing good

A contemporary philosopher attracted to liberal political ideas is likely to object to Aristotle's political philosophy by pointing out that it never crosses his mind to enquire into the limits of what the state may legitimately do. He simply assumes that if some law or institution will promote the common good of the citizens, then it is appropriate for the decision-makers of the political community to adopt that law or create that institution. For example, since he thinks that the institution of common meals fosters a sense of community, and will therefore serve the good of all citizens, he includes it in his design of an ideal city (*Pol.* 7. 10). It does not occur to him that the city has no business requiring its citizens to eat their meals with other citizens on a regular basis, even if doing so would promote the good of all of them.

Liberal political theory has placed jurisdictional questions at the centre of its agenda: one of the great problems of politics is 'Who should decide?', and it is widely assumed that there are many important questions that each person should be allowed to decide for himself, even if he will make decisions that are contrary to his own interest. A liberal political theorist might be attracted to the deontological ethical tradition precisely because it works with a vocabulary that allows questions about what is good for people to be

[30] I take this to be a point made by J. Cooper: having argued that Aristotle is not a teleologist, he denies that he must be classified as a deontologist (*Reason and Human Good in Aristotle* (Cambridge, Mass., 1975), 88). Cooper's reason for saying that Aristotle's theory is not teleological is that *eudaimonia* is not 'specified independently of virtuous action' (ibid.). He assumes, then, that we should take Aristotle's theory of virtue to be a contribution to our understanding of moral rightness.

[31] The assumption I am criticizing—that rightness is a category employed by all ethical theories, the only question being how it is related to goodness and virtue— is taken for granted by G. Santas, *Goodness and Justice* (Oxford, 2001), esp. 2–3, 259–89.

treated as only one kind of question to ask, and not necessarily the most important kind. When one talks in terms of what is morally required and prohibited, or what is right and wrong, then one can use these terms to claim that the state would be morally wrong to interfere with people's lives, even if they benefited as a result. Excessive paternalism can be condemned on the grounds that it is a violation of the moral limits on state action. One need not show that paternalism is, in general and over the long run, harmful. One can instead say that some things are wrong to do, however good they may be.[32]

I leave aside the question whether the kind of politics to which Aristotle is led by his ethical theory constitutes a significant objection to that ethical theory. But at least this much should be recognized: he does not partition ethical theory into two components, one of which advises us about what we are to pursue on the grounds that it is good, and the other of which places limits on what we should pursue on the grounds that to do so would be wrong. That is why his political theory does not contain a discussion of the limits that must be observed by collective decision-making. He sees no reason why anything that is not itself good should be a boundary on that which *is* good.

Those who, like Rawls, believe that moral rightness is no less important for practical life than goodness arrive at this view because they themselves accept a theory of good that makes that concept too weak to serve as the sole basis for practical justification. What is good, they suppose, depends to a large degree on what we happen to care about; but what we ought to do, in many cases, remains something that we ought to do, whether we want to or not. That is why they think we need something else besides what is good if we are to reason well about practical matters.

This way of arriving at a deontological approach to ethics is only as strong as its theory of well-being. If the subjectivism about well-being that is presupposed by deontologists proves to be a weakness, then the question whether we need the category of moral rightness will require re-examination.

In any case, the deontologist owes us some account of what it is

[32] A rather different approach is advocated by J. Raz. He derives the importance of autonomy (a central notion for any defence of liberal institutions) from a conception of the good of human beings, rather than a theory of rightness. See *The Morality of Freedom* (Oxford, 1986), esp. chs. 12 and 14; and *Ethics in the Public Domain* (Oxford, 1994), 3–176.

for something to be morally right or morally wrong, and how we are to determine whether to put an act into one of these categories. Rightness cannot be defined as the property that an act has when there is a reason to do it other than its being good. There must be some distinctive character that right acts have, one that explains why it is so important to do what is right, even when doing so involves some loss of what is good. When we do what is wrong, we step over a limit or boundary; we violate some constraint. But these are metaphors. A philosophical defence of the importance of rightness must explain why the constraints of the right are not mere taboos.[33]

If we have no acceptable theory of rightness, that by itself would not show that goodness does, after all, play the all-important role in practical reasoning that Aristotle claimed for it. We have to answer the same kind of question about it that is properly asked about right: what is the distinctive character something has when it is good for someone? What about it explains why we are justified in attaching such great weight to it in our practical reasoning? That is a question far more difficult than the one posed here, and must be addressed on another occasion.[34] For now, we must rest content with a modest historical conclusion: though there is much *dein* in Aristotle's philosophy, it is no deontology.

Northwestern University

BIBLIOGRAPHY

Annas, J., *The Morality of Happiness* (Oxford, 1993).
Anscombe, G. E. M., 'Modern Moral Philosophy' ['Modern'], *Philosophy*, 33 (1958), 1–19; repr. in *The Collected Philosophical Papers of G. E. M. Anscombe* (3 vols.; Oxford, 1981), iii. 26–43, and in R. Crisp and M. Slote (eds.), *Virtue Ethics* (Oxford, 1997), 26–44 (citations refer to the 1997 reprint).
Barnes, J. (ed.), *The Complete Works of Aristotle* (Princeton, 1984).
Broad, C. D., *Five Types of Ethical Theory* [*Types*] (London, 1930).

---

[33] The importance of T. M Scanlon's *What We Owe to Each Other* (Cambridge, Mass., 1998) lies precisely in its recognition of the need for such a theory. I am not convinced that the central notion of his theory—what would reasonably be agreed to or rejected—provides a sufficient vindication of rightness and wrongness.
[34] I tackle this issue in 'What is Good and Why: The Ethics of Well-Being' (unpublished).

Broadie, S., 'On the Idea of the *summum bonum*', in C. Gill (ed.), *Virtue, Norms, and Objectivity* (Oxford, 2005), 41–58.

—— and Rowe, C., *Aristotle:* Nicomachean Ethics (Oxford, 2002).

Cooper, J., *Reason and Human Good in Aristotle* (Cambridge, Mass., 1975).

Crisp, R. (trans.), *Aristotle:* Nicomachean Ethics (Cambridge, 2000).

Irwin, T., 'Aristotle's Conception of Morality', in J. Cleary (ed.), *Proceedings of the Boston Area Colloquium in Ancient Philosophy*, 1 (Lanham, Md., 1986), 115–43.

—— (trans.), *Aristotle:* Nicomachean Ethics, 2nd edn. (Indianapolis, 1999).

—— 'Aquinas, Natural Law, and Aristotelian Eudaimonism', in R. Kraut (ed.), *The Blackwell Guide to Aristotle's* Nicomachean Ethics (Oxford, 2006), 323–41.

Korsgaard, C., 'From Duty and for the Sake of the Noble: Kant and Aristotle on Morally Good Action', in S. Engstrom and J. Whiting (eds.), *Aristotle, Kant, and the Stoics* (Cambridge, 1996), 203–36.

Kraut, R., *Aristotle: Political Philosophy* (Oxford, 2002).

—— '*Agathon* and *Sumpheron*: *Nicomachean Ethics* 1094a1–2' (unpublished).

—— 'What is Good and Why: The Ethics of Well-Being' (unpublished).

Owens, J., 'The *kalon* in the Aristotelian Ethics', in D. O'Meara (ed.), *Studies in Aristotle* (Washington, 1981), 261–78.

Prichard, H. A., 'Does Moral Philosophy Rest on a Mistake?' (1912), in *Moral Writings* (Oxford, 2002), 7–20.

Rawls, J., *A Theory of Justice*, rev. edn. (Cambridge, Mass., 1999).

Raz, J., *The Morality of Freedom* (Oxford, 1986).

—— *Ethics in the Public Domain* (Oxford, 1994).

Ross, W. D., *Aristotle: A Complete Exposition of his Works and Thought* (Cleveland, 1959).

Rowe, C. (trans.), *Aristotle:* Nicomachean Ethics (Oxford, 2002).

Santas, G., *Goodness and Justice* (Oxford, 2001).

Scanlon, T. M., *What We Owe to Each Other* (Cambridge, Mass., 1998).

Sidgwick, H., *The Methods of Ethics*, 7th edn. (Chicago, 1962).

White, N., *Individual and Conflict in Greek Ethics* [*Conflict*] (Oxford, 2002).

Williams, B., 'Philosophy', in M. I. Finley (ed.), *The Legacy of Greece* (Oxford, 1981), 202–55.

—— *Ethics and the Limits of Philosophy* (Cambridge, Mass., 1985).

—— *Shame and Necessity* (Berkeley, 1993).

A DIFFERENT SOLUTION TO AN ALLEGED CONTRADICTION IN ARISTOTLE'S *NICOMACHEAN ETHICS*

SHANE DREFCINSKI

IN 'Disunity in the Aristotelian Virtues', T. H. Irwin argues that the doctrine of the reciprocity of the virtues is inconsistent with Aristotle's contention that a person can possess the 'small-scale' virtues of generosity and proper pride without the 'large-scale' virtues of magnificence and magnanimity (cf. *NE* 1122^{a}28–9; 1123^{b}5; 1125^{b}1–26).[1] In short, Irwin's objection is this. If Aristotle asserts that (1) these large-scale virtues are genuine and distinct virtues, (2) a person can be liberal without being magnificent or have the right disposition towards small and medium honours without being magnanimous, and (3) one cannot fully possess any of the moral virtues without possessing all of them, including practical wisdom (*phronēsis*), then his position is inconsistent.

   Michael Pakaluk is one of several scholars who have attempted to refute Irwin's argument.[2] In 'An Alleged Contradiction in the *Nicomachean Ethics*',[3] Pakaluk seeks to resolve this contradiction by arguing against (2). Pakaluk argues that Aristotle's claim that 'the magnificent person is generous, but the generous person is not for all that magnificent' (1122^{a}28–9) need not mean that there are generous people who are not magnificent. Rather, it should be

I am grateful to Norman Dahl, John Van Ingen, J. Hubbard, and an audience at the Annual Meeting of the Minnesota Ancient Philosophy Society for their suggestions and encouragement.

   [1] T. H. Irwin, 'Disunity in the Aristotelian Virtues' ['Disunity'], *OSAP*, suppl. vol. (1988), 61–78.
   [2] Others include R. Kraut, 'Comments on "Disunity in the Aristotelian Virtues" by T. H. Irwin', *OSAP*, suppl. vol. (1988), 79–88; E. Halper, 'The Unity of the Virtues in Aristotle', *OSAP* 17 (1999), 115–43; and S. M. Gardiner, 'Aristotle's Basic and Non-Basic Virtues', *OSAP* 20 (Summer 2001), 261–95.
   [3] M. Pakaluk, 'An Alleged Contradiction in the *Nicomachean Ethics*' ['Alleged Contradiction'], *OSAP* 22 (2002), 201–19.

interpreted to mean 'The power of acting magnificently contains within it already the power of acting generously, but the power of acting generously does not contain within it the power of acting magnificently'.[4] Pakaluk further argues that magnificence is not restricted to the rich, because what counts as a 'great' expenditure is relative to the agent, circumstances, and object (cf. 1122^a24–6).[5] Finally, Pakaluk suggests that there is an analogous relationship between magnanimity and proper pride.[6]

Unfortunately, there are some problems with Pakaluk's solution, especially when applying it to the relationship of magnanimity and proper pride. At 1124^a10 Aristotle claims that the magnanimous person 'will utterly despise'[7] honour from casual people and on trifling grounds. But proper pride concerns honours about 'middling and unimportant objects' (1125^b6); apparently the very sorts of honours that the magnanimous person finds beneath himself. Aristotle also suggests that the magnanimous person does not aim at the things commonly held in honour, but rather holds back unless there is some great honour or great work at stake (1124^b23–6). Furthermore, Aristotle claims that magnanimity is a 'crown of the virtues' because 'it makes them greater, and it is not found without them' (1124^a1–3). This makes sense in cases such as courage and justice. But it is difficult to see how magnanimity could make proper pride greater without transforming it into magnanimity itself, thereby collapsing the distinction between the two virtues. These passages suggest that the magnanimous person is not someone with proper pride, nor is the person with proper pride magnanimous. And if proper pride is related to magnanimity as generosity is related to magnificence (1125^b1–4), then it seems that one can be generous without being magnificent.

In what follows I argue for a different solution. Rather than rejecting (2), I contend that Irwin's alleged contradiction is resolved by rejecting either (1) or (3). *Contra* (1), the large-scale virtues are not distinct from their small-scale counterparts in the same way that, for example, courage is distinct from temperance. Instead, generosity and magnificence are species of the virtue that concerns wealth, and proper pride and magnanimity are species of the virtue

---

[4] Pakaluk, 'Alleged Contradiction', 203.   [5] Ibid. 206–8.
[6] Ibid. 216–18.
[7] This and all subsequent citations are from the Revised Oxford Translation, ed. J. Barnes (Princeton, 1984).

that concerns honours. But if Irwin wishes to maintain that it suffices for (1) that the large- and small-scale virtues be distinct species, then (3) is false. Aristotle's doctrine of the reciprocity of the virtues does not require that one have all of the species of the moral virtues and all of the species of practical wisdom. Therefore, Aristotle's ethical theory is not inconsistent in the way that Irwin alleges.

In order to defend Aristotle against Irwin's charge of inconsistency, we first must recognize an ambiguity in his claim that the large-scale virtues are genuine and distinct from their small-scale counterparts. Given Aristotle's various remarks about a variety of virtues, there are at least two ways in which virtues can be distinct. First, the virtues may be distinct in the way in which courage is distinct from temperance and practical wisdom is distinct from scientific knowledge (*epistēmē*). Let us, mindful that what count as genus and species are at least partly relative to a level of analysis, call these virtues 'generically distinct'. A second way in which the virtues may be distinct is illustrated by the differences between legislative wisdom (*nomothetikē*) and political wisdom (*politikē*). These two virtues are types of the kind of wisdom that is concerned with the city. Aristotle claims that the former plays a controlling part—apparently by framing the laws of the state. The latter, which concerns decrees, is related to it as particulars to their universals (1141^{b}23–8). Since these virtues are subgroups of a virtue—practical wisdom—which itself is generically distinct from other intellectual virtues, let us describe them as 'specifically distinct'.

Given this distinction, I make the following assumption: at the generic level, Aristotle distinguishes distinct moral virtues on the basis of their proper subject matter, i.e. on the basis of the actions and passions which are proper to each virtue (cf. 1115^{a}4–5). So courage is distinct from temperance because the actions and passions associated with courage (roughly, standing firm in the right ways in the face of dangers that evoke feelings of fear and confidence) are formally distinct from the actions and passions associated with temperance (roughly, refraining from or partaking of the right ways of the pleasures of the table and bedroom).

Do the large-scale and small-scale virtues have distinct, proper subject matters in the same way that courage and temperance differ from each other? Certainly the actions of the large and small-scale virtues, if they are described rather precisely, are different. Unlike generous people, magnificent people spend large sums of money, often for public benefit. Unlike people with proper pride in areas worthy of small honour, the domain of magnanimous people involves great deeds. Furthermore, if the processes of habituation are described rather precisely, then, as Irwin emphasizes, the kind of habituation required to develop each of these virtues is also different. Generous people who suddenly acquire great sums of money will not automatically know how to use their new resources to finance large-scale projects. They will need further training in order to develop the virtue of magnificence and will probably make mistakes along the way.[8]

Nevertheless, the passions that each pair of virtues is concerned with are clearly the same. Both generous people and magnificent people have the appropriate desire for wealth; their desire for this external good is neither excessive nor deficient. Unlike miserly and niggardly people, who are fond of acquiring money but are pained by spending it (cf. 1120^a30-1; 1121^b11-17; 1123^a27-31; *EE* 1233^b1- 6), they experience the appropriate amount of pleasure in giving money to others (cf. 1120^a27-8; 1120^b30; 1122^b8; *EE* 1231^b27-32; 1233^a31-8). Unlike the prodigal and the vulgar, who take excessive pleasure in spending (cf. 1121^a8-9; 1123^a18-26; *EE* 1233^a38-^b1), they are pleased and pained in the right way by their expenditures (1121^a3-4).[9] Likewise, both magnanimous people and people with proper pride have the appropriate desire for honour and take the appropriate pleasure in receiving honour (cf. 1124^a5-6; $1125^b7, 20-$ 1; *EE* 1232^b10-13).[10] On the other hand, unduly humble people and unambitious people do not desire the honour that they deserve (1125^a19-23; $^b10, 19$; *EE* 1233^a13-15), whereas the vain and the ambitious desire honour excessively (1125^a28-32, $^b9-10, 19$; *EE* 1233^a10-12).

Moreover, because those with the small-scale virtues have the appropriate desires concerning wealth and honour, they are quite capable of making the transition to the corresponding large-scale

---

[8] See Irwin, 'Disunity', 63–5.

[9] Aristotle even claims that generous people are pained if they spend in a manner contrary to what is right and noble (1121^a1-2).

[10] This point is more clearly expressed in Aristotle's discussion of proper pride than in his discussion of magnanimity. For Aristotle delineates the virtue and vices that deal with small honours on the basis of appropriate, excessive, and deficient desire for honour (1125^b7-11), whereas he delineates the virtue and vices that deal with great honour on the basis of one's true or false assessment of the honour that one deserves (1123^a37-^b14).

virtues. This point is clearly made in Aristotle's discussion of magnanimity in the *Eudemian Ethics*. In the Eudemian account he does not name the character state that concerns small honours and he does not treat it as a virtue. But he denies that this character state is either a blameworthy trait or that it is opposed to magnanimity, for it gives rise to actions as reason directs (*EE* 1233ᵃ17–22). Moreover, the person with this character state is 'in fact, similar in nature to the magnanimous man; for both think themselves worthy of what they really are worthy of' (*EE* 1233ᵃ23–4). Aristotle adds that this person 'might become magnanimous, for of whatever he is worthy he will think himself worthy' (*EE* 1233ᵃ25). Hence, while I concede Irwin's contention that people with the small-scale virtues will not automatically exhibit the large-scale virtues when their circumstances change, we must be careful not to exaggerate the difficulties involved. The newly wealthy and the novices in the area of great honour may make mistakes in their attempts to exhibit magnificence and magnanimity. But their mistakes will not be due to disordered desires and so will be dissimilar to the vicious deeds of the vulgar, niggardly, vain, and unduly humble.[11] On the other hand, those who lack the small-scale virtues are more likely to struggle with disordered desires for wealth or honour. Consequently, it is easier for those who have the small-scale virtues to develop their large-scale counterparts than it is for those who entirely lack the small-scale virtues.

Now in order for the large- and the small-scale virtues to be generically distinct, it is not enough that they involve actions and types of habituation which, when rather precisely described, are different. They must also involve different kinds of passions. But magnificence and generosity both deal with desires for wealth, and magnanimity and proper pride both deal with desires for honour. Therefore, these large-scale virtues are not generically distinct from their small-scale counterparts in the way in which courage is distinct from temperance.

But if the large and small-scale virtues are not generically distinct, then how are they related? Aristotle does not provide a clear answer to this question; indeed, he may not have clearly thought

---

[11] Moreover, since they presumably also have practical wisdom, they will recognize their own deficiencies and so will seek the counsel of those with experience. For example, generous people who are newly rich will not attempt to finance a grand project without advice from those who have knowledge in that area.

about this question at all. Consequently, any answer will require some conjecture and there is no guarantee that the same answer will apply to both pairs of virtues. My own view is that there are solid Aristotelian grounds for understanding generosity and magnificence as two species of the generic moral virtue that concerns wealth and magnanimity and proper pride as two species of the generic moral virtue that pertains to the desire for honour.

My interpretation becomes more plausible if there are any indications elsewhere that Aristotle holds that some virtues are species of others. There are at least two examples of just such an arrangement. One occurs in Aristotle's discussion of justice (*NE* 5 = *EE* 4). After distinguishing between general and particular justice, where the former corresponds to the sense of justice that is lawfulness and the latter corresponds to the sense of justice that is fairness (cf. $1129^{a}26-34$), Aristotle distinguishes two forms of particular justice—distributive and rectificatory justice. He notes that the first kind (*eidos*) of justice concerns the distribution of goods such as honour or money among the citizens of a state. The other kind concerns the rectification of transactions between individuals ($1130^{b}30-1131^{a}1$).

A second example occurs in Aristotle's discussion of practical wisdom (*NE* 6. 8 = *EE* 5. 8), where he divides practical wisdom into individual, domestic, legislative, and political. They all share a common subject matter in so far as they all involve actions with regard to the things that are good or bad for human beings as such (cf. $1140^{b}5-6$). Aristotle begins with the remark that political wisdom and practical wisdom are the same character state but their essence is not the same ($1141^{b}23$). Following Aquinas, I understand Aristotle to be distinguishing a form of practical wisdom which pertains to political matters and deals with things that are good or bad for the whole society from practical wisdom itself, which principally deals with things that are good or bad for oneself (cf. $1141^{b}29-30$).[12] Political wisdom is in turn divided into legislative wisdom, which frames the laws of the society, and another form of political wisdom that deals with the implementation of laws and with decrees. This species also goes by the name 'political wisdom' ($1141^{b}24-8$) and it in turn is divided into a deliberative and a judicial

[12] See St Thomas Aquinas, *Comm. on NE*, ##1196–1201; *ST* II-II, q. 50, aa. 1–2. H. Rackham offers an alternative interpretation in his comments in the Loeb translation (Cambridge, Mass., 1934), 346 note c.

part (1141^{b}32).[13] Aristotle further contrasts political wisdom and practical wisdom with a domestic wisdom that deals with household management (1141^{b}31). In sum, he distinguishes three species of practical wisdom: individual, domestic, and political. The third kind in turn is divided into two forms: legislative and political.[14]

On the basis of these examples Aristotle clearly holds that some virtues are species of others and that these species share a common subject matter with the generic virtue in question. Since he applies this distinction to justice and practical wisdom, it is reasonable to think that the same distinction can be extended to the large- and small-scale virtues. Aristotle does not explicitly describe the large- and small-scale virtues as species of a common specific virtue. But this thesis does help make sense of his clearest statement on the relation of the large- and small-scale virtues, which comes at the beginning of his discussion of proper pride in *NE* 4. 4. Aristotle writes:

There seems to be in the sphere of honour also, as was said in our first remarks on the subject, a virtue which would appear to be related to magnanimity as liberality [generosity] is to magnificence. For neither of these has anything to do with the grand scale, but both dispose us as is right with regard to middling and unimportant objects; as in the getting and giving of wealth there is a mean, and an excess and a defect, so too honor may be desired more than is right, or less, or from the right sources and in the right way. (1125^{b}1–8)

Within the same subject matter, one species of the virtue which concerns wealth, viz. generosity, is restricted to the giving and receiving of wealth on a small scale and another species, viz. magni-

---

[13] Aquinas understands this division to apply to both legislative and political wisdom (see *Comm. on NE*, #1199) but this does not seem to be warranted by the text.

[14] If we turn to Aristotle's accounts of the vices associated with generosity and mildness, we find further examples of a division of a character trait into various species. In the *Eudemian Ethics*' discussion of prodigality and illiberality Aristotle notes, 'There are also species of these genera which exceed or fall short as regards parts of the subject matter of generosity, e.g. the sparing, the skinflint, the grasper at disgraceful gain, are all illiberal' (*EE* 1232^{a}10–12). After describing each species (*EE* 1232^{a}13–15), he proceeds to divide prodigality into those who are wasteful through their disorderly expenditures and those fools 'who cannot bear the pain of calculation' (*EE* 1232^{a}16–18). In Aristotle's discussion of irascibility, which is the vice of excess that concerns anger, he notes that since one can get angry with the wrong people, at the wrong times, more than is right, too quickly, or too long, there are several types of irascibility: hot-headedness, being choleric, sulkiness, and bad-temperedness (1126^{a}9–10, 13–26).

ficence, deals with the giving and receiving of wealth on a grand scale. Similarly, one species of the virtue which concerns honour, viz. proper pride, is restricted to the desire for honour on a smaller scale and another species, viz. magnanimity, deals with the desire for honour on a grand scale.

Moreover, this thesis also explicates Aristotle's account of generosity. Many of his comments about generosity are not restricted to a specific virtue that concerns wealth in 'middling and unimportant' matters. For example, Aristotle notes that generosity is concerned with the acquisition and expenditure of wealth (1120^a5– 22; *EE* 1231^b28); he does not indicate that it is limited only to the acquisition and expenditure of wealth in small matters. He also argues that since everything is used best by the people who have the virtue concerned with it, riches are used best by generous people (1120^a6–7). Generous people spend according to their substance and on the right objects, 'alike in small things *and in great*' (1120^b25, 29–30). These remarks clearly indicate that there is a sense of generosity whose scope is not limited to wealth used in small affairs. Thus, although Aristotle does not explicitly mention a generic moral virtue which concerns wealth and which is divided into the species of generosity and magnificence, the supposition that there is one helps account for his remarks about generosity which do not restrict the scope of this virtue to small affairs.[15]

One move remains open to Irwin. Since these large-scale virtues are not generically distinct from their small-scale counterparts, in order for Irwin's objection to stick, Aristotle's ethical doctrine must require that one possess all of the species of moral virtues and all of the species of practical wisdom in order to be fully virtuous and, consequently, in order to be happy. But Aristotle clearly does not require this.

First of all, two such species are distributive justice and political wisdom. Now both of these virtues require a certain amount

---

[15] My thesis also offers an alternative to Pakaluk's treatment of Aristotle's claim that although generous people are not necessarily magnificent, magnificent people are also generous (1122^a28). The remark might mean that magnificent people have both of the species of virtues that concern wealth, whereas those who are generous have only one. Or it might mean that there is a specific virtue concerning wealth which is also called 'generosity'. Both the magnificent and the small-scale generous have this virtue but the magnificent also have a specific virtue that deals with grand matters.

of political power for their exercise. A private person who lacks the authority to ordain laws or issue decrees cannot exhibit distributive justice, the virtue which is manifested in distributions of goods such as honour or money to citizens, or political wisdom, the virtue which concerns the wise ordering of society. But in *NE* 10. 8 Aristotle explicitly denies that one needs to be in a position of political power in order to be happy: 'we can do noble acts without ruling earth and sea; for even with moderate advantages one can act virtuously' (1179^a5-6). Hence, one need not possess the virtues of distributive justice and political wisdom in order to be happy.[16] And since one must be fully virtuous in order to be happy, one need not possess these species of particular justice and practical wisdom in order to be fully virtuous.

Of course, one might worry that Aristotle thinks that happiness none the less requires the specific virtues of magnificence and magnanimity. His subsequent remarks in *NE* 10. 8 resolve that worry. Aristotle cites with approval the remarks of Solon, who describes the happy man as someone 'moderately furnished with the externals' who yet performs the noblest acts and lives temperately; 'for one can with but moderate possessions do what one ought' (1179^a10-12). Aristotle next cites Anaxagoras, who suggests that 'the happy man need not be rich or a despot' (1179^a13-15). Clearly magnificence is not required in order to be happy and, it seems, neither is magnanimity. Since one must be fully virtuous in order to be happy, these large-scale virtues are not required in order to be fully virtuous. As a result, the doctrine of the reciprocity of the virtues should be understood to require, at most, that along with practical wisdom one possess every generic moral virtue and, in cases where there are species, at least one of those species.[17] But the doctrine does not require one to possess every species of these

---

[16] This is not to say that a person who lacks one of the species of the generic moral virtues can possess a vice associated with that specific virtue. Nor do I deny that, on Aristotle's view, in an ideal state all citizens should have an opportunity to govern as well as be governed, and so have an opportunity to develop and exhibit political wisdom and distributive justice; cf. *Pol.* 7. 14

[17] Judging from the paucity of remarks concerning those moral virtues that have species, it seems that Aristotle expects those who have the generic moral virtue in question also to possess one of its species. So, for example, the possession of the generic virtue which concerns the desire for wealth would involve possessing at least one of its species, e.g. generosity. Similarly, the possession of particular justice would involve possessing at least one of its species, e.g. rectificatory justice.

moral virtues.[18] Interpreted in this way, Aristotle is not guilty of the inconsistency that Irwin alleges.

University of Wisconsin—Platteville

BIBLIOGRAPHY

Aquinas, St Thomas, *Commentary on Aristotle's* Nicomachean Ethics, trans. C. I. Litzinger (Notre Dame, Ind., 1993).
—— *Summa Theologiae*, trans. the Fathers of the English Dominican Province (2 vols.; New York, 1947).
Aristotle, *Revised Oxford Translation of the Complete Works of Aristotle*, ed. J. Barnes (Princeton, 1984).
—— *Nicomachean Ethics*, trans. H. Rackham (Cambridge, Mass., 1934).
Gardiner, S. M., 'Aristotle's Basic and Non-Basic Virtues', *OSAP* 20 (Summer 2001), 261–95.
Halper, E., 'The Unity of the Virtues in Aristotle', *OSAP* 17 (1999), 115–43.
Irwin, T. H., 'Disunity in the Aristotelian Virtues' ['Disunity'], *OSAP*, suppl. vol. (1988), 61–78.
Kraut, R., 'Comments on "Disunity in the Aristotelian Virtues" by T. H. Irwin', *OSAP*, suppl. vol. (1988), 79–88.
Pakaluk, M., 'An Alleged Contradiction in the *Nicomachean Ethics*' ['Alleged Contradiction'], *OSAP* 22 (2002), 201–19.

[18] In this respect, I agree with Gardiner's thesis in 'Aristotle's Basic and Non-Basic Virtues'. Gardiner maintains that basic virtues are required for being unconditionally good, and the doctrine of the reciprocity of the virtues applies to them. Non-basic virtues, on the other hand, are not required for being unconditionally good, and the doctrine of the reciprocity of the virtues does not apply to them. Gardiner argues that magnanimity and magnificence are non-basic virtues because they are not required for being unconditionally good. Rather, each virtue governs an essentially relative good: 'magnanimity requires being *relatively* rich, and magnanimity requires having *relatively* higher capacities' (278). While I agree with Gardiner, I am concerned that he leaves the relation between the 'basic' and 'non-basic' virtues underdeveloped. Are the non-basic virtues mere addenda to the basic? Or are they species of the basic virtues, as I argue?

ARISTOTLE ON ACTING UNJUSTLY WITHOUT BEING UNJUST

GILES PEARSON

IN this paper I want to consider a distinction Aristotle draws in book 5 of the *Nicomachean Ethics*. The distinction falls within his account of particular injustice. Recall, Aristotle claims that both (i) the lawless man (ὁ παράνομος) and (ii) the grasping (πλεονέκτης) and unequal man are unjust (*NE* 5. 1, 1129ᵃ32–3). The kind of justice that corresponds to the first kind of injustice relates to complete virtue (ἀρετὴ τελεία), at least in so far as this concerns our relations to another (πρὸς ἕτερον) (5. 1, 1129ᵇ26–7), since

> [t]he law bids us perform both the acts of a brave man (e.g. not to desert our post or take to flight or throw away our arms), and those of a temperate man (e.g. not to commit adultery or outrage), and those of a good-tempered man (e.g. not to strike another or speak evil), and similarly with regard to the other virtues and forms of wickedness, commanding some acts and forbidding others. (5. 1, 1129ᵇ19–24)[1]

Thus, on this notion, 'what, as a relation to others, is justice is, as a certain kind of state without qualification, virtue' (1130ᵃ12–13). On this specification, there is no characteristic motive that picks out unjust acts; they are simply vicious acts more generally. This is in contrast to the injustice that corresponds to the other kind of justice, which picks out *a part* of virtue (5. 2, 1130ᵃ14). Aristotle contrasts the two as follows:

© Giles Pearson 2006

I wish to thank Arif Ahmed for extremely helpful written comments and subsequent discussion on an earlier draft. A version of this paper was read to the philosophy faculty at Edinburgh University in April 2005. Thanks especially to Michael Ridge, Mathew Nudds, and Theodore Scaltsas for their questions. I would also like to thank David Sedley for very helpful comments on an earlier version of the paper submitted to this journal, and David Charles for help with a late correction.

[1] Translations are, unless otherwise stated, based on those in *The Complete Works of Aristotle: The Revised Oxford Translation*, ed. J. Barnes (Princeton, 1984), with a number of emendations of my own.

while the man who exhibits in action the other forms of wickedness acts unjustly but not graspingly [πλεονεκτεῖ] (e.g. the man who throws away his shield through cowardice or speaks harshly through bad temper or fails to help someone with money through meanness), when a man is grasping [πλεονεκτῇ], he often exhibits none of these vices—and certainly not all together, but does exhibit wickedness of some kind (for we blame him) and injustice. (1130ᵃ16–22)

Aristotle thinks that this other kind of injustice is a part of injustice in the broad sense of contrary to the law (1130ᵃ23–4), and he here demarcates the unjust agent in this particular sense by reference to whether or not that agent is 'grasping' (πλεονεκτικός). This, in turn, is explained by reference to whether or not the agent in question is motivated by gain:

if one man commits adultery for the sake of gain [τοῦ κερδαίνειν ἕνεκα], and makes money by it, while another does so at the bidding of appetite [δι᾽ ἐπιθυμίαν] though he loses money and is penalized for it, the latter would be held to be self-indulgent rather than grasping [πλεονέκτης], while the former is unjust not self-indulgent. Clearly, therefore, [he is unjust] because [he acts] for the sake of the gain [διὰ τὸ κερδαίνειν]. (*NE* 5. 2, 1130ᵃ24–8)

Now Aristotle's specifying the narrow kind of injustice in this way has caused a lot of dispute.[2] My aim here is to sort out one crucial issue with respect to this narrow notion of injustice, concerning Aristotle's distinction between unjust acts that are reflective of the agent performing the act and unjust acts that are not reflective in

---

[2] For example, it has been debated (i) whether or not Aristotle's account really enables him to distinguish particular injustice from other vices as he seems to think it does; (ii) whether he can sensibly think that particular justice is a mean; and (iii) what sense can be given to the notions that the *pleonekt* man wants more and that particular injustice is connected to the desire for gain. See e.g. B. Williams, 'Justice as a Virtue', in A. O. Rorty (ed.), *Essays on Aristotle's Ethics* (Berkeley, 1980), 189–99; C. M. Young, 'Aristotle on Justice', *Southern Journal of Philosophy*, 27, suppl. (1988), 233–49; D. O'Connor, 'Aristotlelian Justice as a Personal Virtue' ['Justice as a Personal Virtue'], *Midwest Studies in Philosophy*, 13 (1988), 417–27; H. J. Curzer, 'Aristotle's Account of the Virtue of Justice' ['Virtue of Justice'], *Apeiron*, 28.3 (1995), 207–38; S. E. Foster, 'Virtues and Material Goods: Aristotle on Justice and Liberality' ['Justice and Liberality'], *American Catholic Philosophical Quarterly*, 71.4 (1998), 607–19; D. Sherman, 'Aristotle and the Problem of Particular Injustice' ['Problem of Particular Injustice'], *Philosophical Forum*, 30.4 (1999), 235–48; S. Drefcinski, 'Aristotle and the Characteristic Desire of Justice' ['Characteristic Desire of Justice'], *Apeiron*, 33.2 (2000), 109–23, D. Bostock, *Aristotle's Ethics* (Oxford, 2000), ch. 3; and R. Kraut, *Aristotle: Political Philosophy* [*Political Philosophy*] (Oxford, 2002), ch. 4.

this way. As I see it, Aristotle's account of non-reflective unjust acts has in particular been much misunderstood. Most notably, Bernard Williams argued that there was a straightforward flaw in the way Aristotle was prone to understand such acts.[3] The argument of this paper will not only show that Aristotle's account is not flawed in this way, it will also explain how his view is in fact rather subtle and well worth considering in greater detail.

I

It will be instructive to begin by considering Williams' interpretation in greater detail. He thinks that Aristotle is prone to hold the view that an unjust act in the particular sense must always be motivated by the desire for gain. And Williams argues that such a view is straightforwardly wrong:

To take Aristotle's paradigmatic distribution case, a person could on a particular occasion, be overcome by hopes of sexual conquest, or malice against one recipient, and so knowingly make an unjust distribution, and his act would surely be an unjust act. (191)

I agree, but in the sense of 'unjust act' that Williams is referring to, I do not think that Aristotle believes that an unjust act must be motivated by the desire for gain. What is this sense? Williams draws a distinction between two types of act. With respect to some undesirable characteristic V, there are intentional acts that are

(A) V acts but are not the acts of a V person

and

(B) both V and the acts of a V person.

There can, for example, be cowardly acts performed by agents who are not really cowards—the act, though intentional, was not reflective of their general character—and there can be acts that are both cowardly and performed by someone who is in fact a coward. Williams rightly takes this distinction to be Aristotle's. At the beginning of book 5, chapter 6,[4] Aristotle writes:

---

[3] 'Justice as a Virtue'.
[4] The passage seems to be in the wrong place. It could perhaps work at the very beginning of *NE* 5. 8.

Since acting unjustly does not necessarily imply being unjust, we must
ask what sort of unjust acts imply that the doer is unjust with respect to
each type of injustice, e.g. a thief, an adulterer, or a brigand. Surely the
answer does not turn on the difference between these types. For a man
might even lie with a woman knowing who she was, but the origin of this
act might be not choice but passion. He acts unjustly, then, but is not
unjust; for example, a man is not a thief, yet he stole, nor an adulterer, yet
he committed adultery; and similarly in all other cases. (1134^a17–23)

Aristotle's distinction is precisely the one Williams formulates. We
can perform a V act (unjust, thieving, adulterous, etc.) without
being a V person. And, as the passage indicates, and Williams also
acknowledges (190), a condition for an act to be a (B) unjust act
for Aristotle is that it is chosen (see e.g. *NE* 3. 2, 1111^b5–6; 3. 2,
1112^a1–2; 6. 2, 1139^a31–5). So far, so good. Now, however, comes
the problem. Williams thinks that Aristotle is prone to the view
that an (A) unjust act must be motivated by the desire for gain
(191).[5] And it is this that he finds objectionable about Aristotle's
account. Surely an (A) unjust act can be motivated by desire for
sexual pleasure, or malice, or anger, or whatever. Why should we
think that an (A) unjust act *must* be motivated by the desire for gain?

I agree this would be odd, but I do not think it is Aristotle's
view. So much, I believe, is clear from *NE* 5. 8.[6] In this chapter
Aristotle is still considering injustice in the narrow or particular
sense. This is clear from the end of the chapter, which is plainly
one continuous argument, when he states that if an agent chooses
to perform an unjust act, then the act implies the agent is an unjust
man, 'provided', he immediately notes, 'the act violates proportion
or equality' (1136^a1–3). We have already seen that Aristotle reserves
violations of equality, as opposed to law, for injustice in the narrow
sense, and the notion of proportion is of course central to how

<hr>

[5] Williams thinks that Aristotle is 'disposed' to accept a 'standard model' (192)
linking (A) and (B) acts for some V, which maintains that both have the same
motive. And he thinks that Aristotle is 'certainly tempted by his standard model'
(192) in the case of particular injustice. I contest both these claims. I argue below
that in one of the passages Williams cites (*NE* 5. 2, 1130^a24–32) Aristotle is actually
referring to type (B) unjust acts, not their type (A) counterparts. Equally, at the
end of sect. 1, I argue that Aristotle in general does not hold Williams's proposed
'standard model'. In the light of these points, and given the especially clear *NE* 5. 8,
1135^b19–25, discussed below, the other passage that Williams adduces (*NE* 5. 9,
1136^b34–1137^a3) should probably be understood in the way I suggest in n. 8.

[6] Though Williams (190) mentions *NE* 5. 8, he appears not to notice the crucial
passage that undermines his interpretation (1135^b19–25, quoted below).

he spells out the (in)equality of particular (in)justice in *NE* 5. 3 and 5. 4. So Aristotle here emphasizes that in this chapter he is concerned with acts of injustice in the narrow or particular sense. Now, earlier in *NE* 5. 8 he again discusses the distinction between an unjust act and an unjust man. He writes:

> When a man acts with knowledge but not after deliberation, it is an act of injustice [ἀδίκημα]—e.g. acts out of anger or other passions necessary or natural to man; for when men perform such harmful and mistaken acts they act unjustly, and the acts are acts of injustice, but this does not imply that the doers are unjust or wicked; for the injury is not because of vice. But when a man acts from choice, he is unjust and vicious. (1135ᵇ19–25)

As we have already seen, an act of injustice does not imply that the man who performed the act is unjust. As in the *NE* 5. 6 passage, it is the fact that the agent *chooses* the act that is the crucial factor determining whether it is reflective of his character and the sort of man he is. But, crucially, Aristotle here maintains that (A) acts of injustice can be motivated by anger or the other passions (I shall return to the 'necessary or natural' later). He thus does not insist that an (A) unjust act in the particular sense must be motivated by the desire for gain. Aristotle actually seems to adopt the view that Williams defends as philosophical common sense: all sorts of things can motivate an (A) unjust act.[7]

Was there ever any evidence to the contrary? Again, it is instructive to consider Williams. He appears to get the interpretation from a passage we have already partially quoted.[8] This is it in full (following Williams' translation):

> if one man commits adultery for the sake of gain, and makes money by it, while another does so from appetite, but loses money and is penalized for it, the latter would be thought to be self-indulgent rather than *pleonektês,*

---

[7] This is probably also in the passage quoted above from the beginning of *NE* 5. 6, when Aristotle writes: 'a man might even lie with a woman knowing who she was, but the origin of this act might be not choice but passion' (διὰ πάθος), if we assume 'passion' here is not (or not only) intended to mean 'the desire for gain', and assume that Aristotle is referring to particular injustice.

[8] He also appears to think (192) that the view is present in *NE* 5. 9, 1136ᵇ34–5, where Aristotle writes: 'If (the distributor) judged unjustly with knowledge, he is himself aiming at an excessive share [πλεονεκτεῖ] of gratitude or revenge.' However, in the light of the overall argument of this section, and especially the exceptionally clear *NE* 5. 8, 1135ᵇ19–25, we should probably take 'judge with knowledge' (γινώσκων ἔκρινεν) to imply that something equivalent to a *prohairesis* has taken place. In this way, Aristotle would, as I shall argue he is in *NE* 5. 2, 1130ᵃ24–32, in fact be referring to type (B) unjust acts, not their type (A) counterparts.

while the former is unjust and not self-indulgent; this is obviously because of the fact that he gains. Again, all other unjust acts are ascribed in each case to some kind of vice, e.g. adultery to self-indulgence; deserting a fellow soldier, to cowardice; assaulting someone, to anger. But if he makes a gain, it is ascribed to no other vice but injustice. (5. 2, 1130ᵃ24–32)

Williams comments on this passage as follows: 'Aristotle's point is that the way to pick out acts that are unjust in the particular sense from the whole range of acts that are contrary to justice in the general sense is by reference to the motive of pleonexia' (190). If by 'pick out acts' Williams means 'pick out (A) acts', then he is taking the above passage to support the view that (A) unjust acts must always be motivated by *pleonexia*. But is it not actually more likely that Aristotle is referring to type (B) unjust acts? In the first half of the passage each vicious trait that Aristotle refers to is taken to be a property of a *person*: the person who acts from appetite is self-indulgent, the person who acts for the sake of the gain is unjust. And in the second half of the passage Aristotle is considering acts that are ascribable to 'some kind of vice', and a vice, for Aristotle, is a character trait: that is, is indicative of who that person *is*. Thus, I submit that Aristotle is actually referring to (B) type unjust acts throughout this passage, and is pointing to the non-rational motive that underlies such acts.[9] Now it is a *further* question why Aristotle thinks an unjust *person* must be motivated by the desire for gain, but this is not my concern in this essay.[10]

In fact, it is worth noting that Williams thinks that the formal link he maintains holds between (A) and (B) unjust acts holds in general for Aristotle. He claims that Aristotle is disposed to adopt 'a standard model' (192) linking (A) acts with (B) acts, to the effect that 'the difference between (A) acts and (B) acts is not of motive, but only a difference in the dispositional grounding of that motive' (192). Now Aristotle does indeed think that (A) and (B)

---

[9] Despite Aristotle's language here, he must be emphasizing the importance of the non-rational *motivation* underlying the type (B) unjust act in question, not the actual *outcome* that happens to result. The self-indulgent agent who acts for the sake of appetite, but then by sheer coincidence happens to gain from the act, manifests himself as self-indulgent, not as unjust. The fact that it is motivation, not outcome, that is crucial to Aristotle in this passage is still clearer if we translate 1130ᵃ27–8 as I did in the introduction ('Clearly, therefore, [he is unjust] because [he acts] for the sake of the gain [διὰ τὸ κερδαίνειν]'), rather than in the way Williams does. See also Sherman, 'Problem of Particular Injustice', sect. 1.

[10] See Williams, 193 ff., and, for an interesting defence of Aristotle's view, Sherman, 'Problem of Particular Injustice', sect. 2.

acts for some V have a different dispositional grounding: (A) acts are not reflective of the agent's character, whereas (B) acts are. But the proposed model also claims, as Williams puts it, that '(A) acts are the episodic and later regretted expressions of a motive that regularly motivates the agent who does (B) acts, that is to say, the person who is V' (191). On this account, both (A) acts and (B) acts for some V have the same motive, it is just that (A) acts will later be regretted because the agent is not in fact V, whereas (B) acts will not (because the agent is V). But just as I believe that Aristotle does not think that this link holds with respect to injustice, I doubt he thinks it holds generally. In fact, this is implicit in what has already been said. Adultery is characteristic of self-indulgent agents and with these agents acts of adultery will be motivated by a desire for bodily pleasure. But, as we have seen, Aristotle thinks that we can commit adultery for other motives, e.g. the desire for gain. Now if an agent were to commit adultery for the sake of gain, and choose his act, Aristotle would say that he is unjust, rather than self-indulgent. *But*, he could *also* say of him that he performs an (A) self-indulgent act.[11] Though not self-indulgent himself, he nevertheless performs an act that self-indulgent people characteristically perform. Again, in *NE* 3. 8 Aristotle distinguishes real courage from various states that seem like courage, but in fact are not. People who have political courage, or who act from experience, or from spirit (*thumos*), or people who are sanguine, or ignorant of the situation, can all sometimes appear brave. This suggests that these agents will sometimes perform type (A) courageous acts, without being truly courageous agents. And in some cases the reason these agents will fall short of performing (B) courageous acts will be because their acts are motivated differently from (B) courageous acts (see e.g. *NE* 3. 8, 1116^a29-32). If there is going to be a standard model that Aristotle adopts, it would be, I suggest, that (A) acts for some V need not have the same motive as (B) acts for that V.

II

Aristotle, then, thinks that an (A) unjust act can have a variety of motives. Now I think that this is something that scholars writing

---

[11] Kraut, *Political Philosophy*, 142–3, also seems to recognize something like this point.

since Williams have generally failed to observe.[12] However, it will significantly aid our own subsequent development of Aristotle's view to consider an apparent exception to this. David Sherman has in fact argued that Williams misrepresents Aristotle's act/agent distinction.[13] But, as I see it, Sherman's interpretation, though instructive, also fails to represent Aristotle's view accurately (besides failing to draw attention to the *NE* 5. 8 passage).

Sherman (237–9) thinks Aristotle's act/agent distinction distinguishes between an unjust outcome ('a condition of particular injustice') and an unjust person. Sherman points out that though the unjust person is motivated by *pleonexia*, the desire for gain, this may or may not bring about an unjust outcome—though motivated by the prospect of e.g. financial gain, it may well turn out that the agent loses money in the transaction. Equally, an unjust outcome may be brought about by a person whether or not they are motivated by *pleonexia* because an agent might be motivated by the prospect of bodily pleasure to commit adultery, for example, and yet that act might somehow happen to bring him monetary gain. Sherman thinks that there are several 'necessary conditions' for portraying an agent as particularly unjust, namely, that the agent must know 'the appropriate ends of the other virtues in a given situation', and retain 'a deliberative capacity' (239). But, on Sherman's account, anyone who fails to meet these conditions and yet brings about an unjust distribution 'simply' falls into the category of producing an unjust outcome. As Sherman writes of such an agent: 'he is not particularly unjust, though he does particular injustice' (239). The act/agent distinction, then, on Sherman's account, seems to reduce to this: we either act in a way that indicates we are unjust agents, or we merely bring about an unjust outcome.

Now, I agree that Aristotle recognizes a notion of an unjust outcome, in Sherman's sense, but I do not think this is what he intends to contrast with the acts of an unjust agent. An unjust outcome, 'a condition of injustice', is too weak to do the required work. Again, the crucial chapter is *NE* 5. 8. The opening lines of that chapter run as follows:

Acts just and unjust being as we have described them, a man acts unjustly

---

[12] Young, 'Aristotle on Justice'; O'Connor, 'Justice as a Personal Virtue'; Curzer, 'Virtue of Justice'; Foster, 'Justice and Liberality'; Drefcinski, 'Characteristic Desire of Justice'; Bostock, *Aristotle's Ethics*, ch. 3.

[13] Sherman, 'Problem of Particular Injustice'.

or justly whenever he performs such acts voluntarily; when involuntarily, he acts neither unjustly nor justly except in an incidental way; for he does things which happen to be just or unjust. Whether an act is or is not one of injustice (or of justice) is determined by its voluntariness or involuntariness; for when it is voluntary it is blamed, and at the same time is then an act of injustice; so that there will be things that are unjust but not yet acts of injustice, if voluntariness be not present as well. ($1135^a15–23$)

When we bring about a just or unjust outcome involuntarily (roughly, unintentionally), we do not, Aristotle says, act unjustly or justly, except incidentally. We do of course bring about an unjust outcome; as Aristotle puts it, we 'do things that happen to be just or unjust'—but we should not be blamed for the act, for praise and blame are reserved for intentional acts.[14] Notice, the distinction, as we have it here, states that an act of injustice implies an act with an unjust outcome, but not that an act with an unjust outcome implies an act of injustice: we would not be said to have acted unjustly if we produced an unjust outcome unintentionally, but our act none the less produced an unjust outcome. With respect to the first half of this, it seems to be implicit in Aristotle's notion of 'act of injustice' that such an act has an unjust outcome: that is, he is considering only cases in which an unjust outcome is actually brought about. This is consistent with his conceding that sometimes we may intentionally aim to bring about an unjust outcome, but somehow be thwarted in actually doing so.[15] He would just have to find some other way to describe such cases, e.g. that they were *attempted* acts of injustice.

Now, were Sherman right in his account of the act/agent distinction, we would expect 'acts of injustice' in the above passage to be the acts of an unjust agent. If the act/agent distinction is simply concerned with the difference between unjust outcomes and unjust agents, then an unjust outcome would contrast with acts of injustice *as those are committed by unjust agents*, i.e. type (B) unjust acts. But this is not Aristotle's contrast in the above passage. He claims that whether an act is or is not one of injustice is determined by its voluntariness or involuntariness. But (B) type unjust acts are not simply voluntary, they must also be *chosen*. 'Acts of injustice', in

---

[14] In sect. IV below we shall see that Aristotle actually recognizes that there are some kinds of involuntary act that are not excusable, but this is not important here.

[15] Cf. the stupid akratic agent who ends up doing the right thing only because he (i) mistakenly believes to be good what is in fact bad, and yet (ii) fails to do what he (falsely) thinks good because he is akratic (*NE* 7. 2, $1146^a27–31$).

this passage, thus seems to cover a broader range of acts than those that are indicative of an unjust agent. Aristotle's position becomes still clearer later on in the chapter, in the passage already quoted in Section I, when he distinguishes acting unjustly from acting as the unjust man would act ($1135^{b}19$–25). Aristotle contrasts men who act unjustly from choice with men who act 'with knowledge [εἰδώς] but not after deliberation', and claims that the latter perform 'acts of injustice'—unjust acts that do not imply that the agent is unjust. 'Acts of injustice' here are not simply acts with unjust outcomes. As Williams claimed of (A) unjust acts (190–1), acts of injustice seem to be restricted to unjust outcomes that are brought about intentionally (the agent acts 'with knowledge'). Aristotle, then, actually draws a threefold distinction between:

    (I) acts with a V outcome
    (II) V acts

and

    (III) V acts by a V agent (in so far as that agent is V).[16]

The relation between the three for injustice is as follows. As we have just seen, (II) implies (I), but (I) does not imply (II). Equally, as is evident from above, Aristotle thinks that (II) does not imply (III). But, as seems clear from the following passage, he does think that (III) implies (II):

if a man harms another by choice, he acts unjustly; and these are the acts of injustice which imply that the doer is unjust. (5. 8, $1136^{a}1$–2)

So an unjust man performs an act of injustice (ἀδίκημα) and the act creates an unjust outcome, but one can perform an act of injustice without being an unjust man, and one can act in a way that will bring about an unjust outcome without performing an act of injustice.

    Now, *contra* Sherman, I believe the distinction Aristotle wants to draw when he mentions the act/agent distinction in the domain of injustice is not that between type (I) and type (III) unjust acts, but that between type (II) and type (III) unjust acts. This is suggested, for example, by a passage already quoted at the beginning

---

[16] The bracketed clause is to rule out as type (III) acts those cases in which a V agent might happen to perform V acts that do not actually manifest him as V, i.e. are only type (II) V acts. Unlike type (II) V acts, type (III) V acts must have a specific motivation (e.g. *pleonexia*) and also be chosen.

of Section I (*NE* 5. 6, 1134ᵃ17–23), in which Aristotle considers the distinction between acts that do and acts that do not imply that the agent is unjust. For when Aristotle selects an example to expand his point, he chooses not just a type (I) case, but a type (II) case: a man who has sex with a woman *knowing* who she was—his action is voluntary—but the origin of his act is not choice but passion. In fact, Aristotle sometimes seems inclined to call something that is *only* a type (I) unjust act an act of injustice, but when he does so he always qualifies it by claiming that it is so only incidentally (κατὰ συμβεβηκός). He does this in a passage I quoted at the beginning of Section II (*NE* 5. 8, 1135ᵃ15–19), and again in the following passage:

the man who under compulsion and involuntarily fails to return a deposit must be said to act unjustly, and to do what is unjust, only incidentally. (*NE* 5. 8, 1135ᵇ6–8)

This suggests that when Aristotle refers unqualifiedly to 'acts of injustice' (τὰ ἀδικήματα, τὰ ἄδικα πράττειν) he is referring only to voluntary acts. On the other hand, when one brings about an unjust outcome *un*intentionally, one can at best be said to perform an act of injustice *incidentally*, and, as the first passage above clarifies, this is only because one has in fact brought about an unjust distribution.

In short, Aristotle's act/agent distinction is one that takes place within voluntary acts, between those that reflect an unjust agent and those that need not do so. The bare notion of an unjust outcome is one that does not pertain to this distinction. The difference between acts merely with unjust outcomes and acts of injustice pertains rather to whether or not the unjust outcome is intentionally brought about.

III

I hope this has clarified the broad outline of Aristotle's position. I now want to fill in some of the detail. What I primarily want to examine is precisely what is involved in an act of injustice, i.e. in a type (II) unjust act. These acts, as we have seen, are voluntary acts. Type (III) unjust acts are a subset of type (II) unjust acts, namely those that do have a specific motive (the desire for gain) and must also be *chosen*. As Aristotle writes:

Of voluntary acts we perform some by choice, others not by choice; by
choice those which we perform after deliberation, not by choice those
which we perform without having previously deliberated on them. (*NE*
5. 8, 1135ᵇ8–11)

Chosen acts are those voluntary acts we perform after deliberation.
These acts do imply that the doer is unjust (5. 8, 1136ª1–2), that
the agent is unjust and vicious (5. 8, 1135ᵇ25).¹⁷ But what, exactly,
distinguishes type (II) unjust acts from type (I) unjust acts? In *NE*
5. 8 Aristotle reminds us of what he means by voluntary (ἑκούσιον):

By 'voluntary' I mean, as has also been said before, any of the things in
a man's own power which he does with knowledge, i.e. not in ignorance
either of the person acted on or of the instrument used or of the end aimed
at (e.g. whom he is striking, with what, and to what end), each such act
being performed not incidentally nor under compulsion (for example, if A
takes B's hand and therewith strikes C, B does not act voluntarily; for the
act was not in his own power). (1135ª23–8)

Voluntary acts are performed 'with knowledge' (εἰδώς), rather than
in ignorance (ἀγνοῶν) or under compulsion. Without trying to spell
this out in any great detail, we can say that in order for an act to
be a type (II) act of injustice the agent must actually be aware of
all the relevant features of the situation and the likely outcomes of
his action, and the act must be within his power and not externally
caused.¹⁸ If either of these two features (ignorance, external cause)
is present, then the act can only be a type (I) act of injustice. If both
are absent, the unjust act can qualify for type (II) status.

   Now, when Aristotle comes to acts that are simply type (II) acts
of injustice (that is, are not also type (III) unjust acts), he claims,
as we have seen, that the agent acts with knowledge (εἰδώς) but
without having previously deliberated about the act (ἀπροβούλευτα).
He gives examples of actions that fit this category as 'acts from anger

¹⁷ Aristotle is relying on his familiar connection between choice and character (see
e.g. *NE* 3. 2, 1111ᵇ5–6; 3. 2, 1112ª1–2; 6. 2, 1139ª31–5).
¹⁸ I pursue the ignorance side of the equation in greater detail in sect. IV below.
My argument does not require me to get into the dispute surrounding Aristotle's
distinction between 'mistakes' and 'misfortunes' in *NE* 5. 8, 1135ᵇ12–19; see M.
Schofield, 'Aristotelian Mistakes', *Proceedings of the Cambridge Philological Society*, 19 (1973), 66–70 (criticizing D. Daube, *Roman Law: Linguistic, Social and
Philosophical Aspects* (Edinburgh, 1969)); R. Sorabji, *Necessity, Cause and Blame*
(London, 1980), 278–81; and Bostock, *Aristotle's Ethics*, 119–21. The basic notion
of acting in ignorance, as that has just been specified in the general definition of
voluntariness (1135ª23–8), is sufficient for my purposes.

or other passions necessary or natural to man' (5. 8, 1135^{b}20–2). The last part of the clause ('necessary or natural to man') I shall return to in the next section. The point I want to make now is as follows. The agent in this category is motivated to act by some emotion. *But* the emotion does not prevent the agent from being aware of all the relevant features of the situation (the agent acts 'with knowledge', i.e. not in ignorance). This means that in order for an act to qualify as a type (II) *unjust* act the agent must be aware of the features of the situation that make his act unjust. Emotions may motivate us to do very different things—anger to seek revenge, appetite to pursue bodily pleasure, fear to run away, etc.—but in order for each such act to be an 'act of injustice' the agent must retain awareness of the features of the situation that make his act unjust.

Let me explain this further. If we think back to Williams, his account did have the advantage that it made it clear how (A) unjust acts could be demarcated. Since (A) unjust acts were motivated by the same motive as (B) unjust acts, we could at least clearly identify which acts were (A). But on Aristotle's actual account we might think that this is much less clear. Take adultery, for example. With respect to (B) unjust acts, or—on my classification—type (III) unjust acts, my committing adultery could manifest me as self-indulgent or as particularly unjust (*NE* 5. 2, 1130^{a}24–8). Self-indulgent agents will perform the act for the bodily pleasure involved, whereas unjust agents will perform the act for some gain they expect to achieve, e.g. for financial reward (whether or not they find the act pleasurable).[19] But then surely if (i) we have an act of adultery that is performed by someone who is not actually self-indulgent or unjust, and if (ii) type (A) acts do not necessarily have any special motive, then (iii) it becomes difficult to tell whether the act in question is an act of injustice or an act of self-indulgence. Williams' account at least dealt with this problem. Since, on his view, the motive of (A) acts and (B) acts for some V is the same, those (A) acts of adultery motivated by gain are (A) unjust acts, whereas those (A) acts of adultery motivated by bodily pleasure

---

[19] The financial gain would have to be desired 'at another's expense' or with some such qualification, in order to distinguish particular injustice from the meanness vice corresponding to the virtue of liberality. On this point see especially Young, 'Aristotle on Justice', sect. 2, and Sherman, 'Problem of Particular Injustice', sect. 2. I do not always emphasize this feature in particular examples.

are (A) self-indulgent acts. But, as we have seen, this is not Aristotle's view.

The background I have provided helps us to understand when Aristotle would claim that an act is an act of injustice, in the type (II) sense. Suppose someone is motivated by the prospect of bodily pleasure to commit adultery and yet acts just on the spur of the moment and not after deliberation (that is, the act does not yet fall into the type (III) category). Suppose also that in acting this way the agent will bring about an unjust outcome because he will gain financially at X's expense from the act. If, however, the agent is *unaware* of the particular features of the situation that will make his act unjust (that is, that he will gain financially at X's expense from the act), then though the act could be a type (I) unjust act, it could not be a type (II) unjust act. This is because type (II) unjust acts are restricted to acts in which the unjust outcome is brought about voluntarily, and if the agent is unaware of the particular features of the situation that make his act unjust, he fails to act with knowledge and so acts involuntarily in this respect. Rather than being a type (II) unjust act, since the agent is only aware of the particular features of the situation that make his act self-indulgent (that is, that he is going to get bodily pleasure by sleeping with somebody else's wife), this act would be classified as a type (II) act of self-indulgence. Only when the agent is aware of the particular features of the situation that make his act unjust will his act count as an act of injustice. (This of course has the consequence that some acts could be both acts of injustice and acts of self-indulgence, in so far as, however they were motivated, the agent is aware both of the features of the situation that make his act self-indulgent and also of the features of the situation that make his act unjust.) Type (II) unjust acts need not be chosen after deliberation and may ultimately be driven by the prospect of satisfying any number of emotional states, but in order to move beyond being merely type (I) unjust acts, they do demand that the agent be aware of the features of the situation that make his act unjust. This is needed for him to act unjustly *voluntarily*.[20]

[20] In order for an agent to act unjustly *voluntarily* he has to be aware of the particular features of the situation that make his act unjust, but he does not have to be aware of the fact that his act is unjust. This is because Aristotle thinks that ignorance of the universal does not make an act involuntary, only ignorance of the particular circumstances of the action (*NE* 3. 1, 1110^{b}31–1111^{a}2). I thank Michael Ridge for reminding me of this point.

Now I think this rests on a sensible distinction. Of agents that are motivated by emotional states (whatever they may be) to perform acts that—whatever else they bring about—bring about an unjust outcome, there is a difference between those who act in this way and yet are *unaware* of the particular features of the situation that will make their act unjust, and those that are aware of these features. The former involuntarily bring about injustice, the latter do so voluntarily as a side effect of gratifying their emotion state.[21]

IV

If this much seems fairly clear, let me now complicate matters a little—as this will help us to see a further subtlety of Aristotle's position. We noted that Aristotle claimed that type (II) acts of injustice were motivated by emotions. But he actually claimed that they were motivated by emotions (πάθη) that are 'necessary or natural to man' (ἀναγκαῖα ἢ φυσικὰ τοῖς ἀνθρώποις). This seems puzzling. Does he mean that there are some emotions that are *not* necessary or natural to man, and that if one of these motivated us we would not act voluntarily, and so not perform a type (II) act of injustice? This is in fact exactly what he means. Let me try to explain.

Recall, in Section II I pointed out that Aristotle was sometimes prone to call acts that are merely type (I) unjust acts 'acts of injustice', but when he did so included the qualification 'accidentally' (κατὰ συμβεβηκός). One example he gave was someone who under compulsion fails to return a deposit. Such an agent, he claimed, could be said to act unjustly, but 'only incidentally' (1135^b6–8). But he also provides another case. Aristotle writes:

in the case of unjust and just acts alike the injustice or justice may be only incidental; for a man might return a deposit involuntarily and from fear,

---

[21] Of course, even if, as a matter of fact, the agent is unaware of the features that will make his act unjust, this does not mean that we cannot hold him responsible for the injustice that resulted. In some cases we may, as Aristotle puts it, think that the agent is 'responsible for the ignorance' (1113^b30–1), in so far as he had the power to take care or pay attention but did not in fact do so (see *NE* 3. 5, 1113^b30–1114^a3; *EE* 2. 9, 1225^b14–16). In such cases, we could say that though the agent performed only a type (I) act of injustice (because he did, as a matter of fact, act in ignorance), he was still nevertheless responsible for bringing about the unjust outcome, through his negligence. See also sect. IV below.

and then he must not be said either to do what is just or to act justly, except in an incidental way. (1135^{b}2–6)

At first sight the 'and from fear' might seem very puzzling indeed.[22] It is not merely that later in the chapter Aristotle describes acts motivated by emotions as voluntary. It is also that this seems to be his standard view. In his official account of voluntary action, in *NE* 3. 1, he writes:

Presumably acts performed by reason of anger or appetite are not rightly called involuntary. For in the first place, on that showing none of the other animals will act voluntarily, nor will children; and secondly, is it meant that we do not perform voluntarily any of the acts that are due to appetite or anger, or that we perform the noble acts voluntarily and the base acts involuntarily? Is not this absurd, when one and the same thing is the cause? But it would surely be odd to describe as involuntary the things one ought to desire; and we ought both to be angry at certain things and to have an appetite for certain things, e.g. for health and for learning. Also what is involuntary is thought to be painful, but what is in accordance with appetite is thought to be pleasant. Again, what is the difference in respect of involuntariness between errors committed upon calculation and those committed in anger? Both are to be avoided, but the non-rational passions are thought not less human than reason is, and therefore also the actions which proceed from anger or appetite are the man's actions. It would be odd, then, to treat them as involuntary. (*NE* 3. 1, 1111^{a}24–^{b}3)

For a variety of reasons, then, Aristotle seems committed to the view that acts motivated by emotions or non-rational desires *are* voluntary. The *NE* 5. 8 passage just quoted thus seems not only at odds with the rest of *NE* 5. 8, but also more generally with Aristotle's official view.

However, closer inspection reveals that this is not so. The first

[22] One might not initially find it so puzzling if one understood 'involuntarily' (ἄκων) here non-technically as something like the English 'reluctantly' or 'unwillingly'. But such an interpretation is unlikely. Before this passage Aristotle has just explained a technical notion of voluntary (1135^{a}23–31, quoted at the start of sect. III), and then given a correspondingly (connected by δή) technical account of involuntary (1135^{a}31–^{b}2). It would be exceptionally careless of him then to switch in the very next sentence to using 'involuntary' in a non-technical way, and there is no indication that he is doing so. I suspect the only reason one would want to go this way is because of a failure to understand how the 'fear' may work. See also S. Broadie, 'Commentary' ['Commentary'], in S. Broadie and C. Rowe (trans. and comm.), *Aristotle:* Nicomachean Ethics (Oxford, 2002), 350; as we shall see, unlike Broadie, I think we can make sense of the 'fear' without seeing the passage as in direct conflict with *NE* 3. 1.

thing to consider is whether or not the qualification in the passage in which he characterizes type (II) unjust acts—that we are concerned with those emotions that are 'necessary or natural'—is intended to mark something important. And then one notices that this terminology is picked up again at the very end of *NE* 5. 8. Aristotle writes:

Of involuntary acts some are excusable, others not excusable. For when people make mistakes not only in ignorance [ἀγνοοῦντες] but also from ignorance [δι᾽ ἄγνοιαν], their acts are excusable, while when [people make mistakes] not from ignorance but in ignorance, from a passion which is neither natural nor human, their acts are not excusable. (1136ᵃ5–9)

Here we have a case in which someone acts from a passion that is neither natural nor human (ἀνθρώπινον, which presumably is equivalent to the ἀναγκαῖα ἢ φυσικὰ τοῖς ἀνθρώποις in 1135ᵇ21–2). Aristotle allows that these acts are performed *in* ignorance, but denies that they are *from* ignorance. And his view is that though it is right to call acts performed *in* ignorance involuntary, it is only when the act is both *in* ignorance and also *from* ignorance that it is excusable. Thus an act performed from a non-natural passion and in ignorance is involuntary, but not excusable. Now a fairly natural way to read this passage is as claiming that acting from a non-natural passion can make the act involuntary by *making it* one performed in ignorance. Suppose that we read it this way, and suppose also that we push to one side Aristotle's emphasis on 'non-natural' emotions in the passage. Let us instead just work with the more general distinction between emotions that can cause an act to be performed in ignorance (and so involuntarily), and emotions that will instead leave any resultant act performed 'knowingly' (and so voluntarily). Now if we were to permit some such distinction, we might seem to be endorsing something that would conflict with the official account of voluntary action in book 3, given the passage we have just quoted. In fact, though, I do not think this need be so. The *in/from* ignorance distinction is also present there. Aristotle writes:

Acting from ignorance [δι᾽ ἄγνοιαν] seems also to be different from acting in ignorance [τοῦ ἀγνοοῦντα]; for the man who is drunk or in a rage is thought to act not from ignorance but from one of the things mentioned, yet not knowingly but in ignorance [ἀγνοῶν].[23] (*NE* 3. 1, 1110ᵇ24–7)

---

[23] I am translating δι᾽ ἄγνοιαν as 'from ignorance' and ἀγνοῶν as 'in ignorance'.

The man who is drunk or in a rage (ὀργιζόμενος) acts only in ignorance, not also from ignorance, but even acting *in* ignorance is sufficient for the act to be performed 'not knowingly', and so involuntarily.[24] And surely acting 'in a rage' is acting on an emotion. Again we can naturally read the passage as claiming that drunkenness and extreme anger are capable of *making it* so that I act in ignorance—and, if so, both chapters would now agree that certain passions have this capacity. For that to be so, these emotions would have to be capable of making one unaware of some key feature of the situation. There are at least two ways this might work. First, the passion might just straightforwardly make me unaware of some feature of the situation I otherwise would be aware of. Consider drunkenness. If I am drunk I may not be able to see, for example, that X is a sensitive issue to Y and should not be pursued, and so I may act inappropriately; so too, I suggest, if I am extremely sad or angry. Second, the passion might not make me fail *to see* the feature in question, but it might make me seriously underestimate its *importance*. Again consider drunkenness. If I am drunk I might well retain awareness of the fact that driving whilst drunk is something I should not do, but the alcohol might make me fail to treat this fact with the importance it has. If so, we might say that the alcohol makes me ignorant of the importance of some feature of the situation, even if I am actually aware of that feature itself. Similarly, emotions may make me downplay the importance of some feature; for example, anger may provoke me to certain kinds of violence even though I know they are wrong. Now, if we are ignorant of certain important features of the situation in either of these two ways, our action will be involuntary or unintentional. When this is so, we are, as Aristotle points out, more properly said to act *from* the passion (e.g. δι᾽ ὀργήν, from anger) or *from* drunkenness, rather than *from* ignorance (δι᾽ ἄγνοιαν). But since we are ignorant of certain key features of the situation, our act is still *in* ignorance and so involuntary.

However, we should emphasize right away that Aristotle's position in 1136ᵃ5–9 is that though these states can be classified as involuntary, that does not imply that acts I commit when in them

---

[24] Broadie, 'Commentary', 352, claims that in 3. 1, 1110ᵇ24–7 *from* ignorance and *in* ignorance are mutually exclusive, whereas at 5. 8, 1136ᵃ6–8 *in* ignorance is a subdivision of *from* ignorance. I see no reason to think that the passages conflict in this way. The 3. 1 passage claims only that the two are different because one can act *in* ignorance without acting *from* ignorance. This is consistent with Aristotle also thinking that each case of acting *from* ignorance is also a case of acting *in* ignorance.

are forgivable. The involuntariness of the act I commit when overcome by some non-natural passion may not mitigate the act, just as
the involuntariness of acts I commit when drunk may not mitigate
those acts (see also *NE* 3. 5, 1113^{b}30 ff.). Aristotle is surely right
to make some such point. We can understand him wanting to distinguish, with respect to excusability, acting *in* ignorance but *from*
a passion or drunkenness, on the one hand, and acting both *from*
ignorance and *in* ignorance, on the other. Though in both cases I
can be said to act involuntarily, i.e. in so far as I am unaware of
some key feature of the situation, the case in which I do so because
of a passion or because I am drunk presumably says more *about me
as an agent* than some act I perform both *from* and *in* ignorance.
At the very least I am someone who is capable of undergoing such
mind-altering passions, or who has it in me to get into such a state
of inebriation that I cannot see what needs to be seen. This seems
very different from missing some crucial feature of the situation
that anybody might have failed to foresee.[25]

Now, our argument so far suggests one way we can understand
the fear passage (1135^{b}2–6) without it conflicting with the rest of
NE 5. 8 or even *NE* 3. 1. The passage is intended to provide a
further example (alongside the compulsion case quoted at the end
of Section II (1135^{b}6–8)) in which an agent fails to perform a type
(II) act of (in)justice, and in fact performs only a type (I) act of
(in)justice. Since the agent returns the deposit involuntarily, he
performs only a type (I) just act—that is, involuntarily acts in a
way that happens to bring about a just outcome. If the emotion had
not prompted him to act involuntarily, perhaps the agent would
have voluntarily returned the deposit, or perhaps he would have
voluntarily failed to return his deposit and so acted *un*justly. The
fear makes the agent fail to perform either of these type (II) acts,

[25] Aristotle's view actually appears to be not just that acting on a non-natural
passion *might not* mitigate the act, but that it *will not* mitigate the act (*NE* 5. 8,
1136^{a}6–9). I suppose we might dispute this. Though we might agree that there is
a difference between someone who simply acts from ignorance and someone who
performs the same act but from some emotion (yet still *in* ignorance), might we
still not think that sometimes the emotion or desire *does* mitigate the resultant act?
These would be cases in which we agree the agent acted involuntarily because of
the emotional state or desire, but whose act does not seem to say much about the
agent in question, perhaps because many of us could imagine acting in a similar way
in such a circumstance (for example, if stranded on a desert island for a long time,
one might be overcome by sexual desire to commit adultery if an attractive woman
happened also to be stranded there).

and in fact perform only a type (I) just act. And our understanding
of how an emotion might make an agent ignorant suggests the fear
in question might do this by making him fail to see (the importance
of) some feature of the situation. In this way, the emotion makes
the act fail the 'not in ignorance' criterion for voluntary action, and
so the act is involuntary.

This, I have said, is one way we could understand the fear passage
without it conflicting with *NE* 3. 1 or the rest of *NE* 5. 8. However,
I think there is also another way. Consider the following passage
from the *Eudemian Ethics*:

> many regard erotic desire [ἔρως] and certain cases of spirited desire [θυμός]
> and natural states [τὰ φυσικά] as being too strong for our nature; we pardon
> them as things capable of overpowering nature. A man would more seem to
> act from force and involuntarily if he acted to escape violent than to escape
> gentle pain, and generally if to escape pain than to get pleasure. For that
> which depends on him—and all turns on this—is what his nature is able to
> bear; what it is not, what is not under the control of his natural desire or
> reason, that does not depend on him. Therefore also those who are inspired
> and prophesy, though their act is one of thought, we still say do not have
> it in their own power either to say what they said, or to do what they did.
> And so of acts performed through appetite.[26] So that some thoughts and
> passions do not depend on us, or acts that occur in accordance with such
> thoughts and reasonings, but, as Philolaus said, some arguments are too
> strong for us. (2. 8, 1225ᵃ20–33)

Aristotle's thought seems to be that some desires and passions are
so violent and overpowering that they are beyond that which a
human being can sensibly bear, and so they, and the acts that stem
from them, can be classified as involuntary. But these passions
and desires make the action fail the external-force criterion for
voluntary action, not, it seems, the ignorance criterion. So, on this
scenario, the agent could be aware of all the relevant features of
the situation, but the fear act on him as if it were an external force
(cf. the case of people in a trance). In so far as that description fits
the case, the fear and the resulting returning of the deposit fail to
meet the condition for voluntariness that they are within the agent's
power (5. 8, 1135ᵃ27–8).

But on either the ignorance or the external-force interpretation
of the *NE* 5. 8 fear passage, Aristotle need only be claiming that

[26] I take it that Aristotle does not mean all appetites, just certain very strong or
powerful ones.

in some cases fear may license us to describe the subsequent act
as performed in ignorance or as forced, therefore as involuntary.
And his view would actually closely follow his general account
of voluntary action: he would just be admitting that sometimes
emotions might be able to prevent the 'not in ignorance' or 'not
forced' conditions for voluntariness from being fulfilled. And, as
we have seen, he also appears to allow emotions the power to block
the 'not in ignorance' condition for voluntary action in his official
account in *NE* 3. 1 ($1110^b24–7$).

Finally, though a precise notion of the way in which emotions can
be 'non-natural' is not crucial to the argument of this essay, the *EE*
passage of course also provides us with some such notion. Though
at the beginning of the passage Aristotle somewhat confusingly
refers to natural states (τὰ φυσικά) when he immediately goes on to
say that the states in question overpower nature (though of course
in one sense erotic desire is natural enough), it is at any rate at least
clear that he recognizes a sense in which the states in question can
be said to overpower and go against nature. These emotions are
'non-natural', it seems, because they act on the agent as if from
the outside and force him in certain ways. Aristotle writes: what
depends on him is what his nature is able to bear; and what is
not under the control of his natural desire or reason, that does not
depend on him (that is, is involuntary). But this actually seems
to imply little more than that non-natural emotions are ones that
are capable of making an act involuntary, by forcing the agent to
act in a particular way. 'Natural', here, seems to be equivalent to
something like: 'in accordance with normal voluntary behaviour',
and 'non-natural': 'capable of making one's act involuntary'. Now,
in *NE* 5. 8 non-natural emotions were not tied to external force,
but to causing an agent to act in ignorance ($1136^a6–9$). But the
general notion of '(non-)natural' above could also work there. On
this understanding, 'non-natural' emotions will be those that are
able to make one ignorant of some key feature of the situation, and
so interfere with one's natural (i.e. voluntary) functioning.

I hope I have shown that Aristotle actually has a very subtle account
of type (II) unjust acts. He does not seem inclined to think, as
Williams maintained, that each such act must be motivated by the
desire for gain. For type (II) acts to be specifically type (II) *unjust*
acts the agent must be aware of the features of the situation that

make his act unjust, but all sorts of different emotional state can motivate these acts. Now, this said, in fact Aristotle does recognize a restriction on the possible emotions that can motivate type (II) unjust acts, but this has nothing to do with him wishing to tie these acts to the desire for gain. Rather, it is because type (II) acts are restricted to voluntary acts, and Aristotle accepts that sometimes it may seem plausible to think that certain emotions can overcome us to such an extent that they make acts that stem from them fail to meet the basic conditions for voluntariness. The emotion may seem, for example, to move us 'from outside', or it may seem to prevent us from seeing certain key features of the situation at hand. In so far as some such description plausibly fits the case in question Aristotle will allow that acts resulting from the emotions in question may be classified as involuntary. Because of this, even if the agent could foresee that the act would result in an unjust outcome, he would not be said to have performed a type (II) act of injustice (since these are restricted to voluntary acts). However, though Aristotle thinks that acts that result from such emotions are involuntary, he does not think that this means they must be considered forgivable or pardonable—just as acts we perform involuntarily when drunk might not be forgivable or pardonable.

Christ's College, Cambridge

BIBLIOGRAPHY

Barnes, J. (ed.), *The Complete Works of Aristotle: The Revised Oxford Translation* (Princeton, 1984).

Bostock, D., *Aristotle's Ethics* (Oxford, 2000).

Broadie, S., 'Commentary', in Broadie and Rowe, *Aristotle:* Nicomachean Ethics.

——and Rowe, C. (trans. and comm.), *Aristotle:* Nicomachean Ethics (Oxford, 2002).

Curzer, H. J., 'Aristotle's Account of the Virtue of Justice' ['Virtue of Justice'], *Apeiron*, 28.3 (1995), 207–38.

Daube, D., *Roman Law: Linguistic, Social and Philosophical Aspects* (Edinburgh, 1969).

Drefcinski, S., 'Aristotle and the Characteristic Desire of Justice' ['Characteristic Desire of Justice'], *Apeiron*, 33.2 (2000), 109–23.

Foster, S. E., 'Virtues and Material Goods: Aristotle on Justice and Liberality' ['Justice and Liberality'], *American Catholic Philosophical Quarterly*, 71.4 (1998), 607–19.

Kraut, R., *Aristotle: Political Philosophy* [*Political Philosophy*] (Oxford, 2002).

O'Connor, D., 'Aristotlelian Justice as a Personal Virtue' ['Justice as a Personal Virtue'], *Midwest Studies in Philosophy*, 13 (1988), 417–27.

Schofield, M., 'Aristotelian Mistakes', *Proceedings of the Cambridge Philological Society*, 19 (1973), 66–70.

Sherman, D., 'Aristotle and the Problem of Particular Injustice' ['Problem of Particular Injustice'], *Philosophical Forum*, 30.4 (1999), 235–48.

Sorabji, R., *Necessity, Cause and Blame* (London, 1980).

Williams, B., 'Justice as a Virtue', in A. O. Rorty (ed.), *Essays on Aristotle's Ethics* (Berkeley, 1980), 189–99.

Young, C. M., 'Aristotle on Justice', *The Southern Journal of Philosophy*, 27, suppl. (1988), 233–49.

PSYCHIC DISHARMONY: PHILOPONUS AND EPICURUS ON PLATO'S *PHAEDO*

JAMES WARREN

I

MANY of the Hellenistic philosophers were avid and careful readers of Platonic dialogues. Epicurus was no exception. Despite his generally hostile attitude to other philosophers (and especially to the suggestion that he might have *learnt* anything from them), there is good reason to think that Epicurus read and thought seriously about Platonic works.[1] One might imagine that to any philosopher living and teaching in Athens the Platonic corpus would have been both interesting and available. Further, given the evident interest in Plato's writings shown by his various followers, we should assume that Epicurus himself was similarly aware of them.[2] More

© James Warren 2006

A version of this essay was given at the École Normale Supérieure in April 2005 and a version of part of it was given to a conference in Oxford in June 2005. I would like to thank Alain Gigandet, Pierre-Marie Morel, Julie Giovacchini, José Kany-Turpin, and David Sedley for their comments.

[1] On Epicurus on his predecessors and rivals see D. N. Sedley, 'Epicurus and his Professional Rivals' ['Rivals'], in J. Bollack and A. Laks (eds.), *Études sur l'épicurisme antique* (Lille, 1976), 121–59. Cf. J. Warren, *Epicurus and Democritean Ethics: An Archaeology of Ataraxia* (Cambridge, 2002), esp. 24–8, 186–92. On the question of Epicurus' knowledge of Aristotle see e.g. D. J. Furley, 'Aristotle and the Atomists on Motion in a Void', in P. K. Machamer and R. J. Turnbull (eds.), *Motion and Time, Space and Matter* (Columbus, Oh., 1976), 83–100; O. Gigon, 'Zur Psychologie Epikurs', in H. Flashar and O. Gigon (eds.), *Aspects de la philosophie hellénistique* (Geneva, 1986), 67–98. It is possible that much, if not all, of Epicurus' knowledge of Aristotle came via his knowledge of Theophrastan works. See D. N. Sedley, *Lucretius and the Transformation of Greek Wisdom* [*Lucretius*] (Cambridge, 1998), 182–5.

[2] Colotes wrote works *Against the* Lysis and *Against the* Euthydemus. Although they are omitted from the list at D.L. 10. 24, Metrodorus seems to have written works *Against the* Euthyphro and *Against the* Gorgias (see PHerc. 1005. XI). See Philod. *De piet.* 701–8 Obbink and D. Obbink, *Philodemus on Piety*, pt. 1 (Oxford, 1996), 379–89. Polyaenus wrote a work *Against Plato* (D.L. 10. 25); cf. Cic. *ND* 1. 93. See also G. Indelli, 'Platone in Filodemo', *Cronache ercolanesi*, 16 (1986), 109–12, for a survey of references to Plato in Philodemus.

specifically, there are clearly areas of Plato's thought that would
have spoken to Epicurus' own interests. There are, of course, the
various discussions of the nature of pleasure and pain in such dialogues as *Protagoras, Gorgias, Republic*, and *Philebus*, some of which
would have offered thoughts in sharp contrast to Epicurus' own,
but others of which may not have been so opposed to his views.[3]
Further, the elaborate and complex account of a teleologically organized cosmos given in the *Timaeus* clearly did excite Epicurus'
interest, if not anger and dismay.[4] But perhaps above all one might
imagine that the *Phaedo*, with its twin related topics of the nature
of the soul and the fear of death, would have been high on Epicurus' reading list. There is little evidence that Epicurus did read
and think much about the *Phaedo*, but what indications we have are
very suggestive. We have preserved in Philoponus' commentary on
Aristotle's *De anima* a brief account (followed by Philoponus' own
refutation) of Epicurus' argument against one of Socrates' arguments in the *Phaedo* aimed in turn at refuting Simmias' proposed
harmony theory of the soul.[5]

This brief report is significant in many ways. It is a reliable indication that Epicurus was interested not only in the sorts of ideas
and conclusions which appear in Plato's *Phaedo*, but also in the
detail of specific arguments in the dialogue. His engagement with
Plato and Platonic texts is therefore much deeper than simple dismissal or polemic.[6] Rather, he engaged in close examination of the
various arguments in the *Phaedo* and, moreover, was interested in
examining and criticizing not only the arguments for 'Platonic' conclusions, but also arguments against views he himself did not hold.
More specifically, in the particular brief report we shall go on to

---

[3] See J. Warren, 'Epicurus and the Pleasures of the Future', *OSAP* 21 (2001),
135–79; id., *Facing Death: Epicurus and his Critics* [*Death*] (Oxford, 2004), 137–
42; and T. Reinhardt, 'Readers in the Underworld: Lucretius *De rerum natura* 3.
912–1075' ['Underworld'], *Journal of Roman Studies*, 94 (2004), 27–46.

[4] Cf. Sedley, 'Rivals', 133–4; id., *Lucretius*, 106–7 and 177–9. In Epic. *Nat.* bk. 14
(PHerc. 1148) there seems to be a detailed criticism of the *Timaeus*' account of the
nature of the elements. See G. Leone, 'Epicuro, *Della natura*, libro XIV', *Cronache
ercolanesi*, 14 (1984), 17–107.

[5] H. B. Gottschalk, 'Soul as *Harmonia*' ['*Harmonia*'], *Phronesis*, 16 (1971), 179–
98 at 196–8, should be credited with bringing this passage to light as evidence for
Epicurus' engagement with the idea of the soul as a harmony.

[6] Contrast e.g. Diog. Oen. 38. 3–10 Smith: καθ' ἑαυτὴν μὲν γὰ[ρ ἢ] | ψυχὴ οὔτ' εἶναι
δύνα[ται] | ποτε, εἰ καὶ πολλὰ π[ερὶ] | [τού]του φλυαρεῖ Πλ[άτων | καὶ οἱ] Στωικοί. υ οὔ[τε
κεἠνεῖσθαι], ὥσπερ οὐκ [αἰσθάνεται τὸ σῶμα ἀπαλλαγείσης τῆς ψυχῆς]. The polemic
continues in fr. 39, abusing Plato for thinking that the soul is indestructible.

consider, Epicurus seems to be arguing against Socrates' dismissal of the harmony theory of the soul, although there is no doubt that the notion of a harmony theory of the soul was not at all something which Epicurus himself found appealing. In fact, Lucretius offers an extended discussion and dismissal of some version of a harmony theory early in book 3 of *De rerum natura*. The Epicureans, therefore, find themselves objecting both to such harmony theories and also to the sort of account of the soul which is eventually preferred by the interlocutors in the *Phaedo*. Their conclusion will be that both the harmony and the Platonic dualist accounts of the soul are mistaken.

II

In his commentary on Aristotle, *De anima* 1. 4, 407^{b}27 ff., Philoponus includes an extended discussion of the notion that the soul is some sort of harmony. Aristotle, he tells us, had himself offered further discussion of this theory in his *Eudemus* (so sections from this part of Philoponus are given as fragment 7 in Ross's edition of that lost work) but it was Plato who, in the *Phaedo*, first subjected this view to serious criticism. Philoponus then goes on (*In DA* 142. 5 ff. Hayduck) to give his own analysis and discussion of the Platonic arguments from *Phaedo* 92 E 5 ff., distinguishing five separate arguments against the thesis that the soul is a harmony. The third of these arguments is the one which concerns us here. Philoponus begins his discussion at 142. 22, but the most concise summary of the argument is given at 143. 1–2:

> The attunement [ἡ ἁρμονία] is more and less [μᾶλλον καὶ ἧττον] attunement; but the soul [ἡ ψυχή] is not more and less soul.

The conclusion, left unstated, must therefore be:

> Therefore the soul (i.e. any soul) is not (an) attunement.

Leaving aside for the moment just what the premises mean, the argument has the form of a second-figure syllogism: All As (attunements) are B ('more and less'); no Cs (souls) are B; so no Cs are A.[7]

If we turn to the *Phaedo* itself for some elucidation of what is

---

[7] Philoponus identifies it as such at 143. 7.

going on here, we run immediately into a difficult interpretative controversy. Many modern commentators would resist Philoponus' claim that this constitutes a single, independent argument in the *Phaedo* against the harmony thesis. Rather, it is often thought to be part of a longer stretch of argument running from 93 C 3 to 94 A 11, which forms a *reductio ad absurdum* of the harmony thesis, and concludes that if the harmony thesis were true then it would be impossible for souls to vary morally, for some to be good and others to be bad.[8] Whatever the plausibility of that particular reading, Philoponus is adamant that 93 D 1–E 3 is a separate argument and may well have been encouraged along this line of thinking by Epicurus.[9]

Even accepting Philoponus' divisions, his version of the argument needs clarification, particularly of the meaning of the phrase 'more and less' on which it crucially depends. It seems tolerably clear that we are to understand the claim about harmonies to be that two objects may both be truly designated as 'harmonies' but that one can be 'more' than another. Alternatively, the claim may be that a single harmony can vary over time, at one time being 'more' and at another 'less'. But 'more' and 'less' what? Philoponus himself offers some attempt at explanation in his first version of the argument:

The attunement admits of [ἐπιδέχεται] the more and less. For we say that this lyre is more attuned that that. But the soul does not admit of more and less. For the soul does not become more soul and less soul than itself, nor than any other [soul]. So the soul is not [an] attunement. (142. 22–6)

Consideration of this explanation will serve to highlight important difficulties which most commentators have found with the original Platonic argument. Note first that the argument of *Phaedo* 93 D

[8] D. Gallop, *Plato:* Phaedo [*Phaedo*] (Oxford, 1975), ad loc., and C. C. W. Taylor, 'The Arguments in the *Phaedo* concerning the Thesis that the Soul is a *Harmonia*' ['*Harmonia*'], in J. P. Anton and A. Preus (eds.), *Essays in Ancient Greek Philosophy*, vol. ii (Albany, NY, 1983), 217–31 (esp. 223 ff.), agree that Socrates offers two arguments against the harmony thesis. The section which Philoponus here distinguishes as a separate argument is, according to them, part of a longer argument (argument B, 93 A 11–94 B 3) sandwiched by another (argument A, 92 E 5–93 A 10 and 94 B 4–E 6).

[9] A similar reading, distinguishing this as a separate argument, can be found in Nemes. *Nat. hom.* 23. 10–17 Morani, and cf. Meletius, *Nat. hom., De anima* (*Anecdota Graeca Oxon.*, iii. 145. 3–11 Cramer) = Dicaearchus §22 Mirhady. Damascius' commentary on the *Phaedo* (I §405) makes it clear that this was the standard interpretation of the passage before Proclus. Damascius himself prefers to see this as part of a more extended argument, as do many modern commentators. See the note ad I §§361–70 in L. G. Westerink, *The Greek Commentaries on Plato's* Phaedo, iii. *Damascius* (Amsterdam, 1977).

1 ff. is rather different in form from the simplified version given by Philoponus. Rather than asserting the first premiss of Philoponus' version—that attunements admit of degrees—at *Phaedo* 93 D 1 ff. Socrates instead infers from his opponents' views that (i) the soul is an attunement and (ii) no soul is more or less a soul than any other. Socrates shows that to retain both (i) and (ii), these objectors ought also to think that (iii) no attunement is any more or less an attunement than any other. And it is this concession extorted from the harmony theorists which is then used to generate the absurd conclusions which condemn their theory. In any case, whichever method is used to generate this argument (asserting a starting premiss about attunements which is to be taken as true as Philoponus does, or generating a conclusion about attunements which is shown to have disastrous consequences, as Socrates does), the overall structure of the objection is clear.

Clear though the structure of the objection may be, it is hard to be convinced by either Socrates' or Philoponus' version. For his part, Socrates already at *Phaedo* 93 A 14–B 4 has secured Simmias' agreement that the more an attunement is attuned, the more an attunement it is and that the less an attunement is attuned, the less an attunement it is. This is surely the most puzzling claim in the whole argument, and commentators differ not only in their interpretation of what it might mean, but also in whether they think Socrates himself is asserting this claim or merely leaving the question open.[10] Philoponus and—apparently—Epicurus believe that Socrates himself is asserting that the more an attunement is attuned, the more of an attunement it is. But it is easy to see why one might be reticent to attribute such a claim to Socrates. We can object that although one lyre may be more or better attuned than another, that hardly shows that the attunements themselves are 'more or less' attunements: one is just a better, more precise, or more melodious attunement than another. It is perhaps no accident that Philoponus himself slips into talking about the differing degrees of attunement of different lyres at 142. 22–6, rather than sticking to the original Socratic claim. No one, I imagine, would want to claim that of two lyres, one might be more a lyre than another simply

---

[10] See Gallop, *Phaedo*, ad loc. for a careful discussion. Gallop marks this as his premiss B1 and disagrees with Philoponus' interpretation by denying that Socrates here *asserts* that the greater the degree of attunement, the more an attunement is an attunement. For Gallop, Socrates simply leaves the matter open, neither affirming nor denying that an attunement can be more or less attuned.

by being more 'attuned'. Rather, both are lyres, but one is more attuned than another.[11] Similarly, it is true that no soul is 'more or less' a soul than any other, but that does not rule out their differing in degrees in many other ways. On the harmony thesis, just as two lyres may be attuned to different degrees, so too two souls might be 'attuned' in different ways—perhaps making one more virtuous than another. For present purposes, we do not need to offer a full account of the Platonic source argument. Our interest is focused instead on the discussion between Philoponus and Epicurus, so what matters is how they understood this source argument. In fact, it will turn out that Philoponus' discussion of the *Phaedo* argument will conspicuously leave open just that possibility, noting that just as a lyre is not to be identified with its attunement, but lyres may vary in attunement, so too souls are not to be identified with some attunement, but nevertheless may vary in attunement of some kind.

Epicurus attacks this construal of the Platonic argument by offering what he takes to be an exactly similar but palpably absurd application of just the same sort of reasoning. As Philoponus notes at 143. 10 and 143. 31, Epicurus is employing a *parabolē*, or 'parallel' argument: a dialectical manœuvre which objects to an argument by offering another, with isomorphic premises and an absurd conclusion.[12] Most of the surviving examples of such arguments are aimed at Zeno of Citium's syllogisms, but here we have a striking example of an Epicurean version. It is also presumably a pleasing irony that Simmias' original expression of the harmony argument in the *Phaedo* is itself a *parabolē*; perhaps that is what prompted Epicurus to offer a further such argument in Simmias' defence.[13]

Philoponus records the Epicurean argument as follows:

'The sweet' [τὸ γλυκύ] admits of (ἐπιδέχεται) more and less. But honey does

---

[11] It might be acceptable to think that something with such a small degree of attunement that it cannot be used to play any melody whatsoever might not count as a lyre at all, but nevertheless we would wish to allow that a number of instruments might all be lyres, although tuned to different degrees, without agreeing that of these some are more lyres than others.

[12] Cf. 143. 4, where Philoponus characterizes the Epicurean argument as being διὰ τῶν ὁμοίων.

[13] See *Phaedo* 85 E 3–86 A 3. For *parabolai* aimed at the Stoics see S.E. *M.* 96–7, 109, 134, and see M. Schofield, 'The Syllogisms of Zeno of Citium', *Phronesis*, 28 (1983), 31–58. For an Epicurean account of *parabolai* see Philod. *Rhet.* 1 (PHerc. 1427), II. 17–30 Longo (F. Longo Auricchio, edition of Philodemus *On Rhetoric* bks. 1 and 2, in F. Sbordone (ed.) *Ricerche sui papiri ercolanesi*, vol. iii (Naples, 1977)).

not admit of more and less for it is a substance [οὐσία]. Then honey is not sweet—which is absurd. (143. 4–6)

There are a number of important things to note before we turn to Philoponus' riposte. The argument uses an expression missing from the source text of the *Phaedo* but prominent in Philoponus' first summary of that argument, namely this talk of 'admitting of' more and less. The phrase seems to be a slogan lifted from Aristotle's *Categories* (e.g. 3ᵇ33 ff.) and therefore not, in all likelihood, part of an original Epicurean version. Philoponus, well versed as he is in such Aristotelian works, or perhaps some intermediate Peripatetic source, has recast the argument in the Peripatetics' own terms. (And we shall also see Aristotelian terminology prominent in his diagnosis of Epicurus' error.) However, one likely relic of Epicurus' own argument is the phrase used here for 'the sweet', τὸ γλυκύ, since Philoponus later objects to Epicurus and claims that rather than use this word he should instead have spoken of 'sweetness', γλυκύτης. Had Epicurus been more scrupulous, says Philoponus, he would not have been misled into thinking that his proposed counter-argument was valid.

The combination of these observations might even suggest the ultimate source of Philoponus' report. There is little sign that Philoponus himself had direct knowledge of Epicurus' writings, so he must have discovered Epicurus' argument in some other source, and one candidate seems more likely than any other as the ultimate source of this report, namely Strato.[14] Although Philoponus never mentions Strato by name, the circumstantial evidence is certainly intriguing. Both Strato and Epicurus may have been in Lampsacus at the time Epicurus was writing the section of *On Nature* which probably included the relevant discussion of the nature of the soul.[15] Further, Strato himself compiled a number of objections to Plato's *Phaedo* and would no doubt have been interested in this objec-

---

[14] Philoponus notes that he is reliant on intermediate sources for his information on Epicurus at *In An. Post.* 330. 19 Wallies and *In GC* 12. 6 Vitelli (where his source is Alexander). His other references to Epicurus or Epicureans are very general, noting only that they were atomists (*In DA* 114. 35) or hedonists (*In Cat.* 2. 6 Busse).

[15] Sedley, *Lucretius*, 129–32, dates the composition of *Nat.* 1–13, including bks. 6–9, which, he argues at 116–19, would have contained the discussion of the nature and mortality of the soul, to the years 311/10–307/306 BC. It is not clear where the discussion of the harmony theory would fall within these books but perhaps, like Lucretius, Epicurus would have tackled it early on, before pressing on to give his own account of the nature of the soul, its mortality and corporeality.

tion too.[16] In addition, one of Strato's works listed by Diogenes
Laërtius is a book 'On the more and less' (περὶ τοῦ μᾶλλον καὶ ἧττον,
D.L. 5. 60), precisely the crucial notion at stake in Epicurus' argument.[17] If this suggestion is plausible, then we have a further layer
in the complex history of the discussion of the harmony theory of
the soul—a theory which seems to have preoccupied a number of
Hellenistic thinkers.

The particular choice of counter-example in Epicurus' *parabolē*,
namely the sweetness of honey, is also significant. The sweetness of
honey, like the heat of fire, is often used as an example of an essential
property, and was probably used by the Epicureans to illustrate this
very point. For example, Torquatus at Cic. *Fin.* 1. 30 argues that
to deny that pleasure is to be pursued is as absurd as denying that
honey is sweet or that fire is hot.[18]

---

[16] See D. N. Sedley, 'Plato's *Phaedo* in the Third Century B.C.', in M. Serena
Funghi (ed.), Ὁδοὶ διζήσιος: *le vie della ricerca. Studi in onore di Franceso Adorno*
(Florence, 1996), 447–55, for a discussion of PHeid. G inv. 28 and PGraecMon 21
(edited as parts of one work by A. Carlini, 'Commentarium in Platonis *Phaedonem* (?)
PHeid G inv. 28+PGraecMon 21', in *Corpus dei papiri filosofici greci e latini*, iii.
Commentari (Florence, 1995), 203–20), which contain fragments of a work of the
3rd cent. BC. Col. II includes a concise and semi-formalized summary of Socrates'
arguments against the harmony theory. Sedley conjectures that it might be a copy
of Strato's work criticizing Plato's *Phaedo*. Cf. Strato frr. 118, 122–7 Wehrli and
H. B. Gottschalk, 'Strato of Lampsacus: Some Texts', *Proceedings of the Leeds
Philosophical and Literary Society, Literary and Historical Section*, 11.4 (1965), 95–
182 at 164–7. Strato was also, it seems, interested in Socrates' discussion of the
harmony theory and this argument in particular: fr. 118 Wehrli (=Olymp. *In Phaed.*
2. 134, p. 174 Norvin): ὡς ἁρμονία ἁρμονίας ὀξυτέρα καὶ βαρυτέρα, οὕτω καὶ ψυχὴ ψυχῆς,
φησὶν ὁ Στράτων, ὀξυτέρα καὶ νωθεστέρα.

[17] Based on an analysis of Strato's notion of the void, D. J. Furley, 'Strato's Theory
of the Void', in id., *Cosmic Problems* (Cambridge, 1989), 149–60 [first published in J.
Wiesner (ed.), *Aristoteles: Werk und Wirkung*, i. *Aristoteles und seine Schule* (Berlin,
1985), 594–609] at 159, comments, however: 'We shall never know whether Strato
read Democritus or Epicurus. My own view is that there is nothing in the surviving
reports of his opinions and arguments that requires us to think that he did.'

[18] Polystr. *De irrat. cont.* XXVI–XXVII Indelli appears to class 'sweetness' as a relative
property. Various more sceptically minded authors also use the example of honey for
their own ends. Timon of Phlius ap. D.L. 9. 105 declares that although honey appears
sweet he does not assert that it is so. Cf. S.E. *PH* 1. 20 and, contrasting Pyrrhonism
with Democritus, 1. 213. See also Xenophanes 21 B 38 DK. Philoponus himself,
in other works, also uses the sweetness and colour of honey as an example of the
relation of supervenience which, he argues, holds between a substance's properties
and its ingredients. See his *In GC* 169. 32–170. 5 Vitelli and cf. S. Berryman, 'The
Sweetness of Honey: Philoponus against the Doctors on Supervening Qualities',
in C. Leijenhorst, C. Lüthy, and J. M. M. H. Thijssen (eds.), *The Dynamics of
Aristotelian Natural Philosophy from Antiquity to the Seventeenth Century* (Leiden,
2002), 65–79, who argues (76) that the terms of this debate on the metaphysics
of mixture are borrowed from discussions in the philosophy of mind. See also S.

Having given the Epicurean counter-argument, Philoponus proceeds to refute it:[19]

'The sweet' [τὸ γλυκύ] does not admit of more and less as such [ἁπλῶς], but does so *qua* sweet [καθὸ γλυκύ], not *qua* body [καθὸ σῶμα]. Similarly, honey does not as such not admit of more and less; it does not do so *qua* honey [καθὸ μέλι] but does do so *qua* sweet [καθὸ μέντοι γλυκύ]. In a similar way the soul *qua* soul does not admit of more and less, but does do so in respect of its affections [κατά γε τὰ πάθη]. So we ought in these premisses to grasp in advance the respect in which each of these things admits of more and less and the respect in which it does not. When this is set down in advance, the middle term turns out to be different. And if the middle term is different, the inference is invalid. (143. 23–31)

We can agree, says Philoponus, that the property of sweetness varies by degrees (one thing can be sweeter than another), but if by 'the sweet' (τὸ γλυκύ) Epicurus means to refer to some body, some material stuff, then this does not vary *qua* that stuff by degrees. Honey, therefore, does not vary *qua* honey but can vary in sweetness. (We can imagine two pots, each containing a sticky substance. The substance in pot A may be sweeter than that in pot B, but it is not 'more' honey than that in pot B; both are perfectly good pots of honey.) By specifying for each premiss in what way sweetness does and honey does not admit of more and less, Philoponus thinks we will see clearly that the 'more and less' in question is not the same in both premisses.

This objection alone will not suffice. After all, Epicurus did not advance this argument because he thought the conclusion was true, but rather because he took it to be a patently invalid argument identical in form to the Platonic version. Philoponus therefore needs to show not only that the Epicurean argument is mistaken in some way—since that was its intention all along—but also that there is some relevant distinction between it and its Platonic counterpart. The Platonic argument is sound and the Epicurean argument is not (143. 31–2). And this is what he attempts to demonstrate next.

First he offers to exchange the first premiss of Plato's version

Berryman, 'Necessitation and Explanation in Philoponus' Aristotelian Physics', in R Salles (ed.), *Metaphysics, Soul, and Ethics in Ancient Thought: Themes from the Work of Richard Sorabji* (Oxford, 2005), 65–79.

[19] See Gottschalk *'Harmonia'*, 197 n. 60, for an anonymous writer's more succinct explanation of the fault in Epicurus' reasoning.

for his own rewording, in order to make the argument clearer (σαφέστερος, 143. 44). So rather than:

ἡ ἁρμονία μᾶλλον καὶ ἧττον ἐστιν ἁρμονία

The attunement is more and less (an) attunement

we ought to give:

πᾶσα ἁρμονία τὸ μᾶλλον καὶ ἧττον ἐπιδέχεται.

Every attunement admits of more and less.

The first version does not appear in our text of Plato's *Phaedo*. The closest we have is the agreement to the question posed at 93 A 14–B 2, which asks whether, if the degree of attunement were to increase, we would be left with more of an attunement. Perhaps this is evidence that Philoponus is not working directly with Plato's text or, at least, is not concerned with direct exposition of that text. Perhaps he is working with a version of the argument given by Aristotle in his *Eudemus*.[20] In any case, the second, revised and clearer, version of the premiss, Philoponus assures us, is to be preferred since it does not require any qualification. We need not specify that the attunement *qua* attunement admits of more and less. Why not?

For the attunement [ἡ ἁρμονία] is not some sum composed together with a substrate [μεθ' ὑποκειμένου] like 'the sweet' [τὸ γλυκύ], for this latter means 'the sweetened body' [τὸ ἐγλυκασμένον σῶμα] like 'what has been attuned' [τὸ ἡρμοσμένον], but attunement is something simple [ἁπλοῦν] just like 'sweetness' [γλυκύτης]. (144. 1–3)

Philoponus insists on a crucial distinction between, on the one hand, 'the sweet' (τὸ γλυκύ), a noun formed by adding an article to the neuter adjective and, on the other, the abstract noun, which I have rendered here as 'sweetness' (γλυκύτης). This distinction, which Philoponus explains in terms familiar from Aristotelian ontology, is meant to parallel that between something which is attuned (e.g. a lyre) and an attunement: 'sweetness' (γλυκύτης) is a quality (ποιότης) and therefore the analogue of an attunement, whereas 'the sweet' (τὸ γλυκύ), is a body arranged in a particular way and therefore the analogue of the lyre. Now, it seems, the Epicurean argument

[20] The latter alternative is less likely. 144. 22 ff. marks the move from the discussion of Plato's arguments to the two arguments against the harmony thesis Philoponus finds in Aristotle's *Eudemus*. 142. 4 ff. therefore is most likely to be an excursus, describing the earlier Platonic arguments against the harmony thesis found in the *Phaedo*.

fails to stand as a precise analogue of the Platonic original. Epicurus ought to have given as his opening premiss not 'The sweet [τὸ γλυκύ] admits of [ἐπιδέχεται] more and less', but rather 'Sweetness [γλυκύτης] admits of more and less'. But put like this, Philoponus argues, no absurdity results. It merely turns out that honey is not identical with the quality of sweetness (γλυκύτης), and we do not have to admit the absurd conclusion that honey is not sweet.

Whether the Epicureans could have accepted this particular Aristotelian distinction between the quality of sweetness and the body which possess this quality (even a body such as honey which, we might stipulate, essentially possesses this particular quality) is not crucial. They know that there is something wrong with their *parabolē* argument, however that error is diagnosed. It still remains for Philoponus to show that the Platonic argument is not susceptible to the same problems. The Epicureans' mistake, on Philoponus' account, is their failure to make clear what is meant by 'the sweet' in their first premiss. If Epicurus means 'the sweetened body', something composed with a substrate, then it is true that it admits of more and less only *qua* sweet. And this is true only because sweet flavour, the quality of being sweet, admits of more and less. But the Platonic argument is not similarly flawed. Socrates wants to say that an attunement, here being the analogue of the property 'sweetness' in the corrected Epicurean version, admits of more and less although souls do not. So he is correct to conclude that souls are not attunements, just as the corrected Epicurean argument would be correct to conclude that honey is not 'sweetness'.

Now we can return to the explanation offered at 143. 23–31. Philoponus' central contention, however, is clear: terms like 'sweetness' or 'attunement' are potentially ambiguous between something simple, a property, and something composite, a body arranged in a particular way. This gives him two contrasting pairs of items:

(1a) γλυκύτης—simple, admits of more and less.
(1b) τὸ γλυκύ—composite, 'a sweetened body', admits of more and less only *qua* γλυκύ.

(2a) ἁρμονία—simple, admits of more and less.
(2b) τὸ ἡρμοσμένον—composite, admits of more and less only *qua* ἡρμοσμένον.

Honey, since it does not admit of more and less, cannot be identical with (1a) but could be identical with (1b) once this is understood correctly. As Philoponus himself puts it, honey admits of more and less *qua* sweet but does not do so *qua* honey (144. 18–21). More interesting, however, is the question of where this leaves our conception of the soul. A soul, since it cannot admit of more and less, cannot therefore be identical with (2a). But now it seems that it could be identical with (2b), provided this too is understood in a particular way. This might be surprising, since it seems to allow that there is a sense in which a soul is 'something attuned' as there is a sense in which honey is 'something sweet'. Indeed, Philoponus has already agreed that there is a sense in which a soul does admit of more and less, namely 'in accordance with its affections' (κατὰ τὰ πάθη, 143. 27), presumably meaning that a soul may, for example, be more or less angry at different times or that one soul may, for example, be more irascible than another.

The validity of Socrates' argument in the *Phaedo* has been salvaged at the price of specifying that it shows only that souls are not attunements in one particular sense of attunement: a soul is not an attunement in the same sense as that in which honey is not 'sweetness'. The possibility remains that souls are attunements in a different sense, just as it must be left possible for honey to be sweet. This remaining possibility allows that souls are not to be identified with some kind of attunement just as honey is not to be identified with sweetness, but that just as honey is nevertheless admitted to be susceptible to variety *qua* sweet so too souls can be allowed to vary in accordance with their affections. Now, the fact that both attunements in some sense and souls in some sense admit of 'more and less' does not itself, of course, lend the harmony thesis any independent support. Moreover, that souls can vary and, in some sense, admit of 'more and less' is presumably a conclusion congenial to Socrates in the *Phaedo*, to Aristotle, and to Philoponus himself. They all want to be able to say that souls may differ from one another morally, but that they are all essentially the same. Identifying souls with attunements, they all want to say, prevents this.[21]

[21] For Philoponus' own position on the relationship of the soul to bodily states see the sources collected in R. R. K. Sorabji, *The Philosophy of the Commentators 200–600 A.D.: A Sourcebook*, i. *Psychology* (London, 2004), 199–203 (§6(a) 49–55).

III

At this point we can step back and take stock. Why is Epicurus offering an argument against an argument against a psychological theory he does not accept? Epicurus' purpose here is clearly dialectical since we know that he is no friend of the harmony theory himself.[22] But that observation alone will not explain what Epicurus sought to gain from this kind of dialectical argumentation. The best explanation of Epicurus' practice here is that he is concerned more generally to show not only that the harmony theory of the soul is misguided—which is why he produced a number of other direct refutations of that view which in all likelihood form the basis for Lucretius' dismissal of the theory at 3. 98–135—but also that the Platonic alternative is equally misguided. Indeed, of the two rivals to Epicurus' own materialist theory, at least the harmony theory of the soul would allow one to maintain the important belief that the soul is mortal and does not survive the decomposition of the body.[23] The psychological theory eventually proposed in the *Phaedo*, on the other hand, not only mistakes the nature of the soul but also, and disastrously in Epicurus' eyes, requires one to believe that the soul is immortal and therefore sets obstacles in the way of anyone attaining the correct belief that 'death is nothing to us'.[24] To an Epicurean, this section of the *Phaedo* must have seemed absurd: neither the harmony theorist nor Socrates has any grasp on the true nature of the soul. In that case, it is perhaps not surprising that Epicurus has offered such a ridiculous counterpart to Socrates' argument. To him, the entire discussion is ridiculous.

There is, however, a more positive and important point made by Epicurus' criticism of Socrates' practice. Leaving aside the fact that

---

[22] Cf. Gottschalk, '*Harmonia*', 197.

[23] Cic. *Tusc.* 1. 77 offers the Epicurean view as an ally of Dicaearchus' and Aristoxenus' harmony theories in claiming that the soul is mortal. Philolaus seems to have held both that the soul is an attunement and that it is immortal. See C. Huffman, *Philolaus of Croton, Pythagorean and Presocratic* [*Philolaus*] (Cambridge, 1993), 330–2, and J. Barnes, *The Presocratic Philosophers*, rev. edn. (London, 1982), 488–92.

[24] It is of course true that one of Socrates' intentions in the *Phaedo* is to persuade us not to fear death precisely because the soul *is* immortal (provided we live good lives, that is). The radical disagreement between Platonists and Epicureans on the correct way to combat the fear of death is well exemplified in the pseudo-Platonic *Axiochus*. See Warren, *Death*, 213–15.

Socrates himself has no adequate grasp on the true nature of the soul, a more local problem—again, in Epicurus' eyes—is that he is not tackling the harmony theory in the right way. We can imagine that Epicurus might well have approved of at least one of Socrates' arguments, however, namely the claim that the harmony theorist can make no sense of the soul and body coming into any sort of conflict. At *Phaedo* 94 B–E Socrates makes the sensible point that on the harmony theory it is hard to see how the soul can take its rightful place as the body's ruler. Rather, it seems that the soul will be altered and affected as the body is altered and affected. Second, the harmony theorist will have trouble accounting for cases in which psychic and bodily desires conflict—for example, when the body is thirsty and desires a drink but the soul opposes this (94 B–C).[25] All of these objections would find some favour with Epicurus. But Socrates' own preferred model for accounting for these phenomena certainly would not. Indeed, as Lucretius' refutation of the harmony theory shows, a proper account of why the harmony theory is false will show also that Socrates' brand of dualism cannot be accepted either.

IV

The two principal topics of the third book of Lucretius' great Epicurean poem are (i) the nature of the soul and (ii) the fact that death should not be feared. It is therefore hard to imagine that Plato's *Phaedo* would not be in the background of Lucretius' work, since those are the very same topics which Socrates pursues in that dialogue. Yet Lucretius makes no explicit reference to the *Phaedo* here, nor does he refer to Plato anywhere in his poem.

This does not rule out an awareness of or even engagement with Plato's work, and there are signs that Lucretius is prepared to use motifs from other Platonic dialogues—the *Gorgias* in particular—in book 3.[26] In part, the difference of approach between Lucretius

---

[25] In the *Republic* Socrates will analyse this as a conflict between parts of the soul rather than between the soul and the body. The harmony theorist would likewise be entitled to describe thirst, for example, as a desire of the soul, not the body, and might also be entitled to make psychic conflict compatible with his harmony theory by positing more than one soul harmony in an individual, or even the possibility of internal discord within a single harmony. Cf. Taylor, '*Harmonia*', 229.

[26] See W. Görler, 'Storing up Past Pleasures: The Soul-Vessel-Metaphor in Lu-

and Epicurus is explained by the nature of their respective projects. In *On Nature* Epicurus offers a lengthy and detailed account of his philosophical system which involves the discussion and rejection or modification of various alternative philosophical views. He is writing a work for committed Epicureans and for those already interested in the finer points of philosophical detail. Lucretius, on the other hand, is writing a therapeutic work aimed at those who have not yet declared an allegiance to Epicureanism and, quite possibly, are not well acquainted with philosophy of any sort. This seems to be the pose he adopts by using the internal addressee, Memmius, and the reader is expected to fill a similar role. So, unlike Epicurus, Lucretius is not particularly concerned with the elaboration and refutation of rival theories unless he believes that they are potentially attractive to his imagined audience either because they are commonly held but misguided beliefs, such as the belief that the gods will punish those they dislike and benefit those they favour, or else because they are beliefs which might be mistakenly adopted due to a slight misunderstanding of the correct, Epicurean opinion.[27]

The harmony theory of the soul, which Lucretius discusses early in the third book (3. 98–135), falls neatly into this second category. It is important for Lucretius to inoculate Memmius and us against this view since it is in important ways like the correct Epicurean view while also failing to capture the truth.[28] Lucretius has just as-

cretius and in his Greek Models', in K. A. Algra, M. H. Koenen, and P. H. Schrijvers (eds.), *Lucretius and his Intellectual Background* (Amsterdam, 1997), 193–207; Reinhardt, 'Underworld'.

[27] An interesting possible exception to this general view is Lucretius' polemic against various theories of *primordia* at 1. 635–920. Here various philosophers are named as standard-bearers of different, but equally mistaken, ontological views. Heraclitus is named as an exemplar of a monistic theory, Empedocles of a pluralist theory, and Anaxagoras of a profligate theory which makes all 'homoiomerous' substances fundamental. Lucretius' primary concern is to make clear the comparative virtues of Epicurean ontology, rather than to argue against Heraclitus *per se* or any possible followers of these Presocratics. (Cf. K. Kleve, 'The Philosophical Polemics in Lucretius: A Study in the History of Epicurean Criticism', in O. Gigon (ed.), *Lucrèce* (Entretiens Hardt, 24; Geneva, 1978), 39–75 at 65, who claims that these philosophers are chosen as proxies for Stoic physical theories. This seems unlikely. Lucretius' material even here depends on Epicurus, principally *Nat.* bks. 14 and 15. See Sedley *Lucretius*, 123–6.)

[28] Sedley *Lucretius*, 49, comments that Lucretius' decision to offer the simple transliteration *harmonia* is part of his attempt to dissuade us from the theory: 'An alien concept deserves an alien name.'

serted his first significant claim about the nature of the soul, that no less than hands and feet it is 'part of a person' ('esse hominis partem [dico]', 3. 96) which will already rule out various competing views of the soul, including Platonic notions of the soul as a separable incorporeal thing. But immediately,[29] Lucretius warns us against a related view, the 'harmony theory', which, he tells us, holds that the soul is not located in any *particular* part of the body but is a kind of living condition of the body as a whole (98–9). Before we look at the reasons he offers for rejecting this view, we should pause to wonder why Lucretius should interrupt his exposition so abruptly. We have hardly begun to discover the true nature of the soul and already are being warned away from alternatives.

The harmony theory of the soul is not described in detail by Lucretius, but it does seem to share some important traits with the Epicureans' own view. First, it would follow from this view that the soul is mortal since, it appears, the soul somehow is to be analysed as a particular arrangement or condition of bodily elements and therefore, once that particular arrangement is disrupted, the soul too would cease to be. This is why the theory has to be countered by Socrates in the *Phaedo*, precisely because it would seem to make the soul mortal and then raise fears about death. For the Epicureans, however, this view of the soul manages to produce the correct account of death, namely that it is the destruction of the body and the soul. Their objection to it must lie elsewhere.

Second, it might be thought that the harmony theory of the soul is, like the Epicureans' own account, a materialist theory. This is not so clear. It certainly is like the Epicurean view in that it denies that souls can exist independently of certain material circumstances. However, it is open to a harmony theorist to take a number of routes. It is possible for him either to identify the soul-harmony with the particular material components arranged in some way or, alternatively, to deny such an identification. Both accounts appear in the *Phaedo*. Simmias first specifies that the theory he has in mind rejects the identification of the harmony with its material components. The attunement of a lyre, he says, is invisible, incorporeal, beautiful and divine whereas the physical components of a lyre are not. Still, when the frame or strings break, the attunement

---

[29] It is clear that a line has been lost between 3. 97 and 3. 98 but it is likely simply to have introduced the topic of the harmony theory by offering some subject to govern the reported account in 3. 98 ff.

is destroyed (85 E 4–86 B 3). This appears to offer what we might call a non-reductionist account of the attunement. The attunement depends on the physical constituents arranged in a particular way but is not identical to them. Nevertheless, it is also possible for the harmony theorist to agree with a close identification of the soul and the physical constituents. Indeed, Simmias himself also seems to come close to just this claim when, later in the same passage, he draws an analogy between the physical components of a lyre and the elemental components (the hot, cold, dry, and wet) of organic bodies. He ends his account by asking Socrates to consider how he would answer someone who 'thinks it correct that the soul is a mixture [κρᾶσις] of bodily elements and the first to perish in what we call death' (86 D 2–3, cf. B 7–C 3), apparently identifying the soul and the elements thus arranged.[30] Any serious harmony theorist would no doubt wish to clarify the precise relationship between the soul and the bodily elements. Lucretius' account of the theory (3. 99: 'habitum quendam vitalem corporis *esse*') seems to reject the strong identification of soul with bodily elements and is therefore more like Simmias' first account.[31]

Lucretius therefore has to deal with a theory which is a serious competitor for the Epicurean view since it shares its two major claims: the soul is mortal and corporeal or, if not corporeal itself, then a particular arrangement of corporeal elements. It is more than likely that this proximity of the Epicurean and harmony theories is what provokes not only the prominent rejection of the theory early in Lucretius' third book but also Epicurus' own evident interest in the theory and, more importantly, his interest in pointing out the failings in Plato's own attempts to refute it. He was concerned, for his own purposes, to find the correct method for rejecting this dangerous alternative psychology.

As we saw, Philoponus does not record what arguments Epicurus himself offered as more effective means of countering the harmony theory. But it is not implausible that whatever they were, they might find an echo in Lucretius' account. There, we find three major counter-arguments:[32]

---

[30] For discussion of this lack of clarity see Gallop, *Phaedo*, ad loc., and Taylor, '*Harmonia*', 217–22.

[31] *Habitus* occurs only here in *De rerum natura*. It is probably intended to render the Greek ἕξις.

[32] Cf. P.-F. Moreau, *Lucrèce: l'âme* (Paris, 2002), 20–4.

(1) The soul is not an arrangement of the elements of the body since it is possible for the soul to be healthy and well and the body not, or vice versa (3. 100–11).

(2) The soul can be active when the body is motionless, as in sleep (3. 112–16).

(3) The soul can function even in the case of extreme damage to the body. Also, sometimes a minor physical injury can cause major psychic malfunction (3. 117–29).

These claims seek to outline ways in which the soul and body interact which are incompatible with the harmony theory and, in particular, are incompatible with its assertion that the soul is not located in any specific part of the body (3. 101). This last point is puzzling, since there is no reason why a sophisticated harmony theorist could not specify that only some parts of the body need to be arranged in a particular manner for the soul to exist, just as we can imagine a lyre with physical parts some of which are not themselves essential for the production of an attunement.[33]

Indeed, these three claims are not themselves necessarily fatal to a harmony theory.[34] Lucretius persists in the unnecessarily extreme view that in the harmony thesis all constituents of the body must be perfectly arranged for the soul to function. Further, in his presentation, Lucretius already helps himself to the idea that the soul is composed of atoms of particular sorts, notably atoms of heat and wind (3. 120: 'corpora pauca caloris'; 124–5: 'calidi vaporis semina'; cf. 3. 231–6). We might also note that an imagined 'sophisticated' harmony view, which holds that the soul is an arrangement of certain bodily elements positioned in a particular part of the body, is again very reminiscent of the Epicureans' own theory, which Lucretius outlines later (3. 231–87). Once again, the rival's proximity to the preferred account must have sparked both the Epicureans' interest and their intense desire to put clear water between them-

[33] Huffman *Philolaus*, 328–9, argues that Philolaus 32 B 13 DK shows that he took the soul to be located in the heart and therefore presumably dependent only on the attunement of certain parts of the whole body. D. N. Sedley, 'The *dramatis personae* of Plato's *Phaedo*', in T. J. Smiley (ed.), *Philosophical Dialogues* (Oxford, 1995), 3–26 at 22–6, disagrees, arguing that Philolaus imagines the soul to be the attunement of the whole body, much as outlined in Simmias' theory in the *Phaedo*.

[34] Against (3), for example, the reply might be that the soul may function in the case of extreme damage just as a lyre may be damaged but still play. Similarly, against (1) and (2), provided the necessary physical constituents are appropriately arranged the soul might still be present and healthy.

selves and harmony theorists. Nevertheless, Lucretius' objections do introduce the general method which he employs throughout his presentation of the nature of the soul, namely the deployment of examples of the ways in which we can agree that the body and soul not only interact but also act independently of one another. His central concern with the harmony thesis is that, by identifying too strongly the soul and the arrangement of bodily constituents, it makes it impossible for the body and soul to act independently. Some distinction must be made between body and soul for these phenomena to be explicable and so, in accordance with general Epicurean scientific methodology, any theory which fails to accommodate these phenomena must be rejected.

Crucially, however, Lucretius will also argue that the distinction between body and soul must not be drawn too radically since this will make it impossible to explain the various cases in which the body and soul do interact, the body affecting the soul and vice versa. In short, although we should distinguish between body and soul, these two should not be thought to be metaphysically different kinds of things. A large portion of this part of book 3 is therefore devoted to various arguments demonstrating that the soul and body must both be corporeal. Again, it is profitable to set these arguments in a dialectical context which includes the *Phaedo*, since there too Socrates agrees that any adequate account of the soul must give a reasonable explanation of the interaction between soul and body. One of his complaints against the harmony theory is that it fails to allow the soul to control or oppose the body. Rather, its consequence must be that the soul and its affections are always directed by changes in the composition of the body (92 E 5–93 A 13, 94 B 4–95 A 3).[35] The Epicureans are sure that the body can sometimes, but not always, affect the soul, so they could, had they wished, have borrowed Socrates' argument. But Lucretius does not. Instead, he uses considerations about the soul's ability to be affected by bodily changes to prove something decidedly uncongenial to Socrates, namely the view that the soul must be corporeal.

We can imagine the puzzlement an Epicurean reader would have experienced in encountering this section of the *Phaedo*. Sometimes, such as in the argument about harmonies admitting 'more and less',

---

[35] See n. 8 above. For discussion see V. Caston, 'Epiphenomenalisms, Ancient and Modern' ['Epiphenomenalisms'], *Philosophical Review*, 106 (1997), 309–63 at 322–5.

Socrates seems to be arguing poorly. At other times, such as in the argument concerning the causal power of the soul, Socrates seems to be doing rather well. But on the other hand, to Epicurean eyes Socrates undermines whatever good work he has done by opting for the strange view that the soul is incorporeal and that it survives a person's death. The Epicureans will embrace one of Socrates' arguments against the harmony theory—namely that it does not allow the soul to act upon or oppose the body—but will use this not primarily as an argument against the harmony theory but as an argument against Socrates' preferred view of the soul as well. In their view, the evident ability of the soul to act upon or oppose the body can be explained only by making soul and body metaphysically similar, i.e. by making them both corporeal. Epicurus himself deals with this point rather curtly. Noting that the only *per se* incorporeal existent is the void and that the void can neither act nor be acted upon except by allowing bodies to move through itself, he concludes that the idea that the soul is incorporeal is wildly mistaken:

ὥστε οἱ λέγοντες ἀσώματον εἶναι τὴν ψυχὴν ματαΐζουσιν. οὐθὲν γὰρ ἂν ἐδύνατο ποιεῖν οὔτε πάσχειν, εἰ ἦν τοιαύτη. (*Ep. Hdt.* 67)

So those who say that the soul is incorporeal are foolish. For were it like that it would not be able to act or be acted upon in any way.

Curiously, therefore, Plato has managed to grasp only half of this principle, sufficient for him to cast doubts on the harmony theory. But he has failed to see that it is important to be able to explain both the soul's acting and being acted upon. The harmony theory may fail to explain how the soul can act upon the body but Plato's own theory fails to explain not only how it might act upon the body but also how it might be affected by it. Lucretius can quite happily use similar observations about the interaction between the body and the soul to argue against the view that the soul is incorporeal and immortal (3. 445 ff.). This completes his positioning of the Epicurean account in opposition to both the harmony theory—which denies the soul any independence from the body—and the idea that the soul is incorporeal—which denies the soul any causal interaction with the body. The Epicureans, we might say, want to steer a middle path between Platonism and the harmony theory, doing justice to both the interaction and also the independence of body and soul.[36]

V

Let us step back for a moment and wonder just how much difference there is between the Epicureans' own account and the harmony theory which Lucretius is so insistent we must reject. After all, the Epicureans too will tell us that the soul is a group of physical elements in some sort of arrangement. Furthermore, they occasionally seem almost to agree with the harmony theorists in saying that the soul is some kind of mixture or blending. Aëtius 4. 3. 11 (Us. 315) reports that according to the Epicureans the soul is a mix (κρᾶμα)[37] of various kinds of atoms and it is likely that Lucretius' famous concerns about his ability to express in Latin the precise nature of the composition of the soul centre on the unavailability of a satisfactory Latin counterpart for κρᾶμα.[38] There are differences too, of course. The Epicureans claim that we ought to speak about the soul and the body as two distinct components of a living organism, although both are composed of atoms. Epicurus stresses the distinction between the soul and its container (*Ep. Hdt.* 63–6), a distinction which Lucretius retains.[39] So the Epicureans will dissent from the harmony theory by stressing a kind of dualism of body and soul. And even if the harmony theorist could claim also to recognize a distinction between body and soul analogous to the physical components of a lyre and the attunement of those physical components, this still differs importantly from the Epicureans, since they insist that body and soul, though distinct, are both corporeal. In this way, they will also keep their distance from the sort of dualism espoused by Socrates in the *Phaedo* by insisting that the soul and body are not metaphysically different—they are composed of the same sorts

---

[36] This combination of interaction and independence also has a role in Epicurean ethical theory, which insists that it is possible to retain mental equanimity in the face of physical pain and also that mental pleasures can counteract physical pains.

[37] Cf. Plut. *Adv. Col.* 1118 D, and cf. συγκεῖσθαι in Σ to *Ep. Hdt.* 66 (Us. 311).

[38] G. B. Kerferd, 'Epicurus' Doctrine of the Soul' ['Soul'], *Phronesis*, 16 (1971), 80–96 at 89–91, also has a brief discussion of the Epicurean theory of mixture. Caston, 'Epiphenomenalisms', 320, stresses the common equivalence between *harmonia* and *krasis* in such discussions.

[39] For discussion see J. Annas, *Hellenistic Philosophy of Mind* [*Mind*] (Berkeley, 1992), 147–51.

of items. This observation might lead to further enquiry into the
question of the coherence of that Epicurean attempt to maintain a
position between the Scylla of Platonic dualism and the Charybdis
of the harmony theory.[40] Their account of the soul makes it not
only a group of special atoms, atoms of the most tiny and mobile
kind, but also a group of atoms arranged in a special way. This is an
enquiry of considerable philosophical as well as historical interest
since the Epicureans are looking for what many modern philosophers of mind would like to hold: a vision of the soul or mind which
allows it to be sufficiently metaphysically tied to the physical world
for it to interact with the world but nevertheless retain distinctive
abilities and properties which allow it to be causally independent,
to retain the first-person features of consciousness, and so on.

The philosophical terrain of these three competing psychologies
is clear enough. Epicureanism certainly takes a path which requires
it to dissent from both Platonic dualism and harmony theories
of the soul. But what of the historical question of Epicurus' own
reaction to Plato's *Phaedo*? It might be objected that not only is it
not clear whether Lucretius is interested in attacking Platonism in
particular in his arguments against an incorporeal soul, it is also
not clear whether the harmony theory of the soul which he attacks
is intended to be recognizably the theory outlined by Simmias
in the *Phaedo*. There were certainly other philosophers—known
and unknown to us—who held theories relevantly like the views
which Lucretius attacks. This is all true and, moreover, it would no
doubt suit Lucretius' argument if he were to be able to reject whole
families of related misconceptions about the soul.

Nevertheless, there are still strong reasons to think that an engagement with Plato's *Phaedo* provided much of the material for
Epicurus' development of his own account of the soul and that this
is what we find reflected in Lucretius, although transformed and
re-presented in the way in which Lucretius moulds all Epicurus'
work for his own ends.[41] Peripatetic engagement with the harmony
theory of the soul continues long after Aristotle in the work of

[40] There are different views on their success. It might be objected, for example,
that the Epicureans' reliance on the 'nameless' fourth component of the soul demonstrates the limits of their own physicalist enterprise. See Kerferd, 'Soul', 85–7, and
cf. Annas, *Mind*, 137–43, for a careful and illuminating discussion of this question.

[41] The hypothesis that a reaction to the *Phaedo* lies behind Epicurean psychological theory might also lend weight to the suggestions that other passages in *De rerum
natura* bk. 3 reflect Platonic themes. Commentators have noted, in particular, the

Aristoxenus, Dicaearchus, and Strato, so there is no doubt that this
question was still the subject of lively debate in the Hellenistic
period. It is likely that the *Phaedo* was the source text for much of
this discussion in the Lyceum and, it seems, the debate resonated
in the Garden too.[42] There is also some evidence to suggest that
the argument at *Phaedo* 92 E ff. was one which a number of later
philosophers thought worth further exploration. It would certainly
have been a provocative text for Epicurus, and something he would
have found it profitable to think with. The passage from Philoponus
with which I began gives us a picture of Epicurus at work with a
Platonic text, looking for arguments he might reuse and arguments
he can reject. Happily for him, in looking at the *Phaedo*'s discussion
of the harmony theory of the soul, he can score points against both
that harmony theory and also Socrates' rejection of it.

Corpus Christi College, Cambridge

BIBLIOGRAPHY

Annas, J., *Hellenistic Philosophy of Mind* [*Mind*] (Berkeley, 1992).
Barnes, J., *The Presocratic Philosophers*, rev. edn. (London, 1982).
Berryman, S., 'The Sweetness of Honey: Philoponus against the Doctors
on Supervening Qualities', in C. Leijenhorst, C. Lüthy, and J. M. M. H.
Thijssen (eds.), *The Dynamics of Aristotelian Natural Philosophy from
Antiquity to the Seventeenth Century* (Leiden, 2002), 65–79.
—— 'Necessitation and Explanation in Philoponus' Aristotelian Physics',
in R Salles (ed.), *Metaphysics, Soul, and Ethics in Ancient Thought:
Themes from the Work of Richard Sorabji* (Oxford, 2005), 65–79.
Carlini, A., 'Commentarium in Platonis *Phaedonem* (?) PHeid G inv. 28 +
PGraecMon 21', in *Corpus dei papiri filosofici greci e latini*, iii. *Commentari* (Florence, 1995), 203–20.

description of gradual icy death at 3. 526–30 (cf. *Phaedo* 117 E–118 A) and, perhaps,
the picture of souls queuing for incarnation at 3. 776–83.

[42] For a discussion of harmony theories, particularly Peripatetic versions, see Caston, 'Epiphenomenalisms', 338–45; V. Caston, 'Dicaearchus' Philosophy of Mind',
in W. W. Fortenbaugh and E. Schütrumpf (eds.), *Dicaearchus of Messana: Text,
Translation and Discussion* (Rutgers University Studies in Classical Humanities,
10; New Brunswick, 2001), 175–93; and D. C. Mirhady, 'Dicaearchus of Messana:
The Sources, Text and Translation', ibid. 1–142. Cf. Annas, *Mind*, 30–1. It is possible that Epicurus knew of Dicaearchus' work, for example, and Philodemus uses
Dicaearchus as a source for his history of the Academy.

Caston, V., 'Epiphenomenalisms, Ancient and Modern' ['Epiphenome-nalisms'], *Philosophical Review*, 106 (1997), 309–63.

—— 'Dicaearchus' Philosophy of Mind', in W. W. Fortenbaugh and E. Schütrumpf (eds.), *Dicaearchus of Messana: Text, Translation and Dis-cussion* (Rutgers University Studies in Classical Humanities, 10; New Brunswick, 2001), 175–93.

Furley, D. J., 'Aristotle and the Atomists on Motion in a Void', in P. K. Machamer and R. J. Turnbull (eds.), *Motion and Time, Space and Matter* (Columbus, Oh., 1976), 83–100.

—— 'Strato's Theory of the Void', in id., *Cosmic Problems* (Cambridge, 1989), 149–60 [first published in J. Wiesner (ed.), *Aristoteles: Werk und Wirkung*, i. *Aristoteles und seine Schule* (Berlin, 1985), 594–609].

Gallop, D., *Plato: Phaedo [Phaedo]* (Oxford, 1975).

Gigon, O., 'Zur Psychologie Epikurs', in H. Flashar and O. Gigon (eds.), *Aspects de la philosophie hellénistique* (Geneva, 1986), 67–98.

Görler, W., 'Storing up Past Pleasures: The Soul-Vessel-Metaphor in Lu-cretius and in his Greek Models', in K. A. Algra, M. H. Koenen, and P. H. Schrijvers (eds.), *Lucretius and his Intellectual Background* (Ams-terdam, 1997), 193–207.

Gottschalk, H. B., 'Strato of Lampsacus: Some Texts', *Proceedings of the Leeds Philosophical and Literary Society, Literary and Historical Section*, 11.4 (1965), 95–182.

—— 'Soul as *Harmonia*' ['*Harmonia*'], *Phronesis*, 16 (1971), 179–98.

Huffman, C., *Philolaus of Croton, Pythagorean and Presocratic [Philolaus]* (Cambridge, 1993).

Indelli, G., 'Platone in Filodemo', *Cronache ercolanesi*, 16 (1986), 109–12.

Kerferd, G. B., 'Epicurus' Doctrine of the Soul' ['Soul'], *Phronesis*, 16 (1971), 80–96.

Kleve, K., 'The Philosophical Polemics in Lucretius: A Study in the His-tory of Epicurean Criticism', in O. Gigon (ed.), *Lucrèce* (Entretiens Hardt, 24; Geneva, 1978), 39–75.

Leone, G., 'Epicuro, *Della natura*, libro XIV', *Cronache ercolanesi*, 14 (1984), 17–107.

Longo Auricchio, F. (ed.), Philodemus, *On Rhetoric* bks. 1 and 2, in F. Sbordone (ed.), *Ricerche sui papiri ercolanesi*, vol. iii (Naples, 1977).

Mirhady, D. C., 'Dicaearchus of Messana: The Sources, Text and Trans-lation', in W. W. Fortenbaugh and E. Schütrumpf (eds.), *Dicaearchus of Messana: Text, Translation and Discussion* (Rutgers University Studies in Classical Humanities, 10; New Brunswick, 2001), 1–142.

Moreau, P.-F., *Lucrèce: l'âme* (Paris, 2002).

Obbink, D., *Philodemus on Piety*, pt. 1 (Oxford, 1996).

Reinhardt, T., 'Readers in the Underworld: Lucretius *De rerum natura* 3. 912–1075' ['Underworld'], *Journal of Roman Studies*, 94 (2004), 27–46.

Schofield, M., 'The Syllogisms of Zeno of Citium', *Phronesis*, 28 (1983), 31–58.

Sedley, D. N., 'Epicurus and his Professional Rivals' ['Rivals'], in J. Bollack and A. Laks (eds.), *Études sur l'épicurisme antique* (Lille, 1976), 121–59.

——— 'The *dramatis personae* of Plato's *Phaedo*', in T. J. Smiley (ed.), *Philosophical Dialogues* (Oxford, 1995), 3–26.

——— 'Plato's *Phaedo* in the Third Century B.C.', in M. Serena Funghi (ed.), Ὁδοὶ διζήσιος: *le vie della ricerca. Studi in onore di Franceso Adorno* (Florence, 1996), 447–55.

——— *Lucretius and the Transformation of Greek Wisdom* [*Lucretius*] (Cambridge, 1998).

Sorabji, R. R. K., *The Philosophy of the Commentators 200–600 A.D.: A Sourcebook*, i. *Psychology* (London, 2004).

Taylor, C. C. W., 'The Arguments in the *Phaedo* concerning the Thesis that the Soul is a *Harmonia*' ['*Harmonia*'], in J. P. Anton and A. Preus (eds.), *Essays in Ancient Greek Philosophy*, vol. ii (Albany, NY, 1983), 217–31.

Warren, J., 'Epicurus and the Pleasures of the Future', *OSAP* 21 (2001), 135–79.

——— *Epicurus and Democritean Ethics: An Archaeology of Ataraxia* (Cambridge, 2002).

——— *Facing Death: Epicurus and his Critics* [*Death*] (Oxford, 2004).

Westerink, L. G., *The Greek Commentaries on Plato's* Phaedo, ii. *Damascius* (Amsterdam, 1977).

EPICURUS' ARGUMENT
FOR ATOMISM

GABOR BETEGH

THE cornerstone of Epicurus' physics is atomism: Epicurus follows Democritus[1] in maintaining that our world is ultimately composed of atoms and the void. It is, then, somewhat surprising that
the demonstration of the atomist thesis is apparently confined to
three sentences in the *Letter to Herodotus*, our main source on Epicurus' physics. These are the three sentences that I shall focus on
in this paper. First, I shall argue that the standard interpretation,
which takes the argument to be based on the impossibility of sizeless
parts, is not the correct one. Then, I shall examine the alternative
reconstruction of the atomist argument that focuses on the body–
void distinction. Finally, I shall try to show that Epicurus' defence
of atomism is based on the unalterability of the atoms.

1. The text and its standard interpretation

It will be useful to summarize briefly what we can learn from the
Letter before it gets to the argument for atomism. All the more
so as commentators have often stressed that Epicurus develops his
system in a linear manner and tries to avoid using undemonstrated
premisses for his arguments. Let us see, then, what we can take as
known for the argument for atomism.

© Gábor Betegh 2006

I presented versions of this paper at the University of Pécs, at the Central European
University, Budapest, at the Bibliotheca Classica, St Petersburg, at the University
of Rijeka, and at the Humboldt University, Berlin. Remarks by Howard Robinson,
Katalin Farkas, István Bodnár, László Bene, Péter Lautner, Judit Horváth, and
Christof Rapp were particularly helpful. I am especially grateful to Myles Burnyeat
and David Sedley for detailed comments on the written version.

[1] In this paper I shall not make a distinction between Democritus and Leucippus.
By the name 'Democritus' I mean Abderitan atomism in general.

Epicurus starts the *Letter* by giving his reasons for epitomizing
his monumental work *On Nature*. One can understand that such
a summary was needed: *On Nature* comprised 37 books and was
apparently about double the size of Plato's entire corpus.[2] Epicurus
says that the *Letter* should help those who have no immediate access
either to *On Nature* or even to its most important parts. Yet the
Letter in itself cannot serve as a primary source for learning—
it is only a reminder for those who have already internalized the
doctrines of Epicureanism, either through studying Epicurus' full-
size written works or by receiving teaching from their Epicurean
teachers.

In the next step we learn the foundations of Epicurus' epistemology: primary concepts (πρῶτα ἐννοήματα), sensations (αἰσθήσεις),
and feelings (πάθη) are epistemologically prior and serve as the criteria of truth.

The metaphysical and physical doctrines come next. Epicurus
starts off by establishing three principles of conservation: first, that
nothing comes into existence from nothing, for otherwise things
could spring into being spontaneously, with no regard for the general regularity of nature, which requires that particular outcomes
can be delivered only by particular initial conditions. Generation,
in general, must originate from 'seeds'.[3]

The second principle, which will be of central importance for
us, states that the destruction of a thing cannot mean perishing
into sheer nothing. For if this were possible, all things would have
already passed into not-being, and nothing would exist at all. The
proof for the second principle of conservation already relies on the
first principle. For without the first principle, it would theoretically
be possible that even though things do perish into non-existence,
other things come into existence from nothing, and hence the stock
of existing things will never become empty. Moreover, the argument
will go through only if we assume that physical processes in the
world have been going on for an infinitely long period of time.[4] For

---

[2] On the length of *On Nature*, see D. Sedley, *Lucretius and the Transformation of Greek Wisdom* (Cambridge, 1998), 102–4.

[3] There is some uncertainty whether 'seeds' are meant to be taken here only in the ordinary biological sense of the word or are already pointing towards the technical sense of atoms. The parallel passage in Lucretius elaborates on the conditions for biological generation in great detail, but also refers to atoms as 'seeds' of things (1. 176, 185, 221).

[4] The parallel passage in Lucretius (1. 225–37) makes this premiss explicit.

otherwise it would be conceivable that the world starts out full of beings, and then things gradually go out of existence; eventually there will be nothing at all, but we live in an intermediate period when there is still a considerable number of beings. To rule out such an option, Epicurus has to assume that the history of the universe had no beginning.[5]

The principles of conservation in a third move are applied to the totality of things, stating that nothing can be added to or subtracted from what there is in the universe now. This is supported by further arguments which establish that the universe cannot pass into something else and thereby change *qualitatively*, nor is it possible that something should enter it from the outside and thereby produce a *quantitative* change by addition.[6]

The next step is to establish that bodies and the void are the only *per se* existents. Sensation tells us that bodies exist. The existence of void, on the other hand, is necessary, for if there were no void, bodies could not be in something and could not move.[7] The argument is rounded off by showing that nothing else exists in its own right, but must belong to a body or to the void as a property. Epicurus mentions already at this point, without further elaboration, that there are different kinds of properties: 'accidents' (συμπτώματα) form a subclass of attributes (συμβεβηκότα).[8] The fact that this distinction is introduced already at this point, before the atomist argument is introduced, will prove to be important for us.

---

[5] Even the fulfilment of this condition is not sufficient to render Epicurus' argument conclusive. Even if there is perishing into non-existence, and the process of annihilation has been going on for an infinitely long time, it would still be possible that there is still something in the universe if the initial stock was infinite.

[6] For the reconstruction of the argument, see J. Brunschwig, 'L'argument d'Épicure sur l'immutabilité du tout', in *Permanence de la philosophie: mélanges offerts à Joseph Moreau* (Neuchâtel, 1977), 127–50, repr. as 'Epicurus' Argument on the Immutability of the All', in J. Brunschwig, *Papers in Hellenistic Philosophy* (Cambridge, 1994), 1–20, with refinements in A. A. Long and D. N. Sedley, *The Hellenistic Philosophers* [LS] (2 vols.; Cambridge, 1987), ii. 18.

[7] I shall not embark now on the well-known problem of the Epicurean conflation of empty and occupied space.

[8] Epicurus' language at this point is somewhat confusing, and has in fact caused some confusion. The question is whether we are supposed to take συμβεβηκότα and συμπτώματα as mutually exclusive (when συμβεβηκότα would refer to permanent or inseparable properties) or συμπτώματα should be understood as a subclass of συμβεβηκότα. I am following LS here in opting for the second alternative. For arguments see LS i. 36 and, more fully, D. Sedley, 'Epicurean Anti-Reductionism' ['Anti-Reductionism'], in J. Barnes and M. Mignucci (eds.), *Matter and Metaphysics* (Naples, 1988), 295–327 at 304–11.

This is the point at which Epicurus turns to establishing that the ultimate building-blocks of bodies are atomic. The argument runs as follows:

καὶ μὴν καὶ τῶν σωμάτων τὰ μέν ἐστι συγκρίσεις, τὰ δ' ἐξ ὧν αἱ συγκρίσεις πεποίηνται. ταῦτα δέ ἐστιν ἄτομα καὶ ἀμετάβλητα, εἴπερ μὴ μέλλει πάντα εἰς τὸ μὴ ὂν φθαρήσεσθαι, ἀλλ' ἰσχύοντα ὑπομένειν ἐν ταῖς διαλύσεσι τῶν συγκρίσεων, πλήρη τὴν φύσιν ὄντα καὶ οὐκ ἔχοντα ὅπῃ ἢ ὅπως διαλυθήσεται. ὥστε τὰς ἀρχὰς ἀτόμους ἀναγκαῖον εἶναι σωμάτων φύσεις. (*Ep. Hdt.* 40–1)

Moreover, among bodies some are compounds, others are those from which compounds are formed. These latter are uncuttable and unalterable—if indeed all things are not going to be destroyed into not-being—but are strong[9] enough to stand fast when compounds are decomposed, being full in nature and unable to be decomposed at any point or in any way.[10] Therefore the primary entities are necessarily those among bodies which are atomic.

I shall call this stretch of text 'the argument for atomism'. The passage is very compact and cannot yield an indubitable, obvious interpretation. It seems that, in accordance with the general purpose of the *Letter*, this short passage was meant to be no more than a compressed reminder for those who were already familiar with

[9] Editors have suggested different emendations to replace ἰσχύοντα, found in all manuscripts (Usener: ἰσχύειν τι; Bailey and Bignone: ἰσχῦον τι). I agree with Hicks and LS that there is no need to alter the received text, but I do not follow their constructions. LS translate 'The latter must be atomic [literally "uncuttable"] and unalterable—if all things are not going to be destroyed into the non-existent but be strong enough to survive the dissolution of the compounds—full in nature, and incapable of dissolution at any point or in any way.' I take it that the subject of ἰσχύοντα is ταῦτα, and not πάντα, and thus put the second dash after not-being. In so far as πάντα includes both types of bodies (compounds and their components), Epicurus cannot say that *all things*, including compounds, will survive the dissolution of compounds. The things that are strong enough to survive the dissolution of compounds are their atomic and unalterable components referred to by ταῦτα and described further in the last two participle clauses after the ἰσχύοντα clause. The ἰσχύω + infinitive construction becomes frequent in later Greek and receives the meaning 'being able to' (cf. Lampe s.v.). For relatively close parallels, see e.g. Diod. Sic. 14. 27. 6 ὥστε μηδὲν τῶν ὅπλων ἰσχύειν τὴν βίαν αὐτῶν [sc. τῶν βελῶν] ὑπομένειν, and Philo, *Spec.* 4. 112. 8 ἡ δ' εἰς οὐρανὸν ἄγει τοὺς μὴ προκαμόντας ἀθανατίζουσα, τὸ τραχὺ καὶ δυσαναπόρευτον αὐτῆς ἰσχύσαντας ὑπομεῖναι.

[10] It is not entirely evident how these last two participle clauses are related to what precedes. Moreover, the connection between the two clauses is rendered problematic by textual difficulties. Hicks takes the two participles to be explanatory of the 'strength' of the ultimate components: 'because they possess a solid nature and are incapable of being anywhere or anyhow dissolved'. LS separate the last two clauses from ἰσχύοντα (see previous note). I am closer to Hicks, but do not take the participles to be straightforwardly explanatory of ἰσχύοντα, but rather specifying the physical conditions of 'being strong'.

the argument in its extended form. This is also indicated by a scholion inserted in the first sentence of the text quoted above: 'This [is explained] also in the first book of *On Nature*, and also in books 14 and 15, and in the *Great Epitome*.' Alas, the relevant parts of these texts are not available to help us understand this passage.

The argument, however, is not only dense but quite problematic, too. What seems clear at any rate is that at least some part of it is based on the second principle of conservation. If the ultimate components of compound bodies were not atomic, everything would pass into not-being. But why would it be so? Standard interpretations of the argument take it that Epicurus refers here to an infinite series of divisions resulting in sheer nothing, or thinks that if bodies were not composed of atoms then their decomposition would lead to pulverization into sizeless parts, i.e. nothing. Versions of this reading of the argument can be found in various summaries of Epicurus' philosophy. This is, for example, the way Cyril Bailey paraphrased the argument in his classic work on ancient atomism: 'The idea is that if it were possible to go on dividing and dividing you would ultimately find that matter had disappeared and you had reached "nothing".'[11] As Bailey himself admits, the argument in this form is evidently fallacious. The continuous dissolution or division of compound bodies will never yield 'nothing' itself. If division continued for ever, the ensuing bodies would be increasingly tiny at each stage—but in no way less existing. Bailey finds the argument unworthy of Epicurus and even suggests that 'it is improbable that Epicurus would seriously have maintained the point: it is rather a popular way of putting what he meant'.[12] Even if one does not think that the argument as reconstructed by Bailey is so

---

[11] C. Bailey, *The Greek Atomists and Epicurus* [*Greek Atomists*] (Oxford, 1928), 282. For more recent formulations, see e.g. D. Sedley, 'Hellenistic Physics and Metaphysics' ['Hellenistic Physics'], in K. Algra, J. Barnes, J. Mansfeld, and M. Schofield (eds.), *The Cambridge History of Hellenistic Philosophy* (Cambridge, 1999), 353–411 at 372: '[From the idea that compounds are formed from component parts] it follows in Epicurus' view that there are ultimate components which do not themselves have components. If they did, real destruction would be the compound's separation into those. And if they too had components, and so on *ad infinitum*, a thing's destruction would be pulverization into sizeless bits, i.e. into nothing'; and T. O'Keefe's 'Epicurus' entry in the *Internet Encyclopaedia of Philosophy*: 'the ordinary bodies that we see are compound bodies—that is, bodies which are made up of further bodies, which is shown by the fact that they can be broken down into smaller pieces. However, Epicurus thinks that this process of division cannot go on indefinitely, because otherwise bodies would dissolve away into nothing.'

[12] Bailey, *Greek Atomists*, 282.

catastrophically bad—after all, it is hardly more problematic than some Zenonian arguments we shall consider later—it is not at all certain that we need to impose it on Epicurus. For, indeed, the text itself does not mention either sizeless bits or an endless series of divisions. What is more, Epicurus' doctrine of theoretical minima, his major addition to Abderitan atomism, rules out not only the physical realization of an endless series of cuts, but also the type of thought-experiment required by the standard interpretation of Epicurus' argument for atomism. As we shall see, the argument for theoretical minima does not depend on the argument for atomism, and even if Epicurus has not as yet introduced the doctrine of minimal parts, it would considerably weaken the force of the argument for atomism if it turned out that it was based on an assumption (i.e. that we can divide a magnitude into infinitely small parts at least hypothetically and in thought) that Epicurus later explicitly rules out. Let us see, then, whether we can find an alternative reconstruction of Epicurus' argument for atomism, one that does not involve an infinite series of cuts and infinitely small parts.

2. The Democritean argument

The main reason for understanding Epicurus' argument the way the standard interpretation understands it is its supposed Democritean pedigree. Commentators tend to assume that Epicurus took over not only Democritus' atomism, but also Democritus' argument for atomism. Or even if he did not borrow the argument itself, that he was at least following Democritus in trying to argue for atomism on the basis of an Eleatic or Zenonian type of reasoning.

Democritus' argument, as reported in its fullest form at Arist. *GC* I. 2, 316ᵃ23–34, indeed turns on the impossibility of sizeless parts.[13] Without going now into the details of the interpretation, let me sketch out its structure. Formally, the argument is a *reductio* by which Democritus intends to show that we arrive at impossible

---

[13] For the evaluation of the argument and a defence of its being authentically Democritean, see D. Sedley, 'On Generation and Corruption I 2' ['On GC I 2'], in F. A. J. de Haas and J. Mansfeld (eds.), *Aristotle: On Generation and Corruption, Book I* (Oxford, 2004), 65–89 at 65–77. The historical value of Aristotle's report is also stressed by P. S. Hasper, 'The Foundations of Presocratic Atomism' ['Foundations'], *OSAP* 17 (1999), 1–14 at 1.

consequences if we accept that a body, or any magnitude, is divisible at every point. Therefore the opposite thesis—that bodies are divisible at some but not all points—must be true. And this is exactly what atomism claims. The atomist conclusion is reached through the following steps:

(1) *Hypothesis*: Bodies are divisible at every point.
(2) Now suppose that the body is simultaneously divided at every point.
(3) The resulting parts can have no extension, for if they had, it would mean that the body has not yet been divided at every point.
(4) The resulting sizeless bits are either points or nothing at all.
(5) If the body can be divided into sizeless bits, it means that it can be recomposed from the resulting sizeless points or from sheer nothing—but this is impossible.
(6) Therefore the hypothesis in (1) cannot hold: a body cannot be divisible at every point.
(7) Therefore bodies are not divisible at every point, so the atomist thesis must be true.

The most problematic part of this argument is the step between (1) and (2), because it presupposes a free transition between the following two statements:

(a) A body is divisible at every point.
(b) It is possible that the body is simultaneously divided at every point.

That the transition from (a) to (b) involves an invalid shift of the modal operator becomes even clearer when formalized:

(a) $(x)(P(x, b) \rightarrow \Diamond(D(x, b)))$
(b) $\Diamond(x)(P(x, b) \rightarrow D(x, b))$

(where $P(x, b)$ abbreviates 'x is a point of body b', and $D(x, b)$ abbreviates 'body b is divided at x'). Now who else would see more clearly that this is an invalid move than Aristotle himself, who in his theory on the divisibility of magnitudes accepts (a) but does not accept (b)? For, according to the well-known Aristotelian doctrine, a physical or mathematical magnitude is *potentially* infinitely divisible—that is, there is no point at which the magnitude is not divisible—but it is impossible simultaneously to actualize the divisions at every point.[14] In other words, (a) is true but (b) is false.

Remarkably, Aristotle does not assail the Democritean argument by pointing out that its first step is already invalid. For some reason or other, he provisionally concedes to Democritus that the possibility of a simultaneous exhaustive division follows from the hypothesis of divisibility at every point. Why is Aristotle so lenient? Perhaps he wants to show that Democritus' argument will not go through even if we grant him that initial invalid step. Moreover, this gesture could also be part of the anti-Platonic dialectic of the whole chapter: Democritus' atomism is to be taken seriously, whereas Plato is just fooling around with his triangles.[15]

Yet even if we allow the transition from (a) to (b), we still have to face a 'practical' problem: how can we reach the envisaged state where the body is actually divided at every point? Aristotle includes a sentence which specifies that these two problems have to be temporarily bracketed if we want the Democritean argument to move on:

> For if it [i.e. the body] is divisible everywhere, and this is possible, then it could also be divided everywhere simultaneously even if it did not get divided simultaneously; and if this did happen, there would be nothing impossible in it. (*GC* i. 2, 316ª17–19)

The clause 'and this is possible' indicates that we have to allow the move from (a) to (b). The clause 'even if it did not get divided simultaneously' seems to say, on the other hand, that how we have arrived at the state of simultaneous exhaustive division is of course problematic, but let us ignore this problem for the time being, and suppose that we have already reached that state, no matter how: at a stroke or at the end of an infinite process or in some other way. If we are charitable enough to grant all this to Democritus, the argument from sizeless parts can go on—but only if we grant at least these two points.

An additional problem with Epicurus' argument as understood by the standard interpretation is that it completely ignores these

---

[14] Cf. *Phys.* 8. 8, 263ª4–ᵇ9.

[15] This has been suggested by Sedley, '*On GC* I 2', 85–8. In Sedley's interpretation this is, however, not the main motivation behind Aristotle's generosity. Sedley's main argument is that in what he calls the 'Neo-Democritean argument' Aristotle voluntarily drops his insistence on there being potentialities that can never be actualized.

complications. It does not, with Aristotle, choose to skip the problems surrounding the actualization of the division at every point and jump to the end-state at which, *ex hypothesi*, the body is already divided at every point. Moreover, the Democritean argument is based on a Zenonian type of thought-experiment: let us imagine that the body gets divided everywhere.[16] As opposed to this, and very much in tune with Epicurus' overall methodology, the argument in the *Letter to Herodotus* seems to concentrate on natural physical processes.[17] Remember that the principles of conservation were already based on an argument from the regularity of natural processes, and our empirical experience about them, and not on an Eleatic type of *a priori* reasoning. But, clearly, the natural process of dissolution of a body is a gradual physical progression, so it is even more difficult to see how it could yield in a finite time the hypothetically envisaged end-state of sizeless parts.

To sum up, if we understand Epicurus' argument as referring to the impossibility of sizeless parts, it turns out to be not only problematic—or even distressing, as for Bailey—and in conflict with the doctrine of theoretical minima, but also a considerable step backwards compared with the Democritean argument as reported by Aristotle.

3. Atoms and theoretical minima

The contrast between the two types of argument will become even clearer if we remember that Epicurus does indeed use an Eleatic type of reasoning against infinite divisibility—though not in the argument for atomism, i.e. against infinite *physical* divisibility, but in the argument for minimal parts, i.e. against infinite divisibility *in thought*. Once the atomic nature of the ultimate constituents of bodies has been established, Epicurus goes on to argue that a

---

[16] I am not claiming that the Democritean argument originates from Zeno's arguments; my claim is the much more modest one that Democritus' argument is based on the same methodology and strategy. On the question of the Eleatic inspiration of the Democritean argument, see D. Sedley, 'The Eleatic Origins of Atomism', in P. Curd and D. W. Graham (eds.), *The Oxford Handbook of Presocratic Philosophy* (Oxford, forthcoming).

[17] The body in Epicurus' argument does not get divided up (διαίρεσις) or cut up (τομή), which would indicate an active external involvement as in a physical or thought-experiment, but it dissolves (διάλυσις). This term more readily describes a natural process than some kind of experimental manipulation by an agent.

finite body cannot be divided into infinitely many parts even in thought. Although the proof for minimal parts contains three distinct arguments, at least one of them is an application of a Zenonian argument:

πῶς τ' ἂν ἔτι τοῦτο πεπερασμένον εἴη τὸ μέγεθος; πηλίκοι γάρ τινες δῆλον ὡς οἱ ἄπειροί εἰσιν ὄγκοι καὶ οὗτοι· ἐξ ὧν, ὁπηλίκοι ἄν ποτε ὦσιν, ἄπειρον ἂν ἦν καὶ τὸ μέγεθος. (*Ep. Hdt.* 57)

Moreover, how could this magnitude [i.e. the one we divided by infinitely many divisions in thought] be finite? For it is clear that even these infinitely many bits are of some size, and no matter how small they be, the magnitude composed of them would also be infinite.

This passage is remarkable from our point of view in several respects. First, it shows that Epicurus can be very clear when he wants to build an argument on infinitely many divisions and the size of the resulting parts. This is not what he did in the argument for atomism. Second, the first part of the second sentence stresses that the bits gained via infinitely many splits will always have *some* size. Thus, Epicurus does not even envisage the possibility that an infinite number of divisions will result in sizeless bits, points or sheer nothing—and in doing so he remains consistent with his insistence that we cannot even *imagine* that something is divided into infinitely small, or sizeless, bits.[18]

It is interesting to see, by the way, that it would be possible to construct an argument for atomism on the basis of the thesis of minimal parts. Let us suppose that the thesis of theoretical minima has been established and thus can serve as a premiss in a further argument. Now, finite theoretical divisibility entails finite physical divisibility in so far as physical divisibility cannot go beyond the threshold of theoretical divisibility. Epicurus maintains, however, that independently existing bodies cannot be composed of a single theoretical minimum. There can be multiple justifications for this claim. First, it can be argued that if every atom consisted of one minimum only, atoms could not be different either in size or in shape, and such entirely similar atoms would be unable to account for the diversity of our world.[19] But Epicurus goes further

[18] Clearly, Zeno does both in 29 B 1–2 DK, but he is not committed to a doctrine of theoretical minima.
[19] Lucretius explicitly uses this argument in 1. 628–34. Epicurus also says at *Ep. Hdt.* 55 that we should assume a great variety of atomic shapes in order to account for the great diversity of the phenomenal world.

and says that not even one kind of atom can consist in one theoretical minimum. The reasoning is very condensed, but Epicurus
appears to accept Aristotle's arguments to the effect that what is
partless cannot move on its own.[20] It is also possible, as David
Konstan has suggested, that the impossibility of a single-minimum
independent entity should be understood as an attempt to offer a
solution to the problem of contact between atoms.[21] Be that as it
may, Epicurus explicitly claims that the limits of theoretical and
physical divisibility have to be distinct in bodies.[22] If so, physical
division must necessarily reach a limit before reaching the limit
of theoretical divisibility. This could be a formally valid argument
for atomism on the basis of theoretical minima. Yet Epicurus does
not build his argument for atomism from the side of theoretical
minima, but, in accordance with his empiricist methodology, starts
from perceptible bodies and analyses them into atoms; only then
does he introduce the thesis of theoretical minima.

Some might object, however, that the sentences introducing the
argument for theoretical minima show that Epicurus conceived the
argument for atoms and the argument for minima as analogous.
The relevant part of the text runs as follows:

πρὸς δὲ τούτοις οὐ δεῖ νομίζειν ἐν τῷ ὡρισμένῳ σώματι ἀπείρους ὄγκους εἶναι οὐδ'
ὁπηλίκους οὖν. ὥστε οὐ μόνον τὴν εἰς ἄπειρον τομὴν ἐπὶ τοὔλαττον ἀναιρετέον,
ἵνα μὴ πάντα ἀσθενῆ ποιῶμεν καὶ ταῖς περιλήψεσι τῶν ἀθρόων εἰς τὸ μὴ ὂν
ἀναγκαζώμεθα τὰ ὄντα θλίβοντες καταναλίσκειν, ἀλλὰ καὶ τὴν μετάβασιν μὴ
νομιστέον γίνεσθαι κτλ. (*Ep. Hdt.* 56)

Furthermore, we should not consider that within a limited body there are
infinitely many bits, no matter how small they be. Therefore, not only do
we have to reject the [possibility of] cutting into smaller and smaller *ad
infinitum*, so that we do not make everything weak and become compelled
by our conception of aggregates to waste existing things into not-being by

[20] *Ep. Hdt.* 59: συμφόρησιν δὲ ἐκ τούτων [sc. theoretical minima] κίνησιν ἐχόντων
οὐχ οἷόν τε γίνεσθαι. Cf. Arist. *Phys.* 6. 10, 240b8–241a6. See LS i. 43–4 and 51.
[21] D. Konstan, 'Problems in Epicurean Physics' ['Problems'], *Isis*, 70 (1979),
394–418 at 398–407.
[22] It seems to be that the thresholds of the two types of divisibility coincide in the
case of the void. First, it is clear that the argument showing that it is impossible for
a finite magnitude to contain infinitely many extended bits is applicable not only to
bodies but to any finite part of the void as well. The view that Simplicius, *In Phys.*
934. 23–30 Diels=LS 11G, ascribes to the Epicureans, that atoms move in space in
jerks—i.e. that they cover a spatial minimum not gradually but at once—is entirely
consistent with this tenet. The spatial difference between two consecutive positions
of an atom is exactly one minimum; the movement of the atom divides, as it were,
the void into one-minimum extensions.

rubbing them away. But we should not believe either . . . [*there follows the argument for theoretical minima*].

Bailey invokes this passage when he claims that the argument for atomism is based on the idea of an infinite series of cuts leading to not-being. There is no doubt that these sentences appear to refer back to the argument for atomism, and they do indeed speak of both cutting and the diminishing size of the resulting bits. It is also true that ἀσθενῆ in this passage refers back to the ἰσχύοντα of the argument for atomism. Yet, I would insist, this passage does not say either that by continuous cutting we can ever reach sizeless bits, or that things would pass into not-being because they become too small and thus fade away. For Epicurus clearly says here that even the infinitely many bits reached by infinitely many cuts will have *some* size, however small that may be—so no question of sizelessness.

Moreover, he does not say that the passage from existence to non-existence is a question of size; what he emphasizes instead is that the hypothesis of infinite divisibility would push beings into not-being by making them 'weak'. But 'strength' and 'weakness' are not relative to size. Indeed, Epicurus' central claim, as we shall shortly see, is exactly that atoms, although smaller, are 'stronger' than composite bodies. The hypothesis of infinite physical divisibility would make everything 'weak', in so far as, on that hypothesis, everything could be subject to decomposition and hence would behave as Epicurean aggregates do. Aggregates are 'weak' because they can decompose, but atoms are 'strong' because they resist dissolution. Thus, Epicurus' argument centres on the concepts of 'strength' and 'weakness', but these concepts are not relative to size.

4. Atomicity and 'fullness'

A more promising route for the reconstruction of Epicurus' argument for atomism, preferred by some interpreters, is to understand it as based on the distinction between body and void.[23] On this interpretation one crucial premiss of the argument establishes that

---

[23] See e.g. R. Sharples, *Stoics, Epicureans and Sceptics* (London and New York, 1996), 35–6. Sedley cites it as *the* Epicurean argument for atomism in his discussion of the parallelism between Epicurus' methodology in physics and ethics in 'The Inferential Foundations of Epicurean Ethics', in S. Everson (ed.), *Ethics* (Companions to Ancient Thought, 4; Cambridge, 1998), 129–50 at 133–4.

body and void have opposing characteristics and are therefore mutually exclusive, whereas another crucial premiss specifies the criterion of physical divisibility. As recent studies of atomist physics have emphasized, the atomists accepted the argument going back to Parmenides according to which a continuous, homogeneous being with no internal gaps is not divisible.[24] The atomists could claim on this basis that a body is physically divisible only where void interrupts the internal continuity of body, while a chunk of body with no void articulating it internally is indivisible. The reconstruction of the argument along these lines can in fact gain immediate textual support from the central sentence of the argument for atomism, where Epicurus speaks about the 'fullness' of those bodies which resist decomposition. The 'strength' of such bodies means, then, that they do not decompose because they are 'full'. Their 'fullness' in turn means that they do not contain any void, and, because they do not contain any void, they are not divisible at all.[25]

Even though I agree that this is the correct interpretation of the last clauses of the sentence, I disagree on the status of this part of the sentence. For it seems to me that in this text the fullness of the 'strong' bodies is not the argument for the existence of such bodies, but is rather their physical description: what it takes for a body to be resistant to cutting and decomposition. Epicurus' argument in this sentence is not that there necessarily exist bodies which do not contain any void and are therefore uncuttable, but rather that there necessarily exist such bodies that are resistant to decomposition and destruction, *because* otherwise everything would be destroyed into not-being. The reason given for the necessary existence of such bodies is metaphysical (without atoms things would be annihilated) supported by empirical evidence (we see that things still exist) and takes the form of a *reductio*. The last clauses then explain how it is physically possible to have such 'strong' indivisible bodies which prevent total annihilation.

We can see even more clearly the difference between the two ar-

[24] Cf. Parmenides 28 B 8. 22–5 DK: οὐδὲ διαιρετόν ἐστιν, ἐπεὶ πᾶν ἐστιν ὁμοῖον· | οὐδέ τι τῇ μᾶλλον, τό κεν εἴργοι μιν συνέχεσθαι, | οὐδέ τι χειρότερον, πᾶν δ᾽ ἔμπλεόν ἐστιν ἐόντος. | τῷ ξυνεχὲς πᾶν ἐστιν· ἐὸν γὰρ ἐόντι πελάζει. See I. Bodnár, 'Atomic Independence and Indivisibility' ['Atomic Independence'], *OSAP* 16 (1998), 35–61 at 43, and Hasper, 'Foundations', 5–6.

[25] See n. 10 above. The 'fullness' of the atom as opposed to the 'empty', i.e. the void, is present also in early atomism. See e.g. Arist. *Metaph.* A 4, 985^{b}5, for the use of τὸ πλῆρες as a synonym for atoms.

gumentative strategies when we contrast the argument in the *Letter* with a different argument that indeed argues for the existence of bodies that do not contain any void and are therefore uncuttable. This argument is known to us not from Epicurus, but from Lucretius (1. 503–39). The starting-point of the demonstration is that bodies and the void exist, and only these two exist *per se*. On the basis of the body–void dualism, Lucretius can now go on to argue that body and void are mutually exclusive: that is, that where there is body, there cannot be void in the sense of actually empty space. It is true that visible bodies will always contain a measure of void, for this is needed for their observable differences in relative weight and the observable permeability of even the hardest stuffs. But, because the basic characteristics of body and void are contradictory ('duplex natura duarum | dissimilis rerum', 1. 502–3), body and void cannot form a complete mixture. Therefore, if you keep analysing a visible body, you will necessarily arrive at a level where you will find portions of void unmixed with body and chunks of body unmixed with void. But because without void nothing can be divided or decomposed, these bodies unmixed with void are uncuttable and will never decompose. These bodies are therefore everlasting (*aeterna*). We can set out the argument in the following form:

(1) Only bodies and the void exist *per se*.
(2) Body and void have contradictory characteristics.
(3) Therefore they cannot completely interpenetrate each other.
(4) If so, there are bits of body unmixed with void.
(5) A body can be cut or can decompose only at those points where it has void.
(6) Bits of body containing no void cannot be cut and cannot decompose.
(7) Bits of body containing no void, the existence of which has been shown in (1)–(4), are everlasting.

There are a number of problems with this argument. It can be objected, for example, that (2) cannot yield (3), and that the move either assumes atomism itself—which would result in a *petitio*—or requires the theory of minima, or some other implicit premiss. Indeed, I doubt that the argument as it stands in Lucretius could impress a Stoic adherent of the theory of 'blending through-and-through' (κρᾶσις δι᾽ ὅλου), according to which essentially different components of an entity can totally interpenetrate each other while at the same time retaining their own opposing characteristics.[26] Even apart from this problem, it is no accident that commentators cite only Lucretius for this argument, for there seems to be no way of reading this reasoning into the text of Epicurus' *Letter to Herodotus* 40–1. The argument for atomism in the *Letter* does not say anything about the mutual exclusivity of body and void, which is, after all, the most important premiss in establishing the existence of bits of bodies unmixed with void, and leaves implicit that a body is divisible only where void articulates it.

More importantly, the crucial move in the argument in the *Letter* is that all things would perish into not-being if there were no atoms, and this is why atomic bodies must exist. Yet the argument based on the mutual exclusivity of body and void and the condition of physical divisibility does not say anything about the question of the passage from being to not-being. So even though this argument is a *bona fide* Epicurean argument, and Epicurus may very well refer to it in the last participial clauses of the central sentence of the argument in the *Letter*, it still cannot be the main argument which operates with the passage from being to not-being through decomposition.[27]

Before concluding this section, let me briefly refer to an argument Aristotle attributes to some unnamed monists (surely Eleatics) in *De generatione et corruptione* 1. 8. Similarly to the Epicurean argument we have just seen, this argument is built on the premiss that the void is the condition of divisibility. The argument is one horn of a *reductio* based on a disjunction defending monism. The disjunction states that if what-is is many, then it is divided either everywhere or at some points only. The reasoning can be paraphrased as follows:

(1) What-is is many if it is divided (διαιρετόν).
(2) If it is divided, it is divided either (*a*) everywhere or (*b*) only at some points.
(3) What-is is divided if void articulates it.

Let us first examine horn (*a*):

---

[26] On 'blending through-and-through', see e.g. Alex. Aphr. *De mixt.* 216. 14–218. 16 Bruns and Stob. 1. 155. 5–11 (=LS 48c and 48d on 1. 290–1).

[27] The closest parallel in Lucretius to the argument in the *Letter* comes after the argument based on the fullness of the atom and is introduced as an independent argument by a *praeterea* in 1. 540.

(4) Now if it is divided everywhere, there must be void at every point.

(5) But if there is void at every point, what-is is neither one, nor many, but the whole is void.

The monists then go on to argue that (*b*) is just as impossible because the hypothesis that what-is is divisible at some points but not at others would violate the principle of indifference. Thus, if neither (*a*) nor (*b*) is open, then what-is cannot be many, and therefore it must be one.

As so often, the ambiguity of the -τόν suffix might cause some trouble. Authoritative translations of *De generatione et corruptione*, such as Joachim's and Mugler's, render διαιρετόν by 'divisible' in this passage. It seems to me, however, that the context clearly requires the sense of 'divided'; what-is is many if it is actually *divided*, and not if it is merely *divisible*. Yet the standard way of rendering διαιρετόν as 'divisible' is not entirely incorrect. For if the condition of divisibility is the presence of void at the division point, as the Eleatics and the Abderites seem to maintain, then divisibility in fact *coincides* with the state of being divided. A body is divisible only at those points where there is actual division between chunks of it by the presence of a layer of void—even if this division is not directly perceptible at the macro-level.

This consideration, by the way, might shed some new light on the modal operator shift problem in Democritus' argument as reported by Aristotle in an earlier chapter of *De generatione et corruptione*, which I discussed in Section 2 above. If we understand 'divisibility' as implying the actual presence of a layer of void, then there is safe sailing from (*a*) 'A body is divisible at every point' to (*b*) 'It is possible that the body is simultaneously divided at every point'. We do not even need the modal operator in (*b*): if a body is divisible at every point, it is actually divided at every point—even if the division is not perceptible at the macro-level. The only remaining problem is that such an infinitely divisible body turns out to be no longer a body, but mere void.

Now given that Democritean atomists equated the void with not-being,[28] one could give such a turn to the argument reported by Aristotle that the hypothesis of the total divisibility of a body leads

---

[28] Cf. Arist. *Metaph.* 985^{b}4; Simpl. *In De caelo* 294. 33–4 Heiberg and *In Phys.* 28. 4–5 Diels.

to the absurd consequence that the body is sheer void—that is, sheer not-being. Total divisibility would thus lead to total annihilation. Yet this route is not open to Epicurus because, in contradistinction to Democritus, he defines the void not as not-being, but as a type of being, and calls it 'intangible nature' (ἀναφὴς φύσις).[29]

Let us take stock of what we have seen thus far. The 'standard interpretation' correctly assumes that the argument in the *Letter* is based on the connection between decomposition and the passage from being to not-being. Yet, as I have argued, it mistakenly interprets perishing into not-being as fading away by becoming infinitely small. The alternative interpretation, which takes the argument to be based on the existence of 'full' bodies, picks up a good Epicurean argument which provides us with 'strong' or, as Lucretius puts it, eternal bodies—exactly what the Epicurean needs in order to stop universal perishing into not-being. Yet this interpretation does not explain why the Epicurean needs such 'strong' or eternal bodies in the first place, because it does not offer an account of what it means that the decomposition of bodies leads to not-being. What we need in order to understand the argument as it stands in the *Letter* is a better grasp of the connection between the decomposition of a compound body and its perishing into not-being.

5. Atomicity and unalterability

I have said quite enough of what I think Epicurus' argument in the *Letter* is not about. It is high time to come up finally with some positive suggestions. When we now consider the crucial second sentence of the argument with fresh eyes, we notice at once that Epicurus' demonstrandum is double. The claim at the beginning of the second sentence states that the ultimate ingredients of compounds are *uncuttable* and *unalterable*. Even though the conclusion stated in the last sentence speaks only about atoms, i.e. 'uncuttables', the formulation of the sentence as a whole strongly suggests that the justification serves for both uncuttability *and* unalterability.

The text of the *Letter* provides clear support for this interpretation. Epicurus explicitly discusses the unalterability of atoms at a later point of the *Letter* when he argues for the list of the qualities of atoms:

[29] Cf. e.g. *Ep. Hdt.* 40.

καὶ μὴν καὶ τὰς ἀτόμους νομιστέον μηδεμίαν ποιότητα τῶν φαινομένων προσφέ-
ρεσθαι πλὴν σχήματος καὶ βάρους καὶ μεγέθους καὶ ὅσα ἐξ ἀνάγκης σχήματος
συμφυῆ ἐστι. ποιότης γὰρ πᾶσα μεταβάλλει· αἱ δὲ ἄτομοι οὐδὲν μεταβάλλουσιν,
ἐπειδή περ δεῖ τι ὑπομένειν ἐν ταῖς διαλύσεσι τῶν συγκρίσεων στερεὸν καὶ
ἀδιάλυτον, ὃ τὰς μεταβολὰς οὐκ εἰς τὸ μὴ ὂν ποιήσεται οὐδ' ἐκ τοῦ μὴ ὄντος, ἀλλὰ
κατὰ μεταθέσεις ἐν πολλοῖς, τινῶν δὲ καὶ προσόδους καὶ ἀφόδους. ὅθεν ἀναγκαῖον
τὰ μὴ μετατιθέμενα ἄφθαρτα εἶναι καὶ τὴν τοῦ μεταβάλλοντος φύσιν οὐκ ἔχοντα,
ὄγκους δὲ καὶ σχηματισμοὺς ἰδίους—τοῦτο γὰρ καὶ ἀναγκαῖον—ὑπομένειν. (*Ep.
Hdt.* 54)

Moreover, one should hold that the atoms do not exhibit any of the qualities
of the observable things, except shape, weight, size, and the necessary
concomitants of shape. For all qualities change; but the atoms do not change
in any respect, since something solid and indissoluble must persist when
compounds are dissolved, which can make it so that the changes are not to
and not from not-being, but happen through transpositions in many things,
certain things also being added, and certain others subtracted. Hence those
things which do not admit transpositions are necessarily indestructible, and
do not have the nature of the changing, but their peculiar masses and shapes
must persist—for this is necessary as well.

The claim in the second sentence of the passage that atoms do not
change their qualities functions as a premiss for the thesis of atomic
qualities. However, the premiss of atomic unalterability gets its own
justification, which is the very same as the argument for atomism in
Ep. Hdt. 40–1: if there were no unchangeable ultimate constituents
that we call atoms, the decomposition of compound bodies would
lead to universal not-being. This shows clearly that the reference
to the principles of conservation in *Ep. Hdt.* 40–1 is indeed meant
to be sufficient to prove not only uncuttability but also unalterability. Now, clearly, unalterability is the stronger claim, because
unalterability implies uncuttability, but not vice versa. A body cannot remain unchanged when it is cut, but it can change many of its
qualities without being cut. At least this is so if one does not accept
the atomist theory of qualitative change in advance. But Epicurus
cannot take atomism for granted, because he is just about to argue
for it. The last sentence of the above quotation further strengthens
this conclusion. It states that the ultimate constituents of compound bodies must necessarily retain their masses and *shapes*. This
is a recognition of the fact that for the atomist argument the uncuttability of the atom is not sufficient: the atoms must retain their

shapes as well—that is, it cannot be that atoms retain their masses but, say, are moulded into another shape.

Two questions emerge from these considerations. First, what is the scope of the unalterability requirement? Second, what does it mean that the changes of non-atomic things are to and from not-being?

As to the first question, it is evident that the unalterability claim must receive certain qualifications. For, clearly, atoms *can* change in respect of their relational and dispositional properties. There are an absolute up and down in the Epicurean universe, and atoms are oriented with respect to this absolute directionality. And they are certainly able to change their directionality. Moreover, atoms enter into certain arrangements with other atoms in forming compound bodies. There seems to be no problem in changing these relations either—indeed, Epicurus explains phenomenal processes as the modification of these very relations. And, obviously, 'mere Cambridge change' for atoms is unproblematic. It follows, then, that the unalterability claim is restricted to intrinsic properties of atoms.[30]

The difference between Democritus and Epicurus on the ontology of phenomenal qualities becomes notable at this juncture. Democritus claimed that only intrinsic properties of atoms are real, and phenomenal properties of bodies are nothing over and above the physical states of atomic aggregates. Epicurus, by contrast, maintained that phenomenal properties of observable bodies are just as real as the intrinsic properties of atoms.[31] Thus, Democritus claimed that all the qualities that really exist—i.e. the intrinsic properties of atoms—are unchanging. As opposed to this, when Epicurus also allowed into his ontology the phenomenal properties of bodies (colours, smells, etc.), he had to accept that all the properties of bodies can change; and he then needs to argue that there is an important exception to the general changeability of *per se* existing things: the intrinsic properties of atoms do not change.[32]

---

[30] The Greek term for 'unalterable' (ἀμετάβλητος) could in itself include changes with respect to relational properties; indeed, the etymology of μεταβάλλω implies change of position rather than intrinsic change.

[31] Cf. *Ep. Hdt.* 71, with Polystr. *De contemptu* 23. 26–26. 23. On the motivations and consequences of this important novelty in Epicurean ontology, see T. O'Keefe, 'The Ontological Status of Sensible Qualities for Democritus and Epicurus', *Ancient Philosophy*, 17 (1997), 119–34.

[32] On this ontological difference between Democritus and Epicurus, see D. Furley,

And this is exactly the point that leads us to our second question, that of the relationship between change and passage to and from not-being. The clue in this respect, I suggest, is the metaphysical analysis of bodies in the atomist theory. As Epicurus himself tries to explain in *Ep. Hdt.* 68–71, a body can be analysed in two parallel ways. In physical or material terms, an Epicurean body can be analysed into its material constituents or parts; a compound body can thus be analysed into its constituent atoms and an atom into its minimal parts. From a metaphysical point of view, however, an Epicurean body can be analysed only into its properties. Here the distinction between accidents and permanent properties becomes crucial. As Epicurus puts it, permanent properties are not constitutive parts as material parts are, yet conceptually a body is the complex (ἀθρόον) of its properties. In other words, an Epicurean body *from a metaphysical point of view* is nothing over and above its properties, while the permanent nature of an Epicurean body is nothing over and above its permanent properties. Indeed, this is entirely consistent with Epicurean ontology, which does not include a material substrate (or bare particular) to act as the bearer of properties. In contemporary jargon, Epicurus is, then, best described as a bundle theorist.[33]

Yet one objection to an unrestricted bundle theory is that it makes identity through change problematic. For, if a thing is composed of its properties (or, to put it another way, is a mereological sum of its properties), then if any of its properties changes, the thing

'Democritus and Epicurus on Sensible Qualities', in J. Brunschwig and M. C. Nussbaum (eds.), *Passions and Perceptions: Studies in Hellenistic Philosophy of Mind* (Cambridge, 1993), 72–94 at 93–4.

[33] The central text is still *Ep. Hdt.* 68–71. The Greek is characteristically difficult, and the interpretation is not self-evident. As I see it, Epicurus is struggling to explain the difference between physical parts on the one hand, and conceptual or metaphysical parts on the other. LS understand the passage along the same lines without using the bundle terminology (see i. 36–7). See the helpful explanatory note by Brunschwig and Pellegrin on p. 78 in the French translation of LS, and also Sedley, 'Anti-Reductionism', 313–15, and 'Hellenistic Physics', 381. The fact that our Epicurean sources do not discuss the question of what the 'matter' of the atoms is might well be related to the point that bodies are not to be analysed into properties *plus* some underlying matter, but are conceived of as complexes of their properties. On the point that it is misguided to ask 'What is the constitutive stuff or matter of atoms?', see now A. P. D. Mourelatos, 'Intrinsic and Relational Properties of Atoms in the Democritean Ontology', in R. Salles (ed.), *Metaphysics, Soul, and Ethics in Ancient Thought: Themes from the Work of Richard Sorabji* (Oxford, 2005), 39–63 at 46–8.

ceases to exist. If *a* is the sum of properties FGH, then when H is changed into K, we have FGK instead of FGH, and so *a* has perished. Therefore, a thing, on this view, cannot change.[34]

Had Epicurus accepted an unrestricted bundle theory, he would have been forced to concede that phenomenal bodies perish each time they lose any of their phenomenal properties. Such a radical view would be too high a price for Epicurus—and, surely, had he had such a radical stance, his ancient opponents would have made some nasty remarks about it. Finding a more balanced view, I suggest, might very well be a major motivation for Epicurus in introducing the distinction between permanent attributes (ἀεὶ συμβεβηκότα or ἀίδιον παρακολουθοῦντα) and accidents (συμπτώματα), a distinction that corresponds to the well-known distinction between essential and accidental properties.[35] The ensuing view is that a thing can change with respect to its accidental properties without ceasing to exist, while it loses its nature and ceases to exist when it loses any of its essential properties.[36]

Note that this is not so much a problem for Democritus. For, as Democritus famously claimed, only atoms and the void exist in reality (ἐτεῇ, see e.g. S.E. *M*. 7. 135). Now given that none of them changes with respect to any of their intrinsic properties, none of the ἐτεῇ existents will be subject to perishing through qualitative

---

[34] For a succinct formulation of this objection, see J. Van Cleve, 'Three Versions of the Bundle Theory', *Philosophical Studies*, 14 (1985), 95–107.

[35] *Ep. Hdt.* 68–71.

[36] The trouble is that neither Epicurus nor—as far as I am aware—any of our ancient Epicurean sources provides us with a complete list of essential properties, nor any hint about how one could arrive at such a list. Lucretius does give some examples of both essential properties and accidents: tangibility is essential to body, intangibility to void, heat to fire, liquidity to water, weight to stones. Slavery, poverty, wealth, freedom, war, and peace, on the other hand, are accidents (*De rerum natura* 1. 449–63). The examples offered for accidental properties are relational, and not absolute, properties. Yet, surely, some absolute properties, such as the colour of the house, can be accidental properties. It is also clear that, for example, a visible object *o* will essentially have the property of 'having colour', but it is not certain how far a specific colour can be an essential property of a body. Indeed, it seems to be a daunting task to fix the set of essential properties in a non-circular way and without introducing something like Aristotle's secondary substances. I would suggest, without, however, pursuing the question in this paper, that the clue might be found in the theory of preconceptions (προλήψεις). Preconceptions seem to exhibit recurrent complexes of properties as constitutive of natural classes of bodies. We can fix the essential properties of a house on the basis of our preconception of 'house'. It is crucial in this respect that preconceptions have a criterial role and must therefore be anchored in reality.

change.[37] Epicurus, by contrast, accepted not only the reality of phenomenal properties of composite bodies, but also the *per se* existence of composite bodies. Yet surely such composite bodies can lose their permanent attributes and thereby cease to exist. That Epicurus recognized the connection between qualitative change and the passage into not-being is shown by his remark at *Ep. Hdt.* 54 that we saw earlier: 'For all qualities change; but the atoms do not change in any respect, since something solid and indissoluble must persist when compounds are decomposed, which can make it *so that the changes* [μεταβολάς] *are not to and not from not-being*'. Qualitative change (μεταβολή) can lead to not-being, and this is why the ultimate ingredients must be unalterable (ἀμετάβλητα) in order to guarantee that not all things pass into not-being.

To sum up, from the Epicurean ontology of bodies and properties it follows that even *per se* existents of the world can go out of existence by qualitative change. Yet such a view could easily jeopardize the principles of conservation as set out at the beginning of the *Letter*. What Epicurus wants to guarantee by the unalterability of atoms is not that there is no destruction of existing things at all, and not even that none of the *per se* existing things can cease to exist, but that, even though compounds *qua* compounds do cease to exist, their ultimate components do not admit any qualitative change of their intrinsic properties, and therefore resist dissolution and other forms of destruction;[38] or, as Lucretius puts it, that these bodies are eternal. And in so far as the ultimate components of compound bodies are like that, even if compounds *qua* compounds do cease to exist, the sum total of the universe remains constant. The 'fullness' of the atom, on the other hand, provides a physical account of these 'strong' bodies, and the analysis of qualitative change in terms of transposition, addition, and subtraction explains how a compound body can go through qualitative changes in such a way that its ultimate ingredients do not change at all with respect to any of their intrinsic properties.

Let me finally remark that this way of construing Epicurus' conception of atoms might be able to solve another problem of Epi-

[37] The ontological status of macroscopic objects is debated. Based on Plutarch, *Adv. Colot.* 1110 E–F, R. B. B. Wardy, 'Eleatic Pluralism', *Archiv für Geschichte der Philosophie*, 70 (1988), 125–46, argues that the existence of compounds is 'by convention', just like the existence of sensible qualities. At any rate, the Democritean dictum does not include compounds *qua* compounds among the ἐτεῇ existents.

[38] Note that on this analysis, void too is 'strong'.

curean physics. Interpreters have pointed out that if atomicity is justified merely by the lack of void within the atom (or in other words by the fullness of the atom), then it will remain unclear how atoms can retain their independence when they collide with each other.[39] When atoms collide, they touch each other and hence there is no layer of void between them. If this is so, how come that they do not fuse and form one larger atom from that moment onwards, for at that moment they constitute one continuous extension without the void punctuating it? (The alternative interpretation, according to which there is always a layer of void between atoms, has its own difficulties that I cannot discuss here.) But if, as I have suggested, Epicurus' principal claim is that the atoms are unalterable with respect to shape, size, and weight, and this claim is justified on the basis of independent reasons and not on the basis of the condition of the absence of void within these bits, then these reasons will yield not only uncuttability but also 'inaugmentability'. In other words, Epicurus has a reason for maintaining not only that the ultimate physical components of phenomenal bodies are indivisible, but also that these bits will not lose their individuality by fusion when they collide.

Central European University, Budapest

BIBLIOGRAPHY

Bailey, C., *The Greek Atomists and Epicurus* [*Greek Atomists*] (Oxford, 1928).

Bodnár I., 'Atomic Independence and Indivisibility' ['Atomic Independence'], *OSAP* 16 (1998), 35–61.

Brunschwig, J., 'L'argument d'Épicure sur l'immutabilité du tout', in *Permanence de la philosophie: mélanges offerts à Joseph Moreau* (Neuchâtel, 1977), 127–50; repr. as 'Epicurus' Argument on the Immutability of the All', in J. Brunschwig, *Papers in Hellenistic Philosophy* (Cambridge, 1994), 1–20.

Furley, D., 'Democritus and Epicurus on Sensible Qualities', in J. Brunschwig and M. C. Nussbaum (eds.), *Passions and Perceptions: Studies in Hellenistic Philosophy of Mind* (Cambridge, 1993), 72–94.

[39] For a recent examination of the problem, see Bodnár, 'Atomic Independence'. See also Konstan, 'Problems', esp. 402–7; C. C. W. Taylor, *The Atomists: Leucippus and Democritus* (Toronto, 1999), 186–8; and Hasper, 'Foundations'.

Hasper, P. S., 'The Foundations of Presocratic Atomism' ['Foundations'], *OSAP* 17 (1999), 1–14.

Konstan, D., 'Problems in Epicurean Physics' ['Problems'], *Isis*, 70 (1979), 394–418.

Long, A. A., and Sedley, D. N., *The Hellenistic Philosophers* [LS] (2 vols.; Cambridge, 1987); French translation: *Les Philosophes hellénistiques*, trans. J. Brunschwig and P. Pellegrin (3 vols.; Paris, 2001).

Mourelatos, A. P. D., 'Intrinsic and Relational Properties of Atoms in the Democritean Ontology', in R. Salles (ed.), *Metaphysics, Soul, and Ethics in Ancient Thought: Themes from the Work of Richard Sorabji* (Oxford, 2005), 39–63.

O'Keefe, T., 'The Ontological Status of Sensible Qualities for Democritus and Epicurus', *Ancient Philosophy*, 17 (1997), 119–34.

—— 'Epicurus', in *The Internet Encyclopedia of Philosophy*, http://www.iep.utm.edu/e/ epicur.htm

Sedley, D., 'Epicurean Anti-Reductionism' ['Anti-Reductionism'], in J. Barnes and M. Mignucci (ed.), *Matter and Metaphysics* (Naples, 1988), 295–327.

—— 'The Inferential Foundations of Epicurean Ethics', in S. Everson (ed.), *Ethics* (Companions to Ancient Thought, 4; Cambridge, 1998), 129–50.

—— *Lucretius and the Transformation of Greek Wisdom* (Cambridge, 1998).

—— 'Hellenistic Physics and Metaphysics' ['Hellenistic Physics'], in K. Algra, J. Barnes, J. Mansfeld, and M. Schofield (eds.), *The Cambridge History of Hellenistic Philosophy* (Cambridge, 1999), 353–411.

—— '*On Generation and Corruption* I 2' ['*On GC* I 2'], in F. A. J. de Haas and J. Mansfeld (eds.), *Aristotle: On Generation and Corruption, Book 1* (Oxford, 2004), 65–89.

—— 'The Eleatic Origins of Atomism', in P. Curd and D. W. Graham (eds.), *The Oxford Handbook of Presocratic Philosophy* (Oxford, forthcoming).

Sharples, R., *Stoics, Epicureans and Sceptics* (London and New York, 1996).

Taylor, C. C. W., *The Atomists: Leucippus and Democritus* (Toronto, 1999).

Van Cleve, J., 'Three Versions of the Bundle Theory', *Philosophical Studies*, 14 (1985), 95–107.

Wardy, R. B. B., 'Eleatic Pluralism', *Archiv für Geschichte der Philosophie*, 70 (1988), 125–46.

MATTER, MEDICINE, AND THE MIND: ASCLEPIADES vs. EPICURUS

ROBERTO POLITO

ASCLEPIADES OF BITHYNIA (*fl.* second century BC) was not only an eminent physician, but also a philosopher. As Antiochus of Ascalon puts it, he was 'second to none in the art of medicine and acquainted with philosophy too'.[1] The several traces he left in philosophical literature suggest that he was more than merely acquainted with it. Nevertheless, while the principles of his physiology have been recently investigated in depth,[2] his 'acquaintance' with philosophy has never been pursued as I believe it deserves.[3] It is my intention to take a closer look at this acquaintance, as the

© Roberto Polito 2006

This paper, whatever its remaining defects, has benefited from the criticisms and suggestions of Philip van der Eijk and David Sedley. The latter has accompanied the *Sitz im Leben* of the paper through different versions, and my gratitude to him goes beyond what I can express in this note. Neither of these people, however, should be assumed to agree with the views here expressed. I should also like to thank Geoffrey Lloyd for early discussions of some of the questions I address in this paper, and Patricia Smith Churchland for her encouragement and advice. Asclepiades was the subject of a lecture I gave at the philosophy department of Yeditepe University, Istanbul, in December 2004, and of a shorter paper I gave at the Newcastle 'Approaches' conference in August 2005. I am grateful to both audiences for comments.

[1] S.E. *M.* 7. 201–2. The Greek for 'acquainted' is ἁπτόμενος; see below, n. 148.

[2] J. T. Vallance, *The Lost Theory of Asclepiades of Bithynia* [*Theory*] (Oxford, 1990), and 'The Medical System of Asclepiades of Bithynia' ['System'], *ANRW* 37.1 (1993), 693–727.

[3] Vallance, 'System', 703 ('what may have been explicit claims to philosophical awareness on his [Asclepiades'] part were mere window dressing'), is, I believe, wrong. The best description of Asclepiades' philosophical agenda remains that of M. Wellmann, 'Asklepiades von Bithynien, von einem herrschenden Vorurteil befreit' ['Asklepiades'], *Neue Jahrbücher für das klassische Alterthum*, 21 (1908), 684–703. Later scholarship, with the exception of J. Pigeaud, *La Maladie de l'âme: étude sur la relation de l'âme et du corps dans la tradition médico-philosophique antique* [*Maladie*] (Paris, 1981), 171–96, focuses almost entirely on his particulate theory of matter. As I hope to show, Asclepiades' most innovative contribution to philosophy was his account of the soul. By 'philosophical agenda', as distinct from a medical one, I refer to the set of questions that typically feature in a 'professional' philosopher's

ancient sources understood it. These authors praised Asclepiades' doctrinal consistency, and awarded him, instead of Epicurus, the leadership of the materialist lobby. Beyond their anti-Epicurean purpose, these texts give us insight into the philosophical core of Asclepiades' system, in the form of a consequential application of materialism to the mind–body problem, thus qualifying him as the closest ancient antecedent to modern materialistic accounts of the mind. As I have spoken of a 'materialist lobby', the first topic I shall address (Section 1) is what this lobby's agenda was, and to what other lobby it was opposed.

1. Mechanism vs. teleology

In the *Phaedo* Plato has Socrates complain that earlier philosophers failed to address the question *why* the world is as it is. It is his view that this question is far more important than the one they actually addressed, *how* the world has become as it is. Nevertheless, in the face of his early lack of interest, in the *Timaeus* Plato goes on to rescue natural science, and to put forward his 'likely story' of how the world has become as it is, in the light of geometrical principles and the Demiurge's action. In this way he hoped to reconcile a formal and a material account of things.[4] His pupil Aristotle is critical of Plato's story, and yet Aristotle too was concerned with the role of forms in the phenomenal world, and provided his own teleological account of it. The same goal was pursued by the Stoics, whose active principle is distinguishable from matter only notionally, but mixed with it in reality, so as to give form from inside. Thus, although Plato, Aristotle, and the Stoics disagree on several issues, their doctrines converge in postulating purpose in nature, and could be interpreted as different formulations of one and the same idea.

The ancients at first put forward this picture of the history of philosophy in terms of continuity. This tendency, which touched nearly all schools from the first century BC onward,[5] is called eclec-

---

agenda. I am aware that the borders between the two agendas are thin, and in the course of this paper I shall argue that they are even thinner than normally thought.

[4] D. Furley, *The Greek Cosmologists* [*Cosmologists*] (Cambridge, 1987), 9–15, observes that there is no contradiction between the two tasks: Plato's moral theory *requires* an account of nature suited to it.

[5] Antiochus the Academic was its most convinced upholder (see below, p. 287 and

tic, or syncretist, in the secondary literature.[6] Each ancient author belonging to this tendency attributes different degrees of merit to one or another philosopher, but the emphasis is on agreement. The purpose was, perhaps, to offer a simplified philosophical map for Roman beginners.[7]

However, for all that these authors wished to make the map as simple as possible, they refrained from covering the entire panorama: Epicurean atomism was too distant from the mainstream ideas of nature to fit in. Thus, they resorted to a bipolar scheme of philosophy, reminiscent of Plato's *Phaedo* (96–9), with Epicurus championing materialism and providing a common enemy.[8] This segregation of Epicurus turns into a *damnatio memoriae* in late antiquity and throughout the Middle Ages.[9] As a result, our most detailed source on Epicureanism happens to be a poet, Lucretius, whose verse-making ability prevented the loss of his work, in spite of his heretical ideas.

Antiochus of Ascalon was the leading figure of syncretism in the first century BC, but not much of him survives.[10] To us the author

n. 10). Panaetius is an eminent Stoic antecedent. Centuries later, in spite of their unchallenged hegemony in the philosophical panorama, many Platonists continued to claim for themselves the legacy of both Aristotle and the Stoics (e.g. Porph. *Vita Plot.* 14).

[6] Zeller's label 'Eclecticism', with capital 'E', is challenged by P. L. Donini, 'The History of the Concept of Eclecticism' ['Eclecticism'], in J. Dillon and A. A. Long (eds.), *Questions of Eclecticism: Studies in Later Greek Philosophy* (Berkeley, Los Angeles, and London, 1988), 15–33, as derogatory and failing to see that conflicting school allegiances remain in place. J. Barnes, 'Antiochus of Ascalon' ['Antiochus'], in J. Barnes and M. Griffin (eds.), *Philosophia Togata: Essays on Roman Philosophy and Society* (Oxford, 1989), 51–96 at 79 n. 103, proposes the adjective 'syncretist' for Antiochus.

[7] D. N. Sedley, 'Philodemus and the Decentralisation of Philosophy' ['Philodemus'], *Cronache ercolanesi*, 33 (2003), 31–41 at 32–5, discusses the contemporary delocalization of schools away from Athens subsequent to the Roman conquest, which might have influenced the decline in school loyalty.

[8] Furley, *Cosmologists*, 1–8, provides an outline account of the two 'pictures of the world' which compose the bipolar scheme of philosophy, while the rest of his book focuses on the materialist tradition. The present paper purports to be an addition to it, by bringing into the picture the physician Asclepiades, whom Furley left out.

[9] Cf. Dante's picture of Epicurus paying the penalty of his heresy in the depths of hell (*Inf.* 10. 13–15), while all other philosophers converse in limbo (*Inf.* 4. 130–47).

[10] An account of Antiochus' doctrines is offered by J. Dillon, *The Middle Platonists: A Study of Platonism, 80 B.C. to A.D. 220* (London, 1977), 62–106, and by Barnes, 'Antiochus', 78–89. E. Di Stefano, 'Per una nuova raccolta delle testimonianze e dei frammenti di Antioco di Ascalona' ['Raccolta'], *Quaderni catanesi*, 6 (1984), 95–144, provides a recent assessment of the testimonia.

who best expresses the idea that there existed just two opposite and irreconcilable schools of thought in antiquity is the eminent doctor and Platonist philosopher Galen (late second century AD).[11] Galen's bipolar scheme is as follows. On the one side stand those who posit that matter is a continuum and a unity. These people advocate intentionality and rationality both at the level of nature and as a standard of human knowledge and conduct. On the other side are those who posit void and particles, and who explain life and intelligence in terms of the mechanical processes that inert matter undergoes, thus, in Galen's view, abolishing human responsibility:

Now, speaking generally, there have arisen the following two sects in medicine and philosophy among those who have made any definite pronouncement regarding Nature. . . . The one school supposes that all substance which is subject to genesis and corruption is at once continuous and susceptible of alteration. The other school assumes substance to be unchangeable, unalterable, and subdivided into fine particles which are separated from one another by empty spaces. All people, therefore, who can appreciate the logical sequence of an hypothesis hold that, according to the second teaching, there does not exist any substance or faculty peculiar either to nature or to the soul, but that these result from the way in which the primary corpuscles, which are unaffected by change, come together. According to the first-mentioned teaching, on the other hand, Nature is not posterior to the corpuscles, but is a long way prior to them and older than they; and therefore in their view it is Nature which puts together the bodies of both plants and animals, and this she does by virtue of certain faculties which she possesess. Further she skilfully moulds everything during the stage of genesis; and she also provides for the creature after birth, employing here other faculties again . . . According to the other school, none of these things exist in the natures [of living things], nor is there in the soul any original innate idea, whether of agreement or difference, of separation or synthesis, of justice or unjustice, of the beautiful and the ugly; all such things, they say, arise in us from sensation and through sensation, and animals are stirred by certain impressions and by memories. Some of these people have even expressly declared that the soul possesses no reasoning faculty, but that we are led like cattle by the affections of our senses, and that we are unable to refuse or dissent from anything. In their view, obviously, courage, wisdom, temperance, and self-control are all mere nonsense, we do not love either each other or our offspring, nor do the gods care about us. (Gal. *De nat. fac.* 2. 27–9, trans. Brock)[12]

[11] Cicero already has a basic idea of the bipolar scheme, which he might have borrowed from Antiochus (Barnes, 'Antiochus', 80–1).

[12] Cf. M. Vegetti, 'Historiographical Strategies in Galen's Physiology' ['Strate-

Galen, who claims allegiance to the first sect,[13] does not bother to name its authorities here, but the references are well known, and given throughout the treatise: Plato, Aristotle, and the Stoics, with the addition of Hippocrates as far as medicine is concerned. The terminology is, as such, Stoic. It is a Stoic claim that substance is 'unified' (ἡνῶσθαι) by the divine breath.[14] Galen leaves out breath, because there were different views as to how unity is secured to the world, and yet these differences are not such as to affect the basic idea, on which all members of the sect agree, that the world is a unity (a 'closed world', as Furley describes it) and ordered for the best.[15] Indefinite divisibility is a cornerstone of Stoic physics, because it allows breath to pervade matter through and through. However, not only the Stoics, but also the vast majority of philosophers, including Plato and Aristotle, were opposed to the idea that void could be present in our world, and co-responsible for the way it is.

Stoic terminology can be detected also in Galen's scale of beings, which features 'nature' (*physis*) and the 'soul' (*psychē*). The term 'soul' connotes the mental functions possessed by animals. The term 'nature' connotes the vital functions possessed by both plants and animals.[16] The third and lowest class of beings was, according to the Stoics, that of inanimate things, such as stones, which are held together by a certain 'tenor' (*hexis*) alone. As Galen complains, the members of the second sect, at least those who observed their principles, failed to identify different classes of beings, and attempted to provide a unified account of life and intelligence in terms of in-

gies'], in P. J. van der Eijk (ed.), *Ancient Histories of Medicine: Essays in Medical Doxography and Historiography in Classical Antiquity* (Leiden, 1999), 383–95 at 389–90. Galen offers a similar, albeit more condensed, report at *De usu part.* 3. 17.

[13] On Galen's philosophical allegiances see R. J. Hankinson, 'Galen's Philosophical Eclecticism', *ANRW* 36.5 (1992), 3505–22 at 3508–11.

[14] Alex. Aphr. *De mixt.* 216. 14 Bruns = *SVF* ii. 473 = LS 48c.

[15] Galen displays the same catholic attitude regarding the question whether the soul is corporeal (*De util. resp.* 4. 509; *De foet. form.* 4. 700–2: cf. L. García-Ballester, 'Soul and Body, Disease of Soul and Disease of the Body in Galen's Medical Thought' ['Soul'], in P. Manuli and M. Vegetti (eds.), *Le opere psicologiche di Galeno: atti del terzo colloquio galenico internazionale, Pavia, 10–12 settembre 1986* (Naples, 1988), 117–52 at 124–7). Galen's open-mindedness, however, is no scientific caution. In his view, to establish whether the inborn heat or the *pneuma* is the soul, or only provides its material vehicle, is not the point. What does matter is that this substance, whatever it is, is not inert matter.

[16] Galen defines these notions at the very beginning of his treatise (*De nat. fac.* 2. 1), where he declares his preference for the Stoic terminology over the Aristotelian.

teraction between particles and void.[17] This is anathema to Galen. In his view, not only are life and intelligence essentially different from matter, but matter itself is not just matter: it has been shaped and given a form by Nature. In the absence of a *res extensa* factually independent of a *res cogitans*, there does not exist, for Galen as well as for his authorities, a set of mechanical or physical laws as opposed to teleological ones.[18] While everything in the world has a purpose, life and intelligence none the less are an important reference-point, because they reveal better than inanimate beings that materialism falls short of explaining things.

2. The champion of materialism

On the side opposite to Galen stand those who believe that matter is the only reality, and that it follows mechanical laws alone. I shall refer to this position as 'materialist' for the sake of simplicity, although I am aware that the description is open to question. Vitalistic accounts of nature such as that of the Stoics do not qualify as materialist in the sense thus defined. Only atomism and a few other philosophies—Strato's is one[19]—do. The leading figures of this stance in antiquity are Democritus and Epicurus. To our surprise, however, Galen does not mention either, but the physician Asclepiades of Bithynia instead:

With their views we have dealt at greater length in another work in which we discuss the views of the physician Asclepiades. Those who wish to do

[17] The same point is made by Plutarch at *Adv. Col.* 1111 E–1112 C; cf. also Cic. *ND* 1. 39; S.E. *PH* 3. 187.

[18] As E. Ostenfeld, *Ancient Greek Psychology and the Modern Mind–Body Debate* [*Psychology*] (Aarhus, 1987), 34, puts it with reference to Plato's *Timaeus*. On Aristotle see Ostenfeld, *Psychology*, 37–47; T. H. Irwin, 'Aristotle's Philosophy of Mind' ['Aristotle'], in S. Everson (ed.), *Psychology* (Companions to Ancient Thought, 2; Cambridge, 1991), 84–101, esp. 78. M. Burnyeat, 'Is an Aristotelian Philosophy of Mind Still Credible?', in M. C. Nussbaum and A. O. Rorty (eds.), *Essays on Aristotle's* De anima (Oxford, 1992), 15–26. D. N. Sedley, 'Chrysippus on Psychophysical Causality', in J. Brunschwig and M. Nussbaum (eds.), *Passions and Perceptions: Studies in Hellenistic Philosophy of Mind* (Cambridge, 1993), 313–31, discusses the Stoic view.

[19] Cicero's exclusion of Strato from the mainstream philosophical tradition on account of his antiteleology and lack of interest in ethics is telling (Cic. *Acad.* 1. 9. 34=Strato fr. 13 Wehrli). H. Diels, 'Über das physikalische System des Straton', in *Kleine Schriften* (Darmstadt, 1969), 239–265 [originally in *SB der Akad. Berlin* (1893), 101–27], remains an invaluable contribution, although details of his reconstruction have been called into question.

so may familiarize themselves with their arguments, and they may also consider at this point which of the two roads lying before us is the better one to take. (Gal. *De nat. fac.* 2. 29)[20]

Galen's reference to Asclepiades is primarily bibliographical, and purports to tell us which one of his works to consult for additional information. Nevertheless, if Galen expounded the philosophical system of the second sect in a treatise devoted to Asclepiades, one understands that Galen was thereby attributing to this physician the role of leader. This attribution demands an explanation.

Perhaps the reason is that Galen himself is a doctor, and therefore is more interested in physicians. As a matter of fact, however, Galen is not the only one to have Asclepiades speak for the entire tradition. A similar interpretation is adopted by Calcidius, a Platonic commentator who lived in the fourth–fifth centuries AD, and whose main source is to be sought in the Middle Platonist tradition:[21]

Of those who believed that the substance of matter is discrete [i.e. that it is not a continuum and a unity], some posited that the immense void is interspersed with partless bodies, others that it is interspersed with parts which are, however, undifferentiated and similar to each other, yet others that it is interspersed with atoms or compact molecules—and all of them attributed no certain and definite location to the ruling-part-of-the-soul. (Calc. *In Tim.* 214, p. 251 Waszink, my trans.)[22]

Calcidius reports that all atomists, indeed all upholders of a particulate theory of matter,[23] denied the existence of a localized ruling-part-of-the-soul. This denial was, in effect, distinctive of Asclepiades (who is hinted at by the reference to his 'molecules'—Latin *moles*, Greek ὄγκοι, and who is named in what follows), and Cal-

[20] Vegetti, 'Strategies', 390 ('the second school is characterised by a prevailingly Epicurean terminology, which is seen as the main ideological feature of the whole atomist and mechanistic tradition'), misses the point, but see ibid. 392.
[21] J. H. Waszink, *Timaeus a Calcidio translatus commentarioque instructus* (Leiden, 1962), pp. lxxiv–lxxvii, suggests that Porphyry is the source. O. Phillips, 'Numenian Psychology in Calcidius?', *Phronesis*, 48 (2003), 132–51, argues in favour of Numenius.
[22] I am grateful to Gretchen Reydams-Schils for discussion of interpretative problems in this passage.
[23] J. Mansfeld, 'Doxography and Dialectic' ['Doxography'], *ANRW* 36.4 (1990), 3056–229 at 3113, detects a reference to Diodorus and Anaxagoras too. The continuation, however, makes it clear that the report purports to cover Asclepiades, Democritus, and Epicurus. I shall refer to them as 'atomists' for the sake of simplicity, although Asclepiades himself can be labelled thus only in a loose sense (see below, n. 35).

cidius' attributing the same view to Epicurus and Democritus is in sharp disagreement with reports on them.[24] It is surprising that Calcidius fails to mention differences between the atomists' account of the ruling-part-of-the-soul, which is his topic, while mentioning differences between their accounts of the soul's atoms:

> Either there are light, round, and very frail molecules, from which the soul is made up, and which is entirely breath, as Asclepiades thought, or there are atoms of fire, as in the account of Democritus, who thought that fire and soul were fashioned from the same bodies, or, what is the same, there are atoms which run together by chance and without reason, and which create the soul, as Epicurus thought, on account of their similarity. (Calc. *In Tim.* 215, p. 252 Waszink, my trans.)[25]

The suspicion arises that Calcidius' failure to distinguish between their accounts of the ruling-part is no slip, but a deliberate retrojection of Asclepiades' view onto Epicurus and Democritus. The order that Calcidius adopts, which lists Asclepiades *before* Democritus and Epicurus, and which defies both chronology and relative eminence, lends further support to the hypothesis that Asclepiades is Calcidius' primary reference-point throughout his report on the atomists,[26] in which he expounds a coherent body of doctrines that recalls the one Galen attributes to his second sect.

The agreement between Galen and Calcidius in making up a unitary tradition opposite to Plato's, the spokesman of which is Asclepiades, is remarkable, and it finds a parallel in Sextus, who associates Epicurus and Asclepiades as regards their shared yielding to sense-reports:

> Not far removed, it would seem, from the opinion of these people [the Cyrenaics] are those who declare the senses to be a criterion of truth. For

[24] Epicurus located the mind in the chest (Mansfeld, 'Doxography', 3114 n. 243), while Democritus is reported to have located it in the brain (ibid. n. 242; the alternative interpretation, that the mind is, according to Democritus, widespread within the body, goes back to Asclepiades' own school; cf. R. Polito, *The Sceptical Road: Aenesidemus' Appropriation of Heraclitus* [*Road*] (Leiden, 2004), 109–12).

[25] I tentatively accept the reading *delicatae* ('frail'), as defended by Vallance, *Theory*, 23–4, although *deligatae* ('tied up') is the *lectio difficilior*, and might therefore be preferable. For additional questions concerning the text see below, n. 67.

[26] B. W. Switalski, *Des Chalcidius Kommentar zu Plato's Timaeus: Eine historisch-kritische Untersuchung* (Beiträge zur Geschichte der Philosophie des Mittelalters, III/6; Münster, 1902), 51–2, was the first to hypothesize that Calcidius' entire report on the atomists refers to Asclepiades.

that there have been some who have maintained this view has been made clear by Antiochus the Academic, when in the second book of his *Canonics* he writes thus: 'But a certain other man, second to none in the art of medicine and acquainted with philosophy too, believed that the sensations are really and truly acts of knowledge, and that we apprehend nothing at all with the aid of a reason.' For, in these words Antiochus seems to be stating the view mentioned above [that the senses are a criterion of truth] and to be hinting at Asclepiades the physician, who abolished the ruling-part-of-the-soul, and who lived at the same time as himself . . . Epicurus for his part asserts that there are two things which are correlative, impression and opinion. (S.E. *M*. 7. 201–2, trans. Bury, with minor changes)

Sextus attributes the opposite view, that both reason and the senses contribute to knowledge, to the members of Plato's school (7. 141–89), the Aristotelians (217–26), and the Stoics (227–60). Once again we face an opposition between the mainstream philosophical tradition of the Hellenistic age and an alternative tradition that includes Epicurus and Asclepiades.[27] One recalls that Galen too in his account of the two sects has the materialists yield to sense perception alone.

On closer inspection, not only does Sextus associate Epicurus and Asclepiades, but he also lists the latter *before* the former, as Calcidius does. Sextus tells us that his source is Antiochus.[28] Thus, Antiochus is, for us, the earliest author to couple Asclepiades with Epicurus, and to award him pole position. True, Antiochus' reference is not to an all-embracing philosophical system, as it is in Galen and Calcidius, but to epistemology alone—no wonder, since the *Canonics* was about epistemology. Nevertheless, it was Antiochus' strategy to urge similarities in any area between all major

[27] A third view, that reason alone provides a criterion of truth, is attributed by Sextus to all Presocratics (*M*. 7. 89–140), but he is unable to indicate any more recent upholder.

[28] Antiochus is referred to also at 7. 162, in a way which has suggested to some that he is Sextus' basic source. H. Tarrant, 'Agreement and the Self-Evident in Philo of Larissa' ['Agreement'], *Dionysius*, 5 (1981), 66–97 at 80–2, suggests that Antiochus is the source of Sextus' entire doxography on the criterion; D. N. Sedley, 'Sextus Empiricus and the Atomist Criteria of Truth' ['Criteria'], *Elenchos*, 13 (1992), 19–56 at 45–7, attributes to Antiochus only the post-Socratic section at 7. 141–262; Barnes, 'Antiochus', 64–5, is sceptical about any *Quellenforschung*. For my purposes, it is enough that Sextus at 7. 201 invokes Antiochus not only as a source for Asclepiades, but also for the existence of the doxographical entry to which Asclepiades and Epicurus belong, about those who made sensation a criterion of truth, and the run of the report makes it obvious that Asclepiades was the first of the group that Antiochus mentioned.

philosophical schools with the exception of atomism.²⁹ Galen's reduction of the entire history of philosophy to two opposite and all-embracing systems is but a corollary. While the absence of any reference to Asclepiades' philosophical views from Cicero, who used Antiochus as a source, makes it unlikely that Antiochus himself dwelt upon them in any insistent way, it is hard to believe that Antiochus failed to notice, and to mention, the similarity between Asclepiades' and Epicurus' particulate theories of matter and their anti-teleological stances, a similarity which was to become a topos in later authors. Be that as it may, the Sextus passage makes it tempting to think that Antiochus was at the origin of the pole position that Galen and Calcidius awarded to Aslepiades. This hypothesis squares well with the fact that Galen and Calcidius belong to the same Platonic lobby as Antiochus.

It is disappointing that Sextus gives no indication as to why Antiochus mentioned Asclepiades before Epicurus in his account of their epistemologies. The first thing one understands is that Asclepiades' reputation was far higher than both our scarce evidence and the low level of interest he has provoked among modern scholars might lead us to imagine. He was so well known in his day that Antiochus, a contemporary of him according to Sextus, did not even bother to name him, expecting his readers to understand the reference all the same.³⁰ Sextus is still capable of recovering it three centuries later. Asclepiades' ongoing reputation in Sextus' day was secured by a school still claiming allegiance to him and comparable in size, it seems, to the Epicurean. The survival of both schools is a matter of complaint for Galen:

Almost all other schools depending on similar principles [particles and void] are now entirely extinct, while these two alone [the Epicurean and

---

²⁹ Varro, Cicero's Antiochean speaker, develops this interpretation of the history of philosophy at *Acad.* 1. 2. 7–11. 42. The exclusion of Epicureanism is at *Acad.* 1. 2. 6–7; cf. Barnes, 'Antiochus', 80–1. Antiochus himself took sides, of course, with the mainstream tradition in epistemology against Epicurus (*Acad.* 2. 7. 21; 1. 8. 30; cf. Di Stefano, 'Raccolta', 119; but see Sedley, 'Criteria', 49), as he did in any other philosophical area.

³⁰ Antiochus' failure to name Asclepiades may recall the procedure, not unusual in antiquity, of refraining from naming contemporary authors (e.g. Colotes at Plut. *Adv. Col.* 1120 C as regards Arcesilaus and the Cyrenaics). Yet, even so, this procedure presupposes that the reference is to an author whom readers can easily identify. Moreover, Plutarch complains about Colotes' failure to mention his contemporary opponents, in a way that suggests that this failure was not so normal after all.

the Asclepiadean] maintain a respectable existence still. (Gal. *De nat. fac.*
2. 52, trans. Brock)[31]

Apuleius, who lived in the same period as Galen and Sextus, makes
Asclepiades the most eminent Greek doctor ever, second only to
Hippocrates, thus confirming that he was still enjoying a high reputation.[32] Antiochus himself did not add any such qualification:
Asclepiades was 'second to none'. Dioscurides, a physician of the
first century AD, complains that contemporary pharmacologists explain the action of drugs by differences among molecules (ὄγκοι),
and are all 'followers of Asclepiades'.[33] Indeed, there is evidence
that a school claiming allegiance to Asclepiades flourished throughout the Mediterranean world up to the third century AD.[34]

Galen's rationale for awarding someone a mention is not, however, merely ongoing reputation, but doctrinal consistency (ἀκολου-
θία), as he makes clear at the very beginning of his account of the
two sects:

Now, speaking generally, there have arisen the following two schools of
thought in medicine and philosophy among those who have made any
definite pronouncement regarding Nature. I refer, of course, to those of
them who know what they are talking about, and who realize the logical
consequence of their hypotheses, and stand by them; as for those who
cannot understand even this, but who simply talk any nonsense that comes
to their tongues, and who do not remain definitely attached either to one
school of thought or the other—such people are not even worth mentioning.
(Gal. *De nat. fac.* 2. 27, trans. Brock, with minor changes)

As it happens, Asclepiades is the only affiliate of the second sect
to be mentioned in this context. While it is Galen's usual strategy
to associate Asclepiades and Epicurus as regards their theories of

---

[31] Cf. ibid. 2. 34; *De exp. med.* 86 Walzer. It is not likely that the reference is to
the Methodists, as Vegetti, 'Strategies', 393, hypothesizes, because the Methodists
themselves did not hold a particulate theory of matter of the kind Galen refers
to (Gal. *De meth. med.* 10. 267–8 does not provide evidence to the contrary, *pace*
J. Pigeaud, 'Les fondements du méthodisme' ['Fondements'], in P. Mudry and J.
Pigeaud, *Les Écoles médicales à Rome: actes du 2ème colloque international sur les
textes médicaux latins antiques* (Geneva, 1991), 9–50 at 42–7).

[32] Apul. *Flor.* 19. 1–2. A similar description, however, is applied by Pliny to
Diocles (*NH* 26. 10), and so it should perhaps not be given too much emphasis.

[33] Diosc. *De mat. med.*, pref. 2; cf. Vallance, *Theory*, 14. I owe the reference to
John Scarborough.

[34] V. Nutton, *Ancient Medicine* (London and New York, 2004), 168 and 375
nn. 81–2.

matter,[35] it is not right to say that Galen dismisses Asclepiades as a
plagiarist. Rather, it is his opinion that Asclepiades outbids Epicurus, and qualifies as a leader, because he offers the most consistent
account of things in mechanist terms:

Epicurus, in his desire to adhere to the facts, cuts an awkward figure by
aspiring to show that these agree with his principles, whereas Asclepiades
safeguards the sequence of principles, but pays no attention to the obvious
facts. (Gal. *De nat. fac.* 2. 52, trans. Brock)

Thus, Galen concludes that:

The principles of Epicurus have been refuted by Asclepiades, who adhered
always to their logical sequence, about which Epicurus evidently cares little.
(Gal. *De nat. fac.* 2. 52, trans. Brock)[36]

Galen is talking about attraction, the faculty by which certain organs allegedly draw certain substances towards themselves (e.g. the
kidney's attraction of urine), but his statement is a general one:
while Epicurus inconsistently rescues phenomenal evidence and
common sense, and might mislead someone into thinking that materialism provides a suitable paradigm for explaining the phenomenal world, Asclepiades' explanations are so obviously contrary to
facts and counter-intuitive as to refute the principles he shares with
Epicurus. Thus, making Asclepiades the spokesman of materialism
provides Galen with a shortcut for refuting the entire tradition.

Calcidius plays a game similar to Galen's, but different in presentation. He does not portray Asclepiades as more consistent than
Epicurus—on his story, they held the very same view. Rather, he argues that to abolish a localized ruling-part-of-the-soul, as we know
Asclepiades alone did, is a logical consequence of materialism. In
this way Calcidius not only provides a parallel to Galen, but also

[35] Gal. *De simpl. med.* 11. 405; *De nat. fac.* 2. 45, 51–2; *De usu part.* 3. 74, 571;
873–4; *De plac. Hipp. et Plat.* 5. 3, 18; *De theriaca* 14. 250; *In Hipp. VI epid.* 17b.
162. Some have been misled by Galen into thinking that Asclepiades' theory of
matter is the same as Epicurus', but it is not (Vallance, *Theory*, 10–11).

[36] Surprisingly, Galen in the very same context praises Menodotus for making
the point that Asclepiades' tenets are in opposition to phenomenal evidence, but
also to each other. A passage at *De exp. med.* 85, whose source is arguably Menodotus, suggests that this 'opposition to each other' was a matter of phrasing more
than ideas (see below, n. 150). Be that as it may, the run of the argument against
Epicurus makes it obvious that Galen regarded Asclepiades' alleged inconsistency
as negligible compared with Epicurus' own. I must add, however, that Galen at *De
usu part.* 3. 473, with Epicurus out of the picture, does not hesitate to denounce
inconsistencies in Asclepiades too.

gives us a hint as to which of Asclepiades' teachings qualifies him as a leader, namely his abolition of a localized ruling-part. On closer inspection, the same hint can be drawn from the Galen passage quoted on p. 288. Here Galen refers to certain unnamed members of the second sect who 'have even expressly declared that the soul possesses no reasoning faculty'. These people go further than other members, but Galen considers their addition a consequence of the sect's shared principles. The identification of these people with the Asclepiadeans gains support not only from Galen's subsequent explicit reference to him, but also from his other report:

> While nearly all men believe that there exist . . . intelligence, memory, and deliberation, Asclepiades attempted to dismiss these things, holding that they do not exist at all. (Gal. *In Hipp. de officina medici*, 18b. 660, my trans.)

Galen's 'reasoning faculty' ($\delta\dot{v}\nu\alpha\mu\iota\varsigma$ $\tau\hat{\eta}\varsigma$ $\psi\upsilon\chi\hat{\eta}\varsigma$ $\hat{\eta}$ $\lambda o\gamma\iota\zeta\acute{o}\mu\epsilon\theta\alpha$) is the same thing as the ruling-part-of-the-soul (Lat. *principale*, Greek $\dot{\eta}\gamma\epsilon\mu o\nu\iota\kappa\acute{o}\nu$) of which Calcidius speaks. This part of the soul was deemed to control sensation and motion, and to be in charge of thinking, for those beings that think. From Galen one understands that Asclepiades simply abolished it, and Sextus adopts this interpretation.[37] By contrast, Calcidius' atomists deny only a special location to this part of the soul, and not, it seems, its actual existence. Both formulations of Asclepiades' thesis find parallels in other sources, and while the latter formulation is likely to be his original phrasing, the former appears to be an established interpretation. In what follows, I shall take a closer look at Asclepiades' idea of the soul: I shall ask what his denial of a localized ruling-part was supposed to mean, and why it should make his account of the soul more consistent with materialism than Epicurus' own, which I shall briefly review. Subsequently, I shall turn to epistemology, and shall investigate what may lie behind Antiochus' listing Asclepiades before Epicurus.

3. Asclepiades on the soul

The idea of a ruling-part-of-the-soul, i.e. a control and command centre of our psychic life, anticipates, to some extent, that of a central nervous system. In antiquity there was a dispute as to whether

[37] S.E. *M.* 7. 202 (quoted above, pp. 292–3); 7. 380.

the brain or the heart hosts it.[38] To deny that it has a special location
is peculiar, not least because the argument that Calcidius supplies to
that effect on behalf of the atomists makes the seemingly conflicting
point that the head is the centre of our psychic life:

The breath, as these people maintained, undergoes a process of rarefaction
during respiration, when the breath moves from the mouth to the lungs, and
from here it passes through the heart. Subsequently, it enters the so-called
carotid vessels (those which cause a lethal sleep when injured), carried by
the arteries which depart from the heart. Through these vessels the breath
reaches the head. It is only at this point, they maintain, that the principle
of sensation comes into being, and from the head it spreads through the
entire body through the subtle and narrow orifices of the nerves. (Calc. *In
Tim.* 214, p. 252 Waszink)[39]

The idea is that the soul amounts to air inhaled from outside, and
that internal organs transform it into a substance suited to sensing.
Whose view is Calcidius reporting—Asclepiades', Democritus', or
Epicurus'? His atomists maintain that 'in the head for the first time
[*ibi primum*] the principle of sensation comes-into-being [*nasci ini-
tium sentiendi*; Greek τὴν ἀρχὴν τῆς αἰσθήσεως γενέσθαι?]'. Epicurus
believed that the heart is the centre of our psychic life, and he
never identified the substance of the soul with ordinary air. Calcidius is obviously not reporting his view. The idea that we breathe
the soul's substance from outside goes back to Democritus,[40] except that Democritus' air (in fact, spherical atoms like those of
fire, to be found in the atmosphere)[41] is not in need of being processed by internal organs, the soul being out there, and ready to
be inhaled.[42] Calcidius' atomists too believe that we breathe the
soul. Yet, they attribute to anatomical organs a major role in ge-

[38] P. J. van der Eijk, 'The Heart, the Brain, the Blood and the *Pneuma*: Hippocrates, Diocles and Aristotle on the Location of Cognitive Processes' ['Blood'],
in id., *Medicine and Philosophy in Classical Antiquity: Doctors and Philosophers on
Nature, Soul, Health and Disease* [*Antiquity*] (Cambridge, 2005), 119–35 at 119–24,
discusses problems in ancient doxography on the ruling-part-of-the-soul.

[39] My trans. and emendation of the last line of the text; cf. Polito, *Road*, 144
n. 311.   [40] Arist. *DA* 403ᵇ31–404ᵃ16; *De resp.* 471ᵇ30–472ᵃ5.

[41] Arist. *DA* 404ᵃ16–19.

[42] Arist. *DA* 410ᵇ27–411ᵃ1 finds that Democritus' story veers so dangerously
towards the idea that soul is everywhere that he associates Democritus with the
Orphics. H. Cherniss, *Aristotle's Criticism of Presocratic Philosophy* [*Presocratic*]
(Baltimore, 1935), 289–91, argues against Aristotle's identification of Democritus'
soul- and fire-atoms, and he is probably right in observing that Democritus 'did not
recognise the existence of soul outside of the living body'. Aristotle's report is not
an actual report, but a refutation. Democritus' problem is that his account of the

nerating the 'principle of sensation', by processing and refining the breath (*spiritus . . . attenuatus*). The reference to anatomy invites the hypothesis of a medical pedigree for the theory Calcidius expounds. Asclepiades, who was a physician and better acquainted than Democritus with anatomical organs,[43] is a far more plausible candidate, and, as it happens, the thesis that the soul 'comes-to-be' (Lat. *nasci*, Greek γίγνεσθαι) out of respiration is echoed in reports on him.[44] Remarkably, but, in the light of the syncretist tendency of unifying philosophical traditions, unsurprisingly, Calcidius is not the only one to foist this account onto Epicurus. So does the author of pseudo-Galen's *De historia philosopha*: 'Epicurus believed that the soul is outer air inhaled through respiration.'[45]

The head plays an important role in the view of Calcidius' atomists, just as we know it did for Asclepiades. It was Asclepiades' view that the meninges are the area of the brain affected by mental diseases, presumably on account of a special concentration of soul's breath there.[46] Thus, one would expect him to locate the ruling-part-of-the-soul in the head, all the more so if Calcidius' account of how the soul comes-to-be voices his view. Asclepiades did provide a physiological argument to the effect that neither the head nor any other bodily organ hosts any such part.[47] But his motivation for abolishing a localized ruling-part was, in effect, a genuinely philosophical one. According to Caelius Aurelianus:

He [Asclepiades] denies that the ruling part of the soul is situated in a

soul, in the absence of any explanation of what makes the soul different from fire, and why spherical atoms should become the soul *only* in the body, is liable to incur the criticism that Aristotle applies to it.

[43] It is a widespread assumption that Asclepiades did not appeal to anatomical arguments, but I have called that assumption into question in R. Polito, 'On the Life of Asclepiades of Bithynia' ['Life'], *Journal of Hellenic Studies*, 119 (1999), 48–66 at 63–4.

[44] Gal. *De util. resp.* 4. 471, 492–3; *Comm. in Hipp. VI Epid.* 17b. 320; cf. Wellmann, 'Asklepiades', 697; Vallance, *Theory*, 107–8. Galen distinguishes this thesis from that which attributes to respiration the purpose of 'feeding' the soul. The idea that respiration provides the substance of the soul goes back as far as Hippocrates' *De morbo sacro* (Pigeaud, *Maladie*, 33–41; Vallance, *Theory*, 85 n. 113, adds Timaeus of Locri). [45] [Gal.] *De hist. phil.* 24 (not in Usener).

[46] Asclepiades allows different concentrations of soul *pneuma* in the body (cf. [Gal.] *De hist. phil.* 24), and, according to him, mental diseases affect the area of the meninges (Cael. Aurel. *De morb. ac.* 1. 6; 3. 112). Erasistratus too had identified the meninges as the starting-point of the nerves (Ruf. *De part. corp. hum.* 71–5).

[47] Calc. *In Tim.* 216, p. 253 Waszink, attributes the argument to the atomists in general, but Tert. *DA* 15 correctly attributes it to Asclepiades alone.

definite part of the body. In fact, the soul, he says, is nothing but the combination of all senses [*nihil aliud quam coetum omnium sensuum*]. (Cael. Aur. *De morb. ac.* 1. 115, trans. Drabkin)

Tertullian too understands Asclepiades in this way:

One Dicaearchus, a Messenian, and amongst the medical profession Andreas and Asclepiades, have thus destroyed the ruling part, by letting the senses, for which they claim the job of a ruler, take the place of the mind. (Tert. *DA* 15. 2)[48]

The idea is that the mind is coextensive with the senses. In this way, Asclepiades addresses a distinctive item of the philosophical agenda concerning the relatonship between higher and lower psychic function (*nous* and *psychē*), thinking and sensing (*noeisthai* and *aisthanesthai*). Asclepiades' thesis, that the ruling-part-of-the-soul does not have a definite location in the body, sounds like a transposition of that idea in terms of the physiology of the body. The report that in this way Asclepiades actually abolished that part of the soul, and thereby reason, only makes the philosophical consequence of that thesis explicit.

Asclepiades' idea that the mind is coextensive with the senses logically follows from his description of the soul as such as a 'combined exercise' (συγγυμνασία) of them,[49] i.e. a product of their working, rather than a substance in its own right. In this sense, the soul was for him incorporeal.[50] His incorporeality claim only apparently disagrees with his other claim, that the soul is breath:[51] Asclepiades

---

[48] Trans. Holmes, adapted to Waszink's interpretation of the expression *dum in animo ipso volunt esse sensus* 'by letting the senses . . . take the place of the mind'; cf. J. H. Waszink (ed. and comm.), *Tertullianus: De anima* (Amsterdam, 1947), 219, 223. On Dicaearchus see R. W. Sharples, 'Dicaearchus on the Soul and on Divination' ['Dicaearchus'], in W. W. Fortenbaugh and E. Schütrumpf (eds.), *Dicaearchus of Messana: Text, Translation and Discussion* (New Brunswick and London, 2001), 143–73, esp. 148–51; V. Caston, 'Dicaearchus' Philosophy of Mind', in Fortenbaugh and Schütrumpf, *Dicaearchus*, 175–93 at 175–89. Andreas is the eminent late 3rd-cent. BC Herophilean doctor, perhaps identifiable with Andreas the father of Asclepiades (Polito, 'Life', esp. 53–6), and the Tertullian report is probably a retrojection of Asclepiades' view on to him (Waszink, *Tertullianus*, 222).

[49] Cael. Aurel. *De morb. ac.* 1. 115 (quoted above) speaks of a 'combination' (*coetus*) of all senses. Aët. *Plac.* 4. 2. 12 and [Gal.] *Def.* 19. 373 put it in terms of a 'combined exercise' (συγγυμνασία) of them. The rarity of the Greek word συγγυμνασία suggests that this description of the soul was Asclepiades' *ipsissima verba*.

[50] Aët. *Plac.* 4. 3 1. As Patricia Smith Churchland has suggested to me in private correspondence, Asclepiades' idea could be that 'integration across sensory modalities permits more sophisticated conceptualization than if the sensory signals are kept separate . . . He might think of this combination as "incorporeal" only in the

[See opposite for n. 50 cont. and n. 51

denied a separate existence of the soul *qua* mind, but he posited a fuel that activates the sense-organs, and in this other sense a soul does exist, and it is matter.[52]

Asclepiades identified this material as 'breath'. Thus, his theory belongs to the large family of pneumatic theories of the soul. The difference is that Asclepiades' breath is neither akin to the substance of the stars (Aristotle) nor a fragment of the divine *pneuma* governing the world (the Stoics). Asclepiades' breath is everyday air, which we breathe in and out during respiration. The theory that respiration supplies us with the material of the soul is widely attested in Hellenistic medicine, but is alien to the philosophy of the period,[53] its most recent philosophical upholder being Diogenes of Apollonia.[54] The criticism which the theory incurred from Aristotle, and which is probably responsible for discouraging later philosophers from adopting it, was that vital and mental functions require a special substance, distinct from the substances found in the phenomenal world.[55] Accordingly, Aristotle's own view was that respiration serves the purpose of refrigerating the inner heat,[56] and the breath that he posited as a vehicle of the soul was the 'inborn' (σύμφυτον) one. This adjective describes what is special about this breath, by distinguishing it from the breath 'which comes from outside', i.e. ordinary air.[57]

The conceptual framework of the ancient debate on the substance

loose sense that it does not correspond to activity in any sensory modality, but is an integrative product.'

[51] See above, n. 44, for references, and also [Gal.] *De hist. phil.* 24.

[52] Vallance, 'System', 703, distinguishes between a 'cognitive' and a 'physical' sense in which Asclepiades refers to the soul.

[53] D. Furley and J. Wilkie (eds.), *Galen: On Respiration and the Arteries* [*Respiration*] (Princeton, 1984), 3–39, provide an account of medical and philosophical theories of respiration before Galen.

[54] Simpl. *In Phys.* 151. 28 Diels (=64 B 4 DK): 'Humans and all other animals live upon air by breathing it, and this is their soul and their intelligence.'

[55] Arist. *DA* 411ᵃ7–26 (cf. Cherniss, *Presocratic*, 308–10). Theophr. *De sens.* 46–8 addresses the same criticism to Diogenes; cf. H. Baltussen, *Theophrastus against the Presocratics and Plato: Peripatetic Dialectic in the* De sensibus (Leiden, 2000), 181–2. [56] *De resp.* 475ᵇ16–19; *PA* 668ᵇ33–669ᵃ2.

[57] *GA* 736ᵇ29–737ᵃ1; 741ᵇ37–742ᵃ15; *PA* 659ᵇ17–18; cf. W. Jaeger, 'Das Pneuma im Lykeion', *Hermes*, 48 (1913), 29–74; W. Wiersma, 'Die aristotelische Lehre vom Pneuma', *Mnemosyne*, 11 (1943), 102–7; F. Solmsen, 'The Vital Heat, the Inborn Pneuma and the Aether', *Journal of Hellenic Studies*, 77 (1957), 118–23; V. Caston, 'Epiphenomenalisms, Ancient and Modern' ['Epiphenomalisms'], *Philosophical Review*, 106 (1997), 309–63 at 336 n. 63 ('Aristotle identifies [the natural heat of the body] with ordinary fire'), is, I believe, mistaken.

of the soul is clearly different from that of the later Western tradition about the mind, which is centred upon the dichotomy between consciousness and matter. For there is no question in antiquity that soul and body interact with one another, and that consciousness entails certain physical processes.[58] The controversy concerned, rather, whether or not these physical processes are essentially different from processes involving inert matter. Aristotle's distinction between inborn and external breath, and, relatedly, his rejection of the theory that respiration supplies us with the soul, are to be read against this background.

Against Aristotle, Hellenistic physicians rescued the breathed-soul theory (as I shall call it henceforth), because anatomical findings of that age made workable the idea that internal organs mechanically transform outer air into a substance suited to vital and mental functions.[59] Unsurprisingly, Galen is not sympathetic to this idea:

Thus, every hypothesis of channels as an explanation of natural functioning is perfect nonsense. For if there were not an inborn faculty given by Nature to each one of the organs at the very beginning, then animals could not continue to live even for a few days . . . Let us suppose that they [the living beings] were steered only by material forces, and not by any special powers . . . If we suppose this, I am sure it would be ridiculous for us to speak of natural, and, still more, psychical activities, and, in fact, life as a whole. (Gal. *De nat. fac.* 2. 80, trans. Brock)[60]

By refraining from positing a special substance for the soul, Hellenistic physicians were thereby adopting what one might describe as a reductionist stance. One should not be misled into thinking, however, that they themselves bothered to draw the philosophical consequences of their account of respiration. It is only Asclepiades who made the point that vital and mental activities are a product of the mechanical processes that outer air undergoes inside the body.

---

[58] This consideration applies even to Plato, at least in terms of the unfavourable effects that the body has on the soul.

[59] Erasistratus is a central figure; cf. Gal. *De usu part.* 3. 540; *De util. resp.* 4. 502; *An in art.* 4. 706; cf. C. R. S. Harris, *The Heart and the Vascular System in Ancient Greek Medicine* [*Heart*] (Oxford, 1973), 222–5. Erasistratus went so far as to explain human intelligence in terms of the large number of cerebral cavities in which the breath is processed (Gal. *De plac. Hipp. et Plat.* 7. 3. 10). Harris, *Heart*, 214, describes him as the first iatro-physicist in the history of science.

[60] According to Vallance, *Theory*, 141 n. 57, Galen is here attacking Erasistrateans, Asclepiadeans, and Methodists all at once.

In this way, he did away with the vital and the mental as special domains, thereby doing away with the very explanandum that the breathed-soul theory allegedly failed to explain according to Aristotle.

One thing in particular appears to have intrigued Asclepiades about the breathed-soul theory:

> According to Asclepiades there is no counting how many souls one has: for even the one existing a moment ago is now totally gone, and that which exists now is new, and a moment later this will go too and yet another one will take its place. (Gal. *De util. resp.* 4. 484, trans. Furley–Wilkie)[61]

Flux is foundational to Asclepiades' medical aetiology, based on circulation of fluids and gases.[62] However, unlike other medical upholders of comparable aetiologies,[63] Asclepiades in the quoted passage is making a philosophical point, and one which completes his argument: if each incoming breath supplies us with a new soul replacing the older, this soul will be sufficient to fuel our sensory apparatus and, hence, to keep us sensitive, but will not provide us with a mind, or a self, capable of emerging over and above the body. Calcidius picks up this point:

> According to these people, it happens that our soul is never one and the same, but always different and subject to changes. For, since they maintain that the body precedes the soul, they also give primacy to the body. To be sure, the body is always in flux and subject to changes, and the soul too, which is second in condition, is liable to undergo the same affections as the body. (Calc. *In Tim.* 217, pp. 253–4 Waszink, my trans.)

So also does Galen in his account of the two systems of philosophy, which I quoted at the beginning:

> Some of these people have even expressly [ῥητῶς] declared that the soul possesses no reasoning faculty, but we are led like cattle by the affections of our senses, and we are unable to refuse or dissent from anything. (Gal. *De nat. fac.* 2. 29, trans. Brock)

Epicurus fiercely advocated the possibility for us to make decisions and to resist bodily affections. So did Democritus in his ethical

---

[61] Asclepiades was so fond of the psychic-flux theme that he attributed it to Hippocrates himself (Gal. *Comm. in Hipp. VI Epid.* 17b. 246).

[62] Vallance, *Theory*, 108–10; 'System', 698–9.

[63] Erasistratus in the first place (Vallance, *Theory*, 108).

works.[64] Thus, the view that Calcidius and Galen attribute to the atomists may seem to go far beyond what the atomists themselves, both the early and the Hellenistic ones, were willing to concede. Yet Calcidius does offer, on behalf of the atomists, an argument which could be interpreted as closing that gap:

Either there are light, round, and very frail molecules, from which the soul is made up, and which is entirely breath, as Asclepiades thought, or there are atoms of fire, as in the account of Democritus . . . or, what is the same [*id ipsum*], there are atoms which run together by chance and without reason, and which create the soul, as Epicurus thought, on account of their similarity. For, when one of them is touched, the totality of the breath, i.e. the soul, is touched simultaneously. Hence, it is enough that we hear the sound of the word 'snow', and most often we both think of whiteness and at once feel cold, or, if someone tastes something sour, those around him cannot help spitting because of an increase of saliva, and, if one yawns, others feel like doing the same, and the movement of our body follows the same rhythm as the music we hear. (Calc. *In Tim.* 215, p. 252 Waszink, my trans.)

This passage precedes Calcidius' attack on the atomists, and is apparently not affected by any bias. It merely purports to describe the soul's atoms at work. Their putative similarity is given as a condition for their transmitting stimuli within the body.[65] Remarkably, all instances of actions Calcidius mentions (sympathetic yawning, etc.) are *reflex* actions, and he makes no reference to voluntary ones. If the goal is to explain how the soul's atoms work, the argument receives its point from the assumption that reflex actions are not

[64] C. H. Kahn, 'Democritus and the Origins of Moral Psychology' ['Democritus'], *American Journal of Philology*, 106 (1985), 1–31. There is a controversy whether Democritus' ethics is consistent with his physics: G. Vlastos, 'Ethics and Physics in Democritus' ['Ethics'], in R. E. Allen and D. J. Furley (eds.), *Studies in Presocratic Philosophy* (2 vols.; London, 1975), ii. 381–408 [originally in *Philosophical Review*, 54 (1945), 578–92, and 55 (1946), 53–64], argues that it is; C. C. W. Taylor, 'Pleasure, Knowledge and Sensation in Democritus', *Phronesis*, 12 (1967), 6–27, argues that it is not. A recent assessment of this and other questions concerning Democritus' ethics is in J. Warren, *Epicurus and Democritean Ethics: An Archaeology of Ataraxia* (Cambridge, 2002), 29–72.

[65] Previously Calcidius had identified the common sense in charge of processing data as a kind of 'touch'. The idea that touch provides a model for explaining the working of the senses in general has a long history in atomism (e.g. Arist. *De sensu* 442ª29–ᵇ3; Lucr. 3. 165–6 = LS 14B. 3; cf. A. A. Long and D. N. Sedley, *The Hellenistic Philosophers* [LS] (2 vols.; Cambridge, 1987), i. 84). However, Aristotle too, who was no atomist, identified the common sense as 'touch' (*De somn.* 455ª13–26; *DA* 435ª11–ᵇ8). The Cyrenaics too posited a *tactus interior* or *intumus* (Cic. *Acad.* 2. 24. 76; 2. 7. 20 = Aristippus B 66–7 Giannantoni).

to be distinguished from voluntary ones, but are a paradigm for explaining our behaviour in general.

Calcidius expounds the argument soon after mentioning Epicurus, but the argument has no parallel in Epicurean literature, and it fails to consider the possibility of decision-making of the kind Epicurus posits. The closest parallel describing the soul's atoms at work that we get in Epicurean literature is offered by Lucretius, and the difference is perspicuous:

Now I shall explain how it is that we can step forward when we wish, and move our limbs at will, and what the force is which propels the huge bulk of our body. It is up to you to take in what I say. I maintain, as I have maintained before, that first of all idols of movement present themselves to the mind and impinge on it. Then comes the act of will: for no one can begin to do anything, until his mind has foreseen what it wills to do. (Lucr. 4. 877–84, trans. Smith)[66]

Either Calcidius' argument is incomplete or it is not derived from Epicurus. As a matter of fact, Calcidius himself specifies that the view that he is attributing to Epicurus is the same as (assuming that this is what *id ipsum* means) that of Democritus and Asclepiades,[67] thus hinting at a simplified, group picture. Even if one leaves aside that puzzling expression, one observes that Calcidius describes the soul as 'breath' ('the totality of the breath, that is, the soul'), a description which, as such, is not Epicurean,[68] but which recalls word for word that which Calcidius has attributed to Asclepiades just a couple of lines earlier ('Either there are . . .

[66] Cf. J. E. Annas, *Hellenistic Philosophy of Mind* [*Mind*] (Berkeley, Los Angeles, and Oxford, 1992), 175–88.

[67] The Latin reads: 'aut enim moles quaedam sunt . . . ut Asclepiades putat, aut ignitae atomi iuxta Democritum . . . vel id ipsum atomi casu quodam et sine ratione concurrentes in unum et animam creantes, ut Epicuro placet.' For my translation of *id ipsum* cf. *TLL* viib. 353. 3 s.v. *ipse* (cf. p. 307. 74): 'addit notionem identitatis'. Claudio Moreschini (*Calcidio: Commentario al Timeo di Platone*, ed. C. Moreschini (Milan, 2003), 465) translates it 'precisamente', but it is unclear to me how he arrived at this translation. Gretchen Reydams-Schils has suggested to me in private correspondence the translation 'the very essence [of the soul are] atoms which . . .', but this translation entails a *variatio* in the use of the implied *sunt*, from existential to copula, which is, I believe, not likely. David Sedley has suggested to me in private conversation that the expression *id ipsum* could have an adjectival function in respect of *atomi*: '[there are] atoms as such . . .', as distinct from Democritus' *atomi ignitae*. I am grateful to Luigi Lehnus for discussing this point with me.

[68] Calcidius could have thought his attribution to Epicurus appropriate on account of texts such as *Ep. Men.* 63 ('similar to breath'), and yet Epicurus never identifies the soul as such as breath.

molecules, from which the soul is made up, and which is entirely breath, as Asclepiades thought'). Hence the suspicion arises that the argument, like much of Calcidius' doxography on the atomists, actually voices Asclepiades' own view. So does the physiological argument that Calcidius reports to the effect that, according to the atomists, a localized ruling-part-of-the-soul does not exist, an argument which a parallel in Tertullian enables us safely to attribute to Asclepiades,[69] and which, as I shall argue next, already implies the abolition of any distinction between voluntary and involuntary actions.

The argument is that certain insects and reptiles continue to sense and move for a while in spite of being deprived of their putative ruling part.[70] Asclepiades picks up this observation as evidence that there is no such thing as a localized ruling-part-of-the-soul, this being spread in any part of the body. A comparable case, and one with which readers familiar with the Mediterranean landscape may be acquainted, is that of lizards, whose tail carries on moving for some seconds even if severed from the rest of the body. In the face of Asclepiades' claim that these movements are a token of real and even 'intelligent' life (Tertullian speaks of *vivere et sapere*), what we get are spasms of an inanimate part of the body. If these spasms are what he has in mind, the argument proves his claim upon the assumption that voluntary and intelligent actions, putatively initiated by a centralized organ, are essentially the same as involuntary muscle contractions caused by an external stimulus. The difference, if any, is not in kind, but in degree and complexity.

Caelius Aurelianus, at the end of his report on Asclepiades' theory of the soul, is explicit in attributing to him the view that everything is mechanically determined:

He [Asclepiades] declares that all things happen by necessity, and none without a cause, and nature is nothing but matter and its motion, and so it not only helps, but also harms. (Cael. Aur. *De morb. ac.* 1. 115, trans. Drabkin)[71]

Determinism, materialism, and anti-teleology are the cornerstones of Asclepiades' philosophical system. The mechanical processes

[69] Calc. *In Tim.* 216, p. 253 Waszink; cf. Tert. *DA* 15. 2.

[70] The observation that certain plants and insects carry on living even when divided is also found at Arist. *DA* 411^{b}19–30 and 413^{b}16–24, but for a different purpose. Other parallels are listed in Waszink, *Tertullianus*, 223.

[71] 'Nature' here is the principle of human and animal life.

between particles and void interstices ('matter and its motion') account for the phenomenal world, but also, as the context of a discussion of a mental disease, phrenitis, suggests, for human behaviour, thus leaving no room for any independent source of motivation such as volition. What about our impression that we do make decisions? One may suppose that Asclepiades interpreted this impression as illusory and, by analogy with his interpretation of mental states in general, merely epiphenomenal. Whatever the explanation he offered, he was clearly unwilling to allow self-determination. Thus, Galen's and Calcidius' report that the atomists abolish deliberation could be reliable after all, but with regard to Asclepiades alone. Galen's attribution of this position not to all members of the materialist sect, but only to 'some of them', lends further support to this conclusion.

4. Epicurus on the soul

Thus far I have argued that Asclepiades provided an account of the soul which ancient authors deemed to be a logical consequence of materialism. However, in order to be awarded the championship of the materialist lobby, and to outbid the most obvious candidate Epicurus, Asclepiades' consistency is not enough. Epicurus' inconsistency is required. As we saw, Galen detects this inconsistency in Epicurus' yielding to faculties, quasi-magical forces which, as an atomist, he is not equipped to explain, and should not allow.[72] Galen's Platonist fellow Plutarch specifies that, among the faculties that Epicurus inconsistently allowed, are to be counted vital and mental ones:

Thus by the doctrines of these men [the Epicureans], life and living things are abolished, since the primal elements on their hypothesis are void, impassive, godless, and inanimate, and moreover incapable of mixture or fusion. Then how can they claim to leave room for a thing's nature, for mind, and for a living being? As they do for an oath, for prayer, for sacrifice, for worship: in their manner of speaking, in word, by affirmation, by asserting, by pretending, by naming things that by their ultimate principles and tenets they abolish. . . . Indeed we see that some people [the

---

[72] See above, p. 296. Galen develops the opposition between Epicurus and Asclepiades in a treatise about natural faculties, those governing the physiology of the body. It is, therefore, no cause for surprise if the question of the soul receives little attention. The only reference to it is at *De nat. fac.* 2. 28, quoted at p. 288.

Epicureans] who abolish both mind and thought suppose that they abolish neither living nor thinking. (Plut. *Adv. Col.* 1112 C–E, trans. De Lacy)

Plutarch's argument that Epicurus' yielding to common sense is inconsistent with his atomism is the same as we have found in Galen, thus suggesting that the argument was an established one among Platonists, with or without a reference to Asclepiades. Galen's reference to Asclepiades none the less contributes to the argument, because Asclepiades plainly declared what Epicurus should have but did not, that life and intelligence do not exist in the way we normally conceive of them.

For my purpose, it is irrelevant to establish whether the allegation that Epicurus' account of the soul defies his principles is fair, provided that the allegation was made, and that Galen arguably agreed with it. Nevertheless, a closer look at Epicurus may help us to place Asclepiades in a context, and to appreciate his contribution to ancient materialism better, beyond Galen's disingenuous strategy of playing him off against Epicurus.

In order to make best sense of Epicurus' account of the soul, one should start from ethics, which was his primary concern, and foundational to many of his other views. Here Epicurus is found claiming that the mind can, and should, resist the 'flesh', i.e. bodily affections, when resistance proves wise. But how can the mind resist the flesh, if the mind too is matter? To start with, the material of which the soul is made is not, according to Epicurus, the same as that of the rest of the organism. The substance which he added to fire and wind/air in order to explain what is special about the soul, and which, to use Lucretius' words, provides the 'very soul of the soul', is the 'nameless' substance.[73] Plutarch puts the matter like this:

These 'sages' [the Epicureans] get as far as those powers of the soul that affect the flesh, by which it imparts warmth and softness and firmness to the body, when they manufacture its substance by combining their own varieties of heat, gas and air, but quit before they reach the seat of power. For that whereby the soul judges, remembers, loves and hates—in short its thinking and reasoning faculty—is added, they say, from a quality 'that has no name'. The talk of the thing 'that has no name' is, we know, a confession of embarrassed ignorance: what they cannot make out they assert that they cannot name. (Plut. *Adv. Col.* 1118 D–E, trans. De Lacy)[74]

[73] Lucr. 3. 275; cf. LS 14A, C–D.
[74] Cf. Lucr. 3. 238–45; Aët. 4. 3.11 (= LS 14B); see LS i. 14; S. Everson, 'Epicurean

It is Plutarch's contention that Epicurus' positing a special substance for the soul, other than the phenomenal ones, is a declaration that the mental is an addition to the physical, i.e. not accountable with the aid of the conceptual tools by which Epicurus explains nature at large.

To the extent that the soul is made of atoms for Epicurus, it would be wrong to label his psychology 'dualistic' in the same way as Descartes's.[75] Yet there is no need to posit an incorporeal soul in order to qualify as a mind–body dualist: it is enough to posit that the soul is made of a substance which does not exist elsewhere in the phenomenal world, as the Epicureans and indeed the majority of ancient philosophers did.[76] This other dualism differs from the Cartesian one, because it has the mental as physical (Stoics, Epicureans), or at least as not independent from the physical (Aristotle); it is none the less a dualism, because the physical in question is irreducible to the rest of the physical, and is endowed with special powers. The idea that at least certain entities such as the inborn breath are ensouled in their own right defies the modern concept of matter, and could be interpreted as a kind of animism.[77]

In the case of Epicurus, moreover, there seems to be evidence that he went so far as to posit that volition is independent of the motion of the soul's atoms, regardless of the substance of which these atoms are made:

But many naturally capable of achieving these and those results fail to achieve them, because of themselves, not because of one and the same responsibility of the atoms and of themselves . . . For the nature of their

Psychology' ['Epicurean'], in K. Algra, J. Barnes, J. Mansfeld, and M. Schofield (eds.), *The Cambridge History of Hellenistic Philosophy* (Cambridge, 1999), 542–59 at 544–5.

[75] Cartesian dualism is rare in antiquity. Plato is an antecedent (but see Everson, *Psychology*, 'Introduction', 1–12 at 8–9). Aristotle's active intellect too can be viewed as a token of Cartesian dualism, although Aristotle's psychology as a whole is not (Irwin, 'Aristotle', 70–3, 77–8; Caston, 'Epiphenomalisms', 326–39; P. J. van der Eijk, 'Aristotle's Psycho-Physiological Account of the Soul–Body Relationship', in J. P. Wright and P. Potter (eds.), *Psyche and Soma: Physicians and Metaphysicians on the Mind–Body Problem from Antiquity to Enlightenment* [*Psyche*] (Oxford, 2000), 57–77; C. H. Kahn, 'Aristotle versus Descartes on the Concept of the Mental', in R. Salles (ed.), *Metaphysics, Soul, and Ethics in Ancient Thought: Themes from the Work of Richard Sorabji* (Oxford, 2005), 193–208).

[76] Pigeaud, *Maladie*, 142, speaks of 'interactionist dualism' for Epicurus. I have already discussed above Aristotle's notion of inborn *pneuma*, which became the authoritative philosophical view through the intermediacy of the Stoics.

[77] This consideration applies *a fortiori* to Presocratic hylozoism.

atoms has contributed nothing to some of their behaviour, and degrees of behaviour, and character, but it is their developments which themselves possess all or most of the responsibility for certain things. It is a result of that nature that some of their atoms move with disordered motions, but it is not on the atoms that all responsibility should be placed for their behaviour.

And again:

Thus, when a development occurs which takes on some distinctness from the atoms in a differential way—not in the way which is like viewing from a different distance—he acquires responsibility which proceeds from himself; then he straightaway transmits it to his primary substances and makes all of it (?) one. (LS 20B, from Epicurus' *On Nature* 25. 2–12, 16–22)[78]

According to David Sedley, who first paid the attention that they deserve to these difficult texts, Epicurus is thereby making certain mental states (the 'developments', ἀπογεγεννημένα, of which Epicurus speaks) emergent over and above physical ones, and with a causal efficacy of their own.[79] If this reading is correct, Epicurus would be a dualist not only in the sense described above, but also in the more conventional sense of making the mental ontologically distinct from the corporeal.

It is Sedley's claim that this interpretation makes best sense of Epicurus' theory of the swerve. The swerve is an unpredictable variation in the route of the soul's atoms, which provides the atomic interface of our mind's action in breaking the chain of physical causation, and which Epicurus put forward in order to reconcile self-

---

[78] Trans. Sedley, with the exception of the last line, the translation of which I borrow from S. Laursen, 'Epicurus *On Nature* XXV', *Cronache ercolanesi*, 18 (1988), 7–18 at 9; Sedley's own translation was 'makes the whole of it into a yardstick', but this was based on a now superseded reading. Laursen's article also offers some critical remarks on Sedley's philosophical interpretation of the text.

[79] See D. N. Sedley, 'Epicurus' Refutation of Determinism' ['Refutation'], in Συζήτησις: *studi sull'epicureismo greco e romano offerti a Marcello Gigante* (Naples, 1983), 11–51, esp. 37–40; LS i. 109–10; and D. N. Sedley, 'Epicurean Anti-Reductionism' ['Anti-Reductionism'], in J. Barnes and M. Mignucci (eds.), *Matter and Metaphysics: Fourth Symposium Hellenisticum* (Naples, 1988), 295–327 at 322–3. Other commentators believe that the reference is to atomic developments from the original make-up of the soul (Annas, *Mind*, 125–34; J. E. Annas, 'Epicurus on Agency', in Brunschwig and Nussbaum, *Passions and Perceptions*, 53–71 at 58; cf. Everson, 'Epicurean', 557; R. J. Hankinson, 'Determinism and Indeterminism' ['Determinism'], in Algra *et al.*, *The Cambridge History of Hellenistic Philosophy*, 513–41 at 524; T. O'Keefe, 'The Reductionist and Compatibilist Argument of Epicurus' On Nature Book 25', *Phronesis*, 47 (2002), 153–86).

determinism with atomism.[80] The interpretation that the swerve is the physical cause of volition incurs the objection that a random event by definition rules out intentional action, with the consequence of attributing to Epicurus a very weak line of argument in support of what appears to be a cornerstone of his psychology.[81] Sedley's own interpretation is that Epicurus' swerve is not itself responsible for volition; rather, the swerve represents the fact that two or more alternative motions are physically possible for an atom at any time, and volition is left free to choose between these physical possibilities.[82] Thus, if Sedley is right, Epicurus would be making mental events (volition) the cause of special physical events, and this is definitely incompatible with any materialism whatsoever.

Whatever Epicurus' precise strategy for reconciling self-determinism with atomism, the very fact that he advocated self-determinism creates a breach in his general account of things in terms of mechanism. Lucretius openly declares that the decrees of fate (2. 254 *foedera fati*), i.e. laws of nature (elsewhere *foedera naturai*), do not apply to human behaviour. But how come that human behaviour follows different patterns from all other things? Epicurus' distinction between a domain, the natural, which is ruled by mechanical laws alone, and another one, the mental, which is self-regulating, is, as such, a token of dualism. As Galen puts it in the passage quoted at the beginning (p. 288), genuine materialism entails providing a unified account of life and intelligence in terms of the mechanical interaction between particles. Modern philosophy of mind proposes a more elaborate picture. Materialism need not be reductive, and reductive materialism, in turn, need not eliminate mental talk such as volition: it only requires that one find a suitable account of it in physical terms. Be that as it may, one question is whether the idea that the mental is a self-regulating domain can be accommodated, in one way or another, to materialism; another question is whether this idea is at home there. At least in the case of Epicurus, it is fairly clear that his claim concerning volition is not a conclusion at which he arrives on the basis of his general account of things, but a metaphysical thesis which

---

[80] Cic. *De fato* 21–5 (=LS 20E); cf. Cic. *Fin.* 1. 6. 18; *ND* 1. 25. 69 (=281 Usener).

[81] Sedley, 'Refutation', 11–12, who also provides references to earlier literature.

[82] Ibid. 40–3; 'Anti-Reductionism', 318.

Roberto Polito

he adopts on independent grounds, and which he foists onto his atomism.[83]

One should not be surprised if Epicurus has the soul as a source of autonomous action over and above the body, up to the point of declaring that the wise man will be happy even when being roasted inside Phalaris' bull:[84] it is a shared feature of ancient ethics to detach spiritual welfare, which philosophers claim to provide, from bodily welfare, which is the job of physicians in the first place. Physicians, for their part, are naturally inclined to emphasize the importance of healthy working of the body. To challenge the philosophical assumption that the soul is other than the body and prior to it requires only a small, additional step, which some made. Herophilus (early third century BC) restricts himself to the com- monsensical consideration that 'wisdom cannot manifest itself . . . and reason is powerless, if health is missing'.[85] Tertullian (second century AD), who is no doctor, and yet who expresses the views of Soranus, a major authority both as a medical historian and as a thinker in his own right (*fl.* 98–138), goes further. He identifies the soul as matter, and makes the point that doctors alone are equipped to study it:

I am aware how huge the philosophical literature addressing the topic of the soul is . . . But I did also consult medicine . . . which claims the job of investigating the soul for herself. Why not? To account for the soul may well appear more relevant to medicine, on account of her treating the body. Hence, medicine comes in conflict with her sister [philosophy] most often, because she knows the soul better by visiting it, as it were, in its own domicile. (Tert. *DA* 2. 6, my trans.)[86]

If the soul is matter, philosophical therapies, in the form of spiritual advice, are just useless:

---

[83] Annas, *Mind*, 124–5, argues that Epicurus' defence of self-determination is consistent with physicalism, as long as the atoms' swerving is a physical process. However, Annas herself goes on to admit that Epicurus 'takes very seriously what we believe about ourselves, and where this conflicts with a possible way for his theory to develop, it is the theory he rejects, and not our intuitive picture of ourselves' (134–5).

[84] Cic. *Tusc.* 2. 7. 17.   [85] S.E. *M.* 11. 50 (=Herophil. T. 230 von Staden).

[86] The explicit argument to the effect that soul is matter is at *DA* 5–6. L. Edelstein, 'The Relation of Ancient Philosophy to Medicine' ['Relation']', in *Ancient Medicine: Selected Papers of Ludwig Edelstein*, ed. O. Temkin (Baltimore, 1967), 349–66 at 357, claims that 'the leadership [of discussions on the soul] rested unchallenged with philosophers', but he obviously does not take into account the Tertullian passage.

As, therefore, Soranus has himself shown us, by appealing to facts, that the soul is nourished by material sustenance, let a philosopher demonstrate that it is sustained by a spiritual food. But the fact is that nobody, confronted with a patient whose soul is in danger of leaving the body, has ever treated him successfully with the honey-water of Plato's subtle eloquence or with crumbs from the minute nostrums of Aristotle. (Tert. *DA* 6. 7, trans. Holmes, with changes)

The argument rests upon interpreting the soul solely as a physical life-force, and it deliberately ignores the additional meaning attributed to the term by Plato and others, as referring to a cognitive and moral agent as distinct from the body.

Mental disorders, those putatively affecting the soul, are a borderline field in which medicine and philosophy clash. Drabkin observes that 'ancient medicine . . . considers all [mental] diseases to be essentially organic', i.e. physical.[87] The following passage comes from Caelius Aurelianus, whose source is Soranus, the same as Tertullian's:[88]

There is also a question whether hydrophobia is a disease of the soul or of the body, for some say that it is a disease of the soul, on the ground that desire or longing is a function peculiar to the soul rather than the body . . . But we cannot agree with those who adduce this argument. For a longing for drink or delight in drinking, as in eating, arises from an affection of the body . . . Affections of the soul, in the meaning of the philosophers, are affections of our judgement. But the disease of hydrophobia derives from a bodily force and is therefore a bodily disease, though it also attacks the psychic nature, as do mania and melancholy. (Cael. Aur. *De morb. ac.* 3. 109–11, trans. Drabkin)[89]

By these words Caelius Aurelianus speciously allows a distinction between affections of the body and affections of the soul (in the

---

[87] I. E. Drabkin, 'Remarks on Ancient Psychopathology' ['Psychopathology'], *Isis*, 46 (1955), 223–34 at 226. Van der Eijk, 'Blood', 125–8, discusses the Hippocratic attitude. Galen too, who is a Platonist and yet a doctor, agrees with reducing mental diseases to unbalances in the quality-carrying humours of the body (Drabkin, 'Psychopathology', 229; García-Ballester, 'Soul', 131).

[88] Cael. Aur. *De morb. ac.* 2. 8 claims to be 'Latinizing' Soranus; other references in A. E. Hanson and M. H. Green, 'Soranus of Ephesus: Methodicorum princeps' ['Soranus'], *ANRW* 37.2 (1994), 968–1075 at 979 n. 31; see also P. H. Schrijvers, *Eine medizinische Erklärung der männlichen Homosexualität aus der Antike* [*Homosexualität*] (Amsterdam, 1985), 22–3.

[89] The passage is referred to by M. Frede, 'Philosophy and Medicine in Antiquity' ['Philosophy'], in id., *Essays in Ancient Philosophy* (Oxford, 1987), 225–47 at 227.

Stoic form of affections of 'judgement', *iudicium*),[90] but he nullifies this distinction by positing that not only so-called mental diseases (hydrophobia, mania, and melancholy), but any desire (he mentions desire for food and drink) is causally determined by affections of the body.[91] The point recalls Asclepiades' thesis that our desire for food and drink is brought about by the dilation of passages in the oesophagus and the stomach, which requires to be filled.[92]

In another passage Caelius concedes that philosophical aid none the less may be of some use:

And if he [the sufferer from mania] is willing to hear discussions of the philosophers, he should be afforded the opportunity. For by their words philosophers help to banish fear, sorrow, and anger, and in so doing make no small contribution to the health of the body. (Cael. Aurel. *De morb. chron.* 1. 167, trans. Drabkin)

Remarkably, however, philosophical aid is recommended for patients who ask for it on their own initiative. What if a patient does not? The idea seems to be that philosophical therapies are unequipped to treat diseases, including mental diseases, for real, and yet that they contribute to reassuring patients who believe in their efficacy. In this sense philosophical therapies are, for Soranus, but one of the several placebo techniques in which the doctor does not engage himself, and yet which he allows:

Some people say that some things are effective by antipathy, such as the magnet and the Assian stone and hare's rennet and certain other amulets to which we for our own part pay no attention. Yet one should not forbid their use; for even if the amulet has no direct effect, still through hope

---

[90] Pigeaud, *Maladie*, 112–20.

[91] The only 'disease' that Caelius Aurelianus (*De morb. chron.* 4. 131–7) recognizes as distinctively mental is homosexuality. Drabkin, 'Psychopathology', 228, finds this move 'remarkable', and in sharp contrast with Soranus' usual attitude towards mental diseases. Yet Caelius goes on to quote Parmenides' verses to the effect that homosexuality comes about from a dysfunction in the formation of the embryo, and he also reports that several doctors believed homosexuality to be hereditary, and to affect children and old men more on account of erectile problems. It is hard to see how a congenital disease or physical dysfunction of this kind could be classified as a *passio mentis* in the sense of a misjudgement of the mind. While Caelius attributes to Soranus the idea that homosexuality is a mental disease, at least the idea that divine providence has set fixed roles for male and female is not, as such, attributable to Soranus, who rejected any idea of providence (Hanson and Green, 'Soranus', 980; Schrijvers, *Homosexualität*, 1–3, 17–25).

[92] Cael. Aurel. *De morb. ac.* 1. 114; *De morb. chron.* 3. 49.

it will possibly make the patient more cheerful. (Sor. *Gyn.* 3. 42, trans. Drabkin)[93]

It would be interesting to know exactly how Soranus reconciled the efficacy he allows to placebo remedies with the assumption, which he seems to make elsewhere, that mental states are epiphenomenal, and have no causal efficacy in their own right.

In yet another passage Soranus seemingly permits philosophers exclusive competence regarding the spiritual growth of children:

At what age the child should be handed over to a pedagogue and what kind of a person he should be, and in what manner the child should be prepared by him for the parents if not brought up by them, and all problems of this sort do not belong to the realm of medicine. They belong more to the realm of philosophy, so that, leaving it to others to philosophise on this occasion, contrary to our habit, we ourselves bring to an end the discourse on child-rearing. (Sor. *Gyn* 2. 57)[94]

However, things are less simple beyond the surface. To start with, Soranus' leaving to others to philosophize on this occasion is 'against his habit'. Indeed, Soranus does philosophize on other occasions, as we know from Tertullian.[95] Secondly, other people— and the run of the passage implies that these other people too are physicians—do philosophize on this topic too, thus claiming for themselves the job that Soranus leaves to professional philosophers. No agreement between physicians and philosophers has been reached.

The competition in which physicians engaged with philosophers on this and other issues may well be primarily a matter of professional rivalry, and aimed at increasing their share of the educational market.[96] Whatever their motive, one should not lose sight of the arguments which they put forward, and which hint at a basic disagreement between the philosophical and the medical approaches

---

[93] Cf. Drabkin, 'Psychopathology', 231.

[94] Trans. Drabkin with a change: I accept Burguière's reading of παρὰ τρόπον; Drabkin's own 'we leave it to others to break with customs and philosophise' defies the syntax.

[95] Tert. *DA* 6. 6; 38. 3; see below, n. 107. This consideration provides additional ground, if any were needed, for rejecting Drabkin's reading of παρὰ τρόπον.

[96] Medicine was not regarded as a liberal art in antiquity, in contrast to philosophy. The doctors' ambition to see their discipline counted as such is, presumably, their motive for disputing with philosophers. On this rivalry see Edelstein, 'Relation', 359–60; Frede, 'Philosophy'; E. Romano, *Filosofi e medici: letteratura medica e società altoimperiale [Filosofi]* (Palermo, 1992), 19–48.

to the mind–body problem. In the light of this disagreement along professional lines, it is, then, no cause for surprise if Galen, himself a Platonist, adopts seemingly reductionist arguments when it comes to advertising medical care.[97] Nor is it a cause for surprise if, on the philosophical side, Epicurus, himself a materialist, veers towards dualism, as he approaches his spiritual medicine for the soul, the *tetrapharmakos*. Seneca's fondness for Epicurean ethics need not be just a matter of open-mindness, but also one of acknowledging that all philosophers have a similar attitude to the mind–body problem. Seneca's fierce hostility towards dietetic and health care, which he regards as a dangerous diversion from the care of one's soul,[98] completes the picture.

5. Medicine vs. philosophy

I have suggested that a unified account of mind and the body is a doctrinal feature of the medical tradition about the soul. It remains for us to detect what place Asclepiades occupies in this tradition. The first thing one observes is that his account of the soul received a loud echo in antiquity: of the two works (now lost) which Galen devoted to Asclepiades, one discussed his teachings in general, while the other dealt with his account of the soul.[99] This account is also Sextus' reference at *M.* 7. 202 when it comes to identifying the unnamed upholder of sensation behind Antiochus' enigmatic words. Ancient philosophical handbooks also mention Asclepiades in connection with his account of the soul: he is in fact the only physician whose *placitum* is reported.[100]

[97] G. E. R. Lloyd, 'Scholarship, Authority and Argument in Galen's *Quod animi mores*', in Manuli and Vegetti, *Galeno*, 11–42, esp. 40–2; Caston, 'Epiphenomenalisms', 351–3; see also Edelstein, 'Relation', 355–6.

[98] *Ep.* 95; cf. Romano, *Filosofi*, 115–21. According to Edelstein, 'Relation', 358, ancient dietetics was so demanding that to follow it seriously was like becoming 'a slave of one's body'.

[99] Gal. *De libris propriis* 19. 38. A refutation of Asclepiades' account of the 'elements of the organism' was found in the thirteenth book of the lost treatise *De demonstratione*; cf. *De ordine librorum suorum* 19. 55.

[100] Aët. *Plac.* 4. 2. 12, p. 386 Diels. This is the chapter 'On the Soul'. However, Aëtius at 4. 5 does report the views of Hippocrates, Herophilus, and Erasistratus as regards the location of the ruling-part-of-the-soul. On Aëtius' medical doxography see D. T. Runia, 'The Placita Ascribed to Doctors in Aëtius' Doxography on Physics', in P. J. van der Eijk (ed.), *Ancient Histories of Medicine* (Leiden, 1999), 189–250.

As for Asclepiades himself, he appears to have written a treatise *On the Soul* in more than one book.[101] Medical discussions of this topic date back as far as Hippocrates.[102] However, no physician earlier than Asclepiades is known to have composed a work recorded under that title. Thus, by choosing it, Asclepiades is emphatically intruding into philosophical territory. A medical tradition of treatises *On the Soul* began to flourish from Asclepiades onward. By Tertullian's day this tradition is sufficiently well established for doctors to claim primacy over philosophers, as we have seen.[103] As we learn from Diogenes Laertius, however, rivalry between them started well before Tertullian's day:

Their physical doctrine they [the Stoics] divide in three parts, dealing with the universe, the elements, the aetiological one . . . and the aetiological part is subdivided into two. And in one of its aspects it overlaps with medical investigation, in so far as it involves investigation of the ruling-part-of-the-soul and the phenomena of the soul, seeds, and the like. Whereas the

---

[101] Gal. *De util. resp.* 4. 484. Galen's wording (τοὺς περὶ ψυχῆς λόγους) leaves it open to question whether περὶ ψυχῆς is the title of a work or an indication of the topic under discussion. However, Galen regularly uses the expression for indicating the title of a work, and the fact that Asclepiades' pupil Titus Aufidius gave that title to one of his treatises (Cael. Aurel. *De morb. chr.* 1. 178) lends support to the hypothesis that his teacher had done so before him. Furley and Wilkie, *Respiration*, adopt this interpretation in their translation of the passage. Vallance, 'System', 709–10, provides a list of treatises attributable to Asclepiades, but fails to mention a work *On the Soul*. One assumes that he went for the opposite reading of Galen's words. However, to judge from Vallance's notes on a provisional manuscript of his proposed edition of testimonia, which he privately allowed me to look at, Vallance too now seems willing to concede that the reference is to the title of a treatise.

[102] See D. B. Claus, *Toward the Soul: Inquiry into the Meaning of 'Psyche' before Plato* [*Soul*] (New Haven and London, 1981), 150–5; R. J. Hankinson, 'Greek Medical Models of Mind' ['Models'], in Everson, *Psychology*, 194–217 at 200–8; P. N. Singer, 'Some Hippocratic Mind–Body Problems' ['Problems'], in J. A. López Pérez (ed.), *Tratados hipocráticos* (Madrid, 1992), 131–43; B. Gundert, 'Soma and Psyche in Hippocratic Medicine', in Wright and Potter, *Psyche*, 13–35. The case of early Hellenistic physicians is discussed by H. von Staden, 'Body, Soul, and Nerves: Epicurus, Herophilus, Erasistratus, the Stoics, and Galen', in Wright and Potter, *Psyche*, 79–116 at 87–96.

[103] Tert. *DA* 2. 6, quoted above. To this passage one should add *DA* 13. 2, where he talks in the same breath of the bodies of medical and philosophical works *On the Soul*. Medical authors of treatises bearing that title are Asclepiades' pupil Titus Aufidius (Cael. Aurel. *De morb. chr.* 1. 178), Tertullian's own source Soranus (*DA* 6. 6), and Antipater (*Scholia in Hom. Iliadem*, iii. 14 Cramer). These last two are both members of the Methodist school of medicine, which stems from Asclepiades via his pupil Themison (Gal. *De meth. med.* 10. 268; *De simpl. medic.* 11. 783), and which shares at least some of his ideas (Gal. *De plen.* 7. 515). Sextus' lost treatise *On the Soul* (*M.* 10. 284; 6. 55) was presumably a collection of Sceptical arguments, and does not belong to the genre of medical literature on the soul.

other part, which investigates how vision is to be explained, what causes the image on the mirror, what is the origin of clouds, thunder, rainbow, halos, comets, and the like, is claimed by the mathematicians also. (D.L. 7. 132–3, trans. Hicks)[104]

The adjective 'aetiological', which no Stoic seems ever to have used before Posidonius,[105] is our key to dating the report, to the first half of the first century BC.[106] By this time physicians have become experts in the field. While the point Diogenes makes concerns physicians in general, the dating of his source lends support to the hypothesis that doctors became more and more involved in psychology from Asclepiades onward.

Tertullian, in contrast with Diogenes, goes into the doctrinal details of the rivalry between physicians and philosophers. His source Soranus wrote a long treatise in four books (now lost) *On the Soul*, in which he critically reviewed the opinions of philosophers.[107] Tertullian mentions him nine times,[108] but his debt is far larger than that,[109] starting with the claim that physicians have privileged access to the soul, and with the argument supplied to that effect, that 'medicine knows the soul better by visiting it, as it were, in its own domicile'. The argument is at first sight hopelessly naïve: one might counter-argue that the soul is that special agent which governs the body from inside, without being itself corporeal or at least without

---

[104] The precise meaning of 'overlaps' (ἐπικοινωνεῖν) is spelt out by the corresponding verb used for mathematicians, 'is claimed' (ἀντιποιεῖσθαι), which suggests open rivalry.

[105] Strabo 2. 3. 8 = Posidon. T 85 Kidd–Edelstein.

[106] Diogenes Laertius' doxographical sources are not acquainted with Stoics later than the mid-1st cent. AD; cf. Sedley, 'Philodemus', 37.

[107] Tert. *DA* 6. 6: 'Soranus . . . cum omnibus philosophorum sententiis expertus'; cf. 38. 3 'argumentator'. Waszink's rendering of the sentence, that Soranus 'took up arms against all existing opinions of philosophers' (*Tertullianus*, 239), goes somewhat beyond the text.

[108] Soranus is mentioned at 6. 6–7 (thrice); 8. 3; 14. 2; 15. 3; 25. 5; 38. 3 (referred to anonymously as *argumentator*); 44. 2.

[109] H. Karpp, 'Sorans vier Bücher Περὶ ψυχῆς und Tertullians Schrift De anima' ['Soran'], *Zeitschrift für die neutestamentliche Wissenschaft*, 33 (1934), 31–47, esp. 32, suggests that Tertullian borrowed the entire medico-philosophical part of his discussion of the soul from Soranus; Waszink, *Tertullianus*, 33*–44*, is more cautious; see, more recently, R. Polito, 'Il trattato *De anima* di Tertulliano e i quattro libri sull'anima di Sorano' ['Tertulliano'], *Rivista di storia della filosofia*, 49 (1994), 423–69 at 426–32. Disappointingly, I. E. Drabkin, 'Soranus and his System of Medicine', *Bulletin of the History of Medicine*, 20 (1951), 503–18, fails to mention Soranus' psychological interests. Hanson and Green, 'Soranus', 977–8, 1006–7, do so only very briefly.

being subject to the same laws that govern the rest of the body. However, Tertullian does not consider this possibility, and his argument gets its point from the assumption that to account for the body is to account for the soul as well—that is, that no account other than the material one is required. Here again the soul is regarded solely as a physical life-force, with no concession to philosophical speculations concerning its being a cognitive and moral agent as distinct from the body. Is this Tertullian or Soranus? While Tertullian does sympathize with the argument, the argument as such belongs to 'medicine', it is not his own. Tertullian's own view is, rather, that no human, be he a philosopher or a physician, arrives at a truth, except with the aid of faith.[110] Thus, the argument which he reports, and to which he does not commit himself, is likely to belong to his medical source Soranus.

In what follows, Tertullian/Soranus goes on to claim that the soul is matter,[111] indeed breath, that this breath is ordinary air breathed in from outside,[112] that higher mental functions (*animus*) do not emerge above lower ones (*anima*),[113] and mental functions as a whole do not emerge above vital ones, so much so that plants too have intelligence (*intellectus*).[114] This set of ideas is remarkably close to Asclepiades'. Tertullian admittedly does not mention him as an authority.[115] This suggests that some of Asclepiades' ideas had become such an integral part of the medical vulgate by then

[110] Tert. *DA* 2. 6 explicitly refrains from taking sides on the dispute between doctors and philosophers.   [111] Tert. *DA* 5–6.

[112] Tert. *DA* 10; in ch. 11 Tertullian goes on to specify that our soul is breathed air (*spiritus*) only as regards the way we acquire it, but 'breath of God' (*flatus Dei*) as regards its substance. Whatever he means by that, he is no longer dependent on Soranus.   [113] Tert. *DA* 12–13.

[114] Tert. *DA* 19. [Arist.], *De plant.* 815ᵃ15 attributes the idea to the Presocratics. Strato fr. 48 Wehrli provides a more recent antecedent.

[115] At *DA* 15. 3–6 Tertullian criticizes Asclepiades for abolishing a localized ruling-part, something which, in Tertullian's view (15. 4), defies the Bible. Tertullian tells us that Soranus too challenged Asclepiades on this issue (15. 3). The question of Soranus' attitude to Asclepiades is inextricably linked to that of Asclepiades' role in the genesis of the Methodist school of medicine, to which Soranus was attached (see above, n. 103). Vallance, *Theory*, 14–15, suggests that behind Soranus' hostile attitude to Asclepiades lies the fact that he 'had implicitly taken on board a number of Asclepiadean concepts himself, and had good reasons for keeping quiet about them'. Vallance, ibid. 131–43, discusses borrowings by the Methodists from Asclepiades in more depth; see also Hanson and Green, 'Soranus', 991–2; Pigeaud, 'Fondements', 42–7; P. J. van der Eijk, 'The Methodism of Caelius Aurelianus: Some Epistemological Issues', in P. Mudry (ed.), *Maladie et maladies dans les textes latins antiques et médiévaux* (Nantes, 1999), 47–83 (repr. in van der Eijk, *Antiquity*, 299–327).

that they were no longer understood as individual contributions. Galen's complaint, that 'thousands' of doctors adopted Asclepiades' mechanistic explanation of vital functions, lends support to this hypothesis.[116]

The Stoics, who are mistakenly identified as Tertullian's main source of philosophical inspiration,[117] obtain his approval as regards their argument that the soul is breath, on Tertullian's wrong interpretation that the Stoics were committed to the breathed-soul theory against Aristotle.[118] When it comes to distinctive issues, Tertullian claims allegiance to Democritus, Epicurus, and Strato,[119] thus placing himself well inside the materialist tradition. Accordingly, Tertullian's favourite target is the Platonists, sometimes referred to as 'the philosophers' without any qualification,[120] as if

[116] These 'thousands' of doctors (Erasistratus is mentioned as an antecedent) refrain from positing any 'inborn' agent. It is their view that the heat of a living organism is not magically connate to it, as Galen believes, but the outcome of mechanical processes (Asclepiades refers to particulate friction), likewise phenomenal heat; cf. Gal. *De trem.* 7. 614, 617. I cannot follow Edelstein, 'Relation', 356–7, when he claims that we have to wait until Descartes to get a genuinely mechanistic account of vital functions.

[117] e.g. L. M. Colish, *The Stoic Tradition from Antiquity to the Middle Ages* (2 vols.; Leiden, 1985), ii. 9–29, esp. 24–5.

[118] Tert. *DA* 5. Waszink, *Tertullianus*, 33*, traces Tertullian's putative Stoicism back to Soranus, on the ground that earlier Methodist doctors, most notably Julian, allegedly sympathized with the Stoics (ibid. 25*), and that, therefore, Soranus too might have done so. The so-called Pneumatic school of medicine is deemed to provide the connection between Stoics and Methodists. As a matter of fact, however, the Stoics adopted Aristotle's view that we breathe to cool the inner heat (*SVF* ii. 804, 806–8), and Galen has Athenaeus, the 1st-cent. AD founder of the Pneumatic school, advocate against Asclepiades the thesis that the substance of vital and mental functions is connate with our being (Gal. *De trem.* 7. 614; *De sympt. caus.* 7. 165; *De util. resp.* 4. 475; cf. M. Wellmann, 'Athenaios' (24), in *RE* ii/2 (1896), 2034–6). Therefore, there seems to be no ground for tracing Tertullian's and, relatedly, Soranus' position back either to the Stoics or to the Pneumatists.

[119] I only mention instances of doctrinal agreement on distinctive issues, and omit merely doxographical references, or references where Democritus, Epicurus, and Strato are just some of the several authorities that Tertullian invokes. For Democritus see Tert. *DA* 12. 6. Waszink, *Tertullianus*, 112, observes that 'Soranus frequently quoted Democritus' (the reference is to Caelius Aurelianus' translation of Soranus' *De morbis acutis et chronicis*). For Epicurus see 8. 3 (the argument that Tertullian attributes to Soranus is remarkably close to that of Lucr. 3. 228–30) and 17. 4; Lucretius is explicitly mentioned at 5. 6. Tertullian's fierce hostility to Epicurus for his putative atheism (e.g. 46. 2; 50. 2) provides additional reason to think that he borrowed from Soranus the references in which Epicurus is invoked as an authority instead. For Strato see *DA* 14. 5.

[120] Tert. *DA* 6. 7; 10. 5 (the reference here is to Aristotle, *amicus Platonis*; cf. 5. 1); 24. 11; 33. 10. Occurrences of the term 'philosophers', referring to any pagan thinker whatsoever, are, of course, another story.

Democritus, Epicurus, and Strato were not. Since Tertullian considers philosophy and medicine two equal but opposite stances,[121] one understands that the bipolar scheme mechanism vs. intentionalism, which Plato first conceived of, and which Galen developed, overlaps in Tertullian with another scheme, in which medicine stands for materialism, and philosophy stands for dualism. It is not my intention to discuss how medical materialism contributes to Tertullian's idiosyncratic way to his god.[122] For my present purpose, it is enough to observe that Asclepiades' leadership of Galen's second sect looks by now less surprising than it did.

6. Asclepiades and Epicurus on knowledge

Several of Tertullian's medico-philosophical views are, as I said, mild versions of Asclepiades'. As I shall argue next, Tertullian's epistemology too is a borrowing from Asclepiades. Pursuing this topic will enable me to return to one aspect of Asclepiades' thought, epistemology, which I have only briefly touched upon, as well as to the still unanswered question why Antiochus mentions Asclepiades as first.

In chapter 17 Tertullian discusses epistemology, and argues that the senses never deceive us: they can be inaccurate, because of interferences by the media of sensation, but they always report an actual state of affairs. The idea looks like Epicurus',[123] but Tertullian distances himself from him:

The Epicureans, again, show still greater consistency [than the Stoics], in maintaining that all the senses are equally true in their testimony, and at all times—only in a different way. [According to them,] it is not our organs of sensation that are at fault, but our opinion: the senses only experience sensation, they do not exercise opinion; it is the soul that opines. They [the Epicureans] separated opinion from the senses, and sensation from the soul. Well, but whence comes opinion, if not from the senses? Indeed, unless the eye had descried a round shape in that tower, [the soul] could

[121] Opposition between philosophy and medicine is explicit at Tert. *DA* 2. 6 (quoted above, p. 312). It is less explicit at 13. 2; 14. 5; 15. 3; 26. 1. Here Tertullian refers to the bodies of medical and philosophical discussions of the soul as two distinct bodies.

[122] I briefly discuss this topic in Polito, 'Tertulliano', 423–5.

[123] The instances he gives (oar, tower) belong to Epicurean literature. Tertullian, who is no atomist, neither adopts nor mentions the efflux theory, but his argument seems to imply it.

have had no idea that [the tower] possessed roundness. (Tert. *DA* 17. 4–5, trans. Holmes)

Epicurus' fault is, in Tertullian's view, to believe that opinion, although dependent on sensation, is rational and non-mechanical,[124] the process which leads to it being located in the self, which is a source of autonomous action.[125] In Tertullian's view, by contrast, the mind is the same as the senses,[126] and therefore there is no room for any autonomous action of the self: if sense-reports are true, then opinion, i.e. their verbalization, will be too.[127] Tertullian, however, is no Protagoras, and he does consider the possibility that some reports are more accurate than others, but the senses are for him capable of settling the question by themselves.

Tertullian's position may look naïve, and at least his formulation probably is. However, it has an antecedent as eminent as Democritus, who, according to Aristotle, 'does not employ intellect as a faculty dealing with truth, but identifies it with the soul',[128] and who maintained that 'to think is the same as to sense, and that sensation is, in turn, a physical alteration, and therefore that that-which-appears to the senses is necessarily true'.[129] Whether this is the real Democritus or merely Aristotle's interpretation,[130] Tertullian proudly claims allegiance to him: 'intellect and the soul will be one and the same, and Democritus will carry his point when he suppresses any distinction between the two'.[131] The reference to Democritus enables us to make better sense of Tertullian's argument, in terms of challenging Epicurus' idea that reason and

[124] LS i. 86; E. Asmis, 'Epicurean Epistemology', in Algra *et al.*, *The Cambridge History of Hellenistic Philosophy*, 260–94 at 274–5, 283–94.

[125] Sedley, 'Anti-Reductionism', 323. Lucr. 4. 386 describes error as a *vitium animi* alone.

[126] Tert. *DA* 12–13. Tertullian speaks of *principalitas* of the *anima* over the *animus*. Strato fr. 74 Wehrli provides an antecedent.

[127] Tertullian's goal, as he goes on to explain (*DA* 17. 13–14), is to defend the story of Jesus' resurrection and other biblical tales from the allegation of sensory illusion.   [128] Arist. *DA* 404ᵃ30–1.

[129] Arist. *Metaph.* 1009ᵇ12–15. The reference is to Democritus and Empedocles. A similar report at *GC* 315ᵇ9–10.

[130] Cherniss, *Presocratic*, 79–83, 313–16, believes it is not. R. McKim, 'Democritus against Scepticism: All Sense-Impressions are True' ['Democritus'], in L. G. Benakis (ed.), *Proceedings of the First International Congress on Democritus* (Xanthi, 1984), 281–90, argues in favour of the reliability of the report. M.-K. Lee, *Epistemology after Protagoras: Responses to Relativism in Plato, Aristotle, and Democritus* (Oxford, 2005), 189–200, has recently readdressed the question.

[131] Tert. *DA* 12. 6 (trans. Holmsen).

sensation are two distinct cognitive functions accomplished by two distinct parts of the soul. While Plato and the Academics are Tertullian's primary polemical target in this chapter, the positions of Stoics and Epicureans too were deemed by him to be affected by dualism.

While Tertullian has Democritus as an early authority, his direct source is Soranus. Soranus is not mentioned in chapter 17. One may assume that the argument none the less goes back to him both by analogy with many of Tertullian's philosophical points, and also because it fits nicely in the general picture of Soranus' doctrine, as we can reconstruct it from explicit references in Tertullian and elsewhere.[132] If Soranus is Tertullian's direct source, one may wonder whether the origin too of the position that Tertullian advocates is to be sought in the medical tradition. Do we have any suitable candidate? Indeed we do: according to Antiochus, Asclepiades 'believed that sensations are really and truly acts of knowledge, and that we apprehend nothing at all with the aid of a reason'.[133] The hypothesis that Asclepiades is Tertullian's ultimate source of inspiration gains support not only from the similarity between their views, but also from the similarity between the contexts in which these are expresssed. Both Antiochus and Tertullian are discussing Epicurus. Antiochus couples Epicurus with Asclepiades, but, if the report on Epicurus too goes back to him, also hints at a difference: Epicurus sets out to explain how we can distinguish between true and false opinions,[134] on the assumption that our mind has the power to judge, and to misjudge, sense-reports, and Lucretius expressly attributes to reason (*ratio animi*) the job of validating our ideas on them.[135] Asclepiades, by contrast, bans reason 'totally' (ὅλως).[136] Thus, Asclepiades' position counts as alternative to and in conflict with Epicurus'. This position is Tertullian's too, and his ground for attacking Epicurus. Although we do not possess Asclepiades' original context, and, therefore, we cannot say whether

---

[132] Karpp, 'Soran', 44–5, attributes the argument to Soranus. Waszink, *Tertullianus*, 236–40, is more cautious, on the ground that Soranus, as a Methodist, might have sympathized with the Sceptics' arguments against sense perception. But the very assumption that Soranus sympathized with the Sceptics defies the fact that he entertained several 'dogmatic' views concerning the soul.

[133] S.E. *M*. 7. 201.

[134] S.E. *M*. 7. 203–16.   [135] Lucr. 4. 380–6, 462–8.

[136] A discussion of Asclepiades' epistemology is in Pigeaud, *Maladie*, 95–100, who correctly compares it with that of Epicurus, but fails to notice differences.

he himself was thereby attacking Epicurus, rather than making a general point, so close an agreement of ideas and polemical targets between Antiochus' report on Asclepiades and Tertullian's own argument is hardly a coincidence, and the fact that Asclepiades provides Tertullian's ultimate source of inspiration for other aspects of his psychology makes it plausible that he lies behind this argument too. Tertullian's reference to Democritus does not conflict with the Asclepiades hypothesis, since Asclepiades himself and his followers were fond of Democritus.[137]

Whether or not Tertullian's theory of knowledge is a borrowing from Asclepiades', the distinctively anti-rationalist feature of the latter, as reported by Antiochus, enables us to advance a hypothesis as to why Antiochus mentions Asclepiades as first. As the run of the report suggests, Antiochus' point of interest was neither Asclepiades nor Epicurus, but the actual thesis that the senses, as opposed to reason, provide a criterion of truth, a thesis which Sextus compares with Cyrenaic phenomenalism.[138] This thesis is one of the three possible answers to the question how we gain cognitive access to the outside world (by means of reason, the senses, or both). In this form, it logically precedes both Asclepiades and Epicurus, who merely provide two historical reference-points.[139] Antiochus mentions Asclepiades as first because, I submit, he regarded Asclepiades as voicing most faithfully the thesis that reason does not contribute to knowledge. Epicurus follows because he did away with reason, but not completely. Thus, if I am correct, the sequence that Antiochus adopts intends to establish a hierarchy between Asclepiades and Epicurus, with the purpose of exploiting

[137] Moschion, a follower of Asclepiades, appropriated Aristotle's interpretation that Democritus refrained from distinguishing between mind and the soul, and developed it in the light of Asclepiades' denial of a location to the mind (see above, n. 24). Asclepiades himself at Anon. Lond. 37 invokes Democritus as an authority for the claim that effluences take place from the surface of things, and affect our soul by inhalation.

[138] 'Not far removed, it would seem, from the opinion of these people [the Cyrenaics] are those who declare that the senses are a criterion of truth' (S.E. *M.* 7. 201).

[139] 'For, that there have been some who have held this view has been made clear by Antiochus the Academic' (ibid.). A third reference-point is, of course, Democritus. Sextus adopts the rationalist interpretation of him (*M.* 7. 135–9), but he is acquainted with the alternative interpretation which associates him with Epicurus (*M.* 7. 140; cf. Sedley, 'Criteria', 43–4). It is only a matter of speculation how Antiochus himself interpreted Democritus, since his epistemological doxography putatively excerpted by Sextus covers post-Socratic philosophers alone.

the former against the latter. Cicero offers several instances of anti-Epicurean exploitation of neighbouring philosophers. On Cicero's story, Epicurus has his atomism in common with Democritus and his hedonism in common with the Cyrenaics, and yet Epicurus' own formulation of these ideas is far less consistent than competing formulations.[140] This line of anti-Epicurean argument can be traced back to the Academy, and it would be by no means surprising if Antiochus resorted to it with reference to Asclepiades,[141] thus anticipating Galen's own exploitation of Asclepiades against Epicurus.

Even if one leaves aside Galen, there is at least another instance of exploitation of Asclepiades for anti-Epicurean purposes. This is found in Sextus, with no explicit attribution to any source. Here Sextus sharply distinguishes between Asclepiades and Epicurus, to the point of bracketing the former with Plato (!):

Plato [supposed that only thought-objects are true] because sense-objects are always becoming and never being, as their substance keeps flowing like a river, so that it does not remain the same for two moments together, and, as Asclepiades said, does not admit of being pointed out twice, owing to the speed with which it flows. (S.E. *M*. 8. 7, trans. Bury)[142]

The report on Epicurus' opposite view, that sense-objects are always true, comes next.

It has been suggested that Sextus' basic source here is Academic, and that the report incorporates anti-Epicurean material.[143] The underlying argument can be recovered by comparison with other texts: Epicurus posits ceaseless atomic motion; but how can we have a firm knowledge of things of the kind he claims, if they change continuously?[144] Epicurus' answer is that changes in the shape of

---

[140] e.g. Cic. *Fin*. 1. 18 (Democritus); 1. 26 (Aristippus).

[141] Epicurus' physics and ethics are a polemical target for Cicero's Antiochean speakers at Cic. *Acad*. 1. 2, 6; 2. 45, 139, and Antiochus at Cic. *Fin*. 5. 15 advocates for himself Carneades' scheme for reducing the ethical views of philosophical schools to a limited set of basic options (the so-called *Carneadea divisio*).

[142] Epicurus is mentioned at 8. 8–9. Asclepiades' enrolment in the entry opposite to Epicurus' is still more remarkable in view of the fact that the thesis that Sextus attributes to Epicurus here, that all sense-appearances are 'true' and 'real' (ἀληθῆ καὶ ὄντα), agrees word for word with that which Antiochus attributes to Asclepiades, that 'sensations are "really" and "truly" [ὄντως καὶ ἀληθῶς] acts of knowledge'.

[143] I borrow the argument from F. Decleva Caizzi, 'La "materia scorrevole": sulle tracce di un dibattito perduto' ['Materia'], in Barnes and Mignucci, *Matter and Metaphysics*, 425–70, esp. 454–9.

[144] Plut. *Adv. Col*. 1116 C; *Quaest. conv*. 652 A–B.

aggregates are not so quick as to prevent knowledge of them.[145] Asclepiades' own claim, that one cannot even point out the same thing twice, seems to pick up precisely this answer, and to challenge it.[146] His merit, as an opponent of Epicurus might have understood him, is to refute Epicurus out of shared premisses.

There is a substantial difference between this representation of Asclepiades' theory of knowledge and Antiochus' own representation of it: Antiochus depicts Asclepiades as a more radical upholder of sensation than Epicurus, whereas here Asclepiades is associated, to our surprise, with those who believe that sense-objects are false. This passage none the less provides yet another instance of the anti-Epicurean strategy of making Asclepiades a more consistent Epicurean than Epicurus himself, also as regards epistemology. The hypothesis that Antiochus is playing a similar game in the *Canonics* makes sense not only of the sequence he adopts, but also of his idiosyncratic way of hinting at Asclepiades as 'a certain man second to none in the art of medicine and acquainted with philosophy too'. This description defies any doxographical purpose,[147] but is suited very well to philosophical polemics: can a professional philosopher such as Epicurus, worshipped by his followers as a god, afford to be taught the logical interrelation of his ideas by some unnamed physician, who may be very eminent in his field, and yet has only a superficial knowledge of philosophy?[148]

Whatever the game Antiochus is playing, evidence on Asclepiades' epistemology is controversial. To the Sextus report on the flux of sense-objects, in which Asclepiades is associated with Plato against Epicurus, one may add Sextus' other report that Asclepiades maintained that 'when the pale and the dark are mixed, the sense is unable to discern whether what subsists is a single and

---

[145] Diog. Oen. fr. 4, coll. II. 2–III. 1.

[146] Here I disagree with Decleva Caizzi, 'Materia', 463–5, who hypothesizes that Asclepiades might not be committed to the view attributed to him, his role being merely that of a reporter on Plato.

[147] Barnes, 'Antiochus', 64.

[148] The verb ἅπτεσθαι indicates superficial acquaintance at Plato, *Laws* 694 c; Arist. *EE* 1227[a]1. Plato at *Rep.* 411 c uses it to describe those people who devote themselves to bodily pleasure, and 'have no clue' either in music or in philosophy. Sextus, *PH* 1. 18, makes a distinction between being engaged in physical speculations and being merely acquainted (ἁπτόμεθα) with them. The verb need not have a denigratory nuance, but it does usually refer to the interests/hobbies one has, as distinct from what one is actually engaged in. Plato, *Polit.* 266 A, refers to Theaetetus and Theodorus as having 'touched on' geometry, but that is an ironic understatement.

simple colour or not', an assertion which makes Asclepiades close
to the upholders of the view that reason provides a criterion of
truth.[149] As a result, Asclepiades is in the paradoxical situation of
featuring in both halves of Sextus' epistemological doxography. His
simultaneously yielding to the senses against reason, and to reason
against the senses, is remarkable, and it threatens to create a major
inconsistency in his thought. It is no less remarkable, however, that
none of his opponents is bothered by it.[150] So perhaps no inconsistency is to be found after all. But, then, how to reconcile the two
bodies of reports?

As it happens, reports on Democritus in the first place show
the same specious inconsistency. On the one hand, Democritus
advocated the truth of all sense-reports, and, on the other hand, he
denied the senses cognitive access to external objects.[151] Sextus is
at a loss how to reconcile these two claims:

In the *Confirmations*, despite having professed to ascribe command over
evidence to the senses, he [Democritus] none the less is found condemning
them. (S.E. *M.* 7. 136)[152]

Aristotle is less at a loss: he makes the two claims a consequence
of one another. He refers to the cumulative view of some people,
Democritus among them, who believe that 'appearances are true,
and *therefore* [διὰ τοῦτο] all things are equally false and true, because
they do not appear the same to all, nor always the same to the same
person'.[153] The idea is that sense impressions are bodily alterations,
and therefore always report a state of affairs. However, since they

---

[149] S.E. *M.* 7. 91. We are in the Presocratic section of Sextus' doxography, in
which he develops the point that all Presocratics rejected sense perception, and
adopted reason as a criterion. Asclepiades' 'rationalism' turns up at Gal. *De exp.
med.* 87, where he is brought in as the champion of the Empiricists' opponents, and
it is to Asclepiades, it seems, that Galen owes the anti-Empiricist argument that he
expounds at 88–97. Asclepiades' corpuscles, for their part, are *intellectu sensa sine
ulla qualitate solita* (Cael. Aur. *De morb. acut.* 1. 105; Anon. Lond. 34–7; Gal. *De
diebus decr.* 9. 798).

[150] Galen at *De exp. med.* 85 finds no better instance of inconsistency with which
to reproach Asclepiades than his making experience both 'unreliable' and 'non-
existent'. As he complains, if experience is unreliable, it does exist. He is obviously
short of arguments, and unable to detect any serious inconsistency in Asclepiades.

[151] Democritus too is associated with Plato in the Sextus passage at *M.* 8. 6, and
sense-qualities were for him by convention alone (S.E. *PH* 1. 213).

[152] Trans. Sedley, 'Criteria', 37.

[153] *Metaph.* 1011ᵃ29–33; the reference to Democritus is at 1009ᵃ38–ᵇ15.

conflict with one another,[154] none of them could be regarded as revealing the inner nature of external objects. Hence, Aristotle tells us, Democritus arrived at the conclusion that 'nothing is true or that what is true is hidden to us'.[155] In this sense, sensory data are both true and false, and the reality of things is to be sought beyond them, as Democritus did by invoking atoms and void. Thus, Aristotle's testimony on Democritus gets its point from distinguishing between a phenomenal truth, which covers all sensory data alike, and a cognitive truth, which Democritus denies to them all.[156] It is this distinction between a phenomenal and a cognitive truth that, I submit, is also implied by the reports on Asclepiades, each of which picks up a different part of the argument in isolation, depending on the context and on the source's strategy.

While the distinction between two truths enables us to make sense of Asclepiades' seemingly schizophrenic attitude to sensory data, it still remains for us to make sense of how he arrived at his molecules, which are 'apprehensible by reason alone',[157] in the absence of any power of reason. To start with, Asclepiades argued for his molecules not on the basis of top-down, deductive reasoning, but on the basis of observational data, by proving experimentally that invisible emanations take place from bodies.[158] Still, even so, molecules are not an object of sensory experience, and knowledge of them requires at least some inferential reasoning. Did Asclepiades allow at least this kind of reasoning? And how did he reconcile this allowance with his denial of reason?

As a matter of fact, Asclepiades did *not* do away with reasoning altogether. On the contrary, he did allow the possibility for us to go beyond sensory data and thereby have intelligence of invisible things 'through the swift motion of the senses, this act of apprehension being fulfilled with the help of perceptible objects and previous acts of perception'.[159] Whatever the precise nature of the motion in question,[160] the idea appears to be that the breath that

---

[154] Arist. *GC* 315^{b}11 demonstrates that this consideration was a part of Democritus' original argument.   [155] Arist. *Metaph.* 1009^{b}11–12.

[156] McKim, ' Democritus', 289, speaks of a 'shadow-truth' and 'an atomic truth'.

[157] See above, n. 149, for references.

[158] Anon. Lond. 34–8. Erasistratus provides an antecedent (ibid. 33).

[159] Cael. Aurel. *De morb. ac.* 1. 115 (trans. Drabkin).

[160] The adjective *solubilis* ('swift'; cf. Pigeaud: 'facile'; Pape: 'flüchtige') is crucial. Vallance, *Theory*, 117–19, discusses other occurrences of the adjective. Its meaning in this context remains unclear to me.

fuels the senses processes incoming data by associating them with those previously stored,[161] and that in this way it accomplishes a certain degree of conceptualization. As a result, Calcidius attributes to his atomists the idea that sciences and arts come about from sensation,[162] and Galen attributes to the members of the materialist sect the idea that ethical notions and logical concepts 'arise from sensation and through sensation'.[163]

Thus, Asclepiades' theory of knowledge is in effect less dismissive of reasoning than Galen wants us to believe. Galen fails to distinguish between thinking as an activity of the senses and thinking as a separate faculty, and therefore denies Asclepiades any idea of thinking altogether, because, in Galen's view, any activity presupposes a faculty which carries it out and which is prior to the bodily organs involved.[164] Asclepiades, by contrast, abolishes reason as a separate faculty,[165] and yet allows reasoning as an activity of the senses. His point is not that we do not think. It is, rather, that both thinking and sensing are a product of physical processes that the soul's breath undergoes. The basic idea is thus the same as that which Aristotle attributes to Democritus and other Presocratics.[166] It was Asclepiades' merit to work out this idea in the light of more recent anatomical findings, and on this basis to challenge the distinction, which was first thematized by Plato, between mental activities and bodily processes.[167] In this respect, one should consider that to *fail* to make that distinction, as Plato and Aristotle complained earlier philosophers had done, is not the same thing as to *reject* it, once it has been made, as Asclepiades did.[168] In the absence of any such

---

[161] Pigeaud, *Maladie*, 95, reads *perspectione* instead of *perceptione*, and suggests that the Epicurean idea of *prolēpsis* is in the picture.

[162] Calc. *In Tim.* 216, p. 253 Waszink.　　　　　[163] Gal. *De nat. fac.* 2. 28.

[164] Gal. *De nat. fac.* 2. 10.

[165] Asclepiades abolished any faculty whatsoever, using 'faculty' to refer to a pre-existing force governing physical processes and prior to them; cf. Gal. *De diff. puls.* 8. 713.

[166] Wellmann, 'Asklepiades', 698, was the first to observe the Democritean pedigree of Asclepiades' view.

[167] Claus, *Soul*, offers a full-scale study of the occurrences of the term *psychē* in early Greek literature down to Plato.

[168] For this reason, any interpretation that commits Presocratics and Hippocratics to conscious materialism, as distinct from dualism (e.g. M. R. Wright, 'Presocratic Minds', in C. Gill (ed.) *The Person and the Human Mind: Issues in Ancient and Modern Philosophy* (Oxford, 1990), 207–26, esp. 207; B. Simon, *Mind and Madness in Ancient Greece: The Classical Roots of Modern Psychiatry* (Ithaca, NY, and London, 1978), esp. 215), risks anachronism (Singer, 'Problems', 131–7).

rejection, Democritus too is found perilously veering towards dualism when it comes to his ethics.[169] Indeed, his claim that 'wisdom heals the soul in the same way as medicine heals the body',[170] as if the body and the soul were two separate domains, provided the archetype of a medical simile for describing the job of philosophy, which was destined to become very successful, and which was dualist in essence.[171] Thus, the boast made by the fourth-century BC Democritean Anaxarchus, that to beat his body would have no impact on his self, as if this self could have a life independent of the 'bag' hosting it,[172] does not come out of the blue.

7. Conclusion

In contrast with the philosophical tradition, which seems to have been incapable of resisting the temptation to detach mind and body, there existed in Hellenistic and Roman medicine a radical and aware materialistic tendency, of which Asclepiades was the leading voice. This medical tradition provides an important, but hitherto neglected, antecedent to eighteenth-century iatro-mechanism and to modern materialistic accounts of the mind. While Asclepiades was wrong in thinking that respiration supplies the substance that makes our nervous system work, his paradigm for explaining higher mental functions in terms of the lower ones, and both as a product of bodily processes, is very well suited to modern neuroscience. Whether or not one sympathizes with this paradigm, Asclepiades' commitment to offering a thoroughly mechanistic account of the so-called mental provides a remarkable example of intellectual coherence of the kind other and better-reputed ancient materialists failed to exhibit. In the light of this coherence, it is, then, no cause for surprise if he suffered even more than these other thinkers the *damnatio memoriae* that late antiquity and the Middle Ages applied to upholders of a materialistic account of nature. The goal of this paper has been to do him justice.

Wolfson College, Cambridge

---

[169] As Claus, *Soul*, 142, observes, 'the materialism of Democritus . . . makes him perhaps the least likely of all Presocratics to have anything to do with the development of the Socratic use of psyche. Yet, it is clear at once that the statements on psyche attributed to Democritus are Socratic in tone.'

[170] Clem. *Paed.* 1. 6.

[171] Edelstein, 'Relation', 361–4; Frede, 'Philosophy', 227.   [172] D.L. 9. 59.

BIBLIOGRAPHY

Algra, K., Barnes, J., Mansfeld, J., and Schofield, M. (eds.), *The Cambridge History of Hellenistic Philosophy* (Cambridge, 1999).

Annas, J. E., *Hellenistic Philosophy of Mind* [*Mind*] (Berkeley, Los Angeles, and Oxford, 1992).

—— 'Epicurus on Agency', in J. Brunschwig and M. C. Nussbaum (eds.), *Passions and Perceptions: Studies in Hellenistic Philosophy of Mind* (Cambridge, 1993), 53–71.

Asmis, E., 'Epicurean Epistemology', in Algra *et al.*, *The Cambridge History of Hellenistic Philosophy*, 260–94.

Baltussen, H., *Theophrastus against the Presocratics and Plato: Peripatetic Dialectic in the* De sensibus (Leiden, 2000).

Barnes, J., 'Antiochus of Ascalon' ['Antiochus'], in J. Barnes and M. Griffin (eds), *Philosophia Togata: Essays on Roman Philosophy and Society* (Oxford, 1989), 51–96.

Burnyeat, M., 'Is an Aristotelian Philosophy of Mind Still Credible?', in M. C. Nussbaum and A. O. Rorty (eds.), *Essays on Aristotle's* De anima (Oxford, 1992), 15–26.

Caston, V., 'Epiphenomenalisms, Ancient and Modern' ['Epiphenomalisms'], *Philosophical Review*, 106 (1997), 309–63.

—— 'Dicaearchus' Philosophy of Mind', in W. W. Fortenbaugh and E. Schütrumpf (eds.), *Dicaearchus of Messana: Text, Translation and Discussion* (New Brunswick and London, 2001), 175–93.

Cherniss, H. F., *Aristotle's Criticism of Presocratic Philosophy* [*Presocratic*] (Baltimore, 1935).

Claus D. B., *Toward the Soul: Inquiry into the Meaning of 'Psyche' before Plato* [*Soul*] (New Haven and London, 1981).

Colish, L. M., *The Stoic Tradition from Antiquity to the Middle Ages* (2 vols.; Leiden, 1985).

Decleva Caizzi, F., 'La "materia scorrevole": sulle tracce di un dibattito perduto' ['Materia'], in J. Barnes and M. Mignucci (eds.), *Matter and Metaphysics: Fourth Symposium Hellenisticum* (Naples, 1988), 425–70.

Diels, H., 'Über das physikalische System des Straton', in *Kleine Schriften* (Darmstadt, 1969), 239–65 [originally in *SB der Akad. Berlin* (1893), 101–27].

Dillon, J., *The Middle Platonists: A Study of Platonism, 80 b.c. to a.d. 220* (London, 1977).

Di Stefano, E., 'Per una nuova raccolta delle testimonianze e dei frammenti di Antioco di Ascalona' ['Raccolta'], *Quaderni catanesi*, 6 (1984), 95–144.

Donini, P. L., 'The History of the Concept of Eclecticism', in J. Dillon

Roberto Polito

and A. A. Long (eds.), *Questions of Eclecticism: Studies in Later Greek Philosophy* (Berkeley, Los Angeles, and London, 1988), 15–33.

Drabkin, I. E., 'Soranus and his System of Medicine', *Bulletin of the History of Medicine*, 20 (1951), 503–18.

—— 'Remarks on Ancient Psychopathology' ['Psychopathology'], *Isis*, 46 (1955), 223–34.

Edelstein, L., 'The Relation of Ancient Philosophy to Medicine' ['Relation'], in *Ancient Medicine: Selected Papers of Ludwig Edelstein*, ed. O. Temkin (Baltimore, 1967), 349–66.

Everson, S. (ed.), *Psychology* (Companions to Ancient Thought, 2; Cambridge, 1991).

—— 'Epicurean Psychology' ['Epicurean'], in Algra *et al.*, *The Cambridge History of Hellenistic Philosophy*, 542–59.

Frede, M., 'Philosophy and Medicine in Antiquity' ['Philosophy'], in id., *Essays in Ancient Philosophy* (Oxford, 1987), 225–47.

Furley, D., *The Greek Cosmologists* [*Cosmologists*] (Cambridge, 1987).

—— and Wilkie, J. (eds.), *Galen: On Respiration and the Arteries* [*Respiration*] (Princeton 1984).

García-Ballester, L., 'Soul and Body, Disease of Soul and Disease of the Body in Galen's Medical Thought' ['Soul'], in P. Manuli and M. Vegetti (eds.), *Le opere psicologiche di Galeno: atti del terzo colloquio galenico internazionale, Pavia, 10–12 settembre 1986* (Naples, 1988), 117–52.

Gundert, B., 'Soma and Psyche in Hippocratic Medicine', in Wright and Potter, *Psyche*, 13–35.

Hankinson, R. J., 'Greek Medical Models of Mind' ['Models'], in Everson, *Psychology*, 194–217.

—— 'Galen's Philosophical Eclecticism', *ANRW* 36.5 (1992), 3505–22.

—— 'Determinism and Indeterminism', in Algra *et al.*, *The Cambridge History of Hellenistic Philosophy*, 513–41.

Hanson, A. E., and Green, M. H., 'Soranus of Ephesus: Methodicorum princeps' ['Soranus'], *ANRW* 37.2 (1994), 968–1075.

Harris, C. R. S., *The Heart and the Vascular System in Ancient Greek Medicine* [*Heart*] (Oxford, 1973).

Irwin, T. H., 'Aristotle's Philosophy of Mind' ['Aristotle'], in Everson, *Psychology*, 84–101.

Jaeger, W., 'Das Pneuma im Lykeion', *Hermes*, 48 (1913), 29–74.

Kahn, C. H., 'Democritus and the Origins of Moral Psychology' ['Democritus'], *American Journal of Philology*, 106 (1985), 1–31.

—— 'Aristotle versus Descartes on the Concept of the Mental', in R. Salles (ed.), *Metaphysics, Soul, and Ethics in Ancient Thought: Themes from the Work of Richard Sorabji* (Oxford, 2005), 193–208.

Karpp, H., 'Sorans vier Bücher Περὶ ψυχῆς und Tertullians Schrift De anima' ['Soran'], *Zeitschrift für die neutestamentliche Wissenschaft*, 33 (1934), 31–47.

Laursen, S., 'Epicurus *On Nature* XXV', *Cronache ercolanesi*, 18 (1988), 7–18.

Lee, M.-K., *Epistemology after Protagoras: Responses to Relativism in Plato, Aristotle, and Democritus* (Oxford, 2005).

Lloyd, G. E. R., 'Scholarship, Authority and Argument in Galen's *Quod animi mores*', in P. Manuli and M. Vegetti (eds.), *Le opere psicologiche di Galeno: atti del terzo colloquio galenico internazionale, Pavia, 10–12 settembre 1986* (Naples, 1988), 11–42.

Long, A. A., and Sedley, D. N., *The Hellenistic Philosophers* [LS] (2 vols.; Cambridge, 1987).

McKim, R., 'Democritus against Scepticism: All Sense-Impressions are True' ['Democritus'], in L. G. Benakis (ed.), *Proceedings of the First International Congress on Democritus* (Xanthi, 1984), 281–90.

Mansfeld, J., 'Doxography and Dialectic' ['Doxography'], *ANRW* 36.4 (1990), 3056–229.

Moreschini, C. (ed.), *Calcidio: Commentario al Timeo di Platone* (Milan, 2003).

Nutton, V., *Ancient Medicine* (London and New York, 2004).

O'Keefe, T., 'The Reductionist and Compatibilist Argument of Epicurus' On Nature Book 25', *Phronesis*, 47 (2002), 153–86.

Ostenfeld, E., *Ancient Greek Psychology and the Modern Mind–Body Debate* [*Psychology*] (Aarhus, 1987).

Phillips, O., 'Numenian Psychology in Calcidius?', *Phronesis*, 48 (2003), 132–51.

Pigeaud, J., *La Maladie de l'âme: étude sur la relation de l'âme et du corps dans la tradition médico-philosophique antique* [*Maladie*] (Paris, 1981).

—— 'Les fondements du méthodisme' ['Fondements'], in P. Mudry and J. Pigeaud, *Les Écoles médicales à Rome: actes du 2ème colloque international sur les textes médicaux latins antiques* (Geneva, 1991), 9–50.

Polito, R., 'Il trattato *De anima* di Tertulliano e i quattro libri sull'anima di Sorano' ['Tertulliano'], *Rivista di storia della filosofia*, 49 (1994), 423–69.

—— 'On the Life of Asclepiades of Bithynia' ['Life'], *Journal of Hellenic Studies*, 119 (1999), 48–66.

—— *The Sceptical Road: Aenesidemus' Appropriation of Heraclitus* [*Road*] (Leiden, 2004).

Romano, E., *Filosofi e medici: letteratura medica e società altoimperiale* [*Filosofi*] (Palermo, 1992).

Runia, D. T., 'The Placita Ascribed to Doctors in Aëtius' Doxography on Physics', in P. J. van der Eijk (ed.), *Ancient Histories of Medicine: Essays in Medical Doxography and Historiography in Classical Antiquity* (Leiden, 1999), 189–250.

Schrijvers, P. H., *Eine medizinische Erklärung der männlichen Homosexu-alität aus der Antike* [*Homosexualität*] (Amsterdam, 1985).

Sedley, D. N., 'Epicurus' Refutation of Determinism' ['Refutation'], in Συζήτησις: *studi sull'epicureismo greco e romano offerti a Marcello Gigante* (Naples, 1983), 11–51.

—— 'Epicurean Anti-Reductionism' ['Anti-Reductionism'], in J. Barnes and M. Mignucci (eds.), *Matter and Metaphysics: Fourth Symposium Hellenisticum* (Naples, 1988), 295–327.

—— 'Sextus Empiricus and the Atomist Criteria of Truth' ['Criteria'], *Elenchos*, 13 (1992), 19–56.

—— 'Chrysippus on Psychophysical Causality', in J. Brunschwig and M. Nussbaum (eds.), *Passions and Perceptions: Studies in Hellenistic Philo-sophy of Mind* (Cambridge, 1993), 313–31.

—— 'Philodemus and the Decentralisation of Philosophy' ['Philodemus'], *Cronache ercolanesi*, 33 (2003), 31–41.

Sharples, R. W., 'Dicaearchus on the Soul and on Divination' ['Dicaear-chus'], in W. W. Fortenbaugh and E. Schütrumpf (eds.), *Dicaearchus of Messana: Text, Translation and Discussion* (New Brunswick and London, 2001).

Simon, B., *Mind and Madness in Ancient Greece: The Classical Roots of Modern Psychiatry* (Ithaca, NY, and London, 1978).

Singer, P. N., 'Some Hippocratic Mind–Body Problems' ['Problems'], in J. A. López Pérez (ed.), *Tratados hipocráticos* (Madrid, 1992), 131–43.

Solmsen, F., 'The Vital Heat, the Inborn Pneuma and the Aether', *Journal of Hellenic Studies*, 77 (1957) , 118–23.

Switalski, B. W., *Des Chalcidius Kommentar zu Plato's Timaeus: Eine historisch-kritische Untersuchung* (Beiträge zur Geschichte der Philoso-phie des Mittelalters, III/6; Münster, 1902).

Tarrant, H., 'Agreement and the Self-Evident in Philo of Larissa' ['Agree-ment'], *Dionysius*, 5 (1981), 66–97.

Taylor, C. C. W., 'Pleasure, Knowledge and Sensation in Democritus', *Phronesis*, 12 (1967), 6–27.

Vallance, J. T., *The Lost Theory of Asclepiades of Bithynia* [*Theory*] (Oxford, 1990).

—— 'The Medical System of Asclepiades of Bithynia' ['System'], *ANRW* 37.1 (1993), 693–727.

Van der Eijk, P. J., 'Aristotle's Psycho-Physiological Account of the Soul–Body Relationship', in Wright and Potter, *Psyche*, 57–77.

—— 'The Heart, the Brain, the Blood and the *Pneuma*: Hippocrates, Dio-cles and Aristotle on the Location of Cognitive Processes' ['Blood'], in id., *Antiquity*, 119–35.

—— 'The Methodism of Caelius Aurelianus: Some Epistemological Is-sues', in P. Mudry (ed.), *Maladie et maladies dans les textes latins antiques et médiévaux* (Nantes, 1999), 47–83; repr. in van der Eijk, *Antiquity*, 299–327.

—— *Medicine and Philosophy in Classical Antiquity: Doctors and Philosophers on Nature, Soul, Health and Disease [Antiquity]* (Cambridge, 2005).

Vegetti, M., 'Historiographical Strategies in Galen's Physiology' ['Strategies'], in P. J. van der Eijk (ed.), *Ancient Histories of Medicine* (Leiden, 1999), 383–95.

Vlastos, G., 'Ethics and Physics in Democritus', in R. E. Allen and D. J. Furley (eds.), *Studies in Presocratic Philosophy* (2 vols.; London, 1975), ii. 381–408 [originally in *Philosophical Review*, 54 (1945), 578–92, and 55 (1946), 53–64].

Von Staden, H., 'Body, Soul, and Nerves: Epicurus, Herophilus, Erasistratus, the Stoics, and Galen', in Wright and Potter, *Psyche*, 79–116.

Warren, J., *Epicurus and Democritean Ethics: An Archaeology of Ataraxia* (Cambridge, 2002).

Waszink, J. H. (ed. and comm.), *Tertullianus: De anima [Tertullianus]* (Amsterdam, 1947).

—— *Timaeus a Calcidio translatus commentarioque instructus* (Leiden, 1962).

Wellmann, M., 'Athenaios' (24), in *RE* ii/2 (1896), 2034–6.

—— 'Asklepiades von Bithynien, von einem herrschenden Vorurteil befreit' ['Asklepiades'], *Neue Jahrbücher für das klassische Alterthum*, 21 (1908), 684–703.

Wiersma, W., 'Die aristotelische Lehre vom Pneuma', *Mnemosyne*, 11 (1943), 102–7.

Wright, J. P., and Potter, P. (eds.), *Psyche and Soma: Physicians and Metaphysicians on the Mind–Body Problem from Antiquity to Enlightenment [Psyche]* (Oxford, 2000).

Wright, M. R., 'Presocratic Minds', in C. Gill (ed.), *The Person and the Human Mind: Issues in Ancient and Modern Philosophy* (Oxford, 1990), 207–26.

PYRRHONIAN SCEPTICISM
AND THE SEARCH FOR TRUTH

CASEY PERIN

Two passages at the outset of Sextus Empiricus' *Outlines of Pyrrhonism* raise fundamental issues about Pyrrhonian Scepticism as a way of life:

When people are investigating any subject, the likely result is either a discovery, or a denial of discovery and a confession of inapprehensibility, or else a continuation of the investigation [ἐπιμονὴν ζητήσεως]. This, no doubt, is why in the case of philosophical investigations, too, some have said that they have discovered the truth, some have asserted that it cannot be apprehended, and others are still investigating [οἱ δὲ ἔτι ζητοῦσιν]. Those who are called Dogmatists in the proper sense of the word think they have discovered the truth—for example, the schools of Aristotle and Epicurus and the Stoics, and some others. The schools of Clitomachus and Carneades, and other Academics, have asserted that things cannot be apprehended. And the Sceptics are investigating. [ζητοῦσι δὲ οἱ Σκεπτικοί]. (*PH* 1. 1–3)

The Sceptical way of life [ἡ σκεπτικὴ ἀγωγή], then, is also called 'investigative' [ζητητική], from its activity in investigating and enquiring [ἀπὸ ἐνεργείας τῆς κατὰ τὸ ζητεῖν καὶ σκέπτεσθαι]; 'suspensive' [ἐφεκτική], from the condition that comes about in the enquirer after the investigation [μετὰ τὴν ζήτησιν]; 'perplexed' [ἀπορητική], either (as some say) from the fact that it is perplexed about and investigates everything [ἀπὸ τοῦ περὶ παντὸς ἀπορεῖν καὶ ζητεῖν], or else from its being at a loss [ἀπὸ τοῦ ἀμηχανεῖν] whether to assent or deny. (*PH* 7. 1)[1]

The Sceptical way of life is at least in part a life of philosophical investigation, and it differs in this respect from the way of life exemplified by the philosophical dogmatist. For investigation has no

© Casey Perin 2006

I am very grateful to audiences at Indiana University and Washington University in St Louis for discussion of an earlier version of this paper, and to David Sedley for his detailed written comments.

[1] I use, often modified, the translation in J. Annas and J. Barnes (trans.), *Sextus Empiricus*: Outlines of Scepticism [*Outlines*] (Cambridge, 2000).

place in the life of the dogmatist—either because she claims to have discovered the truth about the matters that concern her and so has no need to investigate them, or because she denies that it is possible to discover the truth about such matters and so in her view any investigation would be futile. The Pyrrhonist, by contrast, neither claims to have discovered the truth about the matters she investigates nor denies that it is possible to do so. That fact, according to Sextus, explains why investigation is an option for the Pyrrhonist but not for the dogmatist. But, as Sextus indicates elsewhere (*PH* 1. 12; 1. 25–9), it is the Pyrrhonist's desire for tranquillity, and the fact that it appears to her that she can achieve tranquillity by discovering the truth, that explains why the Pyrrhonist exercises this option. The Pyrrhonist pursues the subordinate objective of truth as a means to her ultimate objective of tranquillity.

Some of his modern readers, as well as certain critics in antiquity, have argued that Sextus' description of the Pyrrhonist as engaged in the search for truth is a sham.[2] For Sextus himself defines Pyrrhonian Scepticism as the ability to achieve tranquillity through suspension of judgement (*PH* 1. 8). But if the Pyrrhonist possesses this ability, and if she values truth only as a means to tranquillity, then she has no reason to engage in the search for truth. In addition, the Pyrrhonist deploys instances of certain argument-schemas—the so-called 'Agrippan modes'—which collectively purport to show that no one can have any reason to assent to any candidate for belief. But the use of arguments with this negative dogmatic conclusion seems to be incompatible with the search for truth. For genuine engagement in the search for truth requires at least that one does not deny that it is possible to discover the truth, and discovering the truth about some matter requires having a reason to assent to one relevant candidate for belief rather than another.

These criticisms are important but, I shall argue, misplaced. I first survey a number of texts in which, according to some commentators, Sextus' account of the Pyrrhonist or her arguments conflicts with his claim that the Pyrrhonist is engaged in the search for truth. My task here is largely negative: I attempt to show that these texts need not and should not be read in this way. But the completion of

---

[2] For Sextus' unnamed critics in antiquity, see *PH* 2. 1; and for their modern counterparts, see especially J. Palmer, 'Skeptical Investigation', *Ancient Philosophy*, 20 (2000), 351–73, and G. Striker, 'Scepticism as a Kind of Philosophy' ['Scepticism'], *Archiv für Geschichte der Philosophie*, 83 (2001), 113–29.

that negative task leaves unanswered the two important questions raised by these criticisms. So I next try to explain *why* according to Sextus the Pyrrhonist—that is, someone who can achieve tranquillity through suspension of judgement—engages in the search for truth and *how* her use of the Agrippan modes is compatible with her doing so.

I

Louis Loeb has written that although the Pyrrhonist initially sets out to acquire tranquillity by acquiring true beliefs, 'the lower-order aim of truth is renounced as one that cannot be achieved and the higher-order objective of quietude is achieved in another way, by suspending belief'.[3] But Loeb's view here cannot be right, and this for at least two reasons. First, the Pyrrhonist has no grounds for claiming that the discovery of truth *cannot* be achieved. (Nor does Sextus anywhere in the *Outlines* report that the Pyrrhonist takes herself to have grounds for making this claim.) It is true that up to now the Pyrrhonist's investigations have concluded in suspension of judgement, but *that* fact, as the Pyrrhonist herself recognizes, is no reason to deny that it is possible to discover the truth. Thus Sextus writes that, in contrast to the Academic, 'It seems to the Sceptic that it may be possible even for some things to be apprehended' (ὁ δὲ Σκεπτικὸς ἐνδέχεσθαι καὶ καταληφθῆναί τινα προσδοκᾷ, *PH* 1. 226). Second, if, as Loeb claims, the Pyrrhonist does renounce truth as an objective that *cannot* be achieved, then Pyrrhonism collapses into a form of negative dogmatism. Yet Sextus takes great care to distinguish the Pyrrhonist from those negative dogmatists (according to Sextus, the Academics, the Cyrenaics, and the Empiricist school of medicine) who deny that the truth about the matters investigated by philosophers can be known (*PH* 1. 3; 1. 200; 1. 215; 1. 226; 1. 236).

Sextus does tell us, however, that suspension of judgement is an objective for *some* Pyrrhonists. At the conclusion of his discussion of the Pyrrhonist's end or goal (τέλος), Sextus writes:

we say that the Sceptic's end or goal [τέλος τοῦ Σκεπτικοῦ] is tranquillity in matters of belief and moderation in the conditions forced on her. Some

---

[3] L. E. Loeb, 'Sextus, Descartes, Hume, and Peirce: On Securing Settled Doxastic States' ['Sextus'], *Noûs*, 32 (1998), 205–30 at 214.

prominent Sceptics have added to these [ends or goals] suspension of judgement in investigations [προσέθηκαν τούτοις καὶ τὴν ἐν ταῖς ζητήσεσιν ἐποχήν]. (*PH* 1. 30)

According to Diogenes Laertius (9. 107), these prominent Pyrrhonists include Timon and Aenesidemus, and Sextus suggests here that they pursued suspension of judgement as a means to achieving tranquillity. For these Pyrrhonists are said to have identified suspension of judgement as an end or goal *in addition to* tranquillity, and there is no indication in Sextus' text, and no reason to think, that suspension of judgement has some value for these Pyrrhonists independently of its relation to tranquillity. Moreover, Sextus alludes to these Pyrrhonists again in his discussion of the Sceptical phrase 'opposed to every account there is an equal account' (περὶ τοῦ παντὶ λόγῳ λόγον ἴσον ἀντικεῖσθαι). Sextus explains that those who follow the version of Pyrrhonism he is presenting in the *Outlines* utter this phrase to report that they are in the condition (πάθος) in which it appears to them that every dogmatic account they have examined up to now in support of a given candidate for belief is opposed by some equally credible dogmatic account in support of a conflicting candidate for belief (*PH* 1. 203). But, Sextus adds, some Pyrrhonists utter this phrase as an exhortation to their fellow Pyrrhonists to oppose to every dogmatic account they encounter a second, conflicting dogmatic account equal in credibility to the first:

They make this exhortation to the Sceptic to prevent him from being seduced by the dogmatists into abandoning his investigation and through rashness missing the tranquillity apparent to him, which (as we suggested before) they think follows on suspension of judgement about everything [ἣν νομίζουσι παρυφίστασθαι τῇ περὶ πάντων ἐποχῇ]. (*PH* 1. 205).[4]

The Pyrrhonists Sextus describes here pursue suspension of judgement as a means to tranquillity, and, though the text is not clear on this point, it is possible that they do so because they have the view that tranquillity can be achieved *only* by suspending judgement. The important point for our purposes, however, is that Sextus himself takes these Pyrrhonists to represent a version of Pyrrhonism different from the version he is presenting in the *Outlines*. That is

---

[4] I follow Annas and Barnes, *Outlines*, in excising περὶ αὐτοῦ.

why in these passages he contrasts the practices of these Pyrrhonists with his own.[5]

Loeb also claims that 'A hallmark of Pyrrhonian skepticism is the claim that the suspension of belief is the *only* route to tranquility.'[6] But in the texts Loeb cites in support of his claim—*PH* 1. 8; 1. 26; 1. 29; 1. 31—Sextus says that the Pyrrhonist first experiences suspension of judgement, then tranquillity (*PH* 1. 8), or that tranquillity 'followed fortuitously' (τυχικῶς παρηκολούθησεν) suspension of judgement (*PH* 1. 26; 1. 29), or that the Pyrrhonists claimed that tranquillity 'follows' (ἀκολουθεῖν) suspension of judgement (*PH* 1. 31). None of *those* claims is equivalent to the claim that tranquillity comes about *only* through suspension of judgement. None the less, it is true that in the *Outlines* Sextus presents suspension of judgement as the *only* possible route to tranquillity at least with respect to any question about the value, i.e. the goodness or badness, of something. At *PH* 1. 27–8 he argues that anyone who believes that certain things are good and other things bad will be perpetually anxious or distressed (ταράσσεται διὰ παντός).[7] For if I lack something that I believe to be good, I will consider this state of affairs itself as something bad, and so be distressed by it. Yet if I succeed in acquiring something I believe to be good, I will fear the loss of this good and will be anxious about doing whatever I can to prevent myself from losing it. A person can avoid the anxiety and distress associated with the pursuit and retention of things she believes to be good (as well as with the avoidance of things she believes to be bad) only by suspending judgement about whether anything is good or bad. For if I do not believe about anything either that it is good or that it is bad, then I will not be distressed by the fact that I lack certain things and I will not fear the loss of anything I now possess. The argument purports to show, then, that tranquillity at least with respect to questions of value can be achieved *only* through suspension of judgement. Now most commentators have been unmoved by Sextus' argument here, and rightly so. For if I possess something that I not only believe to be a good but also be-

---

[5] So, as we have seen, at *PH* 1. 30 what 'some prominent Sceptics' identify as the aims or goals of Pyrrhonism is contrasted with what 'we say' (φαμεν) they are, and at *PH* 1. 203–5 what 'some' (τινες) mean when they utter the Sceptical phrase 'opposed to every account there is an equal account' is contrasted with what 'I say' (εἴπω) when uttering that phrase.

[6] Loeb, 'Sextus', 218 (emphasis added).

[7] This argument recurs at *PH* 3. 237–8.

lieve to be a good which once acquired cannot be lost—the Stoics, for instance, believe that virtue is a good of this sort—then I will not fear the loss of this good and so I will not experience the distress that, according to Sextus, accompanies my possession of anything I believe to be good.[8] Regardless of the merits of this argument, however, Sextus' use of it commits his Pyrrhonist to the view that at least with respect to matters of value tranquillity can be achieved only through suspension of judgement. For the argument turns on the claim that *any* belief that certain things are good and other things bad—even a true belief formed as a result of investigation on the basis of considerations that establish its truth—is a source of anxiety and distress.

The claim that the belief that certain things are good and others bad is a source of anxiety and distress sounds very much like a piece of dogmatism. It seems to me that the best we can say about the argument at *PH* 1. 27–8 is that while it requires that the Pyrrhonist pursue suspension of judgement rather than the discovery of truth with respect to matters of value, it does not give the Pyrrhonist a reason to do so with respect to other matters. It might seem awkward for the Pyrrhonist that in some or even most, but not all, instances she pursues tranquillity by way of pursuing the discovery of truth, and I think it is. I argue below that Sextus has a good reason to discard the argument at *PH* 1. 27–8

We can understand how an activity whose ultimate objective is tranquillity none the less counts as investigation provided that this ultimate objective is pursued by way of pursuing truth as a subordinate objective. But if truth ceases to be even a subordinate objective, then it is far from clear how that activity can count as investiga-

---

[8] Of course we can restore some force to the argument at *PH* 1. 27–8 by taking one of its premisses to be suppressed, viz. that no good is such that once acquired it cannot be lost. On this reading the argument is directed against those who have been convinced on independent grounds of the truth of this suppressed premiss. However, the rehabilitated argument will still give the Pyrrhonist a reason to pursue—at least with regard to questions of value—suspension of judgement rather than the discovery of truth as a means to tranquillity *unless* the argument is strictly *ad hominem*. If it is directed only against those who have come to believe that no good is such that once acquired it cannot be lost, and if the Pyrrhonist does not hold this belief but suspends judgement about whether there is any good such that once acquired it cannot be lost, then the argument has no bearing on the objectives the Pyrrhonist herself pursues in her investigations. The problem is that Sextus does not present the argument at *PH* 1. 27–8 as strictly *ad hominem*. So at *PH* 1. 29–30 he writes of the Pyrrhonist as being less disturbed by things like cold and thirst because they do not believe that either of these things is bad by nature.

tion. That is why some commentators have argued that Sextus' Pyrrhonist not only replaces truth with suspension of judgement as her subordinate objective, but by doing so abandons the activity of investigation altogether:

The causal principle of Scepticism we say is the hope of becoming tranquil. Men of talent, troubled by the anomaly in things and puzzled as to which of them they should rather assent to, came to investigate what in things is true and what false, thinking that by deciding these issues they would become tranquil. (*PH* 1. 12)

For having begun to do philosophy [ἀρξάμενος φιλοσοφεῖν] in order to decide among appearances and apprehend which are true and which false, so as to become tranquil, the Sceptic came upon equipollent dispute, and being unable to decide it, he suspended judgement. And when he suspended judgement, tranquillity in matters of opinion followed fortuitously. (*PH* 1. 26)

Sextus describes here the experience in virtue of which someone who is *not* a Pyrrhonist *becomes* a Pyrrhonist. He presumably attributes this experience both to the very first or original Pyrrhonists and to anyone who subsequently adopts the Pyrrhonist's way of life. In discussing these passages Gisela Striker claims that 'when he finds himself unable to discover the truth, but nevertheless relieved of his worries once he has given up the project, the Sceptic also loses interest in the investigation of philosophical problems.'[9] On Striker's view, then, abandoning the activity of investigation is

[9] Striker, 'Scepticism', 117–18. A similar view can be found in R. Bett, *Pyrrho, his Antecedents, and his Legacy* (Oxford, 2000), 200–21; Palmer 'Skeptical Investigation', 369; and, perhaps, D. Morrison, 'The Ancient Sceptic's Way of Life', *Metaphilosophy*, 21.3 (1990), 204–22 at 218 (who writes that the Pyrrhonist's suspension of judgement is a matter of being 'in ignorance, but absolved from the responsibility of striving for knowledge by the thoroughgoing blockage of inquiry provided by sceptical training'). In commenting on *PH* 1. 7—where Sextus explains that the sceptical way of life is called 'suspensive' (ἐφεκτική) 'from the condition that comes about in the enquirer *after the investigation*' (ἀπὸ τοῦ μετὰ τὴν ζήτησιν περὶ τὸν σκεπτόμενον γινόμενου πάθους)—K. Janáček, *Sextus Empiricus' Sceptical Methods* (Prague, 1972), 29, writes that 'The main thing is the denial of ἐπιμονὴ ζητήσεως. The ζήτησις lapses and is replaced by the genuine sceptical ἐποχή.' Janáček's view here is endorsed by J. Brunschwig, 'The ὅσον ἐπὶ τῷ λόγῳ Formula in Sextus Empiricus', in id., *Papers in Hellenistic Philosophy*, trans. J. Lloyd (Cambridge, 1994), 244–58 at 244 n. 5. But it seems to me that B. Mates, *The Skeptic Way: Sextus Empiricus' Outlines of Pyrrhonism* (New York, 1996), 226, is right in claiming that *PH* 1. 2–3 (where the Sceptic is said to be still investigating) and *PH* 1. 7 'are consistent if the phrase μετὰ τὴν ζήτησιν in 7 means in effect "after some searching"; certainly some searching is required to bring the Skeptic into a state of *aporia* and from there to *epochē*, but there seems to be no reason why, just because he is withholding assent,

simply part of what it is to become a Pyrrhonist. For Striker appears to think that once the Pyrrhonist has suspended judgement about two conflicting candidates for belief *p* and *q*, and by doing so achieved tranquillity with respect to the conflict between *p* and *q*, the Pyrrhonist no longer has any reason to investigate whether *p* or *q* is the case.[10] Referring to *PH* 1. 12, but apparently intending to refer to *PH* 1. 26 as well, Striker claims that 'here we are told that a Pyrrhonist philosopher is interested in finding the truth *only* as a way of reaching peace of mind'.[11] But we are told no such thing in either passage. Sextus tells us that the Pyrrhonist engaged in the search for the truth in order to achieve tranquillity, but that claim is neither equivalent to nor entails that the Pyrrhonist engaged in the search for the truth *only* to achieve tranquillity. Nothing Sextus says in either passage rules out the possibility that the Pyrrhonist engages in the search for truth *both* for its own sake *and* for the sake of tranquillity. *If* the Pyrrhonist has an interest in the truth that is independent of her pursuit of tranquillity, then even when she suspends judgement about whether *p* or *q* is the case and achieves tranquillity with regard to that conflict, she still has a reason to investigate the matter.

Striker and other commentators also appeal to the following (famous) passage in support of their claim that the Pyrrhonist achieves tranquillity by giving up the search for truth.[12]

A story told of the painter Apelles applies to the Sceptics. They say that he was painting a horse and wanted to represent in his picture the lather on the horse's mouth; but he was so unsuccessful that he gave up, took the sponge on which he had been wiping off the colours from his brush, and flung it at the picture. And when it hit the picture, it produced a representation of the

he must close his mind to all further consideration of the matter in question.' Cf. M. Burnyeat, 'Can the Sceptic Live his Scepticism?' ['Can the Sceptic?'], in M. Burnyeat and M. Frede (eds.), *The Original Sceptics: A Controversy* (Indianapolis, 1997), 25–57 at 56.

[10] For ease of exposition I shall write that the Pyrrhonist investigates or attempts to discover or suspends judgement about whether *p* or *q* is the case, where I use the phrase 'whether *p* or *q* is the case' in place of the more accurate but more cumbersome 'whether it is the case that *p* or the case that *q*'. In using the shorter and less accurate phrase I obviously do not mean that the Pyrrhonist investigates or attempts to discover or suspends judgement about whether the disjunction '*p* or *q*' is true.   [11] Striker, 'Scepticism', 117 (emphasis added).

[12] See G. Striker, '*Ataraxia*: Happiness as Tranquillity', in ead., *Essays on Hellenistic Epistemology and Ethics* (Cambridge, 1996), 183–95 at 192; and 'Scepticism', 118, along with Bett, *Pyrrho*, 109.

horse's lather. Now the Sceptics, then, were hoping to acquire tranquillity by deciding the anomalies in what appears and is thought of, and being unable to do this they suspended judgement. But when they suspended judgement, tranquillity followed as it were fortuitously, as a shadow follows a body. (*PH* 1. 28–9)

It is far from obvious just how we should formulate the moral of the Apelles story. Apelles has a certain objective (representing the lather on the horse's mouth), he is unable to achieve his objective in one way (painting with his brush the lather on the horse's mouth), and as a result he does something else by which he does *not* expect to achieve his objective (throwing the sponge on which he wiped his brush at the painting) but by which none the less he *does* achieve it. The Pyrrhonist, in turn, has a certain objective (tranquillity with respect to a conflict between two candidates for belief *p* and *q*), she is unable to achieve her objective in one way (by discovering whether *p* or *q* is the case), and as a result she does something else by which she does *not* expect to achieve her objective (suspending judgement about whether *p* or *q* is the case) but by which none the less she *does* achieve it. If, therefore, the Apelles story is supposed to reveal something about the relation between the Pyrrhonist's suspension of judgement and her tranquillity, it is that the Pyrrhonist does not suspend judgement in order to achieve tranquillity (just as Apelles did not throw his sponge at the painting in order to produce a representation of the lather on the horse's mouth).[13]

More importantly, I do not think that the Apelles story supports the claim that the Pyrrhonist achieves tranquillity by giving up the search for truth. Sextus does not say here that the Pyrrhonist gives up the search for truth, but only that being unable to determine whether *p* or *q* is the case, the Pyrrhonist suspends judgement about the matter. But in reporting that she is unable to determine whether *p* or *q* is the case, the Pyrrhonist is *not* making the negative dogmatic claim that the truth about this matter cannot be known. It is true that, according to Sextus, Apelles was so unsuccessful in painting the lather on the horse's mouth that he gave up his efforts to do so (οὕτως ἀπετύγχανεν ὡς ἀπειπεῖν), and it might appear that

[13] In fact it may be that the moral of the Apelles story, whatever exactly it is, is supposed to apply only to the person described at *PH* 1. 26 as undergoing the experience in virtue of which she *becomes* a Pyrrhonist. That is, it may be that the Apelles story is not supposed to tell us anything about the relation between suspension of judgement and tranquillity in the case of the converted or practising Pyrrhonist.

we are supposed to conclude from this fact that the Pyrrhonist, too, is so unsuccessful in her search for truth that she gives up that search. But I think this appearance must be misleading. For the Pyrrhonist cannot give up the search for truth because she accepts the negative dogmatic thesis that the truth cannot be known (as Apelles might give up his efforts to paint the lather on the horse's mouth because he is convinced it cannot be done). If the Pyrrhonist suspends judgement about whether p or q is the case, she does so because it appears to her that the considerations she has identified as supporting the truth of p are equally balanced by the considerations she has identified as supporting the truth of q. If there is an analogue for the Pyrrhonist to Apelles giving up his efforts to paint the lather on the horse's mouth, it is this: in suspending judgement about whether p or q is the case, the Pyrrhonist gives up the search for the truth about this matter *as far as those considerations she has surveyed up to now go which bear on the question whether* p *or* q *is the case*. But that simply means that the Pyrrhonist's search for the truth in this case will now be a matter, at least in the first instance, of searching for additional considerations in support of the truth either of p or of q.

Two other texts in the *Outlines* have seemed to some commentators to be especially problematic for the view that the Pyrrhonist is engaged in the search for truth. At *PH* 1. 8 Sextus writes that Scepticism (Σκέψις) is 'an ability [δύναμις] to set out oppositions among things which appear and are thought of in any way at all, an ability by which, because of the equipollence [ἰσοσθένεια] in the opposed propositions and accounts, we come first to suspension of judgement [ἐποχή] and afterwards to tranquillity [ἀταραξία]'. The problem is that here Sextus appears to describe the ability which is constitutive of Pyrrhonism in such a way that the exercise of that ability eliminates any possibility that the Pyrrhonist's investigations will end in the discovery of truth rather than suspension of judgement.[14] And the claim that it is not possible, given the Pyrrhonist's ability, for an investigation to end in the discovery of truth is just a version of the negative dogmatist's thesis that the truth about the matters investigated cannot be known. Since, however, Sextus explicitly claims that Pyrrhonism is not a form of negative dogmatism, we should try to read Sextus' description here of the ability which is constitutive of Pyrrhonism in such a

---

[14] Palmer, 'Skeptical Investigation', 351–2.

way that the exercise of that ability does not commit the Pyrrhonist to negative dogmatism.

It is reasonable, therefore, to construe Sextus' remarks at *PH* 1. 8 along the following lines. Given any candidate for belief *p*, the Pyrrhonist is described as someone who is able to identify a conflicting candidate for belief *q and* to offer an argument which purports to show that there is no reason to assent to *p* rather than to *q*, or vice versa. On each occasion in the past when the Pyrrhonist has set up a conflict of this sort it has appeared to her, given the arguments she has marshalled, that she has no reason to assent to *p* rather than to *q*, and vice versa, and she has suspended judgement about whether *p* or *q* is the case. And it would be unsurprising, at the very least, if it also appears to the Pyrrhonist now that her future investigations, in which she exercises the same ability she has exercised in the past, will result in suspension of judgement. None the less, the Pyrrhonist does not give the form of assent characteristic of dogmatism to the proposition that all of her investigations will or must result in suspension of judgement.[15] That is why the Pyrrhonist is not a negative dogmatist who believes that the truth cannot be known. Of course, the Pyrrhonist does not give the form of assent characteristic of dogmatism to the proposition that her future investigations can and will result in the discovery of truth. She suspends judgement as to whether this is so, but that suspension of judgement is perfectly compatible with her undertaking an investigation which has as one of its objectives the discovery of truth. For it is not a necessary condition of undertaking an investigation with this objective that one give any form of assent to the proposition that it is possible to discover the truth. All that is required is that one not deny, as the negative dogmatist does, that it is possible to do so.

PH 1. 33–4 is a second problematic text. There Sextus writes:

when someone propounds to us an argument we cannot refute, we say to him: 'Before the founder of the school to which you adhere was born, the argument of the school did not yet appear sound, but it was there in nature. In the same way, it is possible that the argument opposing the one you have just propounded is really there in nature but does not yet appear

[15] At *PH* 1. 13 (and see 1. 19–20) Sextus distinguishes two kinds of assent, and claims that only the kind of assent which is voluntary and directed towards propositions which specify non-evident states of affairs yields the dogmatism the Pyrrhonist claims to live without.

to us; so we should not yet assent to what is now thought to be a powerful argument.

The problem here is that Sextus' Pyrrhonist can deploy this argument—let us call it *the possibility argument*—whenever she is presented with an argument which appears sound to her and against which she cannot raise any other objection or counter-argument.[16] And, crucially, *if* it appears to the Pyrrhonist that the possibility argument balances out any argument against which it is directed, then she will never be in a position in which an argument appears sound to her in a way that will lead her to assent to the conclusion of that argument. Given the availability of the possibility argument and given what the Pyrrhonist takes to be its force, her investigation cannot end in anything but suspension of judgement.[17] Now it would be foolish to deny that Sextus' text can be read in this way, but I think another, deflationary reading is plausible as well. In presenting the possibility argument Sextus is indicating that he does not want to deny that it is possible that the argument will seem compelling to some Pyrrhonists. At the same time, however, Sextus can concede that it is possible that the possibility will *not* seem compelling to other Pyrrhonists. It is, after all, easy enough to imagine a Pyrrhonist who does *not* find this argument compelling. (Why should she?) The passage at *PH* 1. 33–4 does not require, as far as I can see, that according to Sextus the possibility argument will seem to *every* Pyrrhonist to be as compelling as any argument against which it is deployed. So for all Sextus has said in this passage, the mere availability of the possibility argument does not guarantee that in every case the Pyrrhonist's investigation will end in suspension of judgement.

II

To this point I have been arguing that none of the texts commonly cited in support of the view that the Pyrrhonist is not engaged in the search for truth needs to be read in this way. But these exegetical

[16] Versions of the possibility argument are presented by Sextus at *PH* 1. 89; 1. 96; 1. 143; 2. 40; 3. 233–4.
[17] Cf. Palmer, 'Skeptical Investigation', 356, and Striker, 'Scepticism', 127–8. The possibility argument has at least one champion in R. J. Hankinson, *The Sceptics* (London, 1995), 30.

arguments leave unanswered the question *why* the Pyrrhonist—
that is, someone who is able to achieve tranquillity by suspending
judgement—engages in the search for truth. There is a genuine
puzzle here, and I think it arises in two ways.

Consider first the case in which the Pyrrhonist encounters and
is distressed by a *new* conflict between candidates for belief. Given
her past experience, it cannot but appear to the Pyrrhonist that her
investigation of this new conflict will result in suspension of judgement. Moreover, it cannot but appear to her that by suspending
judgement about this conflict she will alleviate the distress she is
currently experiencing with respect to it. The puzzle, then, is why
the Pyrrhonist does not pursue suspension of judgement rather
than the discovery of truth as her immediate objective. The answer
cannot be that if the Pyrrhonist were to do so, she would thereby
commit herself to negative dogmatism. For the Pyrrhonist can pursue suspension of judgement as a means to achieving tranquillity
without denying that it is possible to discover the truth. It will just
appear to her, as a result of her past experience, that suspension
of judgement is at least as effective a way to secure tranquillity as
the discovery of truth. I argued earlier that the Pyrrhonist cannot
pursue suspension of judgement rather than the discovery of truth
as a means to tranquillity on the grounds that it is not possible to
discover the truth. The point here is simply that the Pyrrhonist's
pursuit of suspension of judgement need not be based in this way
on negative dogmatism.

Consider next the case in which the Pyrrhonist has suspended
judgement about whether p or q is the case and, as a result, is no
longer distressed by the conflict between p and q. The Pyrrhonist
has now lost her original motive for investigating this conflict—
namely, in order to achieve tranquillity with respect to it. What
reason, then, does the Pyrrhonist have to continue investigating
whether p or q is the case? If she has no reason, how can the Pyrrhonist plausibly claim *still* to be doing so (*PH* 1. 2)? The quick answer
to these questions is that the Pyrrhonist's suspension of judgement is, and is understood by her to be, provisional. That is why
Sextus occasionally remarks that suspension of judgement obtains
only as far as an argument or set of considerations go (ὅσον ἐπὶ τῷ
λόγῳ) or 'up to now' (μέχρι or ἀχρὶ νῦν).[18] It is also the reason why

---

[18] As J. Barnes, *The Toils of Scepticism* [*Toils*] (Cambridge, 1990), 10, has noted,
citing *PH* 1. 25; 1. 200; 1. 201; 3. 70.

when the Pyrrhonist utters one of the sceptical phrases catalogued at *PH* 1. 187–205, her utterance is governed at least implicitly by a temporal qualifier.[19] The Pyrrhonist's suspension of judgement can be disturbed or unsettled by the introduction of a new consideration which bears on the matter about which she has suspended judgement. If this occurs, the Pyrrhonist once again finds herself distressed by a conflict between candidates for belief. This distress, or rather the desire to alleviate it, provides the Pyrrhonist with her reason to continue investigating the matter in question.

This quick answer, however, comes at the price of generating in a second way the same puzzle. Given her past experience, it cannot but appear to the Pyrrhonist that continued investigation of whether *p* or *q* is the case will result in suspension of judgement. Moreover, it cannot but appear to her that by suspending judgement about the conflict between *p* and *q* she will alleviate the distress she is once again experiencing with respect to it. Why, then, does the Pyrrhonist not pursue suspension of judgement rather than the discovery of truth as a means to restoring that tranquillity she has lost?

One possible solution to this puzzle is that for the Pyrrhonist suspension of judgement is not something that can be achieved by pursuing it directly.[20] (In this respect suspension of judgement would require the kind of indirectness familiar from a standard objection to utilitarianism. Just as you cannot maximize good consequences by trying to maximize good consequences, so you cannot come to suspend judgement about a matter by trying to suspend judgement about that matter.) Sextus, however, nowhere attributes this sort of view to the Pyrrhonist. According to him, the Pyrrhonist does *not* pursue suspension of judgement as her immediate objective— that fact is something which distinguishes Sextus' Pyrrhonist from earlier Pyrrhonists such as Timon and Aenesidemus. The question is *why* the Pyrrhonist does not do this, and there is simply no evidence in Sextus that it appears to the Pyrrhonist that suspension of judgement cannot be achieved by pursuing it directly. In addition, and given the Pyrrhonist's distinctive ability and her repertoire of arguments, it is very difficult to see why it would appear to the

[19] See also *PH* 1. 193 (νῦν); 1. 197 (οὕτω πέπονθα νῦν); 1. 200 (ἄχρι νῦν); 1. 201 (πρὸς τὸ παρόν). Contrast Palmer, 'Skeptical Investigation', 372.

[20] This sort of view is suggested by some remarks in J. Annas, 'Scepticism, Old and New', in M. Frede and G. Striker (eds.), *Rationality in Greek Thought* (Oxford, 1996), 239–54 at 242 and n. 14.

Pyrrhonist that she cannot achieve suspension of judgement by pursuing it directly.[21]

We can offer a more promising solution to our puzzle by first noticing that the Pyrrhonist will pursue suspension of judgement rather than the discovery of truth as a means to tranquillity *only if* the Pyrrhonist is interested in the discovery of truth *merely* as a means to tranquillity. For suppose that the Pyrrhonist can achieve tranquillity either by discovering the truth or by suspending judgement, and that the Pyrrhonist is interested in the discovery of truth for its own sake and not merely as a means to tranquillity. In these circumstances the Pyrrhonist's interest in the discovery of truth for its own sake, and the lack of any such interest in suspension of judgement, will favour the choice of truth over suspension of judgement as a means to tranquillity. So the Pyrrhonist will pursue tranquillity by way of suspension of judgement only if she lacks an interest in the discovery of truth for its own sake and, consequently, has no reason to prefer the discovery of truth to suspension of judgement as a means to tranquillity. But—and this is the important point—this lack of interest in the discovery of truth for its own sake, and not merely as a means to tranquillity, undermines the motivation Sextus attributes to the Pyrrhonist for seeking tranquillity in the first place. For according to Sextus, the Pyrrhonist seeks tranquillity because she is distressed by conflicts between candidates for belief (*PH* 1. 12; 1. 26). Yet if the Pyrrhonist has no interest in the discovery of truth for its own sake, then there is no reason for her to be distressed by the fact that candidates for belief conflict and she does not know which member of a given set of conflicting candidates for belief is true. A lack of interest in truth for its own sake renders the Pyrrhonist immune to just the kind of distress which, according to Sextus, motivates the Pyrrhonist to seek tranquillity in the first place. In this way the coherence of Sextus' account of why the Pyrrhonist seeks tranquillity requires that the Pyrrhonist is interested in the discovery of truth for its own sake and not merely as a means to tranquillity. That interest, in turn, gives the Pyrrhonist a reason to pursue tranquillity by way of the discovery of truth rather than suspension of judgement.

---

[21] In fact there are a few passages in *PH* 1 where Sextus presents a certain argument or argument-schema as being deployed *in order to* bring about suspension of judgement. See *PH* 1. 91 (ἵνα .. . . ἐπὶ τὴν ἐποχήν καταντῶμεν); 1. 100 (ἵνα . . . ἔχωμεν καταλήγειν εἰς τὴν ἐποχήν).

This line of thought, incidentally, makes it clear why the argument at *PH* 1. 27–8 is so awkward for Sextus. The source of distress Sextus identifies there is not—as we might have expected given *PH* 1. 12 and 1. 26—a conflict between candidates for belief about the value of something and perplexity about which of these conflicting candidates one ought to endorse. It is, rather, any *belief* that something is good or bad. But in that case the discovery of truth—which involves the acquisition of beliefs about the matter being investigated—is incompatible with the achievement of tranquillity with respect to matters of value. So, on the one hand, Sextus' claim at *PH* 1. 12 and 1. 26 that the Pyrrhonist is distressed by conflicts between candidates for belief presupposes that the Pyrrhonist has an interest in truth for its own sake, and this interest provides the Pyrrhonist with a reason to make the discovery of truth her immediate objective. But, on the other hand, the argument at *PH* 1. 27–8 requires that at least with respect to matters of value the Pyrrhonist abandon her interest in truth for its own sake and make suspension of judgement her immediate objective.

Consider next a passage early in the second book of the *Outlines* where Sextus is responding to the charge that the Pyrrhonist cannot investigate (or even think about) those matters about which the dogmatist holds beliefs. At *PH* 2. 11 he writes:

Consider whether even now the dogmatists are not precluded from investigation. For those who agree that they do not know how objects are in their nature it is not inconsistent [οὐ . . . ἀνακόλουθον] to investigate them; but for those who think they know them accurately it is. For the latter [i.e. the dogmatists] the investigation is already at its end, as they suppose, but for the former, the reason why any investigation is undertaken—the thought that they have not made a discovery—is still present [δι᾿ ὃ πᾶσα συνίσταται ζήτησις ἀκμὴν ὑπάρχει, τὸ νομίζειν ὡς οὐχ εὑρηκάσιν].

According to Sextus in this passage the Pyrrhonist, simply in virtue of withholding her assent both from *p* and from *q*, and hence being in a position in which it appears to her that she does not know whether *p* or *q* is the case, has a reason to search for the truth about *p* and *q*. For Sextus claims here that the reason *anyone*, the Pyrrhonist included, engages in an investigation of some matter is the fact that she thinks she has not discovered, i.e. does not know, the truth about that matter. And any investigation comes to an end when the investigator thinks, as the dogmatist does, that she has discovered, i.e. now knows, the truth about the matter she is investigating. Now the fact that it appears to me that I do not know whether *p* or *q* is the case is *by itself* a reason for me to investigate the matter *only if*, first, I desire to know whether *p* or *q* is the case, and, second, I believe or at least do not deny that it is possible to discover whether *p* or *q* is the case. So in this passage Sextus is, at least by implication, attributing to the Pyrrhonist a desire to know the truth about any matter she investigates. This desire constitutes a reason for the Pyrrhonist to make the discovery of truth rather than suspension of judgement her immediate objective provided that the Pyrrhonist believes, or at least does not deny, that her ultimate objective, tranquillity, can be achieved by discovering the truth. I have already argued that the Pyrrhonist is not in a position to deny that it is possible to achieve tranquillity by discovering the truth. If this is right, then the Pyrrhonist will seek both the discovery of truth and tranquillity, but she will not seek the discovery of truth merely as a means to tranquillity.[22]

So the passage at *PH* 2. 11 suggests the following solution to our puzzle. When the Pyrrhonist encounters a new conflict between candidates for belief or revisits an old one that is now troubling her again, she pursues the discovery of truth rather than suspension of judgement as her immediate objective because she values the discovery of truth independently of any contribution it makes to her achievement of tranquillity.[23] The discovery of truth, unlike

---

[22] Palmer, 'Skeptical Investigation', 368–9, claims that the passage at *PH* 2. 11 can be read 'as a purely *ad hominem* point against the dogmatists who claim that the Skeptic is precluded from inquiring into their own theories: given that *they* conceive of the goal of inquiry as the discovery of truth, then a necessary condition of being able to conduct an inquiry of the type they pursue is the belief that one does not already know the truth, so their complaint against the Skeptic backfires since they suppose that they are already in possession of the truth'. But, first, Palmer does not explain why it is a point against the dogmatist who believes that *p* that she is not *still* investigating or cannot (without giving up her belief that *p*) investigate whether *p* is the case. It is, after all, the Pyrrhonist, not the dogmatist, who claims both that she is *still* investigating and that investigation is a constitutive feature of her way of life. Second, Palmer can read *PH* 2. 11 in the way he describes only by ignoring, as he does, the crucial portion of the text: Sextus explicitly says that those who agree that they do not know what the nature of a given object is—i.e. the Pyrrhonists—have *as their reason for engaging in any investigation* the fact that they think they have not discovered what the nature of that object is.

[23] The claim that the Pyrrhonist values the discovery of truth need not be equivalent to or entail that the Pyrrhonist gives the form of assent characteristic of dogmatism to the proposition that the discovery of truth is something good. According to the argument at *PH* 1. 27–8, as we have seen, doing so would be a source

suspension of judgement, is not merely a means to an end. There is no problem for the Pyrrhonist in pursuing the discovery of truth as an end in itself while also pursuing tranquillity as the ultimate end of the sceptical way of life. In presenting the sceptical way of life as having an ultimate end, Sextus simply employs without endorsing standard dogmatic definitions of the ultimate end (*PH* 1. 25). Tranquillity alone satisfies those definitions. For tranquillity alone is that for the sake of which everything else, the discovery of truth included, is pursued while it itself is not pursued for the sake of anything else.

I now want to turn to a second puzzle about whether and how the Pyrrhonist's use of certain arguments is compatible with the search for truth. At *PH* 1. 164–9 Sextus introduces a set of five modes or argument-forms—the so-called Agrippan modes—which lead, either individually or in combination with one another, to suspension of judgement.[24] The Agrippan modes purport to show that a candidate for belief is subject to undecided disagreement (the mode from disagreement) or that the attempt to establish the truth of a candidate for belief relies on mere assertion (the mode from hypothesis) or involves reasoning in a circle (the reciprocal mode) or generates an infinite regress (the mode from infinite regress). Some commentators have claimed that the Agrippan modes are designed to establish the conclusion that for any candidate for belief *p* (where *p* specifies a non-evident state of affairs), there is not *and cannot be* any reason to assent to *p*. But this conclusion is equivalent to the negative dogmatic thesis that for any proposition *p* which specifies a non-evident state of affairs it is not possible to discover whether *p* is the case or not. The puzzle, then, is how, in searching for the truth about some matter, the Pyrrhonist can use arguments which have as their conclusion, and are taken by the Pyrrhonist to have as their conclusion, that the truth about that matter cannot be discovered. Moreover, as commentators regularly observe, Sextus writes that

of distress or anxiety for the Pyrrhonist. But it might none the less merely appear to the Pyrrhonist that the discovery of truth is something good, and for that reason she might pursue it.

[24] Sextus reports that these modes of suspension of judgement were devised by 'the more recent Sceptics' (οἱ νεώτεροι Σκεπτικοί) in contrast to 'the older Sceptics' (οἱ ἀρχαιότεροι Σκεπτικοί) who are said at *PH* 1. 36 to have handed down the ten modes of suspension of judgement and who include, as Sextus indicates elsewhere (*M.* 7. 345), Aenesidemus. Diogenes Laertius (9. 88) attributes the five modes to Agrippa.

'it is possible to refer every object of investigation to these modes'
(πᾶν τὸ ζητούμενον εἰς τούτους ἀνάγειν τοὺς τρόπους ἐνδέχεται, *PH*
1. 169). If the Agrippan modes have universal application, then
the Pyrrhonist appears to have arguments which can be used in
every investigation she conducts to show that the truth about the
matter investigated cannot be discovered. How can someone who
has arguments of this kind at her disposal be engaged in the search
for truth?[25]

There is a solution to this puzzle, and it is a solution which seems
to me to be available to the Pyrrhonist, but I want to be clear that
Sextus nowhere explicitly formulates it. So I am concerned here
less with exegesis and more with those possibilities that fall within
the logical space of Sextus' Pyrrhonism. The solution I have in
mind turns on two points. First, someone who, like the Pyrrhonist,
takes the Agrippan modes to have universal application is not for
that reason alone committed to a general negative dogmatism. For
the claim that the Agrippan modes can be applied to any matter the
Pyrrhonist investigates is *not* equivalent to the claim that the Agrippan modes can be *successfully* applied in every case. The Agrippan
modes together constitute a formal, and therefore topic-neutral,
argumentative strategy. But while its topic-neutrality guarantees
that the Agrippan strategy has universal application, that topic-
neutrality cannot by itself guarantee that every application of the
Agrippan strategy will be successful. So the fact that the Pyrrhonist
uses an argumentative strategy with univeral application commits
the Pyrrhonist to a general negative dogmatism *only if* the Pyrrhonist *also* believes that every application of the Agrippan strategy will
be successful.

The second point, then, is that the Pyrrhonist has no reason
to believe that every application of the Agrippan strategy will be
successful. Here is one version of the Agrippan strategy.[26] Take any
candidate for belief *p*. Either the truth of *p* is merely asserted or it

<hr/>

[25] For versions of this objection to the Pyrrhonist's use of the Agrippan modes,
see Palmer, 'Skeptical Investigation', 356–9, and Striker, 'Scepticism', 120.

[26] This version of the Agrippan strategy is developed by Barnes, *Toils*, 119, but
it is based on Sextus' own description at *PH* 1. 178–9 of a strategy that employs
three (not, as Sextus curiously says, two) of the Agrippan modes: the mode from
disagreement, the reciprocal mode, and the mode from infinite regress. Barnes
produces his strategy by simply replacing the mode from disagreement with the
hypothetical mode. If the Pyrrhonist's use of this strategy or one of its variants
need not commit her to negative dogmatism, then her use of the Agrippan modes
individually need not do so.

is established on the basis of some reason $R1$. If the truth of p is merely asserted, the hypothetical mode applies. According to that mode the mere assertion of p is no more or less credible than the mere assertion of not-p. If the truth of p is established on the basis of some reason $R1$, then $R1$ is either the same as p or different from p. If $R1$ is the same as p, the reciprocal mode applies. The attempt to establish the truth of p on the basis of $R1$ involves reasoning in a (very small) circle. If $R1$ is different from p, then either the truth of $R1$ is merely asserted or it is established on the basis of a reason $R2$. If $R1$ is merely asserted, the hypothetical mode applies. If the truth of $R1$ is established on the basis of $R2$, then either $R2$ is the same as or different from $R1$. If $R2$ is the same as $R1$ (or p), the reciprocal mode applies. If $R2$ is different from $R1$, then either the truth of $R2$ is merely asserted or it is established on the basis of a reason $R3$; and so on. The effort to establish the truth of p on the basis of a reason generates an infinite sequence of reasons, and the mode from infinite regress applies. According to this mode, an infinite sequence of reasons cannot establish the truth of p.[27]

The crux of the Agrippan strategy is the demand, given any reason $R1$ offered as establishing the truth of p, for a second reason $R2$ which establishes the truth of $R1$, and the dismissal as mere assertion of any reason whose truth is not established by another reason. The question is why the Pyrrhonist would believe that for any reason which is offered as establishing either directly or indirectly the truth of a candidate for belief, it will be reasonable or even intelligible to demand an additional reason which establishes the truth of that first reason. If $R1$ is a reason whose truth is self-evident, then appealing to $R1$ as support for the truth of p without also offering a second reason $R2$ which establishes the truth of $R1$ is *not* an instance of merely asserting $R1$. For the charge of mere assertion, and so the hypothetical mode, can be successfully applied only to a reason whose truth is not self-evident and must be established by some additional reason. And if $R1$ is different from p—as it must be if its truth is self-evident—then the reciprocal mode cannot be successfully applied to the appeal to $R1$ in support of the truth of p. And, finally, if the presentation of $R1$ in support of the truth of p is not an instance of mere assertion and does not involve circular reasoning, then there is no need for an

[27] See Barnes, *Toils*, 44–8, on why this is so or why the Pyrrhonist takes this to be so.

additional reason $R2$ and the mode from infinite regress does not apply.

Call a truth that is self-evident and can be used to establish the truth of some proposition which specifies a non-evident state of affairs a *basic reason*.[28] The Pyrrhonist has a reason to believe that every application of the Agrippan strategy will be successful *only if* she believes that there are not and cannot be basic reasons. In this way her use of the Agrippan strategy commits her to a general negative dogmatism *only if* she is also and independently committed to a form of negative dogmatism about basic reasons. But, I claim, the Pyrrhonist has no reason to believe that there are not and cannot be basic reasons, and she will suspend judgement on the matter.[29] In doing so she must also suspend judgement as to

[28] Barnes, *Toils*, 122–37, sketches an 'externalist' account of basic beliefs or items of knowledge to which the dogmatist can appeal in response to the Agrippan strategy, and he attributes this account to e.g. Galen and certain Stoics. My point here, in contrast, is simply that the Pyrrhonist has no reason to deny the possibility of what I am calling basic reasons (though she need not have any reason to accept their possibility). If the Pyrrhonist does not deny the possibility of basic reasons, then her use of the Agrippan strategy does not commit her to a general negative dogmatism.

[29] David Sedley has suggested to me that the Ten Aenesidemian Modes provide the Pyrrhonist with a reason for denying the possibility of basic reasons. I take it that something like the following is the thought. A basic reason is a self-evident truth. For any proposed basic reason p, the Pyrrhonist can appeal to one or more of the Ten Modes to establish that it appears to some creature under some condition that not-p. But in that case the truth of p is not self-evident and p is not a basic reason. In this way the Ten Modes can be used to show that the truth of any proposed basic reason is in fact something non-evident, i.e. something that needs to be established by argument. But in fact the Ten Modes do not show this at all. For the claim that the truth of p is self-evident is not equivalent to, and does not entail, the claim that the truth of p is evident to every creature under any condition. The claim is only that it is possible to know that p where one's knowledge that p is not derived from some other item of knowledge. Sedley has also suggested to me that if the notion of being apprehended or known by means of itself (τὸ καταλαμβάνεσθαι ἐξ ἑαυτοῦ) is equivalent to the notion of being self-evident, then at *PH*. 1. 178 Sextus assumes that the fact that it appears to one person that p and to another person that not-p is sufficient to show that p cannot be known by means of itself and, therefore, is not self-evident. But it seems to me that in this passage neither Sextus nor those whose argument he is reporting make this assumption. Sextus explains that 'the more recent Sceptics' who devised the Agrippan modes also argued that the fact that nothing is known by means of itself, and therefore that nothing is self-evident, follows from the fact that there is an 'undecided' (ἀνεπίκριτος) dispute among natural scientists (φυσικοί) over all objects of perception and of thought. According to this argument, then, the fact that a given proposition p is not known by means of itself and therefore is not self-evident does not follow, as Sedley suggests it does, from the fact that it appears to one creature that p and to another creature (or to the same creature in different circumstances) that not-p. The conclusion that p is not self-evident, according to this argument, follows only from the fact that the dispute

whether every application of the Agrippan strategy will be successful. That suspension, in turn, allows the Pyrrhonist to use the Agrippan strategy without thereby committing herself to a general negative dogmatism.

III

I have argued here that, according to Sextus, the Pyrrhonist is and takes herself to be engaged in the search for truth, and this is so in part because the Pyrrhonist values the discovery of truth not merely as a means to tranquillity but also as an end in itself. I have also claimed that the Pyrrhonist's use of certain arguments, including the Agrippan modes, does not by itself commit her to negative dogmatism and so is compatible with the search for truth.

The conclusion that Sextus' Pyrrhonist is and takes herself to be engaged in the search for truth has at least two important consequences for our understanding of Pyrrhonian scepticism. First, if the Pyrrhonist takes herself to be engaged in the search for truth, then she will also take herself to be committed to certain basic norms of rationality which she (or anyone else) takes to govern the search for truth. So she will take herself to be committed to, for instance, the principle that if you have no reason to assent to one candidate for belief *p* rather than another conflicting candidate for belief *q*, you ought to suspend judgement about whether *p* or *q* is the case. A commitment to this principle can serve as the basis for a novel explanation of the sense in which, by Sextus' own report, if the Pyrrhonist has no reason to believe *p* rather than *q*, and vice versa, the Pyrrhonist not only suspends judgement about whether *p* or *q* is the case, but it is *necessary* for her to do so.[30] Virtually all commentators think that the necessity which governs the Pyrrhonist's suspension of judgement is causal.[31] But if the Pyrrhonist is

over whether *p* is the case is 'undecided', i.e. from the fact that there is no reason to assent to *p* rather than to its negation, and vice versa. And that is so, the argument continues, because any consideration that could serve as a reason to assent to *p* rather than to its negation, or vice versa, would itself be an object of perception or an object of thought and, for that reason, subject to the dispute it is supposed to resolve.

[30] *PH* 1. 61; 1. 78; 1. 89; 1. 121; 1. 128; 1. 129; 1. 140; 1. 163; 1. 170.

[31] For versions of the view that the necessity with which the Pyrrhonist suspends judgement is causal, see Burnyeat, 'Can the Sceptic?', 39; M. Williams, 'Scepticism without Theory', *Review of Metaphysics*, 41 (1988), 547–88 at 572; J. Barnes,

engaged in the search for truth, then it is possible to see that necessity as hypothetical: suspension of judgement is necessary *if* the Pyrrhonist's epistemic conduct is to conform to the norms which she takes to govern the search for truth.[32]

Second, if Sextus' Pyrrhonist is engaged in the search for truth and committed to certain basic norms of rationality which she takes to govern that search, then the Pyrrhonist does not exemplify the anti-rationalism which some commentators have attributed to her and which is characteristic of, for instance, the early Empiricist school of medicine in antiquity.[33] It is true that reason, in its capacity to construct and assess arguments, leads the Pyrrhonist to suspend judgement and to sustain her suspension of judgement. But it is also reason in this same guise which prevents the Pyrrhonist from becoming one more negative dogmatist. For rational reflection reveals to the Pyrrhonist that neither her past experience of searching for the truth but failing to discover it nor those arguments which led her to suspend judgement about the matters she investigated rule out the possibility of discovering the truth in the future. Of course, the Pyrrhonist does challenge the sometimes extravagant claims made on behalf of reason by dogmatic philosophers. But by subjecting those claims to rational scrutiny that in most cases they cannot withstand, the Pyrrhonist, more than her dogmatic counterpart, emerges as an advocate of reason.

University of Massachusetts

BIBLIOGRAPHY

Annas, J., 'Scepticism, Old and New', in M. Frede and G. Striker (eds.), *Rationality in Greek Thought* (Oxford, 1996), 239–24.

'Pyrrhonism, Belief, and Causation: Observations on the Scepticism of Sextus Empiricus', *ANRW* 36.4 (1990), 2608–95 at 2610–11; Hankinson, *The Sceptics*, 279.

[32] I want to be clear that I am claiming here only that the conclusions of this paper make it *possible*—in the sense that they provide a reason—to see the necessity which governs the Pyrrhonist's suspension of judgement as hypothetical rather than causal. I do not here have the space to provide arguments for the claim that we *ought* to see the necessity in question in this way.

[33] For the charge of anti-rationalism against Sextus' Pyrrhonist, see especially Striker, 'Scepticism', 121–8. For the anti-rationalism of the early Empiricist school of medicine, see M. Frede, 'The Ancient Empiricists', in id., *Essays in Ancient Philosophy* (Minneapolis, 1987), 243–60 at 248–9.

—— and Barnes, J. (trans.), *Sextus Empiricus:* Outlines of Scepticism [*Outlines*], (Cambridge, 2000).

Barnes, J., *The Toils of Scepticism* [*Toils*] (Cambridge, 1990).

—— 'Pyrrhonism, Belief, and Causation: Observations on the Scepticism of Sextus Empiricus', *ANRW* 36.4 (1990), 2608–95.

Bett, R., *Pyrrho, his Antecedents, and his Legacy* [*Pyrrho*] (Oxford, 2000).

Brunschwig, J., 'The ὅσον ἐπὶ τῷ λόγῳ Formula in Sextus Empiricus', in id., *Papers in Hellenistic Philosophy*, trans. J. Lloyd (Cambridge, 1994), 244–58.

Burnyeat, M., 'Can the Sceptic Live his Scepticism?' ['Can the Sceptic?'], in M. Burnyeat and M. Frede (eds.), *The Original Sceptics: A Controversy* (Indianapolis, 1997), 25–57.

Frede, M., 'The Ancient Empiricists', in id., *Essays in Ancient Philosophy* (Minneapolis, 1987), 243–60.

Hankinson, R. J., *The Sceptics* (London, 1995).

Janáček, K., *Sextus Empiricus' Sceptical Methods* (Prague, 1972).

Loeb, L. E., 'Sextus, Descartes, Hume, and Peirce: On Securing Settled Doxastic States' ['Sextus'], *Noûs*, 32 (1998), 205–30.

Mates, B., *The Skeptic Way: Sextus Empiricus'* Outlines of Pyrrhonism (New York, 1996).

Morrison, D., 'The Ancient Sceptic's Way of Life', *Metaphilosophy*, 21.3 (1990), 204–22.

Palmer, J., 'Skeptical Investigation', *Ancient Philosophy*, 20 (2000), 351–73.

Striker, G., '*Ataraxia*: Happiness as Tranquillity', in ead., *Essays on Hellenistic Epistemology and Ethics* (Cambridge, 1996), 183–95.

—— 'Scepticism as a Kind of Philosophy' ['Scepticism'], *Archiv für Geschichte der Philosophie*, 83 (2001), 113–29.

Williams. M., 'Scepticism without Theory', *Review of Metaphysics*, 41 (1988), 547–88.

METHEXIS AND GEOMETRICAL REASONING IN PROCLUS' COMMENTARY ON EUCLID'S *ELEMENTS*

ORNA HARARI

In the opening sentence of his commentary on the first book of Euclid's *Elements* Proclus presents his ontological account of mathematical objects, ascribing to them an intermediate rank between indivisible realities and divisible realities. Following Plato's *Republic* 6, Proclus relates these grades of reality to different cognitive faculties: the indivisible realities are apprehended by the intellect (νοῦς), the divisible realities by sense perception (αἴσθησις), and the intermediate realities (i.e. mathematical objects) by discursive reason (διάνοια) (3. 1–4. 8).[1] The correlation between mathematical objects and the objects of discursive reason does not seem to provide Proclus with sufficient theoretical means to account for *geometrical* objects. These objects, having magnitude, form, and extension cannot be grasped by discursive reason alone. In the second prologue to the commentary on the *Elements*, where Proclus discusses geometry, he relates geometrical objects to *two* cognitive faculties: discursive reason and the imagination (φαντασία). In Proclus' view geometrical objects are projections (προβολαί) of discursive reason-principles (λόγοι) onto the imagination.[2]

© Orna Harari 2006

I am grateful to Alain Bernard, Charles Kahn, Sabetai Unguru, Bernard Vitrac, and the anonymous referee of this journal for their valuable comments on earlier versions of this article.

[1] The references here and throughout are to Friedlein's edition: *Procli Diadochi in primum Euclidis elementorum librum commentarii*, ed. G. Friedlein (Leipzig, 1873).

[2] Throughout his commentary, Proclus employs the terms 'form' (εἶδος) and 'reason-principle' (λόγος) to denote the object of discursive reason. Glenn Morrow in his English translation of the commentary says that 'it is hard to distinguish any difference in signification' between the two (Proclus, *A Commentary on the First Book of Euclid's* Elements, trans. with introduction and notes by Glenn Morrow and

The addition of the imagination to the Platonic account of geometrical objects is aimed at accommodating geometrical certainty
with geometrical reasoning.[3] The correlation between discursive
reason and geometrical objects accounts only for the former; the
immateriality of the objects of discursive reason accounts for the
precision of geometrical objects, the truth of geometrical propositions, and the role of geometry in emancipating the soul from
sensation (49. 7–24). Yet geometrical reasoning requires material
objects. In geometrical proofs the objects under consideration are
constructed and compared with each other. For instance, geometry
considers whether lines, angles, and figures are equal or unequal to
each other and requires one to bisect lines, to construct figures, or
to inscribe them in others. The employment of these procedures
implies, in Proclus' view, that geometrical objects are not separated
from an underlying matter that makes their particularity and constructibility possible (50. 2–9). The imagination serves in Proclus'
philosophy as the medium in which the indivisible and unextended
objects of discursive reason acquire the divisibility and the spatial
extension required for geometrical reasoning. Hence, according to
Proclus, geometrical knowledge is about discursive objects while
geometrical proofs deal with imagined objects:

We grant the geometer that he investigates the universal, and this is the
immanent universal [κατατεταγμένον] in imagined circles; but although he
sees one circle, he studies another—viz. the circle in discursive reason.
Nevertheless, he makes his demonstrations about the former. (54. 23–6)[4]

a new foreword by Ian Mueller (Princeton, 1970), 10 n. 21). Although in the commentary on Euclid's *Elements* no explicit distinction between these terms is made,
in the commentary on Plato's *Parmenides* Proclus does distinguish them, saying that
λόγοι are the causes of things that have no paradigmatic causes (i.e. forms), such as
the parts of animals and accidents (*In Parm.* 825. 36–827. 25 Cousin). Forms and
reason-principles cause different aspects of a certain entity: the former causes its
essential characteristics and the latter its accidental characteristics.

[3] In this respect, Proclus' philosophy of geometry is unique. Neither Plato nor
Aristotle assigns a cognitive role to geometrical constructions and diagrammatic
representations. In *Republic* 7 Plato considers geometrical constructions an un-
avoidable shortcoming of geometry (527 A 6–B 1), whereas Aristotle considers them,
in some contexts, pedagogic means (*De caelo* 279[b]35). Furthermore, it follows from
Dominic O'Meara's analysis of the incorporation of Pythagoreanism into the Neoplatonic tradition that the emphasis on extended representations is Proclus' unique
contribution to this tradition. See D. O'Meara, *Pythagoras Revived: Mathematics
and Philosophy in Late Antiquity* (Oxford, 1989), 168–9.

[4] All translations are mine.

Proclus' attempt to accommodate the cognitive worth of geometry with its mode of reasoning raises two questions: (1) how can
the contention that geometrical objects are projections of discursive reason-principles onto the imagination account for the particularity and constructibility of these objects? and (2) does this
contention provide an adequate analysis of Euclid's geometrical
reasoning? Apart from contributing to the understanding of Proclus' philosophy of geometry, consideration of these questions has
implications for the historiography of Greek mathematics. Proclus' commentary on Euclid's *Elements* is one of the main sources
of information about Greek geometry. Its influence on the historiography of Greek mathematics extends beyond Proclus' strictly
historical remarks, such as his description of the development of
Greek geometry and his attribution of different geometrical proofs
and methods to various ancient sources. Historians of Greek mathematics often understand the structure and methods of Euclid's
proofs in the light of Proclus' interpretation. For instance, they
ascribe to Euclid Proclus' division of geometrical proofs into six
parts and his distinction between theorems that establish the truth
of geometrical propositions and problems that establish the correctness of geometrical constructions.[5] Generally, in treating Proclus'
commentary on the *Elements* as a historical source, historians of
Greek mathematics ascribe little importance to the Neoplatonic
background against which it was composed. The commentary on
the *Elements* is therefore commonly regarded as comprising two un-
related parts: a philosophical part, present in the two prologues to
the commentary, and a mathematical part, where Proclus interprets
Euclid's definitions, postulates, axioms, and proofs. By considering
the relationship between Proclus' philosophy of geometry and his
interpretation of geometrical proofs, the present study may shed a
fresh light on the historical value of Proclus' analyses of geometrical
proofs; it may also lead to jettisoning the artificial separation of the

---

[5] T. Heath, *A History of Greek Mathematics* (New York, 1981), 533; I. Mueller,
'Mathematics and Philosophy in Proclus' Commentary on Book I of Euclid's *Ele-
ments*', in J. Pépin and H. D. Saffrey (eds.), *Proclus: lecteur et interprète des anciens*
(Paris, 1987), 305–18 at 310–11. See also C. B. Boyer, *A History of Mathematics*
(New York, 1968), 212; H. Eves, *An Introduction to the History of Mathematics*
(Philadelphia, 1983), 139–40; M. Kline, *Mathematical Thought from Ancient to
Modern Times* (Oxford, 1972), 26. The discrepancies between Proclus' division of
geometrical proofs into parts and Euclid's proofs are discussed in R. Netz, 'Pro-
clus' Division of the Mathematical Propositions into Parts: How and Why was it
Formulated?', *Classical Quarterly*, NS 49.1 (1999), 282–303.

two components, the 'merely' philosophical and the mathematical, thereby restoring the commentary to its coherence and unity.

To pave the way to an analysis of the relationship between Proclus' philosophy of geometry and his interpretation of geometrical proofs, I discuss in the next section the logical background of Proclus' ontological conception of geometrical objects.[6] This discussion discloses the logical characteristics of the notion of participation (μέθεξις), on which Proclus' philosophy of geometry is based. In view of this discussion, I show, in the second and third sections, how the notion of participation accounts for the particularity and the constructibility of geometrical objects. In the fourth section I go on to consider whether Proclus' notion of geometrical constructions accords with Euclid's. By analysing Proclus' sole example of the theoretical apprehension attained through geometrical constructions, I show that Proclus' metaphysical commitments bear necessarily upon his interpretation of geometrical proofs.

1. The logical background of Proclus' philosophy of geometry

Although Proclus' philosophy of geometry is primarily aimed at establishing the pre-existence of geometrical objects, this ontological view is formulated in logical terms. The characterization of geometrical objects as projections of discursive reason-principles onto the imagination is based on a distinction between three universals: (1) an immanent universal (κατατεταγμένον); (2) a transcendent universal (προτεταγμένον); and (3) a later-born universal (ὑστερογενές), derived from the particulars by collection or abstraction and serving as their *predicate* (50. 18–51. 7).[7] This triple division is central in Neoplatonism; it marks the distinction between the universal that is separate from the particulars (προτεταγμένον), the universal that exists only in each specific and individual instance (κατατεταγμένον), and the universal that exists in our conceptions as an abstraction from individual instances. In other contexts, Proclus

---

[6] My analysis of the relationship between philosophy and mathematics in Proclus' thought differs from extant studies on this topic in focusing on Proclus' logical assumptions and in examining their influence on his account of geometrical practice. For ontological accounts of Proclus' philosophy of mathematics see S. Breton, *Philosophie et mathématique chez Proclus* (Paris, 1971); A. Charles-Saget, *L'Architecture du divin: mathématique et philosophie chez Plotin et Proclus* (Paris, 1982).   [7] A parallel distinction is found in *ET*, prop. 67.

employs various terms to denote the distinction between transcendent and immanent universals. The transcendent universal is also called 'the whole before the parts', 'the unparticipated', 'the unit', and 'form'. The immanent universal is called 'the whole in the parts', 'the participated', and 'secondary entity'. For the sake of clarity, throughout this paper I use the terms 'transcendent universal' and 'immanent universal' in referring to this distinction. For the abstracted universal I use Proclus' technical term—'later-born universal'.

In delineating his philosophy of geometry, Proclus divides the immanent universal into (1a) the universal in which perceptible objects participate and (1b) the universal in which imagined objects participate. Proclus' account of geometrical objects assumes two of the four aforementioned universals: (1b) the immanent universal, in which imagined objects participate, and (2) the transcendent universal, which is the object of discursive reason. The later-born universal (3) has no role in Proclus' philosophy of geometry. The obvious reason for its exclusion is ontological; unlike the first two universals, the later-born universal is not ontologically prior to the particulars but is derived from them. Yet an exclusively ontological understanding of the exclusion of later-born universals does not explain how the assumption of transcendent universals solves the problem that Proclus' philosophy of geometry proposes to solve. If transcendent universals differ from later-born universals merely in their ontological status, what consequences can the assumption of the former have for geometrical reasoning?

Proclus' second argument in support of the ontological priority of mathematical objects makes it clear that the assumption of transcendent universals has logical consequences (*In Eucl.* 13. 27–14. 23). In this argument Proclus contends that the supposition that geometry deals with later-born universals is inconsistent with the priority and explanatory role of universals in scientific demonstrations. Proclus' argument rests on two assumptions. The first is familiar from Aristotle's theory of demonstration; it states that universals, being the starting-points of demonstration (ἐξ ὧν), are by nature prior to the particulars and serve as the causes of the conclusion (14. 17–20). According to the second assumption, the particulars, being the source from which later-born universals are derived, have causal priority over these universals (14. 6–7). These assumptions, taken together, lead to the conclusion that the identification of the principles of demonstration with later-born universals does not accord with the priority of universals in demonstrations.

This argument, however, does not undermine the coherence of Aristotle's theory of demonstration, as Aristotle would reject the second assumption. The priority of the particulars in the process leading to universals does not necessarily amount to logical or explanatory priority. Aristotle's distinction between priority by nature and priority to us renders the explanatory priority of universals compatible with the priority of particulars in the process leading to universals; in this distinction the universals are prior by nature and hence explanatory, whereas the particulars are prior to us. In the commentary on the *Elements* Proclus does not justify the second assumption, yet such a justification can be reconstructed from his commentary on Plato's *Parmenides*. In the fourth book of this commentary Proclus discusses later-born universals, in commenting on Socrates' suggestion that forms are thoughts in the soul. Here, as in the commentary on the *Elements*, Proclus claims that the assumption of later-born universals is inconsistent with the requirement that demonstrations should be based on prior, more honourable (τιμιώτερον), and more universal terms:

How, then, is the universal honourable if it is later-born? For in later-born [universals] the more universal a term is, the less substance it has; from this it also [follows] that the species has more substance than the genus. Hence we should do away with the rules about the truest demonstration, if we lay down only later-born universals in the soul. For these are by no means better [κρείττω] than, causes of, and prior by nature to more particular terms [μερικώτερον]. (894. 24–34 Cousin)

According to this passage, later-born universals cannot serve as the starting-points of demonstration, since they are less substantial (ἀνουσιώτερον) than the particulars. Proclus' contention that the later-born genus is less substantial than the species makes it clear that the expression 'less substantial' does not merely refer to the ontological status of later-born universals. As far as ontology is concerned, genera and species, viewed as later-born (i.e. abstractions), are less real to the same extent; they are both derived from the particulars and subsist in our conceptions. Hence it seems that the expression 'less substantial' bears on the content of later-born universals. This conclusion is confirmed in the fifth book of the commentary on Plato's *Parmenides*, where Proclus contrasts the

definitions that serve as genuine starting-points of demonstration
with definitions that specify the common element abstracted from
the particulars:

Definitions of things common to particulars do not include the particulars as a whole. For how is Socrates as a whole [included in the defini-
tion] 'rational mortal animal', while there are in him other [attributes]
that make up the so-called peculiar quality [ἰδίως ποιόν]? By contrast, the
reason-principle of man in us comprises the whole of each particular, for
it comprises unitarily all the powers that are observed with regard to the
particulars. And similarly 'animal': that which is in the particulars is lesser
than both the particulars themselves and the species; for it does not have
all the differentiae in actuality but merely in potentiality. In that manner
it becomes, like matter, consequent upon the differentiae that make the
species. On the other hand, 'animal' in us is greater and more comprehensive than 'man', for it comprises in a unified way all the differentiae, not
in potentiality like the former but in actuality. If we are, then, to discover
the definition which will be the principle of demonstration, it should be
of such a thing that includes all of the more particular terms. (981. 11–27
Cousin)[8]

In this passage Proclus contrasts common definitions derived from
the particulars and reason-principles (λόγοι), characterized as existing in us (i.e. transcendent universals, existing in the soul). In contrasting common definitions and reason-principles, Proclus criticizes the abstractness of the former. Common definitions are greater
in extension than the particulars but their intension is less than that
of the particulars. In Proclus' view the universal definition of man as
'a rational mortal animal' does not adequately hold for a particular
man, such as Socrates, since it does not include the unique properties that distinguish him from other men. The reason-principles,
by contrast, are no less in intension than the particulars; they include their unique properties. Proclus' account of the relationship
between species and particulars is also applied to the relationship
between genera and species. In the second part of the above passage

[8] In my translation of this passage the expression τὸ καθέκαστον, which appears at
lines 13–14 of Cousin's edition, is omitted. This omission is justified on the following
grounds. First, the claim '*the particular* comprises unitarily all the powers, which
are observed with regard to the particulars' does not accord with Proclus' parallel
claim concerning the genus 'animal', made at lines 20–2. Second, in Moerbeke's
Latin translation the subject of this sentence is *in nobis hominis ratio*; no reference is
made in this translation to 'the particular' (Proclus, *Commentaire sur le Parménide
de Platon: traduction de Guillaume de Moerbeke*, ed. C. Steel (2 vols.; Leuven, 1985),
ii. 292).

he attempts to maintain the correspondence between the extension of genera and their intension. In so doing, he rejects Aristotle's analysis of the relationship between genera and differentiae in terms of the distinction between potentiality and actuality.[9] Unlike Aristotle, Proclus holds that the genus exists over and above its species; in his view the genus is not merely a potential being that becomes actual through the differentiae that make its species, it rather includes all of its differentiae in actuality.[10]

It follows from this comparison that transcendent universals differ from later-born universals in their content as well as in their ontological status. By including in actuality the specific differentiae and the peculiar qualities of the particulars, transcendent universals are richer in their content than later-born universals. Whereas later-born universals include only the common properties of the particulars, transcendent universals include the unique properties of each species and individual. A major implication of this conception is that transcendent universals are not universals in the strict sense. More precisely, they cannot be predicated with the same name and the same definition (i.e. synonymously) of several instances.[11] A species that includes the peculiar qualities (ἰδίως ποῖα) of the particulars cannot be common to several of them. For instance, if the species man includes Socrates' peculiar qualities, it cannot be predicated of Callippus with the same name and the same definition. Similarly, a genus that includes all the differentiae in actuality is not a common predicate, such as 'animal', which holds equally for different species, such as 'man', 'fish', or 'bird'.[12]

---

[9] *Metaph. H* 6, 1045ᵃ23–5.

[10] One of the reasons that led Aristotle to analyse the relationship between genera and differentiae in terms of the distinction between potentiality and actuality is to prevent the genus from having in actuality contrary attributes, such as feathered and featherless (*Metaph. Z* 12, 1037ᵇ19–21). Nevertheless, Neoplatonists held that the actual subsistence of the differentiae in the genus is indispensable for answering the question from what source the differentiae arise in the species. Cf. Syrian. *In Metaph.* 32. 5–6 Kroll. To the best of my knowledge, Proclus does not explain how the genus comprises in a unified way all the differentiae in actuality. I assume that he leaves this issue unexplained since, in his view, the unity of transcendent entities is inexplicable in discursive terms. The third section of this paper touches upon this issue.

[11] See *ET* prop. 110, p. 98. 12–14 Dodds; *In Parm.* 880. 3–10 Cousin.

[12] Anthony Lloyd explains the rationale behind this conception of genera, claiming that from a Neoplatonic point of view a certain genus modified by certain differentiae has a different meaning when it is modified by a different differentia. For instance, 'animal' modified by the differentia 'being capable of flying' differs in its meaning

Nevertheless, transcendent universals do serve as a common element that presides over their particular manifestations. In Proclus' view, the community (κοινότης) between transcendent universals and their manifestations is neither synonymous nor homonymous, but that of being derived from and having reference to a single source (ἀφ' ἑνὸς καὶ πρὸς ἕν) (880. 3–16 Cousin).[13] In this notion of community, the various manifestations of a transcendent universal are not equally subordinated to it, but they differ from each other in their relation to the single source from which they are all derived. Proclus often describes the difference between the particular manifestations of the transcendent universal in terms of different positions of members in an ordered series.[14]

The discussion of transcendent universals brought into light a distinction between two senses of community: predicative community, holding for later-born universals and their instances, and causal community, belonging to transcendent universals and their immanent manifestations. An analysis of the logical characteristics of the other universal which underlies Proclus' philosophy of geometry, i.e. the immanent universal (κατατεταγμένον), should disclose the exact sense of community that holds for it. Proclus, however, does not seem to provide a clear answer to this question.[15] In proposition 19 of *The Elements of Theology* Proclus states that primary terms (τὸ πρώτως ἐνυπάρχον) are present in all instances alike and in virtue of one definition (καθ' ἕνα λόγον καὶ ὡσαύτως).[16] In other

from 'animal' modified by the differentia 'being capable of living in water'. By this view the genus cannot be predicated with the same name and the same definition of different species (A. C. Lloyd, 'Procession and Division in Proclus' ['Procession and Division'], in H. J. Blumenthal and A. C. Lloyd (eds.), *Soul and the Structure of Being in Late Neoplatonism: Syrianus, Proclus and Simplicius* (Liverpool, 1982), 18–45 at 24).

[13] The expression ἀφ' ἑνὸς καὶ πρὸς ἕν is borrowed from Aristotle's characterization of certain terms such as health, medical, and being, whose instances do not have common definition but are nevertheless definable by their various relations to a single term (see e.g. *Metaph. Γ* 2). The exact significance of this relation in Proclus' philosophy will become clearer in sect. 3, where the causal relationship between forms and participants is discussed.

[14] The members are ordered according to their simplicity and creative power. On this see *ET* prop. 62 and sect. 3 below.

[15] The ambiguity concerning the status of the κατατεταγμένον stems from the fact that this universal has an intermediate status between the universal prior to the particulars and the particulars themselves. On this see S. Ebbesen, 'Porphyry's Legacy to Logic: A Reconstruction', in R. Sorabji (ed.), *Aristotle Transformed: The Ancient Commentators and their Influence* (Ithaca, NY, 1990), 141–71 at 152–4.

[16] See also *In Parm.* 981. 1–6 Cousin.

words, he views these terms as predicated synonymously of their instances. Other passages, by contrast, suggest that inasmuch as the immanent universal is *in* its subjects it includes their individualizing properties and hence is not equally realized in them. In proposition 23 Proclus claims that a common property which is present in all things alike (τὸ πᾶσιν ὡσαύτως παρόν) is prior to them and hence transcendent, or in his terms unparticipated, whereas the immanent or participated entity is unique to each manifestation; in Proclus' words, 'it is in one of them and not in the others' (τὸ ἐν ἑνὶ ὂν ἐν τοῖς ἄλλοις οὐκ ἔστιν). Similarly, in proposition 24 Proclus establishes the priority of the transcendent or unparticipated universal over the immanent or participated universal, by claiming that unlike the former, the latter belongs to one particular and not to all (τινὸς ὂν καὶ οὐ πάντων). In proposition 110 Proclus explicitly claims that immanent entities have no common definition, arguing instead that they are related to each other as being derived from and having reference to one source:

> Not all things have the same worth, even if they are of the same class of being [διακόσμησις]; for they have no one definition, but they [all proceed from the appropriate unit] as being derived from and having reference to one source [ἀφ' ἑνὸς καὶ πρὸς ἕν]. (98. 10–14 Dodds)

I do not attempt to settle here the discrepancy between these passages, yet I believe that a non-predicative interpretation of immanent universals accords better with Proclus' general approach.[17] Several passages in Proclus' writings suggest a distinction between two kinds of immanent universals: one which is common to its subjects (i.e. its participants) but separated from them, and another which is in its subjects but not common to them.[18] The introduction of an intermediate entity, which is immanent (i.e. participated) but separate, may reasonably suggest that common and inseparable entities are problematic in Proclus' view. The main problem that such entities raise is their susceptibility to the same criticism that the assumption of transcendent (unparticipated and

---

[17] My argument is not based on an overwhelming rejection of universals but on the claim that Proclus' conception of universals accounts for individual differences between particulars. My discussion in the following two sections further supports this contention.

[18] *In Parm.* 1041. 20–8 Cousin; *ET* props. 63, 64, 81. For a detailed discussion of the distinction between the two kinds of participated entities see Lloyd, 'Procession and Division', 26–8.

hence separate) entities prevents. From a Neoplatonic point of view, transcendent entities have three major advantages over later-born universals. First, they prevent the reduction of the genus to its species, thereby securing the correspondence between grades of universality and grades of reality. Second, they block the infinite regress of the Third Man argument, by denying synonymous community between a common entity and its instances (*In Parm.* 880. 3–10 Cousin). Third, they solve the Sail Cloth dilemma by preventing the distribution of one common entity among many instances. Hence consistency requires that once the separation of the transcendent entity is admitted, no other common entities can be viewed as immanent in the strict sense.[19]

If my interpretation is correct, imagined geometrical objects, being immanent universals (κατατεταγμένα), are not universals in the strict sense; they include the individualizing characteristics that distinguish one particular from another. Likewise, the reason-principles in discursive reason, viewed as transcendent universals, are not related to the geometrical objects in the imagination as a common universal, but as a common source. The consequences of this conception for geometrical constructions are discussed in the third section of this paper. The following section considers the implication of the logical characteristics of immanent universals for Proclus' conception of geometrical objects.

2. Participation and geometrical objects

The notion of imagined matter—the matter in which geometrical objects as immanent universals are realized—is introduced in the second prologue of the commentary on Euclid's *Elements* as originated in Aristotle's notion of 'intelligible matter' (51. 17).[20] Proclus' appeal to this Aristotelian notion raises the question of whether he shares with Aristotle the conception of geometrical objects implied by the notion of intelligible matter. Aristotle's notion of intelligible matter, as it is presented in *Metaphysics Z* 10, gives rise to the following characterization of geometrical objects:

---

[19] This interpretation accords with Anthony Lloyd's discussion of the status of common properties in the Neoplatonic tradition (A. C. Lloyd, *The Anatomy of Neoplatonism* (Oxford, 1990), 67).

[20] *Metaph. Z* 10, 1036ª9–12; 1037ª4–5; and *H* 6, 1045ª33–5.

A part is a part either of the form (and by form I mean the essence) or of the compound out of form and matter or of matter itself. But only the parts of the form are parts of the definition, and a definition is of the universal . . . Now, with regard to the compound, for instance this circle, namely one of the particulars whether sensible or intelligible—by intelligible I mean, for instance, the mathematical and by sensible those which are made, for instance, of bronze or wood—of these there is no definition, but they are known by the aid of intellection or sensation and when they depart from the activity [of these faculties] it is not clear whether they are or are not. But they are always said and known by means of a universal definition; and matter by itself is unknown. Matter is either sensible or intelligible; sensible matter is for instance bronze or wood and all movable matter, and intelligible matter is that which is present in sensible things but not as sensible, for instance the mathematicals. ($1035^b31–1036^a12$)

In this passage Aristotle applies his theory of substance to geometrical objects, considering them compounds of form and matter. Geometrical objects, like other particular objects, have two aspects: form, which can be defined and hence known, and matter, which is excluded from the definition and therefore cannot be known. Thus, only the form of a particular geometrical object can be known; the compound of matter and form can be either perceived or grasped intuitively.

It seems unlikely that Proclus bases his philosophy of geometry on this notion of intelligible matter. In the above passage, the drawn lines, segments, and radii, being parts of the compound of matter and form and not parts of the definition, are excluded from what Aristotle regards as the objects of theoretical knowledge.[21] Proclus, by contrast, introduces the notion of imagined matter in account-

---

[21] I do not venture to infer from this passage a general conclusion regarding Aristotle's conception of mathematical objects and its relationship to Greek mathematical practice. I confine myself to the implications of Aristotle's notion of intelligible matter for a conception of mathematical objects. I disagree here with Ian Mueller, who argues that Aristotle conceives of mathematical objects as particular objects since they have an intelligible matter. Mueller's interpretation is based on an identification of the intelligible matter of mathematical objects with the genus, which is part of the definition of these objects (I. Mueller, 'Aristotle on Geometrical Objects', *Archiv für Geschichte der Philosophie*, NS 55 (1970), 156–71 at 167). This identification, however, seems untenable; the genera 'plane' and 'solid' that Aristotle views as analogous to matter are not equivalent to two-dimensional and three-dimensional extensions, they are rather the concepts of plane figures and solid figures. Hence the 'actualization' of the genus by its differentiae yields a species (e.g. the concept of a circle) and not a particular geometrical object as Mueller argues. In the passage quoted above Aristotle explicitly denies any correspondence between the parts of definitions and the parts of substances.

ing for the theoretical role of diagrammatic representations and constructions in geometry. Hence Aristotle's notion of intelligible matter cannot play the role that Proclus ascribes to imagined matter in his philosophy of geometry. Furthermore, Aristotle's application of the distinction between matter and form to geometrical objects rests on the assumption that various compounds of matter and form can be subsumed under one definition. Thus the incorporation of Aristotle's notion of intelligible matter into Proclus' philosophy of geometry seems to be at odds with Proclus' ontology. Within the framework of Proclus' ontology, imagined matter cannot be identified with Aristotle's intelligible matter, since Aristotle's conception implies that one definition equally holds for several particular instances. This conclusion, however, does not accord with the logical presuppositions of Proclus' ontology. Proclus' immanent universals, as I have shown in the previous section, include the individualizing characteristics that distinguish one particular from another. Hence, one common definition cannot adequately hold for several immanent universals.

It is not clear from Proclus' references to the notion of imagined matter in his Euclid commentary whether his notion of imagined matter accords with his ontology. Yet an examination of his other writings indicates that in forming his concept of matter, Proclus does draw the consequences implied by his ontology. In the fourth book of his commentary on Plato's *Parmenides* Proclus criticizes his predecessors, who likened participation to reflections in a mirror or impressions made by a seal, for viewing matter as utterly passive. In contrast to these views, Proclus distinguishes the substrate in which forms are realized from prime matter in which higher grades of reality are realized (840. 4–7 Cousin), thereby regarding the substrate and not only the form as affecting the process of participation. In Proclus' view, the substrate in which forms are realized, unlike prime matter, is already modified by those grades of reality, which are ontologically prior to the Demiurge or the intellect;[22] these grades of reality are, in descending order: the One, the limit and the unlimited, henads, being, and life. The characteristics derived from these grades of reality yield, in Proclus' terms, the aptitude (ἐπιτηδειότης) of the substrate for receiving forms. The substrate's aptitude accounts, according to Proclus, for different realizations of the same form in various substrates:

---

[22] *In Parm.* 844. 11–31 Cousin; *In Tim.* i. 387. 8–30 Diehl; *ET*, props. 70–2.

Furthermore, if each thing came about according to the divine production alone, all things would be alike. Since this production is steadily the same and present in all things, from where will we derive their variations and the fact that some of them always participate and in like manner, whereas others participate sometimes and in a different manner, unless we state that the difference is derived from their aptitude? (*In Parm.* 843. 7–13 Cousin)

In considering the realization of the form to be unaffected by its substrate, Proclus holds, the proponents of the passive conceptions of matter fail to account for individual differences between the various manifestations of the same form. In the passive conception, matter serves merely as the medium through which one single form is manifested in many instances: matter makes possible merely the *quantitative* pluralization of the form. Proclus, by contrast, regards the substrate's aptitude as affecting the form itself; he thereby views it as yielding *qualitative* differences between the various manifestations of a single form. That is, the unique characteristics of each particular can be explained in terms of defective reception of the form, resulting from the substrate's aptitude. Consequently, differences between particulars can be theoretically known, since they are evident also in the knowable aspect of the particular, namely its form. An application of this conception to geometry facilitates a theoretical understanding of the individual characteristics of geometrical objects, such as their size and position.[23]

This conclusion is confirmed by Proclus' justification of Euclid's definitions of geometrical objects. Opening his discussion of Euclid's definitions, Proclus claims that they assume the priority of composite terms over simple terms; in these definitions the one-dimensional is defined in terms of the two-dimensional and the two-dimensional in terms of the three-dimensional.[24] In Proclus' view, definitions that define points in terms of lines or lines in terms of planes turn simple and limiting terms into accidents contingent on the limited terms. Although this approach is contrary to Proclus' ontological viewpoint, which presupposes the priority of the

[23] Proclus indeed views the realization of geometrical λόγοι in the imagination as yielding such differences (*In Eucl.* 53. 9–18).

[24] Although Proclus presents this characterization as a general description of Euclid's definitions, it holds only for definitions 1. 3 and 1. 6, in which the lower dimensions are indeed defined in terms of the higher dimensions. However, in addition to these definitions Euclid presents the following definitions of the basic geometrical entities: 'a point is what has no parts' (1. 1), and 'a line is length without breadth' (1. 2).

simple over the composite,[25] Proclus justifies Euclid's definitions by appealing to the role of matter in participation. In so doing, Proclus draws a distinction between forms separated from matter and forms embodied in matter, arguing that in the former the simple is prior to the composite, whereas in the latter the composite is prior to the simple:

But more complex, rather than simpler, reason-principles have been assigned to the forms requiring matter, i.e. forms that have their foundation in other things, and departed from their essences, spreading among their substrates and having imported unity. Therefore, in the entities [realized] in the imagination, which appear in the matter of imagined shapes and in the entities [realized] in sensible things, which are generated by nature, the reason-principles of the limited are prior, and those of the limits are consequent, like additions. (*In Eucl*. 86. 7–16)

Proclus' conception of matter, then, resting on his notion of participation, provides a theoretical justification of Euclid's definitions of geometrical objects. The rejection of Aristotle's ontology and its logical implications render Euclid's geometrical objects, despite their particularity and dependence on matter, objects of theoretical knowledge. Proclus' ontology does not require the identification of the objects of knowledge with universal definitions; it requires that the objects of knowledge be considered in their particularity. As a result, differences between geometrical objects, which are excluded from Aristotle's definitions but are represented in geometrical diagrams, can be considered a subject of theoretical knowledge. This approach to geometrical objects is derived from Proclus' ontology. In endorsing the ontological priority of geometrical objects over sensible objects, Proclus bases geometry on immanent universals that include the individualizing characteristics of the particulars. Hence the metaphysical background of Proclus' commentary on Euclid's *Elements* is not accidental to his analysis of geometrical practice; in accounting for individuation, it aims to explain how the drawn figures of Euclid's *Elements* can be considered objects for theoretical enquiry.[26]

[25] e.g. *ET*, prop. 5.

[26] Proclus' contention that geometrical thought involves projection of reason-principles (λόγοι) onto the imagination provides further support for this claim. As pointed out in n. 2 above, according to Proclus reason-principles are the causes of accidental properties and parts of objects. Hence, the conception that geometrical objects are projections of λόγοι reinforces the interpretation that Proclus' geometrical

3. Participation and geometrical constructions

So far, my analysis has dealt with Proclus' conception of geometrical objects in so far as they are immanent universals. A full-
fledged analysis of Proclus' philosophy of geometry also requires
consideration of the relationship between transcendent universals
(i.e. the reason-principles in discursive reason) and their immanent
manifestations in the imagination. Proclus' description of the relationship between discursive reason and imagination suggests that
the exclusion of later-born universals underlies his account of the
imagination's role in the acquisition of geometrical knowledge. In
the first chapter of the second prologue he says:

> Accordingly, when geometry says something about the circle, the diameter,
> and its affections . . . we do not say that it teaches either about sensible
> circles . . . or about the form in discursive reason. For the [discursive]
> circle is one, whereas geometry makes arguments about many [circles] . . .
> For while the discursive reason has the reason-principles, it is too weak to
> see them in their folded form, so it unfolds them and exposes them to the
> imagination. (*In Eucl.* 54. 14–55. 2)

Here the necessity of projecting the content of discursive reason
onto the imagination is explained by reference to the weakness of
discursive reason, which hinders, in Proclus' view, complete attainment of geometrical knowledge. This characterization of the relationship between discursive reason and imagination implies that
the reason-principles of discursive reason do not serve as genera
and species, under which particular instances are subsumed. In a
genera and species classification system, particulars are instances
that exemplify the genera or the species. By contrast, in Proclus'
philosophy of geometry, the projection of the reason-principles of
discursive reason onto the imagination does not merely exemplify
the content of discursive reason; they also reveal content that cannot
be fully apprehended by discursive reason alone. The projections
onto the imagination transform the discursive reason-principles;
they turn them into composite, extended, and divisible entities.[27]
Discursive reason, then, is not related to the imagination as later-

objects are particulars, taken with their accidental properties, rather than genera or
species.

[27] Proclus illustrates this claim in his discussion of Euclid's definition of the point:
the point is not merely a limiting principle, since it contains occultly the potency of

born universals are related to their instances, but as transcendent universals are related to immanent universals. It follows from the foregoing analysis of the logical characteristics of transcendent universals that, unlike later-born universals, they should account for the community as well as for the difference between their immanent manifestations. The following discussion is aimed at explaining this mode of unification; it also clarifies how Proclus' ontology accounts for the role played by constructions in geometry.

Throughout the commentary on the *Elements* Proclus often describes the common principle presiding over geometrical figures in the imagination in terms of a certain activity that brings geometrical figures to perfection. For example, when introducing the distinction between later-born universals and transcendent universals he characterizes the former as predicated of plurality (κατὰ τὴν πρὸς αὐτὰ σχέσιν καὶ καταγορίαν ὑφιστάμενα, 51. 8–9) and the latter as generating plurality (γεννητικὸν εἶναι τοῦ πλήθους, 50. 24–51. 1).[28] Viewed in the light of Proclus' metaphysics, the allusions to causality made in the Euclid commentary seem to be more than metaphors. The relationship between transcendent and immanent universals, in Proclus' philosophy, is not merely logical but also causal. In proposition 21 of the *Elements of Theology* Proclus describes the transcendent universal and plurality as forming an order that advances from a unit to a manifold co-ordinate (σύστοιχος) with that unit. According to this description, the unit and its co-ordinate manifold are ordered in a successive series, whose first member (i.e. the unit) is identified with the transcendent universal, and the other members are its immanent manifestations. In this description the members of a given series (i.e. the immanent universals) are not equally subordinated to the first member (i.e. the transcendent universal), but each differs from the others by the position allocated to it in the series.[29] In the proof of this proposition Proclus

the unlimited. Owing to this potency the point, though unextended, is the cause of extensions and intervals (*In Eucl.* 88. 21–6). This example indicates that the content that becomes overt by unfolding transcendent forms goes beyond the content given in their definitions.

[28] See also *In Eucl.* 50. 24; 53. 5–11; 99. 14; 139. 9; 151. 5; 164. 9.

[29] This view is in keeping with Proclus' description of the relationship between forms and their participants as a relationship between paradigm and copy. Unlike Aristotle's conception of substance, which excludes gradation among substances (*Cat.* 3ᵇ33–4ᵃ9), the terms 'more' and 'less' are applicable to the relationship of similarity between paradigms and copies.

characterizes the relationship between the transcendent universal
and plurality in the following way:

> So since there is in each order something common, continuous, and iden-
> tical, because of which some [members] are called co-ordinate and others
> hetero-ordinate, clearly the identical [characteristic] comes to the entire
> series from one principle. Therefore, there is one unit prior to plurality
> that determines for the members in each order and series the one principle
> of their relation to one another and to the whole. Indeed, of the things
> subordinated to the same series, one is the cause of the other; but it is
> necessary that the cause of the series as a whole be prior to all of them, and
> as co-ordinate they all be generated from it, not each in its particularity
> but as belonging to this series. (24. 12–21 Dodds)

According to this passage the first member of a series unifies the
series in two ways: it determines the relation of the members of
the series to the whole and it determines their relation to each
other. The double role of the first member of the series seems
to be related to the causal relations between the series' members.
According to this passage, the first member of a series as well as
the other members are causes; the first member is the cause of all
of the series' members, whereas each of the subsequent members is
the cause of another member. In what follows, I explain the double
role of the first member in terms of the causal relations between the
series' members. In so doing, I analyse Proclus' main argument for
the identification of the final cause with the efficient cause.[30] This
analysis leads to the conclusion that the first member determines
the relations of the members to the whole as an efficient cause and
that it determines the relations of the members to each other as a
final cause.

In the fourth book of his commentary on Plato's *Parmenides*
Proclus lists several arguments in support of the identification of the
final cause with the efficient cause. I quote here the first argument
in this list, since it is used in Proclus' other attempts to justify this
thesis:[31]

---

[30] On the productive role of forms in Proclus' philosophy see S. Sambursky, 'The
Theory of Forms: A Problem and Four Neoplatonic Solutions', *Journal for the
History of Philosophy*, NS 6 (1968), 327–39. On Proclus' identification of the final
cause with the efficient cause see C. Steel, 'Proclus et Aristote sur la causalité efficiente de l'intellect divin', in J. Pépin and H. D. Saffrey (eds.), *Proclus: lecteur et
interprète des anciens* (Paris, 1987), 213–25.

[31] *ET*, prop. 12; *In Parm.* 842. 24–32; 788. 12–28 Cousin; *In Tim.* i. 2. 15–16; i.
266. 28–267. 13 Diehl.

We are accustomed to use these arguments against those who do not make the intelligibles efficient causes of secondary entities . . . When there is no efficient cause on the one hand and an effect on the other, what would make the desire between one and the other? How would [the effect] desire the cause, having received nothing from it? For everything that desires does so especially for the sake of attaining something. If [the effect] possesses it, the desire in the present case is superfluous, but if [the effect] does not possess it, the desire arises in every case through the lack of something which [the effect] does not possess. Thus if nothing is added to the desiring entity from the object of its desire, the desire is again superfluous, since nothing can be attained from the object of desire. (*In Parm.* 922. 1–20 Cousin)

According to this argument the final cause cannot serve as an object of desire, unless it also serves as an efficient cause that gives something to its effect. This argument rests on the assumption that a cause can serve as a final cause if and only if the desire arises from lack and the desiring object acquires something from the object of desire. In order to meet this requirement the cause, in its role as an efficient cause, should give something to the effect and yet it should also guarantee that the effect would lack something. This requirement can be understood in the light of three theses of Proclus' theory of causality: (1) effects are similar to their causes (*ET*, prop. 28); (2) effects imitate the productive power of their causes (*ET*, prop. 25); and (3) causes differ from each other by the number of effects that they are capable of producing (*ET*, prop. 60).

The similarity between causes and effects implies that the cause gives to its effect a property that it possesses, but it does not make the effect identical with itself. By implying a certain difference between the cause and its effect, the similarity thesis accounts for the lack that gives rise to the effect's desire. This thesis also explains what goal the effect desires to attain; the effect desires to attain the property in virtue of which it differs from its cause. The second thesis explains how the effect attains this goal. The most fundamental difference between the cause and its effect is that the former produces and the latter is produced. Accordingly the effect attains its goal when it turns into a cause—that is, when it imitates its cause by generating another effect. Proclus' argument for the identification of the final cause with the efficient cause requires that the effect, though attaining something from its cause, would also lack something. The third thesis, in which causes differ from one another by the number of effects that they are capable of producing, guarantees that the difference between the cause and its effect will be retained. The original cause is greater than its effect, in spite of the fact that its effect turned into a cause, since the original cause produces more effects. The original cause produces its effect as well as the subsequent members of the series, whereas its effect produces only the subsequent members.

The analysis of Proclus' argument for the identification of the final cause with the efficient cause clarifies how transcendent universals (i.e. the first member of a series) unify their immanent manifestations. The transcendent universal, in its role as an efficient cause, produces all the members of a given series; it unifies the entire series by producing its members in the same manner. In its role as a final cause, the transcendent universal determines the relation between each of the members of the series. Having the greatest productive power, the transcendent universal serves as the criterion by which the productive power of the other members can be measured; in other words, it orders the members of the series according to the number of effects that they are capable of producing. Thus the transcendent universal accounts for the community as well as for the difference between its immanent manifestations. In its role as an efficient cause, it is the common cause of the series' members, and in its role as a final cause, it accounts for the difference between the members of the series by determining their position in the descending order of the first member's effects.

This account of the causal relationship between the transcendent universal and its immanent manifestations leads to two conclusions. First, the common element that presides over Proclus' series is not a common attribute, such as 'rational' or 'mortal', but a common mode of production. The series' members belong to one and the same series because they are produced by the same cause. Second, the first member of the series does not unify the entire series, as a universal term may be said to unify its particular instances. Being one of the members of a series, the first member is a singular entity; as such it cannot comprise other entities. Furthermore, the members of a series are not identical imitations of the first member, hence they are not equally subsumed under it. The second characteristic of the transcendent universal limits our apprehension of the unity of a given series. The first member of a series, being a singular entity, cannot be known in its role as the general principle that unifies the series; it is only through the enumeration of its effects that the role of the transcendent universal as the efficient cause of each of the series' members becomes apparent. This characteristic of the transcendent universal together with its first characteristic determines the method by which the common element of a series can be known. Since the common element of the series is not a common attribute but a common mode of production, and since the transcendent universal cannot be known in its generality, the common element of the series becomes known through the imitations of its mode of production by its effects. This activity discloses the creative power of the first member in a conjunctive way, i.e. in the sum of its effects. The significance of the transcendent universal as a unity that comprises plurality remains occult. In proposition 93 of the *Elements of Theology* Proclus says:

Although [secondary entities] extend towards their cause with whatever reach [ἐφ' ὁσονοῦν], there is still something that transcends them altogether. Although they are all restored to it, there is still something occult and incomprehensible for the secondary entities. Although they unfold the powers in it, there is still something concentrated and unsuppressed that because of its unity extends beyond their explication. (84. 7–12 Dodds)

This passage accords with Proclus' description of the relationship between discursive reason and the imagination in the commentary on the *Elements*. According to Proclus, discursive reason needs the aid of the imagination, because it is 'too weak to see the reason principles in their folded form' (*In Eucl.* 54. 27–55. 2). Interpreted in the light of the passage quoted above, the weakness of discursive reason can be understood as an inability to apprehend the transcendent universal as the unitary cause of each of its manifestations. Proclus' conception of the relationship between transcendent and immanent universals implies that the productive power of the transcendent universal can be apprehended only through its imitation by its effects. The imagination brings into light these effects, thereby enabling discursive reason to apprehend causes. Hence in Proclus' philosophy of geometry imaginary geometrical constructions play the role that effects have in his metaphysics. Geometrical constructions present in a conjunctive way the occult and unitary productive power of transcendent universals. Indeed, in the commentary on the *Elements* Proclus ascribes this role to geometrical constructions:

That is why, then, we draw the constructions, generations, divisions, positions, and applications of figures. Since the form itself is immovable, ungenerated, indivisible, and pure of all substrate, we use the imagination and the extensions [arising] from it. But those things present in it occultly are brought forward to the imagination as extended and divisible. (56. 10–15)

This analysis of the relationship between the transcendent universal in discursive reason and its manifestations in the imagination clarifies why diagrammatic representations and constructions are of theoretical value in Proclus' philosophy of geometry. Proclus' claim that the transcendent geometrical forms cannot be understood on their own but only through the explication of their occult productive power in the imagination is an application of his general conception of the relationship between the transcendent and immanent universals. This conception is based on the replacement of common universals with common creative causes that become partly overt through their effects. It entails a notion of geometrical knowledge in which actual productions and constructions disclose the mode of generation of the geometrical objects, thereby leading to a theoretical understanding of causes.[32]

Justification of constructive procedures is thus made possible in Proclus' philosophy on the basis of three themes central to his metaphysics: the replacement of later-born universals with universals in the particulars, which accounts for the individuality of geometrical objects; the ascription of creative power to the transcendent form, which accounts for their constructibility; and the occult nature of causes, which accounts for the indispensability of geometrical constructions by excluding the possibility of purely intellectual apprehension of causes in geometry. In the following section I show how these metaphysical assumptions find expression in Proclus' analyses of Euclid's geometrical proofs.

---

[32] It follows from this analysis that in Proclus' view the role of geometrical constructions is not, as commonly held, confined to existence proofs. In the light of this analysis, geometrical constructions do not merely answer the question whether a certain geometrical entity exists; they also answer the question what is a certain geometrical entity. That is, since the transcendent form expresses itself in the mode by which its effects are generated, geometrical constructions, carried out in the imagination, reveal the nature of geometrical objects. For the existential interpretation of Proclus' conception of constructions see E. Niebel, *Untersuchungen über die Bedeutung der geometrischen Konstruktion in der Antike* (*Kant-Studien*, suppl. 76; Cologne, 1959), 26–47.

4. Participation and Euclid's geometrical reasoning

In all of Proclus' comments on Euclid's proofs only one illustration is given of the kind of theoretical apprehension attained through geometrical constructions. This illustration is found in Proclus' comments on three related Euclidean proofs that establish various quantitative relations between the angles of a triangle. These proofs (prop. 1. 16, 1. 17, and the second part of 1. 32) establish respectively that (1) the exterior angle of a triangle is greater than either of the interior and opposite angles; (2) any two angles of a triangle are less than two right angles; (3) the sum of the angles of a triangle is equal to two right angles. In Euclid's *Elements* these propositions are based on an auxiliary construction, in which the base of a triangle is extended. In his comments on these proofs Proclus offers an alternative procedure, in which the properties of the triangle's angles are inferred from the construction of the triangle itself. In Proclus' alternative procedure, a triangle is constructed out of two perpendiculars to a given straight line that move towards each other up to their intersection point, which is the triangle's vertex (309. 5–310. 8; 310. 19–311. 14; 384. 5–21). This construction is not directly derived from Euclid's postulates, which allow the drawing of straight lines and circles but do not state that these objects can be generated by the motion of points and straight lines.[33] Yet even if Proclus' construction may be rendered compatible with Euclid's postulates, its introduction raises two questions: (1) why does Proclus offer an alternative to Euclid's construction? and (2) why is this construction kinematic? In what follows I trace the answers to these questions to Proclus' view of the relationship between transcendent and immanent universals.

Proclus introduces the kinematic construction of a triangle as a supplement to a corollary that he derives from proposition 1. 16, according to which if a straight line falling on two straight lines

---

[33] Locomotion is not completely absent from the *Elements*. In the proof of the first congruence theorem Euclid places one triangle on another, and constructs spheres and cones by revolving a semicircle and a right-angled triangle on their axes. Nevertheless, it seems that Euclid tends to avoid such procedures, whenever constructions can be carried out in strict accordance with his postulates. 'Mechanical' considerations do feature in other Greek mathematical sources, most notably in the solutions to the three classical problems (trisection of an angle, the duplication of the cube, and the squaring of a circle). On this see W. R. Knorr, *The Ancient Tradition of Geometric Problems* (Dordrecht, 1986).

makes the exterior angle equal to the interior and opposite angle, these lines cannot form a triangle.[34] Although this corollary presupposes proposition 1. 16, Proclus goes on to show by means of the kinematic construction that if the two straight lines form a triangle by moving towards each other and intersecting, the exterior angle is greater than each of the interior and opposite angles. The introduction of the kinematic procedure in this context is puzzling; why does Proclus establish proposition 1. 16 in proving a corollary of this proposition? His discussion of the demonstrations found in Euclid's *Elements* answers this question:

We shall find sometimes that what is called 'proof' has the properties of demonstration, in proving the sought through definitions as middle terms—and this is a perfect demonstration—but sometimes it attempts to prove from signs. This should not be overlooked. For, although geometrical arguments always have their necessity through the underlying matter, they do not always draw their conclusions through demonstrative methods. For when it is proved that the interior angles of a triangle are equal to two right angles from the fact that the exterior angle of a triangle is equal to the two opposite interior angles, how can this demonstration be from the cause? How can the middle term be other than a sign? For the interior angles are equal to two right angles even if there are no exterior angles, for there is a triangle even if its side is not extended. (206. 12–26)

According to this passage, Euclid's auxiliary construction, in which the triangle's base is extended, is not explanatory: that is, it grounds the triangle's properties in a sign and not in a cause. Proclus' comments on proposition 1. 17 support this conclusion. In these comments, Proclus argues that Euclid's proof of proposition 1. 17 is not causal, since it establishes a necessary truth (i.e. that any two angles of a triangle are less than two right angles) through a contingent fact (i.e. the extension of the triangle's base) (311. 15–21). In Proclus' view, the kinematic construction of a triangle provides the explanation which is missing from Euclid's proof. Similarly, in concluding his proof of the corollary of 1. 16, Proclus says that the kinematic construction brings into light the true causes of the conclusion (310. 5–8). The exact sense in which the kinematic construction is explanatory can be inferred from the passage quoted above. At the end of this passage Proclus says that the extension of the triangle's base does not provide an explanation, since 'there is a triangle even if its side is not extended' (206. 25–6). This re-

---

[34] This corollary is equivalent to proposition 1. 28 in the *Elements*.

mark clarifies Proclus' claim, made in his comments on proposition
1. 17, that the extension of the base is contingent. Construed in
the light of Proclus' characterization of perfect demonstration, the
extension of the base is contingent not only because proposition
1. 17 can be proved without it,[35] but because it has no necessary
relation to the triangle's being. Proclus' construction, by contrast,
derives the triangle's properties from its mode of generation. The
inclination of the perpendiculars towards each other makes the two
interior angles less than two right angles. Therefore, these mutually
approaching perpendiculars will necessarily make a triangle, since
according to the parallel postulate they will intersect each other if
extended indefinitely.

The notion of explanation underlying Proclus' kinematic construction seems to be Aristotelian. Through the kinematic construction, Proclus does not merely show that certain attributes hold
for a triangle, he also shows that these attributes are derived from
the triangle's being. Indeed, in concluding his lengthy discussion
of proposition 1. 32, Proclus refers to the kinematic construction
in justifying Aristotle for viewing the equality of the sum of the
triangle's angles to two right angles as an essential attribute of a
triangle as such (καθ' αὐτὸ καὶ ᾗ αὐτό, 384. 5–21).[36] Yet, although
Proclus here follows Aristotle, his understanding of the kinematic
construction as establishing essential relations is rooted in his metaphysical presuppositions. The attempt to establish essential relations through the kinematic construction of a triangle rests on
the assumption that the mode by which an object is generated constitutes its essence. This assumption, as I have shown, is central
to Proclus' metaphysics, in which the common element in virtue
of which various entities are said to belong to one and the same

[35] Proclus provides such a proof at *In Eucl.* 312. 1–23.

[36] It is not clear whether Proclus regards his alternative to propositions 1. 16,
17, and 32 as demonstrative proofs. From a mathematical viewpoint, the arguments
based on the kinematic constructions are deficient. Regarding propositions 1. 16 and
1. 17, Proclus' argument does not exhaust all possible cases; it ignores the cases in
which both exterior angles decrease or increase in forming a triangle. Furthermore,
the employment of the kinematic construction in the case of proposition 1. 32 does
not entail that the vertical angle of the triangle is equal to the amount subtracted from
the base angles, as a result of the rotation of the perpendiculars. It seems that Proclus
is concerned here mainly with the explanatory force of these arguments rather
than with their mathematical validity. This concern may stem from an attempt to
accommodate these Euclidean proofs to Aristotle's requirement that demonstrations
should be explanatory.

series is not a common property, such as 'rational' or 'bounded by three lines', but a common mode of generation. The kinematic construction accords with this metaphysical conception; it grounds the triangle's attributes in its mode of generation.

Having explained why Proclus offers an alternative to Euclid's construction, I turn to consider why this construction is kinematic. From a mathematical point of view, the derivation of propositions 1. 17 and 1. 32 from the parallel postulate does not require the perpendiculars to move. It is sufficient to assume that the two lines that serve as the triangle's sides incline towards each other, so that the angles that they make with the triangle's base are less than two right angles. Proclus' reasons for basing his construction on the perpendiculars' motion seem to be metaphysical. From the viewpoint of Proclus' metaphysics, the kinematic construction, in order to be considered explanatory, has to meet two requirements: apart from having a necessary relation to the triangle's being, it has to ground its properties in a *common* mode of generation. The kinematic construction may be construed as meeting the second requirement, in the light of Proclus' interpretation of Euclid's postulates. In this interpretation the first postulate, which allows one to draw a line from any point to any point, is identified with the flowing of the point; similarly, the second postulate, which allows one to produce a finite given line continuously in a straight line, is identified with the free flowing of the extremity of the line; and the third postulate, which allows one to describe a circle with any centre and distance, expresses the movement of the line about its stationary point (184. 6–25). This interpretation that incorporates motion into geometrical objects coheres with Proclus' conception of causality. In this conception each of the members of a given series, with the exception of the first member, is not only an effect but also a cause that generates the subsequent members. The first member of a given series serves both as an efficient cause that produces its effects and as a final cause that brings to actuality the activity of the effects, by which they produce other members. Similarly, in Proclus' construction of a triangle geometrical entities (i.e. the perpendiculars) are endowed with inherent motion that generates another geometrical entity, namely the triangle. The motion by which the perpendiculars generate the triangle can be understood as an imitation of the motion that generates the first member in the series of plane figures, which in Proclus' view is the circle (146.

24–5). The circle is produced by the rotation of the extremity of a line about its other extremity and the triangle is produced by the rotation of the perpendiculars. Thus it seems reasonable that Proclus constructs the triangle kinematically, in an attempt to ground the triangle's attributes in a mode of generation which is common to plane figures.

This interpretation of Proclus' comments on propositions 1. 16, 17, and 32 indicates that his metaphysical commitments bear not only on his ontological approach to geometrical objects, but also on his understanding of Euclid's geometrical proofs. His illustration of the role played by constructions in attaining geometrical knowledge does not account for the auxiliary constructions employed by Euclid in proving the propositions discussed above. My interpretation of Proclus' comments on these propositions shows that his metaphysics accounts for a different constructive procedure, a procedure in which the object's attributes are derived from its mode of generation. Nevertheless, Proclus' metaphysical views do not lead to an outright dismissal of proofs based on auxiliary constructions. In the first prologue of the commentary on the *Elements* Proclus praises Euclid for including in his work proofs based on causes and proofs based on signs. He describes Euclid's employment of both modes of reasoning as 'irrefutable, exact, and appropriate to science' (69. 9–12). In Proclus' view, then, the employment of non-explanatory proofs in geometry does not undermine the scientific worth of this discipline. Furthermore, Proclus does not regard all proofs based on auxiliary constructions as non-explanatory. In his view Euclid's first proof, in which an equilateral triangle is constructed by means of auxiliary constructions, is an example of perfect and explanatory demonstration (206. 26–207. 3).[37] Not in all cases, then, do Proclus' metaphysical considerations rub off on his analysis of the constructive methods employed in Euclid's geometrical proofs. Yet, although alternative constructions of the kind that Proclus introduces in his comments on propositions 1. 16, 17, and 32 are not common in his commentary, Proclus seems to achieve by these comments the principal aim of his commentary, which is, according to its concluding sentence, 'to contribute to the ex-

[37] In his comments on this proof Proclus explicitly refers to metaphysical notions in justifying Euclid's auxiliary construction. He argues that an equilateral triangle is reasonably constructed by means of two circles because the circle is the image of intelligible realities and the triangle is an image of the soul. He employs here his idea that lower grades of reality are images or reflections of higher grades of reality.

position of causes, to dialectical judgement, and to philosophical observation' (432. 16–19).

Tel Aviv University

BIBLIOGRAPHY

Boyer, C. B., *A History of Mathematics* (New York, 1968).

Breton, S., *Philosophie et mathématique chez Proclus* (Paris, 1971).

Charles-Saget, A., *L'Architecture du divin: mathématique et philosophie chez Plotin et Proclus* (Paris, 1982).

Ebbesen, S., 'Porphyry's Legacy to Logic: A Reconstruction', in R. Sorabji (ed.), *Aristotle Transformed: The Ancient Commentators and their Influence* (Ithaca, NY, 1990), 141–71.

Eves, H., *An Introduction to the History of Mathematics* (Philadelphia, 1983).

Friedlein, G. (ed.), *Procli Diadochi in primum Euclidis elementorum librum commentarii* (Leipzig, 1873).

Heath, T., *A History of Greek Mathematics* (New York, 1981).

Kline, M., *Mathematical Thought from Ancient to Modern Times* (Oxford, 1972).

Knorr, W. R., *The Ancient Tradition of Geometric Problems* (Dordrecht, 1986).

Lloyd, A. C., 'Neoplatonic Logic and Aristotelian Logic, II', *Phronesis*, NS 1 (1956), 146–60.

—— 'Procession and Division in Proclus' ['Procession and Division'], in H. J. Blumenthal and A. C. Lloyd (eds.), *Soul and the Structure of Being in Late Neoplatonism: Syrianus, Proclus and Simplicius* (Liverpool, 1982), 18–45.

—— *The Anatomy of Neoplatonism* (Oxford, 1990).

Morrow, G. (trans. and comm.), *Proclus: A Commentary on the First Book of Euclid's Elements*, trans. with introduction and notes by Glenn Morrow and a new foreword by Ian Mueller (Princeton, 1970).

Mueller, I., 'Aristotle on Geometrical Objects', *Archiv für Geschichte der Philosophie*, NS 55 (1970), 156–71.

—— 'Mathematics and Philosophy in Proclus' Commentary on Book I of Euclid's *Elements*', in J. Pépin and H. D. Saffrey (eds.), *Proclus: lecteur et interprète des anciens* (Paris, 1987).

Netz, R., 'Proclus' Division of the Mathematical Propositions into Parts: How and Why was it Formulated?', *Classical Quarterly*, NS 49.1 (1999), 282–303.

Niebel, E., *Untersuchungen über die Bedeutung der geometrischen Konstruktion in der Antike* (*Kant-Studien*, suppl. 76; Cologne, 1959).

O'Meara, D., *Pythagoras Revived: Mathematics and Philosophy in Late Antiquity* (Oxford, 1989).

Sambursky, S., 'The Theory of Forms: A Problem and Four Neoplatonic Solutions', *Journal for the History of Philosophy*, NS 6 (1968), 327–39.

Steel, C. (ed.), *Proclus: Commentaire sur le Parménide de Platon. Traduction de Guillaume de Moerbeke* (2 vols.; Leuven, 1985).

—— 'Proclus et Aristote sur la causalité efficiente de l'intellect divin', in J. Pépin and H. D. Saffrey (eds.), *Proclus: lecteur et interprète des anciens* (Paris, 1987), 213–25.

INDEX LOCORUM

Simplicius

Notes for Contributors to Oxford Studies in Ancient Philosophy

1. Articles may be submitted at any time of year. They should be printed, on one side of the paper only, and with double line-spacing throughout. Footnotes may at the stage of initial submission be printed at the foot of the page (however, see point 4 below). Pages should be A4 or standard American quarto ($8\frac{1}{2} \times 11''$), and ample margins should be left.

2. Two identical copies should be submitted to the editor. Authors are asked to supply an accurate word-count (*a*) for the main text, and (*b*) for the notes. The covering letter should provide a current e-mail address, if available, as well as a postal address.

3. Typescripts will not normally be returned to authors, but will be disposed of after all dealings have been concluded.

The remaining instructions apply to the final version sent for publication, and need not be rigidly adhered to in a first submission.

4. Only one printed copy of the final version should be supplied. Foot-notes should be numbered consecutively and located together on se-parate sheets at the end of the typescript, in double line-spacing. They will be printed at the foot of each page. Any acknowledgements should be placed in an unnumbered first note. Wherever possible, references to primary sources should be built into the text.

5. **Use of Greek and Latin.** Relatively familiar Greek terms such as *psychē* and *polis* (but not whole phrases and sentences) may be used in transliteration. Wherever possible, Greek and Latin should not be used in the main text of an article in ways which would impede comprehension by those without knowledge of the languages; for example, where appropriate, the original texts should be accompanied by a translation. This constraint does not apply to footnotes. Greek copy must be supplied in a completely legible and accurate form, with all diacritics in place both on the hard copy and in the computer file. A note of the system employed for achieving Greek (e.g. GreekKeys, Linguist's Software) should be supplied to facilitate file conversion.

6. For citations of Greek and Latin authors, house style should be fol-lowed. This can be checked in any recent issue of *OSAP* with the help of the Index Locorum.

7. In references to books, the first time the book is referred to give the ini-tial(s) and surname of the author (first names are not usually required), and the place and date of publication; where you are abbreviating the title in subsequent citations, give the abbreviation in square brackets, thus:

T. Brickhouse and N. Smith, *Socrates on Trial* [*Trial*] (Princeton, 1981), 91–4.

Give the volume-number and date of periodicals, and include the full page-extent of articles (including chapters of books):

D. W. Graham, 'Symmetry in the Empedoclean Cycle' ['Symmetry'], *Classical Quarterly*, NS 38 (1988), 297–312 at 301–4.

G. Vlastos, 'The Unity of the Virtues in the *Protagoras*' ['Unity'], in id., *Platonic Studies*, 2nd edn. (Princeton, 1981), 221–65 at 228.

Where the same book or article is referred to on subsequent occasions, usually the most convenient style will be an abbreviated reference, thus:

Brickhouse and Smith, *Trial*, 28–9.

Do *not* use the author-and-date style of reference:

Brickhouse and Smith 1981: 28–9.

8. Authors are asked to supply *in addition*, at the end of the article, a full list of the bibliographical entries cited, alphabetically ordered by (first) author's surname. Except that the author's surname should come first, these entries should be identical in form to the first occurrence of each in the article, including where appropriate the indication of abbreviated title:

Graham, D. W., 'Symmetry in the Empedoclean Cycle' ['Symmetry'], *Classical Quarterly*, NS 38 (1988), 297–312.

9. If there are any unusual conventions contributors are encouraged to include a covering note for the copy-editor and/or printer. Please say whether you are using single and double quotation marks for different purposes (otherwise the Press will employ its standard single quotation marks throughout, using double only for quotations within quotations).

10. Authors should send a copy of the final version of their paper on a compact disk (CD) or 3.5″ high density (HD) floppy disk (Macintosh or IBM format), indicating on the disk or in an accompanying note the program in which the text is written, including the system employed for achieving Greek (see point 5 above). **NB. The version on disk must be the *exact* version which produced the hard copy sent in for printing.**